AUTiSM

AUTiSM

Perspectives from Africa | Volume 1

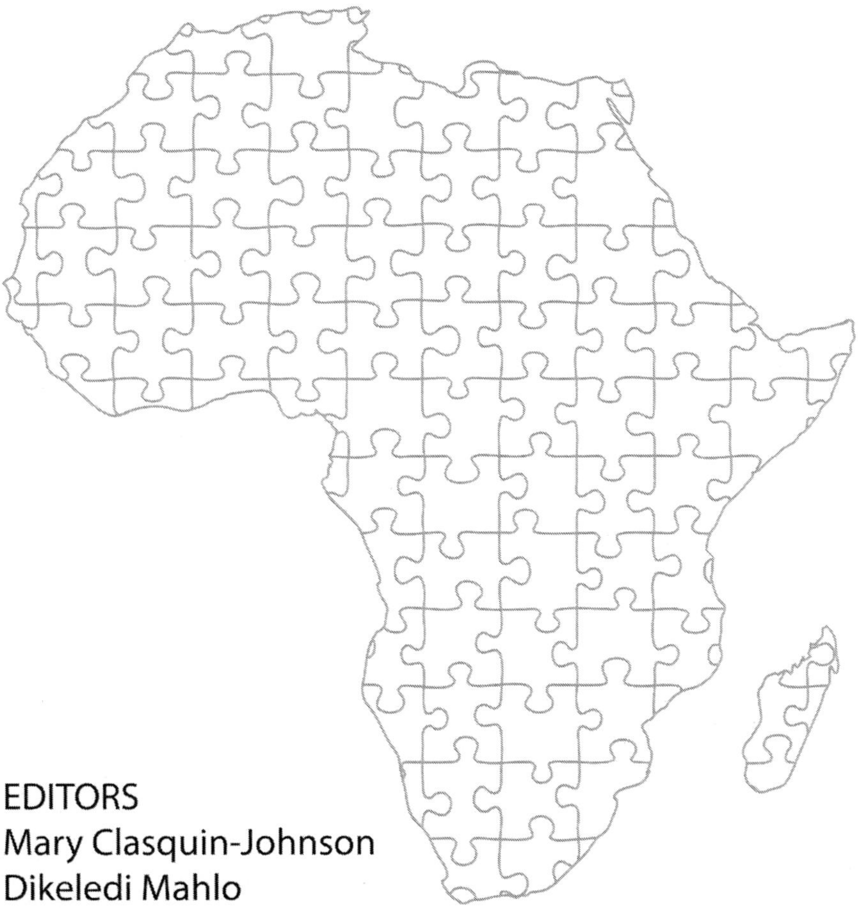

EDITORS

Mary Clasquin-Johnson

Dikeledi Mahlo

Michel Clasquin-Johnson

Foreword by Professor Jonathan D Jansen

Routledge
Taylor & Francis Group
LONDON AND NEW YORK

UNISA university of south africa PRESS

First published 2023
by Routledge
4 Park Square, Milton Park, Abingdon, Oxon, OX14 4RN

and by Routledge
605 Third Avenue, New York, NY 10158

Routledge is an imprint of the Taylor & Francis Group, an informa business

Print edition not for sale in Africa.

British Library Cataloguing-in-Publication Data
A catalogue record for this book is available from the British Library

Library of Congress Cataloging-in-Publication Data
A catalog record has been requested for this book

ISBN13: 9781032430799 (hbk)
ISBN13: 9781032430805 (pbk)
ISBN13: 9781003365631 (ebk)

DOI: 10.4324/9781003365631

Typeset in Times New Roman
by UNISA Press, South Africa

UNISA | university of south africa PRESS

CONTENTS

TABLES

FIGURES

PREFACE

Current teacher education programmes still focus primarily on the normative child. For example, the latest undergraduate bachelor programmes may only include a single module dedicated to Inclusive Education. Yet, a definitive feature of today's educational landscape is diversity. Teacher education programmes must therefore ensure that all teachers are better prepared to accommodate the needs, interests and abilities of learners who are culturally, linguistically and developmentally diverse. Our educational policies on Inclusive Education compel us to educate all learners, including those with autism. This is fundamental for advancing human rights and social justice.

Together with my colleagues working in the fields of Inclusive Education and Special Needs Education, this book represents our attempt to initiate a conversation about autism in Africa. How do we as Africans understand, define and frame autism? Is autism simply a disability? Is autism regarded as a natural form of human diversity? How should we as lecturers prepare our students to teach learners with autism in mainstream or special education settings?

As scholars, we acknowledge the pockets of excellence that exist related to education and therapeutic intervention for children and adults on the autism spectrum in both public and private settings. However, we are critical of the extensive policy borrowing that has characterised post-colonial Africa. While we recognise the extensive international scholarship on autism, very limited research has been conducted in our African contexts. We believe that we need to brainstorm and develop our own context-specific interventions and pedagogies that will be appropriate, affordable and responsive to the needs of our children and adults with autism.

Through our interaction with schools and teachers, we have learned that:

- Many teachers (mis)interpret autism as severe brain injury.
- Few teachers understand that autism is a spectrum condition.
- The overwhelming majority of children and adults with autism are not receiving the support they require to thrive.
- Existing policies and programmes have reinforced segregated placement, which undermines social inclusion, acceptance and support.

This book is also part of a much larger research project on *Curriculum Adaptation for Learners with Autism*, funded by the Women-in-Research Programme at the University of South Africa. It is the first scholarly book on autism in Africa. The main purpose of the book is to explore African perspectives on autism. At the end of the book, we will critically reflect on whether we achieved our purpose.

FOREWORD

South Africa's original sin was not race but difference. Fixed into our DNA, the social genetics that is our inheritance, is a low tolerance level for anything outside of what our society has come to define as normal. The most obvious defect in our social DNA shows up in a long history of anti-Black racism but there are loci on those genes for anti-Semitism, misogyny, xenophobia and any number of targets that fall outside the norm. The social construction of an able-bodied person is one of those normative conditions that leads to the exclusion, marginalization and suppression of those deemed less able including autistic persons. Sadly, that inattention to children with autism is also found in the research literature in South Africa. I was very surprised to hear that this is the first scholarly book on autism in Africa.

That is why this excellent collection of research and thinking on autism is such an important contribution to scholarship on the subject under the broad conceptual umbrella of Inclusive Education. The topics covered are wide-ranging including religion, technology, rurality, sexuality, and the law. Given my own field of interest (education), I was particularly drawn to the insightful chapters on early childhood education, curriculum differentiation and classroom assessment.

We should not underestimate the level of ignorance in the South African society about autism and why this book is therefore so important because it offers a rich compendium of concepts, methods, and interventions for creating more inclusive classrooms. I found it useful, for example, to think of autism as a spectrum condition and to engage the fascinating question as to whether autism is in fact a disability or simply a naturally existing form of human diversity. How we see autism, in other words, could be highly consequential for how we see human beings with autism and how we design teaching and learning in response to such conceptions of others.

This otherwise powerful idea that how we "see" autism has many positive possibilities such as a humane response that goes beyond biomedical treatments of an illness – but also some potential downsides. In this regard it is important to distinguish between normative ideals (what we would like to see autism research, policy and practice look like) and empirical realities (what actually exists on the ground as documented through high quality research). Given its understandable emotional content and the moving voices of its most ardent advocates, disability education in general and autism education in particularly veers far too much in the direction of a spirited advocacy rather than a sustained research programme on the basis of which more impactful policies and practices might emerge.

In this respect, I do believe that the value of Ubuntu as an all-encompassing description of the African condition needs to be endowed with a healthy dose of intellectual criticism. I cannot sense Ubuntu empirically in the unravelling of South African society made so much more visible as the result of an invisible virus. The institutionalized corruption, the waves of xenophobic attacks on other Africans, and the everyday criminality and violence towards women makes me wonder why Ubuntu is still advanced in politics and scholarship as some kind of ideal state inherent in African society and the African condition. It makes no sense.

I also think that our theorizing about inclusion has to move beyond the language of the 1970s about an Afrocentric versus Eurocentric world of knowledge and research to examining the ways in which our understandings of complex events are entangled through scientific collaborations, exchange and productive work. The idea that Africa serves simply as a source of raw materials for processing in the West is as misleading in economic terms as it is insulting in intellectual terms. African scholarship, such as represented in this important book, not only offers something powerful to scholars in the West, it does so using concepts and methods from both worlds.

That said, it is the case that African scholars need to develop substantive research within the disciplines and the professions, for example, that becomes the basis for a much more elaborate theorizing beyond worn-out concepts such as Ubuntu and Afrocentricity. Is that all we have to offer? There is a reason that vaccines are not going to come out of Africa or that new online learning platforms are going to emerge from North America. It is not primarily resources. It is the poverty of ideas in the absence of which recycle the same old, tired concepts from the early postcolonial period.

What makes this book so critical for a broader African scholarship with worldwide import is its promise – the first book on autism from the continent. It now requires incredible intellectual courage and determination to build the second and third books on a much more formidable base of empirical work and much more courageous theoretical labour that expands on how we "see" autism in a post-pandemic world.

Jonathan D Jansen
Distinguished Professor of Education
Stellenbosch University
26 August 2020

ABBREVIATIONS

AAC	Augmentative and Alternative Communication
ABA	Applied Behaviour Analysis
ABI	Activity-Based Intervention
ANA	Annual National Assessments
ACRWC	African Charter on the Rights and Welfare of the Child
ACHPR	African Charter on Human and Peoples Rights
ADDM	Autism and Developmental Disabilities Monitoring
ADHD	Attention-Deficit/Hyperactivity Disorder
ANS	Autonomic Nervous System
APA	American Psychiatric Association
Apps	Technology Applications
ASA	Autism South Africa
ASC	Autism Spectrum Condition
ASD	Autism Spectrum Disorder
ASAN	Autistic Self Advocacy Network
APSI	Autism Parent Screen for Infants
AYC	African Youth Charter
BCEA	Basic Conditions of Employment Act
BGSU	Bowling Green State University
BPA	Beijing Platform for Action
BTh degree	Bachelor of Theology degree
CAPS	Curriculum and Assessment Policy Statements
CAS	Critical Autism Studies
CBT	Cognitive-Behavioural Therapy
CCMA	Commission for Conciliation, Mediation and Arbitration
CCTV	closed-circuit television
CDC	Centers for Disease Control and Prevention
CEC	Council for Exceptional Children
CEWFCL	Convention on the Elimination of the Worst Forms of Child Labour
Cf	compare
CFTMEA	Classification Française des Troubles Mentaux de L'Enfant et de L'Adolescent
CORC	United Nations Committee on the Rights of the Child
CPA	Criminal Procedure Act
CPCCTICA	Convention on the Protection of Children and Cooperation in Respect of Inter-Country Adoption
CRE-SVs	Cis-Regulatory Element Structural Variants
CSEC	Comprehensive Sexuality Education
CVEs	Collaborative Virtual Environments
DBE	Department of Basic Education
DWCPD	Department of Women, Children and People with Disabilities
DoE	Department of Education
DBSTs	District Based Support Teams

DoJ	Department of Justice
DPI	Disabled People's International
DPSA	Disabled People South Africa
DS	Disability Studies
DSD	Department of Social Development
DSM-IV	Diagnostic and Statistical Manual of Mental Disorders, Fourth Edition
DSM-IV-TR	Diagnostic and Statistical Manual of Mental Disorders, Fourth Edition, Text Revision
DSM-V	Diagnostic and Statistical Manual of Mental Disorders, Fifth Edition
DRGs	Disability Rights Groups
DTT	Discrete Trial Training
DVD	Digital Versatile Disc or Digital Video Disc
DWCPD	Department of Women, Children and People with Disabilities
EBI	Evidence-Based Intervention
ECD	Early Childhood Development
ECE	Early Childhood Education
ECEC	Early Childhood Education and Care
EEA	Employment Equity Act
EELC	Equal Education Law Centre
EIBI	Early Intensive Behavioural Intervention
Ed Support	Educational Support
ESRC	Economic and Social Research Council
FEW	Facial Expression Wonderland
FBA	Functional Behavioural Assessment
GBV	Gender Based Violence
GRSA	Government of the Republic of South Africa
HANDLE	Holistic Approach to Neuro Development Learning Efficiency
HANDS	Helping Autism-diagnosed Teenagers Navigate and Develop Socially
HHH Model	Head, Heart and Hands Model
HCI	Human-Computer Interface
HEP	Home Education Policy
HFA	High-Functioning Autism
HIV	Human Immunodeficiency Virus
HIV/AIDS	Human Immunodeficiency Virus, Acquired Immunodeficiency Syndrome
HMDs	Head-Mounted Displays
HMD-VRTs	Head-Mounted Display – Virtual Reality Technologies
HRW	Human Rights Watch
ICCC	International Convention on Cyber Crime
ICCPR	International Covenant on Civil and Political Rights
ICD-10	International Statistical Classification of Diseases and Related Health Problems 10th Revision
ICESCR	International Covenant on Economic, Social and Cultural Rights
ICF	International Classification of Functioning
ICTs	Information and Communication Technologies
IDDC	International Disability and Development Consortium
IE	Inclusive Education
IEPs	Individual Education Plans

IESA	Inclusive Education South Africa
IF	Independent Functioning
ILO	International Labour Organization
INDS	Integrated National Disability Strategy
INSSSCD	Integrated National Strategy on Support Services to Children with Disabilities
iPSCD	Induced Pluripotent Stem Cells Disease
IQ	Intelligence Quotient
ISP	Individual Support Plan
K-ASD Project	KwaZulu-Natal Autism Spectrum Disorder Project
LAA	Legal Aid Act
LC	Labour Court
LFA	Low-Functioning Autism
LSA	Learner Support Agent
LWA	Learners with Autism
MEC	Member of the Executive Council
MHCA	Mental Health Care Act
MTs	Mobile Technologies
NASRHRFS	National Adolescent Sexual and Reproductive Health and Rights Framework Strategy
NCCA	National Council for Curriculum and Assessment
NCS	National Curriculum Statement
NDP	National Development Plan
NELDS	National Early Learning and Development Standards for Children Birth to Four Years
NEPA	National Education Policy Act
NET	Natural Environment Training
NGOs	Non-Governmental Organisations
NIMH	National Institute of Mental Health
NINDS	National Institute of Neurological Disorders and Stroke
NLP	Natural Language Paradigm
NNSSF	National Norms and Standards for School Funding
NPA	National Prosecuting Authority
NPD	Neuro-Psychiatric Disorders
OCALI	Ohio Center for Autism and Low Incidence
O-O spectrum	Orthodoxy and orthopraxy also reinforce one another (Clasquin-Johnson, Chapter 3 in this volume.)
OT	Occupational Therapy
PECS	Picture Exchange Communication System
PEPUDA	Promotion of Equality and the Prevention of Unfair Discrimination Act
PCs	Personal Computers
PCPs	Primary Care Providers
PDAs	Personal Digital Assistants
PDD-NOS	Pervasive Developmental Disorder – Not Otherwise Specified
PhD	Doctor of Philosophy Degree
PMI	Peer-Mediated Instruction
PROMPT	Prompts for Restructuring Oral Muscular Phonetic Targets
PRT	Pivotal Response Training

SASA	South African Schools Act
SBSTs	School Based Support Teams
SIAS	Screening Identification Assessment and Support Strategy
R&D	Research and Development
RMT	Rhythmic Movement Training
RMTs	Remote Microphone Technologies
RNCS	Revised National Curriculum Statement
RRR	Relationship-Resourced Resilience
SAC	School Assessed Coursework
SAHRC	South African Human Right Commission
SASL CAPS	South African Sign Language Curriculum and Assessment Policy Statements
SARs	Socially Assistive Robotics
SDGs	Sustainable Development Goals
SFT	Systems Factorial Technology
SGDs	Speech-Generating Devices
SNA	Support Needs Analysis
Stats SA	Statistics South Africa
ST	Systems Theory
STI	Sexually Transmitted Infection
TEACCH	Treatment and Education of Autistic and Related Communication Handicapped Children
TBI	Technology-Based Interventions
UDHR	Universal Declaration on Human Rights
UDL	Universal Design for Learning
UK	United Kingdom
UN	United Nations
UNAIDS	Joint United Nations Programme on HIV/AIDS
UNESCO	United Nations Educational Scientific and Cultural Organisation
UNCRC	United Nations Convention on the Rights of the Child
UNCRPD	United Nations Convention of Rights for Persons with Disabilities
UNGACC	UN Guidelines for the Alternative Care of Children
UNICEF	United Nations Children's Fund
UNISA	University of South Africa
USA	United States of America
VB	Verbal Behaviour
VCE	Victorian Certificate of Education
VM	Video-based Modelling
VSM	Video Self-Modelling
VRTs	Virtual Reality Technologies
WHO	World Health Organisation
WIMP	Window, Icon, Menu and Pointer
WP6	White Paper 6 on Special Needs Education: Building and Inclusive Education and Training System
WSSD	World Summit for Social Development

CONTRIBUTORS

Mary G Clasquin-Johnson (ORCID: 0000-0002-0750-6579) is a senior lecturer in the Department of Inclusive Education at the University of South Africa, and the grant holder of the Women in Research grant from which this volume originates.

Michel Clasquin-Johnson (ORCID: 0000-0003-2780-9718) is a professor in the Department of Religious Studies and Arabic at the University of South Africa.

Thersia Du Toit-Smit (ORCID: 0000-0003-3282-0225) is a Senior State Advocate at the NPA with an interest in education, constitutional and employment law.

Leila Goosen (ORCID: 0000-0003-4948-2699) is a professor in the Department of Science and Technology Education at the University of South Africa, and a former holder of a Women in Research grant.

Moyagabo Kate Malahlela is a lecturer in the Department of Inclusive Education at the University of South Africa

Dikeledi Mahlo (ORCID: 0000-0002-1793-4382) chairs the Department of Inclusive Education at the University of South Africa

Hlabathi Maapola-Thobejane is a lecturer in the Department of Inclusive Education at the University of South Africa

Tawanda Majoko (ORCID; 0000-0001-9655-4881) is an associate professor in the Department of Inclusive Education at Great Zimbabwe University.

Joyce Mcgogo works for the Mpumalanga Department of Education.

Serefete M Molosiwa (ORCID: 0000-0002-3055-7446) lectures at the University of Botswana.

Jabulani Mpofu (ORCID: 0000-0001-5634-8581) lectures in the Department of Disability Studies and Special Needs Education at the Zimbabwe Open University.

Penny Round (ORCID: 0000-0001-9638-6144) is a lecturer at Monash University (Australia) in the area of Inclusive and Special Education.

Pearl Subban (ORCID: 0000-0002-2904-976X) is a lecturer at Monash University (Australia) in the areas of literacy and Inclusive Education.

Mahlapahlapana J Themane (ORCID: 0000-0002-2097-8538) is a professor of Education Studies at the University of Limpopo.

AN AFROCENTRIC PERSPECTIVE ON INCLUSIVE EDUCATION AND UBUNTU

Tawanda Majoko

The Salamanca Statement and Framework for Action on Special Needs Education (UNESCO, 1994) reaffirmed the fundamental right to education of everyone as enshrined in the Universal Declaration of Human Rights (United Nations, 1948). It renewed the pledge of the World Conference on EFA (Jomtien, 1990) to safeguard the rights of all irrespective of individual differences. Consequently, the world shifted in paradigm from exclusive to Inclusive Education. Civil rights movements as expressed in various international human rights instruments including the Convention on the Rights of the Child (United Nations, 1989) and the Convention of the Rights of Persons with Disabilities (United Nations, 2006) propels the global impetus for Inclusive Education (De Boer & Simpson, 2009; Majoko, 2017). Inclusive Education champions the human rights and social justice agenda (Eldar, Talmor & Wolf-Zukerman, 2010; Majoko, 2016; Phasha, 2016; Symes & Humphrey, 2010, 2016). Access, participation, acceptance and success of all learners including those with autism in ordinary education underpin Inclusive Education. Worldwide, inclusion in education is the best option of service delivery in education (Humphrey & Lewis, 2008; Leach & Duffy, 2009; McGillicuddy & O'Donnell, 2013). Inclusive Education is a catalyst for elimination of societal discriminatory attitudes towards persons with disabilities including autism.

Although Inclusive Education is popularly perceived as a western philosophy, it is embedded in Afrocentricity. According to Phasha (2016), Inclusive Education is not a foreign phenomenon in Africa because of the embedded-ness of its practices and ideals in the lives of Africans. The alignment of the principles and values of Inclusive Education with the principles and values of African theories reveals that it is not an exclusively western fundamental pedagogical innovation of aspiration and contention of the century (Phasha, 2016). Terms such as "primitive, backward, archaic, outdated, pagan and/or barbaric" (Ocholla, 2007:239) were employed to keep other ways of knowing at the margins because the European epistemology had hegemony over African epistemology (Phasha, 2016; Van Wyk, 2014). An Afrocentric perspective of Inclusive Education is entrenched in theories originated in the African continent including Ubuntu, Africanisation and Indigenous Knowledge instead of imported from elsewhere, as is the case with Eurocentric theories

(Anderson, 2012; Sotuku & Duku, 2014). Nevertheless, not all aspects of African theories resonate with Inclusive Education. Similarly, not all Eurocentric theories resonate with Inclusive Education.

Ubuntu is an Afrocentric or indigenous theoretical ideology that is consistent with the humanistic spirit that defines the ethos of Africans (Letseka, 2013; Nussbaum & Weichel, 2010, see also chapter 12 in this volume). It is found in diverse forms in diverse African societies. Different words are used to refer to Ubuntu in different African countries. In Zimbabwe, Ubuntu is referred to as "hunhu" while in eastern Nigeria Ubuntu is referred to as "igwebuike". Ubuntu emanated from the political tumult before the 1990s as a defining component of a democratic vision (Msila, 2008). In several African countries including South Africa, Ubuntu is popularised in democratic dispensations since it constitutes basic values of humanity and compassion (Sotuku & Duku, 2014).

Aspects of kin and village relations underpin Ubuntu in several contexts in contemporary African societies. Consequently, Ubuntu is a social survival strategy that mushroomed from adverse geographical and social circumstances in which people cooperated for survival (Msila, 2008; Pellerin, 2012). Most Eurocentric theories do not account for these sentiments. Therefore, it is imperative to advance Afrocentric approaches including Ubuntu in theorising about African educational, political, social and economic domains (Letseka, 2013; Phasha, 2016; Swanson, 2007).

Throughout Africa, Ubuntu is practised in different forms in several societies. In Southern Africa, Ubuntu is a short for an isiXhosa proverb, which is derived from "Umuntu ngumuntu ngabantu" which is translated into "a person is a person through their relationship with others" (Sotuku & Duku, 2014). Similarly, teaching and learning of all learners including those with autism in the community of the ordinary classroom underpin Inclusive Education (Lindsay, Proulx, Scott & Thompson, 2013; Majoko, 2017). Ubuntu can be viewed as integral to all African values and entails collective morality and collective personhood (Brown & Shumba, 2011).

Ubuntu is perceived as an African philosophy of humanism which links the individual to the collective. According to Tutu (1999:34), Ubuntu "speaks to the essence of being human… When you want to give high praise to someone, we say, 'Yu u nobuntu': he or she has Ubuntu." In their discussion of Ubuntu Brown and Shumba (2011:35) utilise Nelson Mandela as an example. They express that: 'Madiba's humanism […] is reflected in the qualities of Ubuntu. We can infer from this that when others are tortured or treated as if they are less than who they are, Madiba feels equally diminished, humiliated and undervalued." This resonates with the pursuit for equity and equality for all learners including those with autism in Inclusive Education. Policies and legislation in several African countries including the Constitution of the Republic of South Africa (1996) enshrines Ubuntu (Phasha, 2016). The Constitution protects several values and principles including Ubuntu (human dignity), non-racism and non-sexism, an open society, accountability, the rule of law, respect and reconciliation. Consistent with Ubuntu, the South African Schools Act Number 84 of 1996 also enshrines human rights and human dignity through prohibition of administration of corporal punishment and the policy on language in education (Sotuku & Duku, 2014).

Ubuntu constitutes several elements including valuation of humanness. Overall, Ubuntu translates as personhood, humanness, justice and morality (Khoza, 21012; Letseka, 2012;

Tutu, 1999). Ubuntu is translated through human rights and social justice (Kunene, 2009). Consequently, it is in alignment with the inclusion of learners with unique needs including autism in ordinary education that is entrenched in promotion of human diversity, respect for human dignity and celebration of human diversity. Interdependence and dependence also underpin Ubuntu. According to Khoza (2004), Ubuntu values humanity and consultation as a value orientation and interdependence as a value to dependence. Mbigi (1997) explains such virtues using the African Collective Fingers Theory. The theory postulates that the thumb requires the cooperation of the other fingers to work effectively. The African Collective Fingers Theory, therefore, lobbies for inclusive open forms of communication. It is embraces the African proverb 'It takes a village to raise a child' (Sotuku & Duku, 2010). Consistent with collaborative structures and cultures in inclusion of learners with unique needs including autism in ordinary education, Ubuntu is embedded in cooperation, supportiveness and solidarity. Ubuntu is social contract that emanates from, but transcends the restricted narrow confines of the nuclear family to be extended kinship network, the community (Letseka, 2013; Sotuku & Duku, 2010). Nevertheless, the family is the hub for the successful inclusion of learners with unique needs including autism in ordinary education. A spirit of interconnectedness and social cohesion underpins Ubuntu (Brown & Shumba, 2011; Letseka, 2013). Similarly, multi-disciplinary teams that transcend into trans-disciplinary teams are integral in successful inclusion of learners with unique needs including autism in ordinary classrooms. Interconnectedness, respect and dignity, collectivism and solidarity, communal enterprise and leadership legitimacy are the cornerstones of Ubuntu (Sotuku & Duku, 2010). '[Ubuntu] speaks to the very essence of being human. We belong in a bundle of life [...]. Harmony, friendliness, community, are great goods. Social harmony is for us [...] the greatest good. Anything that subverts or undermines this sought-after good is to be avoided like the plague' (Tutu, 1999:34-35).

Inclusive education which is confronted with the legacy of special education requires Ubuntu. Self-protection, in-group collectivism, consensus building, and a 'being your brother's keeper-type' of humane orientations inform Ubuntu (Littrell, 2011:6). Therefore, Ubuntu is embedded in supportiveness, cooperation and solidarity (Khoza, 2004). Similarly, the inclusion of learners with unique needs including autism in ordinary school education requires consultation and partnership of stakeholders including parents and professionals such as therapists, educational psychologists, assistant teachers, social workers, mainstream teachers and specialist teachers.

According to Oppenheim (2012), Ubuntu is a spiritual ideal, which requires humans need to perpertuate. Spirit of compassion, hospitality and sharing underpin Ubuntu (Swanson, 2007). Compassion and hospitality are central values in the life of Africans (Broodryk, 2006). Compassion entails depth caring and understanding of each other. Because of such caring and understanding, team members or community can have a shared vision and share a burden during hard times (Brown & Shumba, 2011). Embedded in Ubuntu, Africans care during both times of joy and times of sorrow; hence 'Your joy is my joy, and your sorrow is my sorrow' (Sotuku & Duku, 2010). Support of learners with unique needs including autism is indispensable in realisation of successful inclusion in ordinary education.

The premise that people have different talents, qualities and resources, which should be shared in a spirit of cooperativeness for positive existence, underpins Ubuntu (Brown & Shumba, 2011; Phasha, 2016). This includes values such as supportiveness and openhandedness in alignment with needs. Similarly, Inclusive Education is founded on provision of services and programmes that meet the individual needs of learners with unique needs including autism in ordinary classrooms. In his explanation of the inherent spirit of sharing and caring in the spirit of Ubuntu, Tutu expressed that, "We Africans share everything and share nothing". This means that Africans share whatever they possess, even when they possess nothing. Similarly, articulating on sharing and compassion as attributes of Ubuntu, Broodryk (2006) articulates that if an individual is progressing materially and receiving more than others, the extras are shared with the underprivileged brothers and sisters. "Africa does not allow that some to eat while others go hungry, or some sleep warm whilst others are left in the cold."

Nelson Mandela cited in Oppenheim (2012) articulates that in Ubuntu sharing is not only limited to material things but is also linked to human capital including knowledge and skills. Nussbaum and Weichel (2010) posit that a spirit of harmony can be achieved through sharing human capital. These authors refer to the African adage that "when there is peace in an individual, there is peace in a family. When there is peace in a family, there is peace in the community. When there is peace in the community, there is peace in the nation and ultimately in the world." The spirit of caring, sharing and collective personhood can be viewed as underpinning the inclusion of learners with unique needs including autism in ordinary education. The need for educational theories that relevantly reflect political, social, economic and educational lives propels the imperative for Africanisation (Pellerin, 2012; Wyk, 2014). Africanisation is embedded in re-telling of the historical experience of Africa to de-emphasise over-dependence on Eurocentric theoretical interpretations of the continent and its development (Shockley & Frederick, 2010). It calls for education that is inherently inclusive. African indigenous knowledge refers to the totality of the knowledge and skills possessed by a specific group of people that facilitate their survival in a specific geographic community. It is a lived world, a form of reasoning that informs and sustains people who resides in a specific local area (Van Wyk, 2014). Indigenous knowledge systems link people with their nature (Pellerin, 2012). Similarly, Inclusive Education is founded on the education of learners with disabilities in their neighbourhood ordinary classrooms in their natural proportions in the community of their typically developing peers.

References

Anderson, W. (2012). Ex-prisoners deserve chance. *The Columbia Daily Tribune*, Sunday, May 27, D3.

Broodryk, J. (2006). uBuntu African life coping skills: Theory and practice. *Paper delivered at CCEAM Conference*, 12-17 October 2006, Lefkosia, Cyprus.

De Boer, S., & Simpson, R. (2009). *Successful inclusion for students with autism: Creating a complete, effective ASD inclusion program*. San Francisco, CA: Jossey-Bass.

Eldar, E., Talmor, R. & Wolf-Zukerman, T. (2010). Successes and difficulties in the individual inclusion of children with Autism Spectrum Disorder (ASD) in the eyes of their coordinators. *International Journal of Inclusive Education*, 14(1): 97-114.

Humphrey, N. & Lewis, S. (2008). Make me normal: The views and experiences of pupils on the autistic spectrum in mainstream secondary schools. *Autism*, 12 (1): 23-46.

Khoza, R.J. (2004). Challenges Facing African Leadership. *Business in Africa*, Online available at: http://www.businessinafrica.net/thoughtleadership [accessed on the 11/8/2005]

Khoza, R. (2012). *In defence of Ubuntu*. Johannesburg: Politicsweb.

Leach, D. & Duffy, M., L. (2009). Supporting students with ASD in inclusive settings. *Intervention in School and Clinic*, 45(1): 31-37.

Letseka, M. (2012). In defence of Ubuntu. *Studies in Philosophy and Education*, 31(1): 47-60.

Letseka, M. (2013). Educating for Ubuntu/Botho: Lessons from Basotho indigenous education. *Open Journal of Philosophy*, 3(2): 337-344.

Lindsay, S., Proulx, M., Scott, H., & Thompson, N. (2013). Exploring elementary school teachers' strategies for including children with autism spectrum disorder in mainstream classroom classes. *International Journal of Inclusive Education*, 18(2): 101-122.

Littrell, R.F. (2011). Contemporary Sub-Saharan African managerial leadership research: Some recent empirical studies. *Asia Pacific Journal of Business and Management*, 2(1): 65-91.

McGillicuddy, S. & O'Donnell, G.O. (2013). Teaching students with autism spectrum disorder in mainstream post-primary schools in the Republic of Ireland. *International Journal of Inclusive Education*, 18(4): 323-344.

Majoko, T. (2016). Inclusion of children with ASD: Listening and hearing to voices from the grassroots. *Journal of Autism and Developmental Disorders*, 46(4): 1429-1140.

Mbigi, L. (1997). *Ubuntu: The African dream in management*. Randburg: Knowledge Resources.

Msila, V. (2008). Ubuntu and school leadership. *Journal of Education*, 44: 67-84.

Nussabaum, B. & Wiechel, K. (2010). The spirit of Ubuntu. http://www.peacexpeace.org/2010/07/the-spirit-of-Ubuntu. Accessed 17 December 2018.

Ocholla, D. (2007). Marginalised knowledge: An agenda for indigenous knowledge development and integration with other forms of knowledge. *International Review of Information Ethics*, 7(9): 1-10.

Oppenheim, C.E. (2012). Nelson Mandela and the power of Ubuntu. *Religions,* 3(2): 369-388.

Pellerin, M. (2012). Benefits of Afrocentricity in exploring social phenomena: Understanding Afrocentricity as a social science methodology. *The Journal of Pan African Studies*, 5(4): 149-160.

Shockley, K.G. & Frederick, R.M. (2010). Constructs and dimensions of Afrocentric education. *Journal of Black Studies*, 40(6): 1212-1233.

Sotuku, N. & Duku N.S. (2014). Indigenous African theories in multicultural education. In Okeke, C, Van Wyk, M and Phasha, N (Eds.). *Schooling, society and inclusive education: An Afrocentric perspective*. Cape Town: Oxford University Press.

Swanson, D.M. (2007). Ubuntu an African contribution to (re)search for/with a 'humble togetherness. *Journal of Contemporary Issues in Education*, 2: 53-67.

Symes, W. & Humphrey, N. (2010). Peer-group indicators of social inclusion among pupils with autistic spectrum disorders (ASD) in mainstream secondary schools. *School Psychology*, 31(2): 123-130.

Tutu, D. (1999). *No future without forgiveness*. London: Rider.

UNESCO. (1994). *The Salamanca Statement and Framework for Action on Special Needs Education*. Paris: Unesco.

United Nations. (1948). *Universal declaration of human rights*. New York, NY: United Nations.

United Nations. (2006). *Convention on the rights of persons with disabilities*. New York, NY: United Nations.

Van Wyk, M.M.(2014). The nama stap as indigenous identity and cultural knowledge. *Journal of Human Ecology*, 48(1): 181-188.

FRAMING AUTISM

Mary Clasquin-Johnson

Abstract

This chapter examines how South African organisations frame autism on their websites. I illustrate how the resultant narrative shapes public opinion and proceed to disturb the dominance of the medical model and clinical description of autism. This model is in stark contrast to the social model of inclusion, which South Africa formally adopted in 2001. Drawing on the concept of empathetic scholarship introduced by the emerging field of Critical Autism Studies, I analyse 64 South African organisations' websites. My analysis exposes that the dominant narrative on autism as an undesirable medical condition creates panic and perpetuates stigma. Moreover, the economic drivers of pathology render autism advocates complicit. In contrast, the counter-narrative of neurodiversity recognises autism as natural human difference to be respected as any other difference. This holds promise for how parents and teachers view individuals with autism and respond to their needs.

2.1 Introduction

Many parents experience their child's autism diagnosis as frightening, overwhelming (McCollum, 2012:101) and traumatic (Dale, Jahoda & Knott, 2006:464). Similarly, Navot, Jorgenson, van der Stoep, Toth and Webb (2016:605) have described the diagnosis of autism as a significant stressor for parents. Moreover, studies such as those conducted by Kaniel and Siman-Tov (2011) and Giallo, Wood, Jellett and Porter (2011) have found that parents of children with autism experience more fatigue, stress, depression and anxiety, compared to parents of children with other disabilities. This is consistent with Dudley-Marling and Gurn's (2010:5) argument that 'living on the boundary of the normal curve' affects the life quality of parents of children with disabilities. People search for meaning and justifications (Dale, Jahoda & Knott 2006:464) to make sense of stressful events and often seek online information related to education, practical help and support (Clasquin-Johnson & Clasquin-Johnson, 2018:4; Meadan, Stoner & Angell, 2015:1679; McCollum, 2012:108). I therefore conducted a literature review of South African websites to illuminate how autism is framed on these websites.

The internet shapes public opinions about autism (Thibault, 2014:60). While only about half of South Africans have access to the internet (De Villiers 2019), that is an increase from approximately one-third a decade earlier (Statistics SA, 2011:66), and it is an important source of information for those who do have access. Although this is the most recent statistic I could find, I suspect that it has increased owing to the availability of smartphones. Many South African organisations' websites have links to international organisations. However, these were not included in my analysis as it was out of the scope of the study.

According to Autism South Africa (ASA) (2018), parents are the primary advocates for their children with ASD. Internationally, debates in the field of disability studies focused on whether the emphasis should be on the individual, or the condition, continue unabated. Ellis (2014:5) for example, argues that 'child with autism' puts the child before the condition and 'humanises the individual', while positioning disability as an individual problem rather than a social one. In contrast, 'autistic child' emphasises that 'the child is disabled by society and not the condition' (Ellis, 2014). Extending the latter argument, Johansson (2014) asserts, "I see my autism as part of me, not something I have as 'an add on'".

In addition to being their primary caregivers, parents mediate the outside world for their children by providing information and insight into their behaviour for teachers and therapists (Johansson, 2014:430). The process of adapting to the diagnosis requires parents to rally the family's adaptive resources, advocate for social support, form a positive cognitive assessment of autism and become resilient (Navot *et al.*, 2016:606). Research reveals that parents' cultural beliefs influence their decisions, based on their interpretation of the symptoms, causes and course of autism (Johansson, 2014:418). For example, in a study conducted in India, Daley (2004) found that culturally-shaped beliefs about child development determine what parents perceive as 'abnormal'. Moreover, cultural norms influence the support parents seek before and after diagnosis. Gibson (2014:514) studied parents' perceptions, experiences and emerging stories on autism and highlighted parent-child relationships as crucial to healthy child development. Similarly, de Wolf (2014:4) examined how parents who described themselves as "left with the diagnosis but no other help" search for explanations. Participants in de Wolf's study on "the meaning of autism parenthood" defined themselves as "autism parents" and "autism warriors" since they embrace and manipulate the autism label in order to access services and support for their children. Similarly, Davidson and Orsini (2013:9) recognise parents' role as pioneers in treatment models owing to their feelings of attachment.

There are a number of South African autism-related organisations (we have listed over sixty in an appendix to this chapter), and they generally have websites. In this chapter, I will examine how the websites of South African autism-related organisations present and discuss autism and will then reflect on the consequences of these findings. To enable us to examine the websites, we first need to study the definition of autism.

2.2 Defining autism

There is no consensus among either the persons with autism, their families, friends and supporters or the scientific (clinicians, researchers and other professionals) communities on how autism should be defined (Kenny, Hattersley, Molins, Buckley, Povey & Pellicano, 2016). A literature search on the term autism yielded the following definitions: Autism is a highly variable neurological disorder (Lokhandwala, Khann & West-Strum, 2012:95; Wang, Zhou, Xia, Sun, Wu, Wang & Tomoda, 2012:1) and is characterised as a wide spectrum of complex, life-long developmental disorders that typically emerge during the first three years of life (Meadan, Stoner & Angell, 2015:1680). According to the Oxford

Dictionary, the term autism is derived from the Greek word 'autos' meaning 'self, same, spontaneous; directed from within'. The term, 'autism', was initially coined in 1911 by the Swiss psychiatrist, Eugen Bleuler (1857-1939) to describe a subset of symptoms in schizophrenia. It was Leo Kanner (1894-1981) who first used the word "autism" in the current sense to describe the solitary nature of the children he observed (Kenny et al., 2016:442; Uddin, 2011:201). The term is based on the pathological perspective that autism is an undesirable medical condition (Hughes, 2015:6) and therefore, an impairment to be cured (Kim, 2012:536). These perspectives emanated from the medical model where focus was mainly on what is medically "wrong" with a person. Clasquin-Johnson and Clasquin-Johnson (2018) have illustrated that autism is presented as a condition for which children require costly long-term intensive remediation, therapy and biomedical intervention. As a result, autism is a deeply discrediting attribute (Lilley, 2013:515).

Diagnostic criteria continue to evolve, as reflected by the Diagnostic and Statistical Manual of Mental Disorders (DSM-V) (American Psychiatric Association, 2013). Researchers such as Kenny *et al.* (2016:443) as well as Volkmar and McPartland (2017:194) noted that changes in diagnostic criteria reflect the fluidity of knowledge and conceptual understanding about autism. Individuals who previously would have received a diagnosis of

- autistic disorder;
- Asperger's disorder;
- childhood disintegrative disorder; or
- pervasive developmental disorder not otherwise specified (PDD-NOS).

under the DSM-IV, now all receive an umbrella diagnosis of ASD under the DSM-V (Sawchuk & Clarke, 2015:147). There has been a debate about this new classification because in many countries it has altered who is eligible for services (Volkmar & McPartland, 2014:194). Furthermore, revisions to classification systems accompanied by new definitions invariably alter the nature of conditions (Lai, Lombardo, Chakrabarti & Baron-Cohen, 2013). Within the DMS-V, two critical issues have not adequately been addressed namely clarification of the term "spectrum"; and the need for subgrouping of symptoms (Lai, et al., 2013).

Autism is defined according to behaviour (Lester, Karim & O'Reilly, 2014:139; Uddin, 2011) since it is not possible to use the biology of autism diagnostically (Lai et al., 2013). Recent descriptions of autism emphasise social and communicative deficits, restricted interests or rigid thinking and repetitive or self-stimulating behaviours (American Psychiatric Association, 2013; Hughes, 2015:4). However, researchers such as Root, Case, Burrus and Ramachandran (2015:206) have pointed out that there is no unifying explanation for all three categories of symptoms. Gibson (2014:569) and Thibault (2014:60) concur that the general definition of autism based on the 'triad of impairments', deficit, disability, distress and impairment is overly simplistic, and disregards human diversity. Kenny et al. (2016:443) note that autism is also described as a "way of being".

Many clinicians describe individuals with autism as either low or high functioning. However, the degree of 'impairment' or level of functioning is subject to interpretation and social context (Gibson, 2014:569). The emerging Neurodiversity Movement regards the 'symptoms' associated with autism "simply [as] differences related to autistic neurology that must be accepted rather than fixed or cured" (Hughes, 2015:4). Furthermore, the Autistic Self Advocacy Network (2015) lists seven common features of autism:

- Different sensory experiences such as heightened sensitivity and synaesthesia, any combination of mixed perception (e.g., hearing colour, seeing words and letters as particular colours);
- Non-standard ways of learning and approaching problem solving;
- Deeply focused thinking and passionate interests - what persons with autism commonly refer to as 'special interests' and diagnostic literature calls 'perseveration;'
- Atypical, sometimes repetitive, movement;
- Need for consistency, routine, and order;
- Difficulties in understanding and expressing language as used in typical communication, both verbal and non-verbal, as well as difficulties expressing emotions or feelings in words; and
- Difficulties in understanding and expressing typical social interaction.

Hughes (2015:6) notes that:

> Medical discourses equate 'normal' with healthy and atypical differences with disease; medical researchers portray autistics as defective individuals and genetic mistakes; [in contrast social discourses are based on] the conception of autism as normal neurological variation and neurotypicality as a delusional "obsession with conformity"; Characterising autistic differences in terms of neurodiversity is a way of highlighting the value of autism as a development of human evolution.

Nearly all South African autism-related organisations provide a definition of autism. I will analyse how these definitions are constructed, which model they reflect, including the words that are used to describe the characteristics, needs and challenges experienced by individuals with autism, and their families.

2.3 Framing autism

The dominant discourse of persons without disabilities utilises the metaphor of "autism as disease" to frame autism and constitute it as a disability label that determines policy and intervention practices. Common metaphors include "aliens", portraying children with autism as "locked inside a shell" or the result of "refrigerator mothers" (Broderick & Ne'eman, 2008:462,468). Furthermore, the dominant narrative about the suffering of family members portrays autism as a negative force. As a consequence, autism is widely regarded as an epidemic and an urgent public health crisis (Davidson & Orsini, 2013:1,6; Government of South Africa, 2017).

Childhood is constructed as increasingly risky or precarious, especially for children viewed as suffering from developmental delays or diagnosable mental health difficulties (Sawchuk & Clarke, 2015:148). These researchers assert that owing to the psychiatrisation of children, common behaviours are pathologised as disorders requiring biomedical intervention and treatments. Gibson (2014:6) illustrates how marginalising storylines frame autism according to sources, issues, dominant themes, ideas and labels (Kang, 2013) as well as representations, narratives and images that have implications and consequences (Waltz, 2012). Similarly, Hughes (2015:22) scrutinised how media discourse represents autism and reproduces detrimental medical storylines. In addition, her study revealed that frames describing autism as a "heartbreak" and a "tragedy" were pervasive in magazine discourse directed at women while discourse directed at mixed (both women and men) audiences presented autism from a more scientific and biological viewpoint. Furthermore, television programmes frequently reinforce the association of autism with fear and isolation (Hughes, 2015). Similarly, Kang's (2013:248) analysis of network TV news reports of autism over a 21-year period exposed isolation with the emphasis on individual responsibilities rather than societal support or solutions.

When it comes to autism, language is critical because it has the power to mirror and contour people's perceptions of autism (Kenny *et al.*, 2016). Marginalising narratives dominate the internet in general and, as I will demonstrate, South African websites in particular.

2.4 Research design

I analysed the websites of 64 national and regional organisations and associations, parent support sites and services for children and adults including public and private special schools, autism-specific schools, inclusive schools, vocational training centres (workshops), consultancies related to autism, therapy centres and tutor centres serving the South African autism community. Initially, organisations were discovered via a search engine. I then continued by following links from the websites found this way. I am confident that I have discovered all relevant organisations that have a web presence. Over the past two years, the number of schools have increased, as well as their web presence.

2.4.1 Theoretical framework

In this chapter, I employ Davidson and Orsini's (2013) conception of Critical Autism Studies (CAS) to make sense of autistic experience. My intention is to elucidate how South African websites produce cultural meanings through their representation of concepts and ideas about autism. In other words, how they frame autism. I concur with Waltz (2012:220) that representations via language create meaning and understanding. I align my research with other studies that take a critical standpoint in working to expose and dismantle stigmatising conceptions of autism and disability, as recommended by Hughes (2015:22). Moreover, I draw on the concept of empathetic scholarship introduced by Osteen (2007) to guide my analysis as a parent-practitioner, since I concur that parents in particular, have a critical role to play in teaching others about with and learning from individuals with autism (Osteen, 2010; 2013).

The prevailing medical model of teaching others about and learning frames non-normative embodiments as individual deficiencies demanding prevention, cure, medication and remediation (Hutcheon, 2015:12). While the medical model describes disability as deviancy from normal development or a disease that causes 'difficulty' or 'affects' individuals, the social model describes disability in terms of "the social barriers, restrictions and/or oppressions" that persons with disabilities experience (Hughes, 2015:4). In addition, the medical model compels individuals with disabilities to 'get better', through treatments and therapy. Conversely, the social model views society as responsible for accepting and accommodating disabled people who are entitled to equal opportunities to participate in society.

In their book titled *The Myth of the Normal Curve*, Dudley-Marling and Gurn (2010:4) contend that "to be considered outside the boundaries of normal has consequences. In western cultures difference has long been equated with deviance, and people who are deemed to be different have faced marginalisation and discrimination – or worse." In contrast to the medical model, Disability Studies (DS) situates disability as a social, cultural and political phenomenon that can be interrogated (Ashby, 2008:28). It began as a grassroots rights movement during the 1960s, stressing human rights for persons with disability as a minority group and disputing the obsolete socio-cultural construction of disability as deficit (Ashby, 2008:29; Garland-Thomson, 2013:916; Hutcheon, 2015:12). Moreover, DS celebrates human diversity since "it's normal to be different" (Dudley-Marling & Gurn, 2010:4; Kim, 2012:536), and disability is common and universal (Garland-Thomson, 2013:924). According to Goodley (2013:14), "Disability is the space from which to think through a host of political, theoretical and practical issues that are relevant to all". Critical Disability Studies (CDS) symbolises a shift from disability and disablement to "ableism". In this way it strives to empower the powerless and transform prevailing social injustices and inequalities (Ashby, 2008:30) as well as discrimination and social exclusion (Hughes, 2015:38).

Davidson and Orsini (2013:12) have extended CDS to reflect the "kaleidoscopic complexity of autism" through

- critical attention to ways in which power relations characterise the autism arena;
- new, empowering storylines of autism to contest the dominant deficit and deprecating constructions that shape public opinion, popular culture, and policy; and
- innovative critical frameworks via non-reductive and inclusive methodological and theoretical approaches to autism scholarship.

My research is grounded in Critical Autism Studies (CAS) as I concur with Davidson and Orsini (2013) that there is an urgent need to de-stigmatise autism and cease framing it in either/or terms. In particular, the enduring tensions between the medical and social models of disability are impeding the field. Instead, the most useful facets of each model should be used strategically. In this chapter, I employ CAS to illustrate how South African organisations construct disablement in how they frame autism.

To extend my analysis I draw upon the four sets of rules identified by Osteen (2013) that many writers have applied as formulas for narrating autism. While Osteen's (2013) analysis centred on literature and the portrayal of persons with autism in the visual media, my analysis centres on how South African organisations construct disablement in how they frame autism on their websites.

- Rule #1: The person with autism must be a savant.
- Rule #2: The person with autism must be charmingly quirky but not too severely disabled.
- Rule #3: The person with autism must be a catalyst to advance, or a yardstick to measure the moral progress of non-autistic characters.
- Rule #4: The person with autism must experience a miraculous cure. It makes explicit the subtext hidden in the other rules: autism (and people with autism) must be erased.

2.5 Findings and discussion

In answering the question, "what is autism?" websites construct a medical model of disability containing an overwhelmingly negative message about autism. Consequently, South African websites resemble the websites of many disability charities since they focus on a single disability, namely autism, and its causes, and situate it as an individual problem (Waltz, 2012). One of the first realisations parents will arrive at is that their child is disabled and therefore needs long-term professional help that will cost unlimited amounts of money, as he/she is unlikely to be accommodated at an ordinary public school. There are only six autism-specific public schools in South Africa, accommodating 1.7% of learners with autism (Department of Basic Education & Department of Women, Children and People with Disabilities, 2013:14). Since January 2016, 18 new autism units for learners diagnosed with autism have been opened at special schools in Gauteng Province alone (Evans, 2016), each accommodating between 25 and 50 learners. In contrast, ASA in its 2016 Autism Awareness Day Media Release (2 April 2016) claims that approximately one million South Africans are living with autism.

2.5.1 Autism is framed as a deficit, disability, disorder, disaster and disease Rule #4

Medically constructed definitions of autism follow Rule #4 and individuals need to be cured. To quote some examples:

- Autism is "a severe, life long, developmental disability of neurobiological cause" (http://www.vera.co.za). Autism spectrum disorder (ASD) and autism are both general terms for a group of complex disorders of brain development (http://www.aut2know.co.za).
- Autism is a whole body disease, which presents as a neuro-developmental disorder and is affecting a growing number of children in different ways (Dr Louise Lindenberg – http://www.autismdoctor.co.za/; http://www.thestaracademy.co.za).
- The nature of the disability drives the family into isolation. Managing autism is about taking children who exhibit this bizarre social behaviour, and giving them interventions to make them less bizarre" (http://www.johannesburghospitalschool.co.za).

- "… Quality intervention for children aged between 18 months and nine years who have difficulty with social interaction, communication and behaviours. This includes children suffering from ASD" (www.centre4playandlearning.co.za).
- "Autism is a lifelong condition that impacts on all areas of communication and social interaction. The condition can sometimes manifest itself in severe behavioral problems and cognitive impairment" (http://www.actioninautism.org.za).

The above definitions frame autism as a disorder to be cured, which disrespects diversity and disregards the autistic child's right to exist.

2.5.2 Autism is framed as a tragedy Rule #4

Autism Western Cape outlines the stages of grief that parents should anticipate following their child's diagnosis (http://www.autismwesterncape.org.za). This equates the presence of an autistic child with a death in the family. In order to cope with the tragedy, parents are offered extensive options for therapeutic interventions, consistent with Rule #4.

- As neither the presentation of symptoms of ASD nor the profile of a child is universal, effective intervention requires the 'cocktail approach' – the combination of a vast array of different techniques. They include the following Applied Behaviour Analysis (ABA); Verbal Behaviour (VB); Pivotal Response Training (PRT); Teach Me Language; Relationship Development Intervention (RDI); Treatment and Education of Autistic and Related Communication Handicapped Children (TEACCH); Floortime (DIR); NEW SCERTS; Holistic Approach to Neuro Development Learning Efficiency (HANDLE); Brain Gym; Prompts for Restructuring Oral Muscular Phonetic Targets (PROMPT); Makaton; Sensory Integration; Social Skills Training; Social Stories; Assisted and Alternative Communication; and Rhythmic Movement Training (RMT)" (http://www.asapautism.co.za).
- A variety of methods are used with a high success rate (http://www.ablecentre.org).
- It is also important that the parents and extended family receive guidance, advice and support in terms of how to adequately cope with the situation. These can only be provided by those who have in–depth training and experience in this field (http://www.cherebotha.co.za).

2.5.3 Autism is framed as an epidemic

Recent suggestions of an "autism epidemic" (South African Government, 2018) are uncritically reported on many South African websites since they fail to consider if the ostensible escalation in autism is socially constructed. In fact, there are no reliable existing data on the prevalence of autism in South Africa. Some researchers assert that while international statistics are 1:68, it may be considerably greater in developing-country contexts such as South Africa (Van Biljon, Kritzinger & Geertsema, 2015). According to Kim (2012:535) the prevalence rate in the United States of America (USA) has progressively increased from

- 1 in 5000 children in 1970; to
- 1 in 500 in 1987; to 1 in 150 in 2007; to
- 1 in 110 in 2009; to
- the current 1 in 68 children (1 in 42 boys and 1 in 189 girls) (Centers for Disease Control and Prevention, 2014).

Notably, in South Africa, Van Biljon et al. (2015:53) found a significantly higher gender bias of 9:1. These prevalence rates communicate a sense of urgency as autism is portrayed as 'unstoppable' (Davidson & Orsini, 2013:1) meanwhile knowledge about autism is constantly altering. At the same time, Gernsbacher, Dawson and Goldsmith (2005:55) argue that the increase in diagnosed cases of autism is attributable to expanded diagnostic criteria, combined with intentionally increased public awareness.

Private providers and their profit-driven therapeutic interventions dominate South African websites. Consequently, the prevailing narrative or framing is that autism is a disorder, a tragedy (or disaster) and a lifelong disability characterised by a complex triad of impairments (in communication, social interaction and imagination). Yet Kim (2012:536) contends that autism is socially constructed differently in various cultures. Furthermore, there are significant differences regarding how autism is constructed in the USA as opposed to other countries without epidemiological studies. According to Kim (2012), the majority of studies promote pathological perspectives that autism is an impairment to be cured. However, there is very little evidence of treatment and intervention efficacy given on South African websites, which appear to uncritically represent the dominant Euro-Western view. Note in this context, the dominance of stereotypes and social stigma associated with the representation of autism (Garner, Jones & Harwood, 2015:2) in film, and the impact of media portrayals of the autism spectrum on viewers. Nevertheless, this is strongly associated with Rule #4.

2.5.4 Mixed, contradictory messages

Several websites contain contradictory messages by purporting both medical and social models. They offer a clinical definition of autism that reinforces stigma and yet proclaim acceptance Rule #3, as illustrated below:

- "We regard ASD as a neurological disorder. Our interventions are based on respect for human variety and dedication to understanding the experience of living from the perspective of the individual with autism" (www.vera.co.za).
- "Autism South Africa (ASA) aspires to achieving a society in which persons with Autism Spectrum Disorder (ASD) enjoy all the rights and opportunities to meet their needs and fulfil their potentials, throughout their lives, as loved and valued members of their families and communities" (http://www.aut2know.co.za).
- "… Autism is not a death sentence. We will provide the best one-on-one teaching to Autistic children to help them reach their full potential as adults... to better understand the disease and to obtain ways to ensure a better adult life prognosis for all Autistics." http://www.autismfs.org.za).

- "On the Spectrum celebrates the diverse abilities of children and adults on the autism spectrum and guides them in realising their potential" (http://www.onspectrum.co.za).
- "At CARE, we emphasise the ethos of being 'different, not less'" (http://www.thecarecentre.co.za).
- "We believe in the worth, dignity and unique character of the individual... An embracing environment of tolerance and understanding must be sought after to ensure that all feel accepted and secure" (http://www.unicaschool.co.za).
- "Our main objective is to improve the quality of life for people with ASD and their caregivers by building partnerships between people with ASD, their families and the community to provide information, services, learning and research" (http://www.actioninautism.org.za).
- Through individual objectives determined for each child, we work toward improving every child's functional prognosis and enhancing their potential to become a functional adult, able to contribute to society in a meaningful way (http://www.chrysalispreschool.org.za).

So, while the principles of social inclusion are reflected above, it is severely constrained by the medical definitions and descriptions. Moreover, parents have to make sense of these contradictory messages. Notwithstanding, this may provide the basis for integrating the medical and social models and using the benefits of each.

2.5.5 Admission criteria

Although schools acknowledge the existence of the DSM-V, they still use the previous DSM-IV criteria, for example:

- "The school admits the following sub-groups: Autistic Disorder also referred to as Kanner's Autism or Classic Autism, Asperger's Disorder and Pervasive Developmental Disorder not otherwise specified {PDD (NOS)} also referred to as Atypical Autism" (http://www.vera.co.za/index.php/admission-criteria/).

This suggests that they disagree with the broad definition of autism under the DSM-V. It should however be noted that schools put their own interests first by indicating conditions of admission linked to probationary periods. This implies that they can ask parents to leave it they feel that they are unable to work with a specific child.

- "Our school is for children with a primary diagnosis of Autism Spectrum Disorder (ASD)" (http://www.randburgclinicschool.co.za/autism-centre).
- "A primary diagnosis of autism by a medical professional who is registered with the HPCSA" (http://www.thekeyschool.org).
- "If your child is suitable for admission, he or she will attend the Centre for a ten-day observation and assessment period" (http://www.thecarecentre.co.za).
- "Learners are referred to us by the Department of Education after detailed assessment and special permission" (http://www.espotch.co.za).

- "A probationary period of up to 6 months will be applied. A review will be held to consider the child's needs and the ability of the school to meet these needs, and the level of resources required for the child" (http://cslc.co.za/).

2.5.6 Recovery and cure

While some websites state that, "there is no known cause for autism and there is no cure for autism" (http://www.ernieelscentre4autism.co.za) authors such as Shute (2010) note that many parents are desperate for a cure. Two South African organisations (http://www.thestaracademy.co.za; http://www.ablecentre.org) claim that "Recovery is possible". This reflects Rule #4 as autistic self-advocate Jim Sinclair (1993) in his notorious speech, "Don't mourn for us", recognised when he cautioned parents that if their autistic child was cured, he or she would cease to exist. Yet parents' fears concerning who will care for their autistic child when they no longer can is valid, since contemporary society is unlikely to do justice to this task.

2.5.7 Only "high-functioning" autistic children can be included

Owing to an autistic learners' need for long-term, intensive specialist interventions, such as individual development plans, and their weighting of six (i.e. one child with autism equals 6 neurotypical learners), they are seldom referred to ordinary schools. Autism Western Cape (http://www.autismwesterncape.org.za) provides a list of private schools that accommodate learners with high functioning autism. This is consistent with Rule #2 that learners can only be included on condition that they are "not be too severely disabled". This narrative appears to focus exclusively on academic ability and disregards psychosocial, emotional and other practical support needs such as physically moving between classes during the school day.

Several schools stipulate high functioning autism as an admission criteria, even though this is not clearly defined; for example, "We are proud to announce that we will be opening an Autistic Unit in January 2015 which will primarily help high functioning autistic children. Using individual programmes created for each child (IEP), we will endeavour to increase each child's skills to a level where in time, they will be able to transfer to the Special Needs Class at Capulum College (http://www.capulumcollege.co.za). In other words, even high functioning autistic learners will still only be accommodated in the Special Needs Class.

While Lilley (2013:518) argues that parents find themselves between social justice arguments advocating inclusive schooling and special education arguments advocating expertise and the promise of the partial remediation of deficits, this does not appear to apply in the South African context. Following a child's diagnosis as being on the autism spectrum, parents are referred to special education institutions as the most appropriate educational placement (See http://www.aut2know.co.za).

In fact, the majority of public and private special schools make the case that autism is highly specialised and therefore requires autism-specific settings and approaches. For example, "We are a Public Benefit organisation that provides affordable, specialised education to learners with Autism Spectrum Disorder between the ages of 3 and 18" (http://www.unicaschool.co.za). This reflects the continuing commitment to the provision of segregated education placements and the lack of adequate resources available in public schools to make inclusion work (Lilley, 2013:518). Again, this reflects Rule #4.

2.6 Alternative framing: autism as 'differ-bilities'

Recognising the voice of the individual appreciates autism as a difference rather than a disorder (Gibson, 2014:569; Jones, Zahl & Huws, 2001). Autistics' perceptions and definitions should therefore be considered, as they are the people most affected by autism who know it most intimately (O'Neil, 2008:788). First-hand accounts from the autistic community as well as evidence from the scientific literature challenges the idea that ASD are simply illnesses or disorders.

> Human life is precious and deserving of the respect implied by the Declaration of Human Rights in the Constitution of the Republic of South Africa. People with disabilities have the right to live a life free from discrimination. They are entitled to appropriate care, education and training, with adequate scope for the exercising of their abilities and interests. We use terminology like autistic, which is not politically correct, as this seems to be preferred by people with autism who have expressed themselves on this issue (http://www.vera.co.za).

Although autism can be associated with distress and impairment, autistics thrive and astonish those around them because their autistic qualities may equate to giftedness (O'Neil, 2008:795) or they possess the 'ideal cognitive profile' to succeed in our knowledge economy (Cowen, 2009). From a religious perspective, parents are encouraged to see their child's disability as part of a "divine plan," "gift" or "blessing" (Sawchuk & Clarke, 2015:151). Dr Genevieve Kumapley, Director of Haven International Autism Centre in Ghana, urged Ghanaians to understand autism as a disorder rather than a curse from God (GhanaWeb 9 July 2016).

I concur with O' Neil (2008:795) that if we disregard the voices of autistics, we will never come to a genuine understanding of autism. The growing neurodiversity movement as a disability rights movement promotes autism acceptance based on understanding autism as natural neurological variation. However, some have argued that they do not represent severely affected individuals (Kenny et al., 2016).

2.7 Conclusion

As I have illustrated, the dominant narrative of South African websites frames autism as deficit, disability, disorder, disaster and even disease. They overwhelmingly reflect Rule #4. While I was able to identify some traces of Rule #2 and Rule #3, I was unable to find a single example of Rule #1. In other words, it appears that South African websites do not recognise savant abilities.

Combined with the representation of autism as an epidemic, it creates fear and panic. Moreover, being disabled, autistic, neurodivergent or 'low-functioning' is clearly undesirable. In South Africa, many websites related to autism appear to reinforce exclusion instead of advancing social inclusion, acceptance and support. Parents are introduced to special schools as their best option. This is fertile ground on which to convince parents that their children require intensive early intervention. In reality the cost of intervention is so prohibitive that families cannot afford it for long (Byford, Cary, Barrett, Aldred, Charman, Howlin, Hudry, Leadbitter, Le Couteur, McConachie, Pickles, Slonims, Temple, Green & the PACT Consortium, 2015; Cidav, Marcus & Mandell, 2012:Jian-Jun, Li-Juan, Guang-Lei, Chen, Ren-Rong, Xue-Rong, Yeng-Ye & Jing-Ping, 2015). As a result, very few autistic children currently receive the support they need to develop optimally.

The increase in prevalence can be linked to the proliferation of private remedial schools that seldom declare their registration or accreditation status. South Africa urgently needs large-scale cost-effective interventions appropriate for its developing country context. This should include systemic change in the school system in order to cater to the needs and aspirations of diverse learners. Regardless of inclusive policies, this is unlikely to happen since schools operate in an increasingly competitive academic environment, making them reluctant to accept students with disabilities who may perform poorly in testing (e.g. Annual National Assessments) and lower the measures of academic performance in the regular classroom (Lilley, 2013:519).

2.8 Recommendations

There is an urgent need for the authors of autism websites to be educated about the importance of being sensitive towards their readers. Parents who are already deeply affected do not deserve to be disrespected by the very people they turn to for help and support. I agree with Hughes (2015:11) that discrimination and exclusion will persist unless the conversation around autism changes. One key aspect will involve reconsidering autism as a medical condition and the purview of clinicians. South African organisations should consider an alternative narrative on autism in keeping with its constitutional imperatives of human rights, equity, redress, social justice and inclusion. Therefore, when writing websites, the alternative perspective of neurodiversity should be considered. Rather than leaving parents with a sense of panic and despair, they should be reassured that their child can learn and that appropriate support and help is available.

I do not advocate misleading parents. No one understands a child better than their parents. Assessment reports very seldom come as a complete surprise. However, it is essential to moderate the clinical message with empathy and understanding. Nothing is more personal for parents than a discussion related to their children's development and learning or more stressful than trying to address any barriers that their children may encounter.

Organisations involved in advocacy should carefully examine the content of their messages. The central focus of increasing autism awareness must be on fostering understanding and respect for human diversity. Becoming autism-aware will then enable us to recognise individual strengths and needs, and to provide appropriate support to reduce and overcome barriers. Therefore, we need to pay special attention to how we could align reframing or alternatively framing autism with our policies on inclusion. Davidson and Orsini's (2013:12) call for empowering storylines of autism should guide us here.

As a university lecturer involved in teacher education, I believe that universities are well placed to take the lead in alternatively framing autism, as well as disability in general through our tuition, community engagement and research. After all, we are modelling alternative framing for our students – the teachers of the future.

References

American Psychiatric Association. (2013). *Diagnostic and Statistical Manual of Mental Disorders*. (5th ed.). Washington, DC: APA.

Ashby, C.E. (2008). Cast into a Cold Pool: Inclusion and Access in Middle School for Students with Labels of Mental Retardation and Autism. PhD diss., Syracuse University.

Autistic Self Advocacy Network. (2016). About Autism. http://www.autisticadvocacy.org

Autism South Africa. (2016). World Autism Awareness Day (United Nations Resolution (A/RES/62/139) https://www.facebook.com/AutismSouthAfrica.

Bateman, C. (2013). Autism: Mitigating a global epidemic. *South African Medical Journal* 103(5): 276-277. doi:10.7196/SAMJ.6915 http://www.samj.org.za/index.php/samj/article/view/6915/5045

Bennett, P.L. (1996). Practitioners' Perceived Usefulness of 'Autism' and Related Terms: Implications for Diagnostic Procedures. *Educational Research* 38(3): 343-349. doi: http://dx.doi.org/10.1080/001318896038030.

Broderick, A.A., & Ne'eman, A. (2008). Autism as Metaphor: Narrative and Counter-narrative. *International Journal of Inclusive Education* 12(5): 459-476. doi: 10.1080/13603110802377490http://dx.doi.org/10.5130/portal.v11i2.3279.

Byford, S. M.C., Barrett, B., Aldred, C.R., Charman, T., Howlin, P., Hudry, K., Leadbitter, K., Le Couteur, A., McConachie, H., Pickles, A., Slonims, V., Temple, K.J., Green, J. & the PACT Consortium. (2016). Cost-effectiveness analysis of a Communication-focused Therapy for Pre-school Children with Autism: Results from a Randomised Controlled Trial. *BMC Psychiatry* 15:316. doi: 10.1186/s12888-015-0700-x.

Centers for Disease Control and Prevention. (2014). CDC Facts: Autism Spectrum Disorder. http://www.cdc.gov/ncbddd/autism/addm.html

Nicolas, C. (2014). More on the Ontological Status of Autism and Double Empathy. *Disability & Society* 29(10): 1672-1676. http://dx.doi.org/10.1080/09687599.2014.949625

Cidav, Z., Marcus, S.C. & Mandell, D.S. (2012). Implications of Childhood Autism for Parental Employment and Earnings. *Paediatrics* 129(4): 617-623. https://www.ncbi.nlm.nih.gov/pmc/articles/PMC3356150/

Cowen, T. (2009). *Create Your Own Economy: The Path to Prosperity in a Disordered World*. New York: Dutton.

Daley, T.C. (2004). From Symptom Recognition to Diagnosis: Children with Autism in Urban India. *Social Sciences & Medicine* 58(7): 1323-1335 doi: 10.1016/S0277-9536(03)00330-7

Dale, E., Jahoda, A. & Knott, F. (2006). Mothers' Attributions following Their Child's Diagnosis of Autistic Spectrum Disorder: Exploring Links with Maternal Levels of Stress, Depression and Expectations about Their Child's Future. *Autism* 10(5): 463-479. doi: http://dx.doi.org/0666001362-3613.

Davidson, J., & Orsini, M. (Eds). (2013). *Worlds of Autism: Across the Spectrum of Neurological Difference*. Minneapolis: University of Minnesota.

Department of Basic Education and Department of Women, Children and People with Disabilities. (2013). *Report on the Status of Learners with Disabilities in Special Schools. In the Department of Basic Education's Year of Inclusive Education (2013) – Are things being done differently?* 30 September 2013. Pretoria: DBE/DWCPD.

De Villiers, J. (2019). South African internet users spend much more time online than Americans and Europeans. *Business Insider SA*, Feb 05 2019. https://www.businessinsider.co.za/south-africa-one-of-the-worlds-top-internet-users-hootsuite-report-2019-2, Accessed 13 January 2020.

De Wolf, J. (2014). *Parents of Children with Autism: An Ethnography*. New York: Palgrave Macmillan. doi: 10.1057/9781137436238.

Di Tore P.A., De Giuseppe, T. & Corona, F. (2017). Autism Spectrum as an Empathy Disorder. *Autism Open Access* 7: 198. doi: 10.4172/2165-7890.1000198

Dudley-Marling, Curt, & Gurn, A. (Eds.) (2010). *The Myth of the Normal Curve*. New York: Peter Lang.

Ellis, S.J. (2014). *Perspectives of the Autistic 'Voice': an Ethnography Examining Informal Education Learning Experiences*. Sheffield Hallam University. http://shura.shu.ac.uk/8317/

Evans, J. (2016). Gauteng rolling out schools for autistic children. *News24*. https://www.news24.com/SouthAfrica/News/gauteng-rolling-out-schools-for-autistic-children-20160512

Garland-Thomson, R. (2013). Disability Studies: A Field Emerged. *American Quarterly* 65(4): 915-926. doi: 10.1353/aq.2013.0052

Garner, A., Jones, S. & Harwood, V. (2015). Authentic Representations or Stereotyped 'Outliers': Using the CARS2 to Assess Film Portrayals of Autism Spectrum Disorders. *International Journal of Culture and Mental Health* 8(4): 414-425. doi: http://dx.doi.org/10.1080/17542863.2015.1041993.

Gernsbacher, M.A., Dawson, M. & Goldsmith, H.H. (2005). Three Reasons Not to Believe in an Autism Epidemic. *American Psychological Society* 14(2): 55-58.

GhanaWeb. (2016). Autism is a disorder not a curse. Dr. Genevieve Kumapley, *Health News* Sat, 9 July mobile.ghanaweb.com

Giallo, R., Wood, C.E., Jellett, R. & Porter, R. (2011). Fatigue, Wellbeing and Parental Self-efficacy in Mothers of Children with an Autism Spectrum Disorder. *Autism* 17(4): 465-480. doi: 10.1177/1362361311416830.

Gibson, K.A. (2014). Appreciating the World of Autism through the Lens of Video Interaction Guidance: An Exploration of a Parent's Perceptions, Experiences and Emerging Narratives on Autism. *Disability & Society* 29(4): 568-582. doi: http://dx.doi.org/10.1080/09687599.2013.844096.

Government of South Africa. (2017). World Autism Awareness Day 2 April 2017. https://www.gov.za/speeches/world-autism-awareness-day-2017-15-nov-2016-1401

Hall, S.S., Hannah F. Wright, H.F. & Mills, D.S. (2016). What Factors Are Associated with Positive Effects of Dog Ownership in Families with Children with Autism Spectrum Disorder? The Development of the Lincoln Autism Pet Dog Impact Scale. *PLoS ONE* 11(2):e0149736. doi:10.1371/journal.pone.0149736

Higashijima, J, Miura, Y., Nakagawa, C., Yamanouchi, Y., Takahashi, K. & Nakamura, M. (2012). Public Opinions Regarding the Relationship between Autism Spectrum Disorders and Society: Social Agenda Construction via Science Café and Public Dialogue using Questionnaires. *Journal of Science Communication* 11(4): 1-12.

Hughes, J.M.F. (2015). Changing Conversations around Autism: A Critical Action Implicative Discourse Analysis of U.S. Neurodiversity Advocacy Online. PhD diss., ProQuest 3721820.

Hutcheon, E.J. (2015). 'Cripping' Resilience: Generating new Vocabularies of Resilience from Narratives of Postsecondary Students who Experience Disability. Master of Science diss., Calgary, Alberta.

Huws, Jaci C., & Jones, R.S.P. (2010). They just seem to Live their Lives in their own little World': Lay Perceptions of Autism. *Disability & Society*, 25(3): 331-344. http://dx.doi.org/10.1080/09687591003701231.

Jian-Jun, O., Li-Juan, S., Guang-Lei, X., Chen, C., Ren-Rong, W., Xue-Rong, L., Yeng-Ye, Z., & Jing-Ping, Z. (2015). Employment and financial burden of families with preschool children diagnosed with ASD in urban China: results from a descriptive study. *BMC Psychiatry* 15(3). doi: 10.1186/s12888-015-0382-4

Johansson, S.T. (2014). He is Intelligent but Different: Stakeholders' Perspectives on Children on the Autism Spectrum in an Urban Indian School Context. *International Journal of Disability, Development and Education* 61(4): 416-433. doi: http://dx.doi.org/10.1080/1034912X.2014.955786.

Jones, R.S.P., Zahl, A, & Huws, J.C. (2001). First-hand Accounts of Emotional Experiences in Autism: A Qualitative Analysis. *Disability & Society* 16(3): 393-401. doi: http://dx.doi.org/10.1080/09687590120045950.

Kang, S. (2013). Coverage of Autism Spectrum Disorder in the US Television News: An Analysis of Framing. *Disability & Society* 28(2): 245-259. http://dx.doi.org/10.1080/09687599.2012.705056.

Kaniel, S., & Siman-Tov., A. (2011). Comparison between Mothers and Fathers in Coping with Autistic Children: A Multivariate Model. *European Journal of Special Needs Education* 26(4): 479-493. http://dx.doi.org/10.1080/08856257.2011.597186.

Kenny, L., Hattersley, C., Molins, B., Buckley, C., Povey, C., & Pellicano, E. (2016). Which Terms should be used to Describe Autism? Perspectives from the UK Autism Community. *Autism* 20(4): 442-462. doi: 10.1177/1362361315588200.

Kim, H.U. 2012. Autism across Cultures: Rethinking Autism. *Disability & Society* 27(4): 535-545. doi: http://dx.doi.org/10.1080/09687599.2012.659463.

Kumapley, G. (2016). Autism is a Disorder not a Curse. *Health News of Saturday*, 9 July 2016 GhanaWeb https://www.ghanaweb.com/GhanaHomePage/health/Autism-is-a-disorder-not-a-curse-Dr-Genevieve-Kumapley-454065

Lai, M, Lombardo, M.V., Chakrabarti, B. & Baron-Cohen, S. (2013). Subgrouping the Autism Spectrum: Reflections on DSM-5. *PLoS Biol* 11(4): e1001544. https://doi.org/10.1371/journal.pbio.1001544

Lester, J.N., Karim, K., & O' Reilly, M. (2014). Autism itself actually isn't a Disability: Negotiating a 'Normal' Versus 'Abnormal'. *Autistic Identity, Communication and Medicine* 11(2): 139-152. doi: http://equinoxpub.com

Lilley, R. (2013). It's an Absolute Nightmare: Maternal Experiences of Enrolling Children Diagnosed with Autism in Primary School in Sydney, Australia. *Disability & Society* 28(4): 514-526. doi: http://dx.doi.org/10.1080/09687599.2012.717882.

Lokhandwala, T., Khanna, R. & West-Strum, D., (2012). Hospitalization Burden among Individuals with Autism. *Journal of Autism and Developmental Disorders* 42: 95-104. DOI 10.1007/s10803-011-1217-x

McCollum, M. (2012). A Look into the World of Autism in Australia: Autism Spectrum Australia (Aspect). *Journal of Consumer Health on the Internet* 16(1): 101-109. doi:http://dx.doi.org/10.1080/15398285.2012.646918.

Meadan, H., Stoner, J.B.S. & Angell., M.E. (2015). Fathers of Children with Autism: Perceived Roles, Responsibilities, and Support Needs. *Early Child Development and Care* 185(10): 1678-1694. http://dx.doi.org/10.1080/03004430.2015.1019876.

Navot, N., Jorgenson, A.G., Van der Stoep, A. Toth, K. & Webb. S.J. (2016). Family Planning and Family Vision in Mothers after Diagnosis of a Child with Autism Spectrum Disorder. *Autism* 20(5): 605-615. http://dx/doi.10.1177/1362361315602134.

Mio, B., Matthews, M. & Takeyama, Y. (2014). Visualising 'Unacceptable' Lives? The Moving Story of Hikari to tomo ni (With the Light: Raising an Autistic Child, 2001–2010). *Journal of Multidisciplinary International Studies*, 11(2): 1-22. The Unacceptable Special Issue, guest edited by John Scannell.

O'Neil, S. (2008). The Meaning of Autism: Beyond Disorder. *Disability & Society* 23(7): 787-799. doi: http://dx.doi.org/10.1080/09687590802469289.

Reynolds, C.R., & Goldstein, S. (1999). *Handbook of Neurodevelopmental and Genetic Disorders in Children*. New York: The Guilford Press.

Root, N.B., Case, L.K., Burrus, C.J. & Ramachandran, V.S. (2015). External Self-representations Improve Self-awareness in a Child with Autism. *Neurocase* 21(2): 206-210. http://dx.doi.org/10.1080/13554794.2014.888455

Sawchuk, D., & Clarke, J. (2015). Representations of Autism and Autism Spectrum Disorder (ASD) in the North American Roman Catholic Print Media, 1990–2013. *Journal of Disability & Religion* 19(2): 146-167. http://dx.doi.org/10.1080/23312521.2015.1024910.

Shute, N. (2010). Desperate for an Autism Cure. *Scientific American* 303: 80- 85. doi: http://dx.doi.org/10.1038/scientificamerican1010-80.

Sinclair, J. (1993). "Don't Mourn for Us." Presentation to the International Conference on Autism in Toronto. Autism Network International Newsletter, *Our Voice* 1(3). http://www.autreat.com/dont_mourn.html.

Statistics South Africa. (2011). *Census 2011: Statistical Release (Revised) P0301.4*.Pretoria: Statistics South Africa. http://www.statssa.gov.za/publications/P03014/P030142011.pdf

Thibault, R. (2014). Can Autistics Redefine Autism? The Cultural Politics of Autistic Activism. *Trans-Scripts* 4.

Uddin, L.Q. (2011). The Self in Autism: An Emerging View from Neuroimaging. *Neurocase* 17(3): 201-208. doi: 10.1080/13554794.2010.509320

Van Biljon, S., Kritzinger, A. & Geertsema, S. (2015). A Retrospective Case Report on Demographic Changes of Learners at a School for Children with Autism Spectrum Disorder in the Gauteng Province. *South African Journal of Childhood Education* 5(1): 42-61.

Volkmar, F.R. & McPartland, J.C. (2014). From Kanner to DSM-5: Autism as an Evolving Diagnostic Concept. *The Annual Review of Clinical Psychology* 10:193-212. https://doi.org/10.1146/annurev-clinpsy-032813-153710.

Waltz, M. (2012). Images and Narratives of Autism within Charity Discourses. *Disability & Society* 27(2): 219-233. http://dx.doi.org/10.1080/09687599.2012.631796.

Wang, J., Zhou, X., Xia, W., Sun, C., Wu, L., Wang, J. & Tomoda, A., (2012). Parent-reported Health Care Expenditures Associated with Autism Spectrum Disorders in Heilongjiang Province, China. *BMC Health Services Research* 12: 1-7. http://www.biomedcentral.com/1472-6963/12/7

Webster, A., Feiler, A., & Webster, V. (2003). Early Intensive Family Intervention and Evidence of Effectiveness: Lessons from the South West Autism Programme. *Early Child Development and Care* 173(4): 383-398. http://dx.doi.org/10.1080/030044303200007907.

Zaidman-Zait, A., Mirenda, P., Duku, E., Vaillancourt, T., Smith, I.M., Szatmari, P., Bryson, S., Fombonne, E., Volden, J., Waddell, C., Zwaigenbaum, L., Georgiades, S., Bennett, T., Elsabaggh, M. & Thompson, A. (2016). Impact of Personal and Social Resources on Parenting Stress in Mothers of Children with Autism Spectrum Disorder. *Autism* 1-12, http://dx.doi:10.1177/1362361316633033.

Websites

Action in Autism http://www.actioninautism.org.za Accessed 13 September 2018.

Alma Special School https://www.almaschool.co.za Accessed 23 September 2018

Alpha School for Autism https://www.westerncape.gov.za/facility/alpha-school Accessed 12 September 2018.

Amazing K, Randburg http://www.amazingk.co.za Accessed 15 September 2018.

Ashton International College Ballito, The Grace Wing Autism Unit http://www.ashtonballito.co.za Accessed 23 September 2018.

Association for Autism http://www.afa.org.za Accessed 18 September 2018.

Autism and Behavioural Learning Environment (ABLE) Centre, Richards Bay http://www.ablecentre.org Accessed 17 September 2018.

Autism Eastern Cape http://www.autismec.co.za Accessed 15 September 2018.

Autism South Africa http://www.aut2know.co.za Accessed 12 September 2018.

Autism Spectrum Adaptive Programme South Africa www.asapautism.co.za Accessed 23 September 2018.

Autism Western Cape http://www.autismwesterncape.org.za Accessed 18 September 2016.

Boland School for Autism http://www.bolandautism.org.za/autism Accessed 15 September 2018.

Blaze Academy for Specialised Education http://blazeacademy.co.za Accessed 23 September 2018/

Capulum College, Hilton KZN http://www.capulumcollege.co.za Accessed 15 September 2018.

Cape Autism Charity Trust http://www.cact.co.za/what_is_autism.html Accessed 21 September 2018.

Care Centre for Autism, Research and Education http://www.thecarecentre.co.za Accessed 22 September 2018.

Casa Do Sol School https://www.casadosolschool.com Accessed 17 September 2018.

Centre for Play and Learning https://www.centre4playandlearning.co.za Accessed 11 September 2018.

Chere Botha http://www.cherebotha.co.za Accessed 11 September 2018.

Chrysalis preschool http://www.chrysalispreschool.org.za Accessed 23 September 2018

Cornerstone Learning Centre http://www.cslc.co.za Accessed 17 September 2018.

Craiglands Remedial School Randburg http://www.craiglandsremedialschool.co.za Accessed 23 September 2018.

Crossroads School http://www.crossroadsschool.co.za Accessed 23 September 2018

Duncan Sinclair Academy http://www.autismacademy.co.za/index.php/autism-education-and-training Accessed 23 September 2018

EduExcellence Private Therapeutic Remedial Schools http://www.eduexcellence.co.za Accessed 15 September 2018.

ES le Grange School http://www.espotch.co.za Accessed 18 September 2018.

Faery Glen Therapy Centre http://www.faeryglen.co.za Accessed 12 September 2018.

Flutterbys Special Education and Therapy Centre http://www.flutterbys.co.za Accessed 23 September 2018

Footprints School http://www.footprintschool.co.za Accessed 18 September 2018.

Free State Association for Autism Spectrum Disorders http://www.autismfs.org.za Accessed 15 September 2018.

Glenoaks School https://glenoaks.org.za Accessed 23 September 2018

I am school for autism https://www.iamautismschool.com Accessed 23 September 2018

Johannesburg Hospital School http://www.johannesburghospitalschool.co.za Accessed 17 September 2018.

Khuluma Education http://www.khulumaeducation.co.za Accessed 15 September 2018.

Kidstart Early Intervention Centre http://www.kidstartcentre.com Accessed September 2018.

Lethabo Le Khutso www.autism-llk.org.za Accessed 23 September 2018

Little Gems https://www.little-gems.co.za Accessed 23 September 2018

Little Leaps School for Autism http://www.littleleaps.co.za Accessed 12 September 2018.

L.U.C.C.A Support and Care Centre for Children with a Difference http://www.luccaspecialkids.co.za Accessed 22 September 2018.

Mind Stretch http://www.mindstretch.co.za Accessed 18 September 2018.

Okuhle Autism School

On the Spectrum http://www.onspectrum.co.za Accessed 22 September 2018.

Pathways https://www.ptapathways.co.za Accessed 23 September 2018

Randburg Autism Clinic Centre http://www.randburgclinicschool.co.za/autism-centre Accessed 22 September 2018.

Situla – Education and Therapy https://situla.co.za Accessed 23 September 2018

SNAP Special Needs Adapted Programme http://www.snap.org.za Accessed 15 September 2016.

Special Kids http://www.specialkids.co.za Accessed 18 September 2018.

Tamarisk Special School for Autism (TASSFA)

The Baby Therapy Centre http://www.babytherapy.org.za Accessed 28 September 2018.

The Claremont Practice http://www.claremontpractice.co.za Accessed 15 September 2018.

The Dream Tree School http://www.thedreamtreeschool.co.za Accessed 18 September 2018.

The Ernie Els Centre for Autism http://www.ernieelscentre4autism.co.za Accessed 15 September 2018.

The Key School http://www.thekeyschool.org Accessed 18 September 2018.

The Star Academy http://www.thestaracademy.co.za Accessed 24 September 2018.

The Talk Shop http://www.thetalkshop.co.za Accessed 24 September 2018.

The Way Christian School http://www.theway.co.za Accessed 23 September 2018.

Triad Schools, KZN http://www.triadschools.co.za Accessed 18 September 2018.

Unica School for Autism http://www.unicaschool.co.za Accessed 24 September 2018.

Van Kervel Special School, George http://www.vankervel.wcape.school.za Accessed 15 September 2018.

Vera School for Autism http://www.vera.co.za Accessed 15 September 2018.

Via Nova Special School http://www.vianovaschool.co.za/vns Accessed 23 September 2018

Wings for Life School for Special Education http://www.wingsforlife.co.za Accessed 23 September 2018

Wandsworth School https://www.wandsworthschool.co.za Accessed 23 September 2018

Zenith Academy www.pretoriadirectory.co.za/home/education/special-needs/zenith-academy Accessed 23 September 2018

3

EARLY IDENTIFICATION AND CURRICULUM DIFFERENTIATION FOR LEARNERS WITH AUTISM

Dikeledi Mahlo and Hlabathi Maapola-Thobejane

Abstract

This chapter will focus on the significance of early identification and Curriculum Differentiation for learners with autism in the inclusive classrooms. Autism Spectrum Disorder (ASD) is a condition that affects many children in South Africa and around the world. Early identification of learners with ASD is very crucial as it facilitates the process of early intervention such as Curriculum Differentiation. Learners who experience barriers to learning perform better and benefit from educational settings, which are inclusive and have the ability to respond to their needs. When individual needs are met, the individual has the ability to access education at the relevant and appropriate level to succeed. Learners with autism have specific needs which when ide-ntified early, will enable them to thrive and lead a successful life like all other individuals and contribute meaningfully to society.

3.1 Introduction

Inclusive Education is practised in many countries globally. South Africa embarked on the implementation of Inclusive Education in 2001, with the aim of providing quality education and accommodating all learners including those who have additional learning needs such as autism into regular classes. Advocates of inclusion encourages a shift from a medical model to the one that embraces diversity (Bornman & Donahue, 2014; Chireshe, 2013; Majoko, 2016; Phasha, 2016; Subban & Mahlo, 2017; Watson, 2018). There are tremendous benefits for learners to learn in an inclusive setting with their peers who are different from them (Shaik, 2015) because all learners are given access and equal educational opportunities to succeed. Teachers are expected to identify learners with autism early in their school career and meet their individual needs (DoE, 2001). This can be realised when teachers use innovative pedagogies such as Curriculum Differentiation to teach learners with autism. The principle of inclusivity signifies the value of every person to be included in the society, regardless of their unique characteristics (Phasha, 2016), including autism.

As mentioned in the introduction, an Afrocentric viewpoint of Inclusive Education is entrenched in theories that originated from Africa such as Ubuntu, Africanisation and Indigenous Knowledge in addition to Eurocentric theories. Inclusive Education cannot be understood using western theories and practices only, but also non-western theories should be acknowledged as they are culturally and contextually relevant to Africa, these theories include Ubuntu (see also the Introduction to this volume). Ubuntu advocates that human beings should demonstrate humanness by being good themselves and by acting sensitively towards their fellow human beings and their needs. In this light, learners should be accepted unconditionally in inclusive classrooms, diversity in the community should be acknowledged and all children should be treated equally in the education system.

The values that are common to African people and reflect inclusion are interdependence, communalism and humanism, therefore the ideals of Inclusive Education are not new to African communities (Phasha & Moichela, 2011). Not all aspects of African theories resonate with Inclusive Education and not all Eurocentric theories are in agreement with Inclusive Education. Hence, both theories can work interchangeably to benefit learners with autism through early identification and Curriculum Differentiation in inclusive settings.

Ubuntu is against any form of discrimination and supports the idea of equality in terms of treatment of all people with respect and dignity. The treatment of people who are different reflects the absence of Ubuntu in most communities; yet society is supposed to embrace people who are different so that they can live a successful and fulfilling life. Phasha and Moichela (2011:375) argue that human beings should perceive each other as valued individuals who deserve to be treated with dignity and respect irrespective of their characteristics. This implies that the diversity in the community should be embraced; human beings need to acknowledge that learners will never be the same: they have different cultural orientations and their physical characteristics are different. In inclusive classrooms, learners who are different should be accepted and provided with appropriate support so that they can succeed.

Teachers in regular classrooms need to identify learners early in their school careers and provide them with the necessary support regardless of their individual characteristics. They should demonstrate a caring and humane behaviour in the spirit of Ubuntu. According to Broodryk (2002), Ubuntu is characterised by the values of humanness, caring, sharing, respect and compassion. Learners with autism can succeed if teachers identify them early in their academic careers. Waghid and Smeyers (2012:12-13) argue that Ubuntu is a form of moral consciousness of which communal Africans care and welcome each other with respect and forgiveness so that humanity can be realised. It is important to note that a person is incomplete unless he or she maintains an active connection with their society or culture (Letseka, 2013:352). Ubuntu demonstrates that the ideals of inclusivity are not new to African communities because they have been caring, showing compassion and accepting people who are diverse in the communities they live in. Inclusivity means that everyone is accepted, feels a sense of belonging and is connected to the community and each other, even though they have different needs.

Some societies struggle to acknowledge diversity. This often leads to undesirable labels and stereotypical tendencies towards learners with disabilities. Letseka (2013:351) asserts that early introduction into Ubuntu morality is a positive indication that the young people will be able to treat others with respect and dignity, that way they will be practising Ubuntu. Learners with autism must be treated with respect and dignity similar to all learners in the classroom. The White Paper 6 (DoE, 2001) on Inclusive Education mandates all schools to admit and accommodate all learners with barriers to learning and development provided there is appropriate support. This policy further encourages that all learners irrespective of race, gender, class, religion, disability, HIV/AIDS status and culture have a right to access education and acknowledges that all children can learn with support (DoE, 2001:28). Similarly, the notion of Ubuntu encourages humanity to others, and Inclusive Education can be seen as a vehicle that promotes or support the principles of Ubuntu. To be able to accommodate and support learners with different barriers such as autism in class, the teacher should be able to appreciate and demonstrate the principle of Ubuntu.

An inclusive environment demonstrates the value system that all are people accepted, feel a sense of belonging, are connected to the community and each other and have different needs (CSATDP, 2005). Inclusivity involves supporting other people with what they are unable to master or do on their own. As such it requires one to be able to cherish the fact that we need to help or be human to others so that our life can have a meaning to us because we are who we are because of others. Support cannot be ignored when we speak of Ubuntu. It involves not only having assistance in the day-to-day experiences but also emotional. It is important to recognise that inclusivity is complex, but it should not be seen as an issue of placing learners with diverse needs and barriers in regular classes, without the support related to their actual barriers (Mahlo, 2017). It is in the spirit of Ubuntu and caring for others that including learners with autism can become reality. Schools need to have teachers who are able to realise the importance of identifying learners early in their academic careers so that they can thrive as other learners do.

3.2 Early identification of learners with autism

Early identification of learners should be a collective effort, parents, teachers and other stakeholders should all be involved in the process. From an African perspective, even if parents are not educated, they have an important role to play in the early identification of learners with autism while Eurocentric approaches leave the responsibility to teachers and schools (Phasha & Moichela, 2011). According to Carmata (2014) parents, clinicians and teachers are readily able to detect severe disruptions in social abilities that can be the symptoms of autism. It takes a village to raise a child; this means that raising children should be a collective effort of a community. Mbiti (2009) argues that in African culture, the society assumes the responsibility of transforming the child into a social human being who is connected to the community. Therefore, responsibility of identifying children at an early age should not be left to teachers alone, but to all stakeholders including community members because education of children is a communal effort. Parents' responsibility in early identification of learners with autism should not be ignored, as they are the first to notice any delays in the development of children. In inclusive classrooms, the value of each child as an individual is recognised. This resonates well with Ubuntu, which condemns any form of discrimination and promotes equal treatment of all learners in inclusive classrooms. It is acknowledged that all learners can learn and need support.

Early identification involves careful observation of an individual learner's behaviour over time. The American Psychiatric Association (APA) (2013) has identified two categories of diagnostic criteria in the Diagnostic and Statistical Manual of Mental Disorder, 5th edition (DSM-V), namely (i) impaired social communication and/or interaction; and (ii) restrictive and/or repetitive behaviours, activities and interests. It is vital to note that although teachers and parents are not qualified to diagnose ASD, they still need to know the diagnostic criteria and have an important role to play in providing information related to the learner's developmental history.

Early identification of learners with barriers is core to the success of Inclusive Education (Phasha, Mahlo & Maseko, 2013) as it facilitates the process of early intervention such as Curriculum Differentiation. Early diagnosis and intervention can have a positive impact on the developmental outcomes of children with ASD (Zwaigenbaum, Bauman et al., 2015). When individual needs are met, the self-image and the confidence of learners are enhanced/ boosted. Early intervention can improve the developmental trajectory of learners with autism (Koegel, Koegel, Ashbaugh & Bradshauw, 2014). Teachers can include learners with autism successfully in the classroom by planning strategies to differentiate the curriculum that sets up a child with autism to succeed in an inclusive classroom (Majoko, 2016). This implies that learners with autism can flourish in a well-planned and welcoming environment that focuses on the strength of the learner and not on their weaknesses. Accurate early identification and intervention in an inclusive classroom is core if teachers are to support learners with autism. Learners who experience barriers to learning perform better and benefit from inclusive educational settings and have the ability to respond to their needs (Mahlo & Condy, 2016). Early identification and intervention such as Curriculum Differentiation during the early years of schooling is beneficial to learners as it increases the prospect of enriched long-term results.

In line with Inclusive Education principles, the South African government developed a policy on Screening, Identification, Assessment and Support (SIAS) (DoE, 2014). Its main thrust is to target all learners in urban and rural settings who need support, and not only learners with disabilities, but even those from the poorest communities in townships, informal settlements or rural areas, as they have previously suffered from the unavailability of and lack of access to services (DoE 2005:3). Advocates of Afrocentrism argue that support is not about fixing or correcting the behaviour, rather it should be understood as the development of all children in reaching their full potential and the acknowledgement that learners are not the same. Therefore, they will perform and behave differently in an inclusive classroom.

This policy outlines the role of teachers (especially in the Foundation Phase), parents, managers and support staff within the new framework of a completely new vision of how support should be structured. According to DoE (2005: 58), teachers in schools should identify learners who are in need of an enriched programme, are in need of a support programme, require diagnostic help in specific aspects of a learning programme or have a learning barrier. These include over-aged learners, those who have problems because of a mismatch between home language and the language of teaching, learning and assessment, have physical disabilities, e.g., vision, speech, have health problems, e.g., illnesses, hunger, have problems with emotional stability; for example, owing to harassment or violence, do not attend school regularly and show signs of abuse or neglect.

The SIAS policy is therefore very clear on which learners could be in need of support including learners with autism. It is declared that previously, assisting learners with barriers to learning was the responsibility of specially qualified persons employed by either educational support services or special schools. The practice of Inclusive Education mandates teachers to identify and support all learners in their classrooms with high quality support in the spirit of caring and humanness, Ubuntu.

The provision of high quality support services and resources, including personnel, may lead to long-term benefits of early identification and intervention for learners with autism. The White Paper 6 on Inclusive Education requires classroom teachers to teach learners with diverse needs including autism since they are being educated in the ordinary classes. The importance of classroom teacher support to the success of Inclusive Education cannot be overemphasised. On the contrary, a study conducted by Abubakar, Ssewanyana and Newton (2016) found out that there is scanty information to plan adequately for effective intervention strategies for children with ASD in sub-Saharan Africa because there is lack of expertise in African countries. Although classroom teachers are not expected to have all the answers or undertake the task of Inclusive Education alone, they must realise that while the foundational principles of teaching and learning do not change, those principles may need to be applied differently or used more systematically. Giangreco, Carter, Doyle and Suter (2010) acknowledge that support provided by classroom teachers is essential in an inclusive environment. Teachers have to use different pedagogies and innovative strategies to be able to provide support for learners with autism. According to Carmata (2014), there is a need to increase the evidence base in the area of early diagnosis and intervention services for children with ASD because early diagnosis and early intervention can improve long-term outcome of learners with autism.

3.3 Curriculum Differentiation for learners with autism

Teacher's pedagogical insights of teaching with learners with autism are still a challenge to most teachers on the African continent. Since the democratic dispensation in South Africa, policies regarding admissions of learners in schools were developed and one of the important factors is that, parents have a right to enrol their child (including those with autism) were they deem fit. Prater (2007: 232), Smith, Pollway, Patton and Dowdy (2008: 168) and Miller (2009: 457) contend that curriculum adaptation refers to the adaptations in the classroom environment, the content, the process and the product. The following paragraphs highlight how teachers should adapt the classroom environment, the content, the process and the product for learners with autism. Classrooms are diverse and a one-size-fits-all approach to teaching and learning is no longer relevant. Teachers need to use more innovative ways to teach all learners with diverse needs.

The inclusion of learners with autism in regular classrooms provides opportunities for teachers to identify learners' needs and differentiate the curriculum to meet the individual needs of learners (Majoko, 2016). Theorists operating from anti-colonial lens such as Freire (1984), Dei (2012), Phasha, Mahlo and Dei (2017) argue for the provision of anti-colonial inclusive teaching that will allow all learners to develop a strong sense of identity, collective respect, agency and empowerment. Curriculum differentiation is reflected in African theories such as Ubuntu, which promotes the social, interactional relationship between the teacher and the learner. Inclusive educational approaches must incorporate multiple learning methods and experiences. Teachers must find ways to make the critical link of culture, identity, history, pedagogy, instruction and education. Learners from disadvantaged situations created by socio-cultural contexts are mostly affected (Tschombe, 2017). Differentiation of the curriculum should be according to the individual needs of the learners, as no two learners will present with the same needs.

Darko (2017) argues that social inequalities, along the lines of gender, class and religious differences impact on the abilities for local populations to have equal access to education. If learners with autism are not provided with the same quality education as the other learners, then schools should consider differentiating the curriculum to meet their needs. School curriculums need to be reframed for Africa as a way to decolonise education (Nyaga, 2017). It cannot be business as usual while these learners are not benefiting from the education system. Schools need to be practically inclusive to learners with autism, not only on paper. Exclusionary practices in the education system impede inclusion in Africa (Watson, 2017). Most policies like Inclusive Education policy are good on paper but the practical implementation remains a challenge when learners are excluded from schools because of their characteristics.

The anti-colonial lens promote indigenous teachings that focus specifically on values such as social justice, equity and fairness. One of the strategies that teachers need to use is differentiating the curriculum for learners with autism in inclusive classrooms. This can become a reality if teachers embrace the values such as caring and humanness, and promote that no child should be left behind in the process of teaching and learning. “Curriculum adaptation” and “Curriculum Differentiation” can be used interchangeably since they both mean the processes of modifying the curriculum.

The United Nations Educational, Scientific, and Cultural Organization (UNESCO) (2004) defines Curriculum Differentiation as the process of modifying or adapting the curriculum according to the different ability levels of the learners in one class. Tomlinsons (2005) defines Curriculum Differentiation as practice, which is based on the premise that learners learn best when their differences are accommodated and all learners have the ability to learn.

According to the Department of Basic Education (DBE) (2010), a differentiated curriculum offers a variety of ways for learners who differ in abilities, knowledge and skills to access the curriculum. Teachers are encouraged to use Curriculum Differentiation because they will be responding constructively and proactively to learners needs (Munro, 2012). Curriculum differentiation refers to differentiating adaptations in content, process and product: what learners learn (content), how learners learn (process) and how learners demonstrate what they have learned (product).

This involves adjusting tasks to appeal to the various interests, needs, aptitudes, experiences and previous achievements of individual learners (DoE 2010). Curriculum Differentiation should not be regarded as a teaching strategy only but an innovative way of thinking about teaching and learning (Tomlinsons, 2000). Diverse needs of learners can be met if teachers differentiate their instruction, teachers in an inclusive classroom should be able to create positive experiences for learners with autism so that they experience success like all the other learners.

Teachers find themselves at the crossroads because of lack of skills and knowledge of teaching learners with autism. Teacher’s professional development is important as most of the teachers were not trained to teach learners with autism in their initial teacher training. Teachers play a critical role in the successful implementation of Inclusive Education, and new teachers should be adequately prepared to work in “diverse classrooms” (Forlin & Chambers 2011). Teachers require additional training in Curriculum Differentiation and teacher education programmes should be designed in a way that pre-service teachers will be able to identify and differentiate the curriculum especially for learners with autism

3.3.1 Professional development of teachers in Curriculum Differentiation for learners with autism

The new system of education in South Africa has strengthened the need for Curriculum Differentiation, its point of departure and the recognition of the school curriculum as one of the most significant barriers to learning is the classroom. One key strategy for responding to diversity is through Curriculum Differentiation.

Tomlinson and Imbeau (2010) maintain that classroom practice should be treated as a learned art, which is deliberately planned for, and teachers need to work hard to master it. Professional development of teachers involves providing them with necessary materials and 'tools' they need for effective teaching (Egbo 2011). This includes equipping teachers with knowledge of Curriculum Differentiation and skills for planning lessons and organising classroom activities guided by such knowledge. One of the most significant current discussion in the education sector is the practice of including learners with autism in mainstream schools. Many teachers, however, lack knowledge and skills needed to adapt curriculum to the individual needs of learners with autism (UNESCO 2005; Vaillant 2011). The attention now shifts to teachers' capacity to differentiate the curriculum. With growing number of learner diversity, teachers' pedagogical knowledge needs to be strengthened. Inclusion has been a practice in Africa's holistic developmental education (Nsamenang, 2011; Tschombe, 2011). Traditional epistemology of human relationships has been based on humanness, communality and interdependence (Phasha & Moichela, 2011). This implies that educating children with autism should be approached in a human way because the learners should be developed holistically. Classrooms are complex spaces where teachers require appropriate teaching strategies to respond to student diversity (Subban & Round, 2015; Suprayogi, Valcke & Godwin, 2017). Therefore, it is necessary to develop teachers in Curriculum Differentiation so that they can be able to respond to the needs of a diversity of learners in the class. The effective inclusive school requires reflective teachers who are willing to change their attitudes, teaching, classroom management practices and curricula to accommodate individual learner needs.

Teachers in the 21st century should be equipped to respond constructively and proactively to different kind of learners needs which is based on modification of four elements, content, process, product and learning environment (Tomlinsons & Imbeau, 2010; Munro, 2012). The traditional way of teaching does not have a place in contemporary classes because learners are not the same. Phasha, et al. (2017) maintain that Africa's schooling and education is still at crossroads, as teachers should teach a diversity of learners with strategies, which can make them global citizens, and to effect social and personal change. It is at these inclusive schools where teachers are reflective, flexible, responsive and aware of learners needs.

The one-size-fits–all approach is no longer applicable in contemporary classes (Fox & Hoffman, 2011; Subban, 2006). In contrast, these teachers think critically about their values and beliefs. They consistently examine their own practices for self-improvement to ensure that diverse learners' needs are met. When teachers are not given the autonomy to create appropriate curricula, the planned curricula, especially when scripted, is informally modified through instructional delivery (Tomlinson, 2000). One question that needs to be asked, however, is whether curriculum implementers, teacher trainers and subject advisors have a clear understanding of Curriculum Differentiation. They should be able to demonstrate to the teachers how it is done it practice. The entire staff should have a sound knowledge and understanding of autism. Conducting training in ASD for all staff members will be beneficial because a teacher might be exposed to a learner who has autism in their teaching career. The training should include detailed classroom training as well as general training for members of the support staff at the school. Therefore, provisions should be made at schools to address barriers to learning of learners with autism. The schools should make reasonable accommodations so that learners with autism are able to receive education in close proximity to their peers (UNESCO, 2004).

One of the most significant current discussions in the education sector is the fact that autism is a neglected barrier, as stated in the consolidated report on the implementation of WP6, (2015), the DBE identifies autism as the most neglected barrier. Research has shown that autism is an individual condition. Therefore, supporting learners with autism should not be a blanket approach as the needs of learners are not the same. DoE (2001b: 19) in White Paper 6 stipulates that the curriculum is the most significant barrier to learning. Therefore, teachers are required to differentiate the curriculum so that learners with autism could benefit and achieve educational outcomes.

It is important to note the four classroom elements available to teachers for differentiation, based on the learner's readiness, interest, or learning profile, according to Tomlinson's model, namely, content, process, product and learning environment.

3.3.2 Classroom environment

Classroom environment refers to the manner in which the classroom is organised and the atmosphere that prevails therein. Examples include sitting arrangement organisation of learners in groups (Marishane, 2013). Differentiation should be practised in any learning situation because no two learners learn the same way. The classroom environment is an essential component of a productive learning initiative for diverse learners. Teachers should adapt the learning environment by creating a positive climate in the classroom that caters for everyone, including learners with autism. Emotions and feelings, which are created by the experiences and reactions to current experiences, influence the self-concept as well as the motivation to learn and ability to collaborate (Strickland,2007). When the climate is positive, both the teacher and the learner demonstrate mutual respect and courtesy, and everyone feels safe to express thoughts and opinions without fear of embarrassment or ridicule. An essential element of a positive classroom environment is a caring teacher who communicates respect and concern for others. Learners with autism will have a sense of belonging if the classroom is organised so that learners with autism are aware of their expectations and roles (Gibson, 2011).

Gibson (2011) further advises that, schedules should be clearly displayed, students should know when activities will occur and how will they be involved in that particular activity. That way the effectiveness of the lesson will be improved and the class will be well managed. Learners with autism react positively to the learning environment that responds to their needs. Classroom environment should respond to the learner's emotional needs for example if the learner needs a little bit additional attention to be able to stick to the task. Modification of the learning environment is needed for learners with autism to ensure effective learning (Tomlinsons & Imbeau, 2010). For example, there are learners who cannot sit still for a long time and the teacher can move around the room. There are also learners who do not work well where there is excessive noise. For those learners, earplugs can be supplied.

3.3.3 Content

Content refers to what the teacher would like learners to learn and how to access it. As Watts (2010:5) puts it, content includes "essential knowledge, skills, facts, concepts, principles, and generalisations that the teacher conveys to students through instruction". One example of differentiated content that may be cited here is the use of different teaching and learning support materials (videos, computer programmes, voice recorder and slides) to teach the same content to different learners, including learners with autism. When the content is differentiated, learners are given access to what they need to learn. These may include the amount or difficulty level of the work to be achieved. The knowledge, understanding and skills that the students need to learn is the content (Tomlinsons & Imbeau, 2010). The learning goals should always remain the same for all learners especially for learners with autism.

Learners with autism can benefit and text materials can be adapted in the following ways:

- using voice-recorded materials and DVDs;
- using simplified versions of the classroom text;
- changing the modality of text input by reading it aloud;
- allowing a peer to read a text to a learner;
- decreasing the amount of content by using easier vocabulary, highlighting key concepts, omitting unnecessary or distracting parts of context, or writing abridged versions of text; and
- adding definitions of key terms; adding interest to important content and adding cues, signals and questions.

As mentioned in the previous sections, individual learners with autism have different needs. One-size-fits-all approach is no longer applicable in contemporary classes. In responding to the learners' needs, teachers can provide scaffolding when working with the content by teaching prerequisite content to learners with autism, allowing progressive students to move ahead of the class or changing the content based on their individualised education plan (Tomlinsons & Imbeau, 2010). By doing this, the teacher will be acknowledging that learners with autism learn differently and the teacher is responding to their needs.

3.3.4 Process

Marishane (2013) maintains that process involves activities in which learners engage in order to gain and enhance their understanding of the curriculum delivered to them. An example may be a classroom situation in which different learners are given the same assignment with varying difficulty different completion times while pursuing the achievement of the same learning outcome.

Leading scholars in Curriculum Differentiation, Tomlinsons and Imbeau (2010) define process as "how learners come to understand and make sense of the content". Process adaptation involves how the teacher teaches, how much support is provided to the learner, how much time is allocated to instruction, the degree of complexity of the instruction and teachers' various activities and strategies needed by the individual learner. According to Dettmer et al. (2009: 244), the following are examples of how teachers could adapt the process for learners with autism:

- use a multisensory approach for presenting materials;
- provide a written copy of material on the chalkboard;
- demonstrate skills before a learner does seated work;
- mark the material that must be mastered;
- reduce the amount of material on paper;
- decrease the pace of instruction; and
- have a learner follow text while looking at a visual illustration.

The instructional needs of learners with autism vary because autism is an individual condition and no two learners with autism have the same needs. Teaching should be made available orally, visually and in writing. Prater (2007) states the following possible types of adapting the teaching and learning process:

- The manner in which instruction occurs (e.g. cooperative learning groups versus direct instruction); and
- The modality of instruction (e.g. visual, auditory).

When adapting teaching strategies, teachers can use concrete objects to demonstrate concepts and use voice changes to stress points and repeat important information. Regarding the amount of time that needs to be adapted for learners with autism, the teacher needs to consider adjusting the amount of time allowed for learning and for completing activities. These differentiated teaching and learning strategies should be prioritised so that learners with autism can access the curriculum.

3.3.5 Product

Product refers to the variety of modalities through which learners can demonstrate to the teacher what they have learned from the curriculum. Such modalities include written work, projects, models and oral presentation (Marishane, 2013). Products are ways for students to demonstrate what they have come to know, understand and be able to do after an extended period of learning (Tomlinsons & Imbeau, 2010).

The DoE (2011b: 22) emphasises that the minimum requirements for achieving grades may not be compromised. The product refers to the manner in which the learner will be evaluated in the form of tests, projects, written work or oral presentation to see whether the learner has mastered the content or not. Marishane (2013) views continuous instruction-linked assessment and adjustment as involving an on-going formal and informal assessment of learners' work to identify differences in learners' learning weaknesses and strengths. Knowledge gained from such assessment enables the teacher to adjust teaching to the learners' abilities to maximise their self-confidence.

However, this should be done within a flexible learner based and learner paced approach to the curriculum so that all learners could achieve their full potential. For an example, activities that respond to varied interests or learning profiles and adopting criteria for success from the learners who have limited knowledge to those who are advanced. Learners can acquire new knowledge through reading independently or with a partner, reading a book or listening to an audiotaped material. To achieve that, alternative forms of assessment should be employed for the learner with autism. Alternative assessment refers to any change in the standard form of assessment, examination or condition relating to assessment, which is established to accommodate a learner experiencing barriers to learning.

3.4 Conclusion

This chapter is based on Afrocentric approaches to Inclusive Education. It is entrenched in theories that originated from Africa such as Ubuntu, Africanisation and Indigenous Knowledge. In addition to Eurocentric theories, this chapter is assimilated with theories appropriate and relevant to African contexts. Such theories include Ubuntu, which advocates that human beings should demonstrate humanness by being good themselves and act sensitively towards their fellow human beings and their needs. Learners with autism should be accepted unconditionally in inclusive classrooms and diversity in the community should be acknowledged and all children should be treated equally in the education system. The anti-colonial lens promote indigenous teachings that focus specifically on values such as social justice, equity and fairness. One of the strategies that teachers need to use is differentiating the curriculum for learners with autism in inclusive classrooms. This can become a reality if teachers embrace the values such as caring and humanness, and promote that no child should be left behind in the process of teaching and learning.

Learners who are identified with autism can perform better and benefit from educational settings, which are inclusive and have the ability to respond to their individual needs. When individual needs are met, the self-image and the confidence of learners are enhanced. Learners with autism have specific needs which when identified early and interventions made, these learners can be able to thrive and lead a successful life like all other individuals and contribute meaningfully to society.

Proceeding against the background of Inclusive Education with its emphasis on catering for the different needs of all learners in education, the importance of differentiating curriculum in the teaching cannot be ignored. While literature provides evidence of the benefit of such differentiation in the form of academic achievement of all learners, such benefit cannot be realised in the absence of competent, skilled and professionally developed teachers, whose inclusive pedagogies are well thought and executed. Critical decisions about relevant and appropriate pedagogy are vital for learners with autism.

References

Abubakar, A., Ssewanyana, D., & Newton, C. R. (2016). A systematic review of research on autism spectrum disorders in Sub-Saharan Africa. *Behavioural Neurology*, 2016.

Broodryk, J. (2002). *Ubuntu: life lessons from Africa*. Ubuntu School of Philosophy.

Canada South Africa Teacher Development Project (CSATDP). (2005). *Towards Inclusive Classrooms: An Educator's Guide*. Mpumalanga Department of Education.

Camarata, S. (2014). Early identification and early intervention in autism spectrum disorders: Accurate and effective? *International Journal of Speech-Language Pathology*: 16(1): 1-10.

Chireshe, R. (2013). The state of Inclusive Education in Zimbabwe: Bachelor of Education (Special Needs Education) students' perceptions. *Journal of Social Sciences*, 34(3): 223-228.

Darko, I.N. (2017). Concealed Market and the Commercialization of Education and its implications on Inclusivity. In Phasha, N., Mahlo, D. and Dei, G.J.S. (Eds.). *Inclusive schooling and education in African contexts*. Rotterdam: Sense Publishers.

Dei, G. S. (2012). Indigenous anti-colonial knowledge as 'heritage knowledge' for promoting Black/African education in diasporic contexts. *Decolonization: Indigeneity, Education & Society*, 1(1).

Department of Education (2001). *Education White Paper 6. Special needs education. Building an Inclusive Education and training system*. Pretoria, South Africa: Government Printers.

Department of Basic Education. (2010). *Guidelines for Inclusive Teaching and Learning. Education White Paper 6, Special Needs Education: Building an Inclusive Education and Training System*. Pretoria: Government Printers.

Department of Basic Education. (2011). *National Protocol for Assessment: Grades R – 12*. Pretoria: Government Printers.

Department of Education (2014). *Policy on Screening, Identification, Assessment and Support*. Pretoria, South Africa: Government Printers.

Dettmer, P., Thurston, L.P., Knackendoffel, A. & Dyck, N. (Eds.) (2009). *Collaboration, Consultation, and Teamwork for Students with Special Needs*. Upper Saddle River: Pearson.

Donohue, D. & Bornman, J. (2014). The challenges of realising Inclusive Education in South Africa. *South African Journal of Education*, 34(2).

Egbo, B. (2011). Teacher capacity building and effective teaching and learning: A seamless connection. A keynote speech delivered at the *International Conference on Teaching and Learning organised by African Association for Teaching and Learning (AATL)* held at the Federal College of Education (Technical) Omoku, Rivers State, Nigeria, September 5-8, 2011.

Fox, J. & Hoffman, W. (2011). *The Differentiated Instruction Book of Lists*. San Francisco: Jossey-Bass.

Fukunaga, G.A., Simonelli, S. & Sperry, L. (2015). Individualised educational support strategies for students with autism in inclusive classroom settings. Effective Practices Brief. Retrieved from http://www. sig. hawaii. edu/final_products.

Freire, P. (1984). Education, liberation and the church. *Religious Education*, 79(4): 524-545.

Gawande, A. (2009). *The checklist manifesto: How to get things right*. New York: Metropolitan Books.

Giangreco, M.F., Carter, E.W., Doyle, M.B. & Suter, J.C. (2010). Supporting students with disabilities in inclusive classrooms. In Rose, R. (Ed.). *Confronting obstacles to inclusion: International responses to developing Inclusive Education.* (pp. 247-264). London: Routledge.

Gibson, V. (2011). *Differentiating instruction: Teaching differently to improve reading instruction.* Saint Paul, Minnesota: Read Naturally.

Gibson, S. & Blandford, S. (2005). *Managing Special Educational Needs: A Practical Guide for Primary and Secondary Schools.* London: Paul Chapman.

Koegel, R. L., Bradshaw, J. L., Ashbaugh, K. & Koegel, L. K. (2014). Improving question-asking initiations in young children with autism using pivotal response treatment. *Journal of Autism and Developmental Disorders*, 44(4): 816-827.

Letseka, M. (2000). African Philosophy and Educational discourse. In Higgs, P., Vakalisa, N.C.G., Mda, T. & Assie-Lumumba, N.T. (Eds.). *African Voices in Education.* (pp. 179-191). Cape Town: Juta and Co.

Letseka, M. (2013). Anchoring Ubuntu Morality. *Mediterranean Journal of Social Sciences*, (4): 351-359.

Mahlo, F., & Condy, J. L. (2016). *Learning support in Inclusive Education settings*. Cape Town: Oxford University Press Southern Africa (Pty) Limited.

Majoko, T. (2016). Inclusion of children with autism spectrum disorders: Listening and hearing to voices from the grassroots. *Journal of Autism and Developmental Disorders*, 46(4): 1429-1140.

Marishane, M.A. (2013). Capacity Building for Curriculum Differentiation in the teaching of Foundation Phase Mathematics in Ngwaritsi Circuit Limpopo Province. M Ed Thesis.

Meidl, T. & Meidl, C. (2011). Curriculum Integration and Adaptation: Individualizing Pedagogy for Linguistically and Culturally Diverse Students. *Current Issues in Education*, 14(1). http://cie.asu.edu/

Mbiti, J. (2009). Challenges of Language, Culture, and Interpretation in Translating the Greek New Testament. *Svensk Missionstidskrift SMT/Swedish Missiological Themes*, 97(2): 141-164.

Miller, S.P. (2009). *Validated Practices for Teaching Students with Diverse Needs and Abilities* (2nd ed.).Upper Saddle River: Pearson.

Mills, M., Monk, S., Keddie, A., Renshaw, P., Christie, P., Geelan, D. & Gowlett, C. (2014). Differentiated learning: From policy to classroom. *Oxford Review of Education*, 40(3): 331-348.

Munro, J. (2012). Effective strategies for differentiating instruction. Paper presented at the *Research Conference: School Improvement – What does research tell us about effective strategies*? Melbourne.

Nieman, M.M. & Monyai R.B. (Eds.). (2006). *The Educator as Mediator of Learning*. Pretoria: Van Schaik.

Nsamenang, A. B. (2011). The culturalization of developmental trajectories. Bridging cultural and developmental approaches to psychology. *New Syntheses in Theory, Research, and Policy*, 235.

Nsamenang, A. B. & Tchombe, T. M. (2011). *Handbook of African educational theories and practices*. Presses Universitaires d'Afrique, Bamenda, Cameroon.

Nyaga, D. (2017). New possibilities for school curriculum: Praxis of Indigenous people in Kenya. In Phasha, N., Mahlo, D. & Dei, G.J.S. (Eds.). *Inclusive schooling and education in African contexts*. (pp. 1-17). Rotterdam: Sense Publishers.

Peters, S. (2002). Inclusive Education in accelerated and professional development in schools: A case based study of two schools reforms efforts in the USA. *International Journal of Inclusive Education*, 6: 287-308.

Phasha, N.T., Mahlo, F.D. & Maseko, N. (2013). In Davin, R. (Ed.). *Handbook for Grade R Teaching*. Cape Town: Pearson Education South Africa (Pty) Ltd.

Phasha, N.T. & Moichela, Z. (2011). Inclusive Education in South Africa. In Nsamenang, A.B. & Tchombe, T.M. (Eds.)*Handbook of African Educational Theories and Practices*. Cameroon: Human Development Resource Center (HRDC).

Phasha, N., Mahlo, D. & Dei, G.J.S. (2017). Inclusive schooling and education in African contexts. In Phasha, N., Mahlo, D. & Dei, G.J.S. (Eds.). *Inclusive schooling and education in African contexts*. (pp. 1-17). Rotterdam: Sense Publishers.

Prater, M.A. (2007). *Teaching Strategies for Students with Mild to Moderate Disabilities*. Boston: Allyn and Bacon.

Seidman, W.H. (1983). Transactive curriculum: A practical guide to curriculum adaptation. *Theory into Practice*, 22(3): 216-223, DOI: 10.1080/00405848309543064

Shaik, N. (2015). Who is the Grade R teacher? In Excell, L. & Linington, V. *Teaching Grade R.* Cape Town: Juta & Co (Pty) Ltd.

Smith, T.E.C., Pollway, E.A., Patton, J.R. & Dowdy, C.A. (2008). *Teaching Students with Special Needs in Inclusive Settings* (5th ed.). Boston: Allyn and Bacon.

Subban, P. (2006). Differentiated instruction: A research basis. *International Education Journal*, 7(7): 935-947.

Subban, P.K. & Round, P.N. (2015). Differentiated Instruction at Work. Reinforcing the art of classroom observation through the creation of a checklist for beginning and pre-service teachers. *Australian Journal of Teacher Education*, 40(5). http://dx.doi.org/10.14221/ajte.2015v40n5.7

Subban, P. & Mahlo, D. (2017). 'My attitude, my responsibility' Investigating the attitudes and intentions of pre-service teachers toward Inclusive Education between teacher preparation cohorts in Melbourne and Pretoria. *International Journal of Inclusive Education*, 21(4): 441-461.

Subban, P.K. & Round, P.N. (2015). Differentiated instruction at work. Reinforcing the art of classroom observation through the creation of a checklist for beginning and pre-service teachers. *Australian Journal of Teacher Education*, 40(5):1-7.

Smit, R. & Humpert, W. (2012). Differentiated instruction in small schools. *Teaching and Teacher Education*, 28(8):1152-1162.

Smith, T.E., Polloway, E.A., Patton, J.R. & Dowdy, C.A. (2014). *Teaching students with special needs in inclusive settings* (Vol. 6). Upper Saddle River, NJ: Pearson.

Tchombe, T.M.S. (2017). Inclusive schooling and education in African contexts. In Phasha, N., Mahlo, D. & Dei, G.J.S (Eds.). *Inclusive schooling and education in African contexts*. (pp. 1-17).Rotterdam: Sense Publishers.

Tomlinson, C.A. (2000). Reconcilable differences? Standards-based teaching and differentiation. *Educational Leadership,* 7-11.

Tomlinson, C.A. & Imbeau, M.B. (2010). *Leading and managing a differentiated classroom*. ASCD.

Tomlinson, C.A. & Strickland, C. (2005). *Differentiation in practice: a resource guide for differentiating curriculum, grades 9-12.* Alexandria, Virginia: Association for Supervision and Curriculum Development.

UNESCO. (2004). *Changing Teaching Practices: Using Curriculum Differentiation to Respond to Students' Diversity*. Paris: UNESCO.

Vaillant, D. (2011). *Preparing teachers for Inclusive Education in Latin America.* Paris: UNESCO.

Waghid, Y. & Smeyers, P. (2012). Reconsidering Ubuntu: On the educational potential of a particular ethic of care. *Educational Philosophy and Theory*, 44(2): 6-20.

Walton, E. (2017). Inclusive schooling and education in African contexts. In Phasha, N., Mahlo, D. & Dei, G.J.S. (Eds.). *Inclusive schooling and education in African contexts*. (pp. 1-17). Rotterdam: Sense Publishers.

Walton, E. (2018). Decolonising (Through) Inclusive Education? *Educational Research for Social Change*, 7(1): 31-45. http://dx.doi.org/10.17159/2221-4070/2018/v7i2a3

Watts J. (2010). *A Foundational Research Study Connecting Carol A. Tomlinson's Model of Differentiated Instruction to the Study Island Program*. Charlottesville, VA: Mongolia Consulting.

Zwaigenbaum, L., Bauman, M.L., Stone, W.L., Yirmiya, N., Estes, A., Hansen, R.L., McPartland, J.C., Natowicz, M.R., Choueiri, R., Fein, D. & Kasari, C. (2015). Early identification of autism spectrum disorder: recommendations for practice and research. *Pediatrics*, 136(Supplement 1), S10-S40.

4

RELIGION AND AUTISM: INTEGRATING THE PERSON WITH AUTISM INTO A COMMUNITY

Michel Clasquin-Johnson

Abstract

Religion remains one of the key social institutions and in this chapter, we will consider religious responses to autism. There is a possibility, albeit a speculative one, that persons with autism were an important contributing factor in the genesis of religion itself. Given that, one might imagine that religious organisations would be safe havens for people with ASD today. The available literature does not support this intuition. Churches have gone as far as to take out court orders barring "disruptive" persons diagnosed as autistic from their premises, and religions other than Christianity fare little better. There are indications that people with autism have a marked tendency towards irreligion to the point of outright atheism. This has to do not only with a general pattern of rejection from the world of organised religion, but also from the respective natures of religion and ASD themselves. However, those religions that favour orthopraxy over orthodoxy will tend to be more accommodating, and also more successful in their attempts at intervention.

From this, it emerges that the approach we need to take to teach religion to learners with autism is to focus on religiously correct ritual behaviour. Educators and religious professionals will need to let go of insisting that religion is something to believe, and see it as equally, or more, as a way to behave, and thereby to be. Integrating a young person into a religious community is a challenge at the best of times. Integrating a young person with autism requires a specific approach.

***

Imagine what it is like. Someone begins to tell you stories about a man dying and being resurrected and living inside of you. Where exactly does he live? Heart? Lungs? Kidneys? What a disturbing thought! Then they tell you that God is here but you cannot see him, although he is in control of your life nevertheless! And such truths for Christians come before anyone suggests that they gouge their eyes out if tempted by lust! (Swinton & Trevett, 2009, p. 2)

4.1 Introduction

South Africa is, at least on the surface, a religious country. Census reports continue to show that the vast majority of South Africans report an affiliation to a religious organisation. It is also a diverse country. Christianity is the largest religious bloc, but it is present in almost all its many varieties. All the other major religions of the world (Islam, Judaism, Hinduism, Buddhism etc.) have a presence in this country. Furthermore, traditional African religious practices thrive, both as a visible separate religious tradition and as an underlying substratum that affects even much of the officially Christian population.

The religiously diverse nature of the country complicates our quest for a coherent analysis of the relationship between religion, autism and education. Moreover, education in this country has seen several waves of upheaval in recent decades and autism itself has recently been subjected to a radical redefinition. We therefore have three broad concepts, at least two of which are in a state of flux. Establishing a relationship between them will not be easy. Nevertheless, it is necessary that we try. Learners with autism are part of this country, with all its religious diversity and educational challenges. Leaving them ignorant of their heritage implies that they are less than full citizens (see the chapter on Autism and the Law in this volume).

> [I]t would be very easy ... to suggest that religion is clearly detrimental and potentially dangerous. 'Surely we should not encourage people who have such neurological challenges as part of their lives to engage in such practices!' And yet, the fact remains that many people with autism clearly want to engage with religion, sometimes at quite a deep level. Furthermore, if we are to believe that spirituality is a basic human need and indeed a basic human right, then the option of discouraging or failing to accommodate those with autism is really not available (Swinton & Trevett, 2009, p. 2).

Let us consider what autism (or Autistic Spectrum Disorder) is. A condensed version of the DSM-V (Diagnostic and Statistical Manual of Mental Disorders, Fifth Edition) reads as follows:

> People with ASD tend to have communication deficits, such as responding inappropriately in conversations, misreading non-verbal interactions, or having difficulty building friendships appropriate to their age. In addition, people with ASD may be overly dependent on routines, highly sensitive to changes in their environment, or intensely focused on inappropriate items (American Psychiatric Association, 2013).

The ICD-10 (International Statistical Classification of Diseases and Related Health Problems 10th Revision) groups various types of autism together under the category of Pervasive Developmental Disorders, including variants such as Asperger's Syndrome, which have recently been dropped from the DSM. It describes this group of conditions as follows:

> A group of disorders characterised by qualitative abnormalities in reciprocal social interactions and in patterns of communication, and by a restricted, stereotyped, repetitive repertoire of interests and activities. These qualitative abnormalities are a pervasive feature of the individual's functioning in all situations (World Health Organisation, 2016).

However, research shows that the DSM5 and ICD-10 criteria, which focus on social and cognitive *deficits*, are not the whole story of autism. Baron-Cohen and Wheelwright (1999, p. 5), for example, found that while persons with autism are deficient in "folk psychology", they may actually be *superior* in "folk physics", the instinctive understanding of how the natural world works. How can the religious traditions not merely accommodate, but employ the specific abilities of the person with autism, rather than merely alleviating their problems, and how can the educational system work alongside religion in this respect?

We do not know what causes autism, and there are other conditions easily confused with it. For instance: "West Indian children in Britain were frequently described as displaying a syndrome akin to autism, in which the children appeared aloof, apathetic and withdrawn ... this phenomenon was unique to West Indian children who had emigrated to Britain" (Bailkin, 2012, p. 191). It is known in the UK as "Brought over Child Syndrome". Autism is being diagnosed or recognised in different societies at wildly different rates and there are a number of socially-determined responses to it that reflect a given society's views on the role and worth of the individual in the community (Dyches et al., 2004; Ecker, 2010; Gona, Newton, Rimba et al., 2015) even before we start taking the further complicating effect of religion into account.

Religion is a complex mixture of emotional attachments, prescribed behaviours and intellectual assent to theories about the way the world is constituted. The relationship between religion and mental health is a complex one, but there are indications that religious practice can lead to a reduction in stress levels (Basu-Zharku, 2011). However, such findings are undercut by a disagreement on the role of religion among autism researchers. We see one study classifying "religious coping" among parents of autistic children as a "beneficial coping method", while another classifies it as a form of "denial" (Benson, 2010, p. 225). Popular culture too, seems uneasy with the idea that ASD and religion can mix within the same individual, one prominent exception being the film "My name is Khan" (Erndl, 2016).

It is usual to distinguish between "low-functioning" and "high-functioning" persons with autism. It can be asked whether such a stark binary opposition accurately represents the totality of people on the spectrum, and even if such a distinction undercuts the entire concept of people being "on a spectrum" (cf. Sowell, 2003). Nevertheless, I must concede that what will follow will largely focus on relatively high-functioning persons. The truly low-functioning person with autism has different priorities, and while the care for such people may be motivated by religious conviction, it will not include the inculcation of, for example, the Christian concept of the Incarnation, the Mahayana Buddhist understanding of Śūnyatā or the Hindu theory of Maya. We need to presuppose a reasonable basis for communicating with the autistic learner, whether verbally or by means of assistive and augmentative technology.

However, this does not mean that lower-functioning autists are to be cut off from the religious community or religious practice. With time and patience, even the most low-functioning person with autism can be integrated into such a community. The spiritual state of such individuals is a matter for each religion's theologians to debate. We are here concerned with their social integration.

The issue of autism and religion is not just one that concerns educators. Parents will want their children to experience the comforts of religion, preferably their own. Therapists will come across individuals from various religious backgrounds (or lack of the same). Religious professionals (priests, ministers, imams, rabbis etc) will likewise encounter autistic individuals, mostly from within their own tradition. It is to the position of persons, especially children, with autism within religious communities that we shall turn first.

4.2 Autism in religious communities

Autism might have been a contributing factor in the rise of religion itself. The hermit, the mystic and the antisocial prophet are powerful symbols in the histories of many religions. Annus (2015) traces the existence of such figures as far back as the Epic of Gilgamesh and into the early Christian era. In addition, Annus (2015) argues that even in the absence of religious belief, being on the autistic spectrum itself produces behaviour that strongly resembles that of these religious roles: food fetishes, sleep disturbance, mobility-constricting devices, lack of hygiene – all these are shared symptoms of autism and extreme religious withdrawal. Likewise, Huntington (2015, p. 639) remarks on the relationship between Asian religions and mental disorders when he speaks of "the morally ambiguous figure of the hermit or the yogi, a solitary contemplative who often exhibits behaviors lifted straight out of the pages of the Diagnostic and Statistical Manual of Mental Disorders".

Annus gives the contemporary example of Christopher Knight, the "North Pond Hermit", who survived in the woods of Maine for 27 years, as an example of the same impulse being present in some individuals today (MacQuarrie, 2013; Finkel, 2014; Adams, 2015). But Knight did not become a religious figure: he was arrested for petty larceny and forcibly reintegrated into mainstream society. Had he lived in another time (say, 3rd-century Egypt) or place (India, even today), he might have gone down in history as a holy figure. Twenty-first century western culture, sadly, has no use for hermits, holy or otherwise.

Given an appropriate religious framework, the solitary lifestyle preferred by many people living with autism becomes associated with supernatural power, and by extension, with sanctity.

> All behaviours associated with the ascetic movement were institutionalised as cultural norms in due course. Therefore, these institutions also attracted people who had no neurological inclinations towards the behaviours discussed above (Annus, 2015, p. 16).

The first hermits may have had autistic tendencies, but later generations need not have them. If being a hermit becomes a desirable occupation, people who lack the innate attraction to this lifestyle will attempt it.

In the long run, however, religions rarely tolerate such loose cannons indefinitely. Eremiticism is changed into a collective monasticism, a tamed, less solitary existence that is acceptable to the non-autistic populations. While Annus does not extend this argument beyond the western tradition, exactly the same process can be observed in the history of the Hindu and Buddhist traditions: An initial emphasis on solitary withdrawal is subverted into a communal and religiously sanctioned monasticism. Over time, monasticism moves so far from its autistic roots that the person with autism who craves solitude has no choice but to trek into the wilderness and inadvertently start yet another new religion.

Given the striking coincidences between autism and the roots of religion, one might expect that religious communities would be more accommodating and helpful to the families of people with autism than the surrounding secular society. Unfortunately, existing research does not entirely bear out this assumption. "Some findings indicate that religious groups provide positive social support and have positive effects on well-being, while other findings illustrate negative effects from putting problems in the hands of religion" (Brown, 2014, p. 8). Coulthard and Fitzgerald (1999) found that while parents of children with autism in Ireland reported that their personal religious beliefs were a comfort to them, they had received little or no support from their religious organisations. Indeed, across religious traditions, we find patterns of misunderstanding and persecution.

> Chicago immigration officials recently decided to grant political asylum to a 10-year-old autistic boy whose mother had claimed his disability and sporadically violent behavior is so misunderstood in Pakistan, their homeland, that he would be tortured and persecuted if he returned there. In her successful application to the Chicago Office of Asylum, she stated that: "He was forced to undergo various degrading and dangerous mystical treatments consistent with the curse of Allah, which is how the Islamic majority in Pakistan view his condition". In Muslim societies such as Pakistan or Saudi Arabia, the religious community is obliged to recognise the asocial behaviour of an autistic child or schizophrenic a social problem requiring forceful intervention of the religious community. From the secular standpoint of US immigration officials and their medical advisers, this leads the boy's homeland community to "violate" the individual's rights (Atran, 2002, p. 11).

This typification of Pakistani attitudes towards autism conflicts starkly with the one given by Jegatheesan's (2010) study among British Pakistani immigrants. That should remind us that we tend to paint with excessively broad brushes when we talk about religion. There is no single "Pakistani Islam", and immigrant communities may retain practices that have changed considerably in the home country.

In Mann's work on Mothers of autistic children in Jamaica, we see religion playing an equally ambivalent role:

> Although several mothers reported that they would recommend a mother of a newly diagnosed child keep the faith and have God or their religion to rely upon, only one mother mentioned her religious community as a source of support. Another mother described her experience of attempting to attend church services, but deciding she could no longer attend due to her child's challenging behaviors (Mann, 2013, p. 147).

Such attitudes are not restricted to the Third World. Poston and Turnbull, reporting on their research in Kansas City, found that for every respondent who managed to have their child integrated into the religious community, another would report great difficulties in doing this: "There's a lot of people (in the church) that don't know how to deal with your autistic child" (Poston & Turnbull, 2004, p. 103). Howell and Pierson (2010), working in Southern California, report that "mothers in the sample described attitudinal, communicative, and programmatic barriers in their congregations, although not all reported experiencing them in precisely the same way". However, mere attitudinal barriers are by no means the extreme end of the scale here. A particular offshoot of American Evangelicalism denounces autism as demonic possession (DeRogatis, 2009, p. 288). In 2008, a Minnesota Catholic parish went so far as to obtain a court order banning a 13-year old autistic boy from attending Mass (Terry, 2015, p. 460).

It even seems to be the case that prejudice against autism is greater in religious communities and organisations than against other disabilities. Terry, quoting research by Ault, Collins and Carter(2013) notes that

> In a study of 416 parents of children with disabilities, of which autism was one, a full third of the parents surveyed had changed their places of worship due to a lack of inclusive welcome, and 46% refrained from participating in any activity because their child was not included or welcomed. This research further found that parents of children with intellectual disabilities were much more likely to say their place of worship was supportive than the parents of children who have autism (Terry, 2015, p. 459).

A recent case goes beyond neglect and gives us a case of outright abuse. An organisation calling itself the Genesis II Church of Health and Healing markets a supposed cure for autism. Investigation shows it to be a powerful and poisonous industrial solvent (Galli, Kreider & Ross, 2016).

The above examples imply that there is a considerable educational task ahead within religious communities. Religious professionals are not prepared during their professional training to deal with the issue, and there is so far little theological reflection on autism. There is some, however, at least within Christianity. The dissertation by Cox (2015) and the book by Gillibrand (2010) are important turning points in the development of a Christian theological perspective on autism. Brock (2009, p. 25), reflecting on his son "Adam", points out how Christian theological reflection on the issue will inevitably end up as a critique of modernist society:

> Modern public institutions, oriented as they are to serving large groups of people, are marked almost inevitably by a trajectory toward "one-size-fits-all" care. If the autistic are not to be violently made to fit into modern society, communities will have to exist where people can learn that to truly care is always an individual affair. Thus, one of the sharp thrusts of a theological focus on responsibility to individual neighbors is to affirm the work of carers and people with autism as they search for holes or gaps in institutions within which individual care can be given in systems organised by a concept of "equality of provision.

It seems that the Biblical name "Adam" has become a default pseudonym for parent-practitioners describing their sons' experiences, and their own, auto-ethnographically. It is also used by Gillibrand (2010, ch 2), for example. It was also used as the title of a UK film that came out in 2009 (http://www.imdb.com/title/tt1185836/).

It is necessary to bring in a cautionary note at this point. Religious professionals, like teachers, are asked to deal with an enormous variety of issues, from poverty to political upheaval. Just in terms of psychological disorders, Johnson and Johnsons' (2014) influential guide on the issue for ministers can spare just three of its 200 pages on the issue of autism (six if we include the section on ADHD). Even so, considering all the recent media attention claiming that the prevalence of autism is on the rise, it is legitimate to ask why the religious world has not become more involved in this issue.

There even is less evidence of systematic theological reflection on autism when we look at religions other than Christianity. There are, however sociological case studies and reports that briefly give the main doctrinal background of a particular religion (e.g. Jegatheesan & Witz, 2013). Kamei (2013) does some comparative work between Christianity and Buddhism, but only as a small part of a larger project which does not allow for an in-depth consideration of concepts such as "karma" and "the will of God". Also, Kamei's project reflects another common theme in the available research on religion and autism: it focuses on the parents, and more specifically the mothers, not on the people with autism themselves (cf. Ekas et al. 2009; Howell & Pierson 2010, Poston & Turnbull 2004, Jegatheesan et al. 2010, White 2009).

There are indications that the religions are, in fact, not particularly successful at reaching the (high-functioning) autistic community. Studies indicate that atheism is more heavily represented among autists than the population in general (Caldwell-Harris et al., 2011). However, these studies have been criticised for not using representative samples (Kilsdonk-Gervais, 2015; Reddish, Tok & Kundt, 2016, p. 96). Still, this should not surprise us. As McCauley(2000) puts it, people with autism "... are destined to possess no more knowledge about human conduct than what the methods of behaviourism can afford. ... as a result of their disability, religion is something that even persons with autism functioning at such a high level do not readily comprehend or acquire." A series of studies showed that there is " ... compelling evidence that religious belief is positively associated with various measures of empathy and negatively associated with analytic thinking" (Jack et al., 2016). That is to say, religious belief is positively associated with the person with autism's greatest weakness and negatively associated with the strongest point of at least the higher-functioning ones.

McFall (2016), a theologian, recognises this relationship, in a sense, by reversing it. In his account, someone unable to establish a relationship with God suffers from "spiritual autism" (McFall, 2016). He offers this metaphor as an update to the old Christian metaphor of spiritual blindness. Arguing from the other side, Megil and Lindford (2016, p.42) use this same relationship as part of an argument in favour of atheism. That the same data can be interpreted in such different ways shows that the relationship between autism and religion is, at best, a work in progress.

Now how does this work in a religious environment? That depends on the religion. In evangelical Christianity, for example, there is a strong emphasis on the personal encounter and on-going relationship with Jesus Christ. We can expect the person with autism, who already has problems building friendships with real, physical people, to struggle with the concept of building a relationship with a trans-physical personality. Recent research by Reddish, Tok and Kundt (2016), however, interrogates this assumption. They argue that "... gods may be arguably easier to interact with than humans: Communication is one way and does not require complex deconstruction of social behaviours in a particular social situation to understand and predict the behaviours that are unfolding before you. Gods do not use sarcasm" (2016, p. 108). Their research, however, as they duly note, interrogated one religious behaviour pattern with a select group of high-functioning people with autism, and needs further investigation before it can be extended as a general observation of religion and autism. Also, no religious tradition would accept their secularist assumption that communication with the divine is a one-way process.

The same is true when the relationship the believer has to establish and maintain is with the ancestors, Krishna, or Buddha Amitabha. "[T]he intersection of marked autistic traits in a single individual might lead us to expect a highly distinctive sensibility, which is unlikely to support more typical forms of religiosity or spirituality" (Deeley, 2009, p. 82) such as Asperger syndrome or high functioning autism, present with difficulties in social understanding (including 'theory of mind'. In Visuri's qualitative research, the typical pattern was that the (high-functioning and articulate) subjects did not reject the idea of god, but saw it in a deist rather than theist fashion, as an impersonal spiritual force rather than a personal presence (Visuri, 2012).

Other religions, however, can be seen as more friendly to the person with autism. In both Judaism and Hinduism, for example, *orthopraxy* (performing approved behaviour) is generally more important than *orthodoxy* (holding approved beliefs). We can infer that autistic individuals born into these traditions would be accepted to the extent that they are able to perform the minimum prescribed ritual. Given the autistic love for routine, this should be possible for all but the lowest-functioning people with autism and lead to a greater acceptance of such people in society. And this is what we see in the studies quoted by Ecker (2010), especially those by Jegatheesan, Miller and Fowler (2010) and Shaked (2006). In both the Pakistani Muslim and the Ultra-Orthodox Jewish community, we see a theological justification that regards the child with autism as having been sent down from the divine realm to test the piety and care of parents and community (Yes, a religious community called "Orthodox" actually emphasises orthopraxy. It is just one of the ironies scholars of religion learn to live with). But there is nothing to prevent such a theological justification from existing in the above-mentioned Evangelical movement – a movement that instead denounces autism as demonic possession (DeRogatis, 2009). What, then, made the difference?

I suggest that the division between orthodoxy and orthopraxy is where we need to look when we try to determine the extent to which a given religious tradition will be able to work with individuals on the spectrum. In the academic study of religion, this distinction is so foundational that it is even used to analyse a completely fictional religion that exists only among online Harry Potter fans (Alderton, 2014, p. 221). We have briefly touched on these terms above, but a more complete definition is needed at this stage.

Orthodoxy, when used as a technical term in the academic study of religion, has to do with what one believes to be true, and whether those beliefs accord with those maintained by one's religious community. If your religion accepts you as a member in good standing if you are capable of standing up and saying: "I accept Jesus Christ as my personal Lord and Saviour", or "There is no god but God and Muhammad is his messenger" then your religion favours orthodoxy.

Orthopraxy is the other side of religion. It is the totality of behaviour required by your religion. What you are required to eat, or not to eat, how you pray, and how often, how to dress, how to use certain words – all these define the orthopraxy of a religion. A religion that stresses orthopraxy will accept you as a member in good standing if, for example, you regularly visit a temple to offer praise and libations to the gods, *even if you privately think they do not exist*. Orthopraxy is concerned with religion as social bonding through ritual, not with truth-claims. In addition, ritual, repetitive action that is intrinsically meaningless but personally meaningful, just happens to be a characteristic of autism. In the person with autism, it happens at a personal rather than a collective level and we refer to it as "stimming".

The more a religious tradition inclines to orthodoxy as the key criterion of religiosity, the more difficult it will be to fit in as an individual with autism. The more it inclines towards orthopraxy on the other hand, the easier it will be. No religion is completely orthodox or completely orthoprax. The vast majority of religions will be found somewhere in the middle. However, they will generally be on either side of the middle. Think of it as the

O-O spectrum. Orthodoxy and orthopraxy also reinforce one another. What you believe will lead you to certain behaviours. More surprisingly, perhaps, repeated performance of specific behavioural patterns will also lead to a change (or intensification) of belief. This principle lies at the heart of the religious formation of children. In a more sinister sense, it also lies at the heart of political propaganda and brainwashing (Selisker, 2016).

Needless to say, I am here isolating a single variable, which is always an oversimplification. There are larger societal patterns involved. If one lives in a society where the overall pattern is one of acceptance, then even someone belonging to a minority religion that favours orthodoxy will have to accommodate the larger societal picture somewhat. Conversely, if one lives in a community where having an autistic child leads to loss of face, such as Korea, then one's personal religious background may lead to a greater acceptance of one's child, but the loss of face in the outer community remains in place. In a multicultural society like South Africa, we need to constantly ask ourselves what community, as well as what religion we are dealing with, and considering the woeful shortage of research regarding the perception of autism among South Africa's communities, this is likely to be a difficult endeavour. Therefore, the persistent negative framing (See chapter 2 in this volume) among service providers is not helpful in this regard.

4.3 Autism in educational communities

Religion is a controversial topic in the sphere of education even when we deal with neurotypical learners. The South African government has produced the National Policy on Religion and Education (Department of Education, 2003) one of the most progressive statements on the issue ever produced, but it is silent on the issue of Inclusive Education. Indeed, even the most cursory inspection of practice in South African schools today reveals that the policy is not being enforced and is largely ignored by teachers and school governing bodies (SGBs) (Rousseau, 2010).

Despite this, we need to consider the position of learners with autism when it comes to religion, and here the policy makes a useful distinction between different activities. *Religion Education* is education about religion as a historical human activity, as this has developed into the various religions of the world. On the contrary, *Religious Instruction* is the induction of people into a specific religion (a related concept, *religious formation*, is sometimes used to express the further development of religious belief and practice within a specific faith). Finally, *Religious Observances* at schools are dealt with by the policy.

According to this policy, Religion Education is the public school's task while Religious Instruction is the responsibility of the parents and the religious community to which they belong. Things get murkier when we consider private schools, which may be (and often are) established on a religious basis. Private schools in South Africa are not entirely free to do as they please. Nevertheless, they do have greater leeway in adapting official curricula to be in line with a philosophical or religious vision. Considering that the private sector plays a significant role in the provision of specialised education for learners with autism in South Africa (Clasquin-Johnson & Clasquin-Johnson, 2018), we should consider both Religion Education and Religious Formation.

There is a prescribed curriculum for Religion Education, partly subsumed under Life Orientation and partly an independent Grades 10-12 subject. The objective of this curriculum falls squarely within the ambit of Religion Education. It teaches the "facts", the who, where and what of the history of religion. If the learner is sufficiently high functioning, this material should be no harder to impart than geography or biology. If not, then the same principles would apply that we use to present material to otherwise cognitively impaired learners. But when we consider curriculum adaptation of religious learning content for the autistic learner, there is a decision we must make.

Is the objective to help the autistic child to fit into his or her existing religious community? Then we need to reach for orthopraxy. All religions have rituals and performances: even religion analogues like atheism, if we care to look deeply enough. It is entirely possible to train teachers to teach these ritual requirements and to pass them on to the learner. If the learners remain in the same faith tradition for the rest of their lives, they will be able to go through the motions. The extent to which the religious community will accept that as sufficient will depend on where it stands on the O-O spectrum. In addition, if the autistic learner or their family decides to convert to a different religion, we have wasted our effort. Nevertheless, it is an achievable goal for us as educators.

Within an Indonesian Muslim context, we see such an approach described by Fithri (Fithri, 2011) in which "religious therapy" (in a Muslim context) consists of teaching learners the correct way to recite the Koran and the way to do the ritual washing required before the daily prayers. Note that the learners are not asked to explain the text or its meaning to their lives. It is enough to be able to recite it in correctly pronounced Arabic. A learner might not be able to give intellectual assent to the higher reaches of Islamic theology, but the repeated, doctrinally correct performance of these rituals will nevertheless foster an emotional attachment, a recognition that "this is what we do as Muslims". Contrast this with the situation in nearby Brunei, where "children with intellectual impairments are not considered to be able to perform the necessary religious obligations of the Islamic faith" (Tait & Mundia, 2012, p. 200)

Similarly, Swanson (2010, p. 253), working in a Christian context, describes her work in the religious formation of "Justin" and points out that

> Religious experiencing requires that the person be actively interacting with the environment and those within it. For children with autism this means being actively engaged in experientially based and meaningful learning opportunities embedded in everyday routines. (Emphasis added)

However, if the objective is to foster orthodoxy: to bring the learner with autism to a reasoned, voluntary decision to commit to the truth-claims of a specific religion, then we are looking at a different process. I have a PhD in Buddhist Studies, and I would hate to have to convince a teenager with Asperger's Syndrome and internet access that Buddhism is true. It can be done, of course, but it would take more time and more debate: a process more akin to postgraduate theological training than to the complex mixture of reason and emotion that makes up religion for most of us. The average teacher is simply not trained to this level, unless we start requiring teachers to have three-year BTh degrees, and the equivalent in other religions, over and above their educational qualifications.

We do not need to know the Laws of Thermodynamics to teach someone to drive a car, even though those laws form the theoretical basis of the internal combustion engine.

By analogy, teachers (and parents) of autistic learners cannot be required to have detailed knowledge and understanding of, say, the 2 000 years of debate regarding the Christian doctrine of the Trinity, or the even older and equally debated Hindu concept of Avatara. What they can and must do is teach the learner what it means to live as a good Christian, Jew, Hindu, Muslim and so on. If we can let go of insisting that religion is something to *believe*, and see it as equally, or more, a way to *behave*, and thereby to *be*, the road to curriculum adaptation becomes clear. For the learner with autism, religion must be introduced as something to do, repeatedly and correct in the tiniest detail. In that way, we will be leveraging the teaching of religion to learners with autism in a way that speaks to the strengths of the person with autism, not to his or her challenges.

References

Adams, B. (2015). *'North Pond Hermit'* Knight Completes Specialty Court Program, centralmaine.com. http://www.centralmaine.com/2015/03/23/north-pond-hermit-completes-specialty-court-program/ (Accessed: 1 January 2016).

Alderton, Z. (2014). "Snapewives" and "Snapeism": A Fiction-Based Religion within the Harry Potter Fandom *Religions*, 5(1): 219-267. doi: 10.3390/rel5010219.

American Psychiatric Association (2013). Autism Spectrum Disorder Fact Sheet, APA DSM5. American Psychiatric Publishing. http://tinyurl.com/k77bwpq (Accessed: 26 July 2016).

Annus, A. (2015). Asceticism in the Ancient Mesopotamia: Metaphor or Reality? A Study on Autism in Antiquity, ResearchGate. https://www.researchgate.net/publication/277330272_Asceticism_in_the_Ancient_Mesopotamia_Metaphor_or_Reality_A_Study_of_Autism_in_Antiquity (Accessed: 17 May 2016).

Atran, S. (2002).The Neuropsychology of Religion. In Joseph, R. (Ed.) *NeuroTheology: Brain, Science, Spirituality & Religious Experience*. University Press California.

Ault, M., Collins, B. & Carter, E. (2013). Factors associated with participation in faith communities for individuals with developmental disabilities and their families. *Journal of Religion, Disability and Health*, 17: 184-211.

Bailkin, J. (2012). *The Afterlife of Empire*. Berkeley, CA: University of California Press.

Baron-Cohen, S. & Wheelwright, S. (1999). "Obsessions" in Children with Autism or Asperger Syndrome. Content Analysis in Terms of Core Domains of Cognition *The British Journal of Psychiatry*, 175(5): 484-490. doi: 10.1192/bjp.175.5.484.

Basu-Zharku, I. O. (2011). The Influence of Religion on Health. *Student Pulse*, 3(1). http://www.studentpulse.com/articles/367/the-influence-of-religion-on-health (Accessed: 14 April 2016).

Benson, P. R. (2010). Coping, distress, and well-being in mothers of children with autism *Research in Autism Spectrum Disorders*. 4(2): 21-228. doi: 10.1016/j.rasd.2009.09.008.

Brock, B. (2009). 'Autism, care, and Christian hope. *Journal of Religion, Disability & Health*, 13(1): 7-28. doi: 10.1080/15228960802581404.

Brown, S. (2014). *Coping, Resolution and Advocacy in Parents of Children with Autism.* Purchase College, State University of New York.

Caldwell-Harris, C., Murphy, C. F., Velazquez, T. & Mcnamara, P. (2011). Religious belief systems of persons with high functioning autism *Annual Meeting of the Cognitive Science Society*. 3362-3366.

Clasquin-Johnson, M.G. & Clasquin-Johnson, M. (2018). 'How Deep Are Your Pockets?' Autoethnographic Reflections on the Cost of Raising a Child with Autism. *African Journal of Disability* 7

Coulthard, P. & Fitzgerald, M. (1999). In God we trust? Organised religion and personal beliefs as resources and coping strategies, and their implications for health in parents with a child on the autistic spectrum. *Mental Health, Religion & Culture*, 2(1): 19-33. doi: 10.1080/13674679908406329.

Cox, J. A. (2015). *Autism, Humanity and Personhood: A Theological Perspective*. Murdoch University.

Deeley, Q. (2009). Cognitive Style, Spirituality, and Religious Understanding: The Case of Autism *Journal of Religion, Disability & Health*, 13(1): 77-82. doi: 10.1080/15228960802581479.

Department of Education (2003). *National Policy on Religion and Education*. Tshwane: Government of the Republic of South Africa. http://www.gov.za/sites/www.gov.za/files/religion_0.pdf (Accessed: 26 July 2016).

DeRogatis, A. (2009). Born Again is a Sexual Term: Demons, STDs, and God's Healing Sperm. *Journal of the American Academy of Religion*, 77(2): 275-302. doi: 10.1093/jaarel/lfp020.

Dyches, T. T., Wilder, L. K., Sudweeks, R. R., Obiakor, F. E. & Algozzine, B. (2004). Multicultural Issues in Autism. *Journal of Autism and Developmental Disorders*, 34(2): 211-222.

Ecker, J. (2010). *Cultural Belief Systems in Autism and the Effects on Families*. Barnard College, Columbia University.

Ekas, N. V., Whitman, T. L. & Shivers, C. (2009). Religiosity, spirituality, and socioemotional functioning in mothers of 1children with autism spectrum disorder. *Journal of Autism and Developmental Disorders*, 39(5): 706-719. doi: 10.1007/s10803-008-0673-4.

Erndl, K. M. (2016). Religious and National Identity in My Name is Khan. *Journal of Religion and Film*, 20(1). http://digitalcommons.unomaha.edu/jrf/vol20/iss1/5 (Accessed: 14 April 2016).

Finkel, M. (2014). The Strange & Curious Tale of the Last True Hermit GQ. http://www.gq.com/story/the-last-true-hermit (Accessed: 24 October 2016).

Fithri, H. (2011). Religious Therapy As One of an Alternative Ways in Getting Educational Betterment for Children With Autism Spectrum Disorder *Procedia - Social and Behavioral Sciences*. Elsevier B.V., 29, 1782-1787. doi: 10.1016/j.sbspro.2011.11.425.

Galli, C., Kreider, R. & Ross, B. (2016). Wacky Church Under Fire Over 'Miracle Cure' for Autism, *abc News*. http://abcnews.go.com/US/wacky-church-fire-miracle-cure-autism/story (Accessed: 26 October 2016).

Gillibrand, J. (2010). *Disabled Church, Disabled Society*. London: Jessicah Kingsley Publishers.

Gona, J. K., Newton, C. R., Rimba, K., Mapenzi, R., Kihara, M., Van De Vijver, F. J. R., Abubakar, A. & Eapen, V. (2015). Parents' and Professionals' Perceptions on Causes and Treatment Options for Autism Spectrum Disorders (ASD) in a Multicultural Context on the Kenyan Coast. *PLoS ONE*, 10(8): 1-13. doi: 10.1371/journal.pone.0132729.

Howell, E. J. & Pierson, M. R. (2010). Parents' Perspectives on the Participation of Their Children with Autism in Sunday School. *Journal of Religion, Disability & Health*, 14(2): 153-166. doi: 10.1080/15228961003622302.

Huntington, C. W. (2015). The Triumph of Narcissism: Theravāda Buddhist Meditation in the Marketplace. *Journal of the American Academy of Religion*, 83(3): 624-648. doi: 10.1093/jaarel/lfv008.

Jack, A. I., Friedman, J. P., Boyatzis, R. E. & Taylor, S. N. (2016). Why Do You Believe in God? Relationships Between Religious Belief, Analytic Thinking, Mentalizing and Moral Concern *Plos ONE*, 11(3): p. e0149989. doi: 10.1371/journal.pone.0149989.

Jegatheesan, B., Miller, P. & Fowler, S. (2010). Autism From a Religious perspective: A Study of Parental Beliefs in South Asian Muslim Immigrant Families *Focus on Autism and Other Developmental Disabilities*, 25(2): 98-109.

Jegatheesan, B., Miller, P. J. & Fowler, S. A. (2010). Autism From a Religious perspective: A Study of Parental Beliefs in South Asian Muslim Immigrant Families. *Focus on Autism and Other Developmental Disabilities*, 25(2): 98-109. doi: 10.1177/1088357610361344.

Jegatheesan, B. & Witz, K. (2013). An Ethnographic Study on Religion, Spirituality, and Maternal Influence on Sibling Relationships in a Muslim Family with a Child with Autism. *Review of Disability Studies*, 9(1): 4-21.

Johnson, W. B. & Johnson, W. L. (2014). *The Minister's Guide to Psychological Disorders and Treatments*. New York: Routledge.

Kamei, A. (2013). *Perceptions and Experiences of Mothers who have Children with Autism Spectrum Disorders: Cross-Cultural Studies from the US and Japan*. The University of North Carolina at Greensboro.

Kilsdonk-Gervais, N. (2015). Atheism, autism and naivety. https://nkilsdonkgervais.wordpress.com/2015/09/18/atheism-autism-and-naivety/ (Accessed: 18 May 2016).

MacQuarrie, B. (2013). In Rural Maine, a Life of Solitude and Larceny. *Boston Globe*, 26 May. https://www.bostonglobe.com/metro/maine/2013/05/25/north-pond-hermit-discovered-arrested-after-years-maine-woods/xSXsUlDOQVhqUMb8nkslxN/story.html (Accessed: 24 October 2016).

Mann, A.R. (2013). *The Experiences of Mothers of Children with Autism in Jamaica: An Exploratory Study of Their Journey*. University of South Florida. http://scholarcommons.usf.edu/etd/4722.

McCauley, R.N. (2000). The Naturalness of Religion and the Unnaturalness of Science'. In Keil, F. and Wilson, R. (Eds). *Explanation and Cognition.* (pp.61-87). Cambridge, Mass: MIT Press.

McFall, M.T. (2016). Divine Hiddenness and Spiritual Autism. *Heythrop Journal*, (Early View). doi: 10.1111/heyj.12324.

Megill, J. & Linford, D. (2016). God, the meaning of life, and a new argument for atheism. *International Journal for Philosophy of Religion*. Springer Netherlands, 79(1): 31-47. doi: 10.1007/s11153-015-9538-x.

Poston, D.J. & Turnbull, A.P. (2004). Role of Spirituality and Religion in Family Quality of Life for Families of Children with Disabilities. *Education and Training in Developmental Disabilities*, 39(2): 95-108.

Reddish, P., Tok, P. & Kundt, R. (2016). Religious Cognition and Behaviour in Autism: The Role of Mentalizing. *The International Journal for the Psychology of Religion*, 26(2): 95-112. doi: 10.1080/10508619.2014.1003518.

Rousseau, J. (2010). Religion Education in South African Schools. *Synapses*. http://synapses.co.za/religious-education-south-african-schools/ (Accessed: 11 April 2016).

Selieker, S. (2016). *Human Prograsmming. Brainwashing, Automatos, and the American Unfreedom.* Minneapolis: University of Minnesota Press.

Shaked, M. & Bilu, Y. (2006). Grappling with affliction: Autism in the Jewish ultraorthodox community in Israel. *Culture, Medicine and Psychiatry*, 30(1): 1-27. doi: 10.1007/s11013-006-9006-2.

Sowell, T. (2003). The Autism Spectrum. *Capitalism Magazine.* http://capitalismmagazine.com/2003/09/the-autism-spectrum/ (Accessed: 14 April 2016).

Swanson, S. (2010). Experiential religion: A faith formation process for children with autism. *Journal of Religion, Disability & Health,* 14(3): 238-255. doi: 10.1080/15228961003622393.

Swinton, J. & Trevett, C. (2009). Religion and Autism: Initiating an Interdisciplinary Conversation. *Journal of Religion, Disability & Health*, 13(1): 2-6. doi: 10.1080/15228960802606193.

Tait, K.J. & Mundia, L. (2012). The Impact of a Child with Autism on the Bruneian Family System. *International Journal of Special Education*, 27(3): 199-212.

Terry, K. (2015). A Wrinkle in the Fold: Inclusion of People with Autism Spectrum Disorders in Faith Communities. *Social Work and Christianity*, 42(4): 449-469.

Visuri, I. (2012). Could Everyone Talk to God? A Case Study on Asperger's Syndrome, Religion, and Spirituality. *Journal of Religion, Disability & Health*, 16(4): 352-378. doi: 10.1080/15228967.2012.731888.

White, S.E. (2009). The Influence of Religiosity on Well-Being and Acceptance in Parents of Children with Autism Spectrum Disorder. *Journal of Religion, Disability & Health*, 13(2): 104-113. doi: 10.1080/15228960802581503.

World Health Organisation (2016). Pervasive Developmental Disorders, ICD-10 Version:2016. http://apps.who.int/classifications/icd10/browse/2016/en#/F84 (Accessed: 14 May 2017).

5

VOICES AND VIEWS OF SENIOR STUDENTS WITH ASD

Penny Round and Pearl Subban

Editors' note

As the sole exception in this African volume, we include this Australian contribution. While the purpose of our book is to initiate an All-African discussion on autism, we also wish to engage in a South-South discussion on the subject. The authors have long-standing ties with South Africa and the South African debate on the educational implications of autism.

Abstract

The purpose of this study was to develop an understanding of the support required by students with a diagnosis of high functioning autism undertaking the senior secondary school years. Diagnosed students often experience significant challenges with accessing the curriculum, as particular support accommodating their unique needs, is limited. The study employed a qualitative methodology incorporating both case studies and semi-structured interviews. Data were collected from four young adults with a diagnosis of high functioning autism (HFA) to ascertain what needs were required and to gather the students' perspective. The perspectives of these four teenagers provided valuable insight into their perceptions of the supports needed to assist them through their senior secondary classes. An inductive and exploratory approach to data analysis identified multiple themes. These included visual cues, the role of the teacher, support with organisation and general support strategies. The study adds new information to the growing body of research in this field by yielding a functional checklist which can be utilised by teachers in the senior secondary school years, as they accommodate students with HFA. While much research has revolved around the need to support the full inclusion of students with HFA, there is little research on the practicalities of this, particularly for those students undertaking their final years of secondary school.

5.1 Introduction

Much has been written about the deficits of students with autism spectrum. However, little attention has been paid to the high functioning students who are undertaking senior secondary schooling and what strategies can support them through this process (McKeithan & Sabornie, 2017). Recent research on the learning of students with High-Functioning Autism (HFA) indicates that they may have comparable academic strengths compared to their peers, or may even exceed their peers (Klin, Danovitch, Merz, & Volkmar, 2004; Volkmar, Lord, Bailey, Schultz, & Klin, 2004; Roberts, 2010; McKeithan & Sabornie,

2017). Students with HFA have post-secondary school aspirations, but they have to contend with workload increases, more complicated methods of assessment, combined with the pressures of undertaking senior school examinations. This may well determine the student's future study and career pathways (Dixon & Tanner, 2013; Lindsay, Proulx, Thomson, & Scott, 2013).

Students with a diagnosis of HFA require that teachers focus on the students' visual strength and understand that organisation is also a frequent issue (Attwood, 2007). Students with HFA are particularly in need of an understanding and supportive teacher. The teacher's responses to, and behaviour toward, students with HFA are significant predictors of how well students respond to the environment, and of their subsequent success (Luiselli, Russo, Christian, & Wilczynski, 2008). Therefore, this chapter focuses on a collection of student voices, which would allow teachers in this context to modify or change conditions within the classroom setting in order to increase the potential for academic success among students with HFA, in the senior secondary schooling years. The study is informed by antecedent based interventions. Antecedent based interventions were deemed preferable for students with HFA, as they allowed teachers to implement these preventative and proactive strategies with minimal effort (Conroy, Asmus, Sellers, & Ladwig, 2005; DiGennaro Reed, Hirst, & Hyman, 2012). In the case of students in the senior secondary school years, manipulating antecedent variables is an effective strategy as it is pre-emptive and can support students by eliminating or minimising any potential negative triggers for students with HFA. Previous research has demonstrated that controlling antecedents have produced positive outcomes for students with HFA (Boyd, Conroy, Asmus, & McKenney, 2008; Prupas & Reid, 2001; Rapp, Patel, Ghezzi, O'Flaherty, & Titterington, 2009). Following systematically from this conceptual approach, the researchers were able to devise a checklist for teachers of students with HFA, in the senior secondary school years, outlining effective strategies for intervention in the classroom.

The study sought to represent an authentic "voice" as students with HFA expressed participants' views in the senior secondary years. Ashby (2011) asserts students with disabilities often do not have the voice with which to self-advocate. Young people with disabilities are often marginalised, or silenced within academic communities, rendering them powerless to act on their own behalf (Ashby, 2011; Cefai & Cooper, 2009; Fielding, 2010). As such, the senior secondary school students who formed part of this study were not just subjects, but participants in the research process. Studies in the field of Inclusive Education often perceive students as "subjects" instead of "participants" in a study (Ashby, 2011; Fielding, 2010). Furthermore, Fielding (2010) posits that "tokenistic" involvement of students with disabilities into research scenarios is "condescending" and "suffocating" to students. Nevertheless, the need to acknowledge and recognise student voices and their right is becoming increasingly warranted in the contemporary age (Bragg, 2007). This study consequently offered a forum to students with HFA in the senior secondary school years, allowing them to express their thoughts and ideas within settings and frameworks that suited them.

Contemporary society places a huge emphasis on secondary school success, linking such success with future careers and successful lives (Fleury et al., 2014). Consequently, many students strive to not only persevere through to the senior secondary school years, but work hard to do their best under test and examination conditions. Many students diagnosed with HFA have often shied away from the senior secondary school years, despite being quite able and intelligent (Varney, 2015). They often opt for less academic options, as the highly pressured academic workload deterred them from completing their secondary school studies. The Australian Bureau of Statistics (2012) reported that 81% of students with HFA do not further their studies after leaving school, therefore, suggesting that many have not performed well enough to seek tertiary study, or that many have not completed secondary school. In the United States, 58 percent of students with autism spectrum disorder (ASD) have participated in some form of postsecondary education, either a two-year community college (43%), vocational, business or technical school (27%) or 4-year college (22%) (http://www.nlts2.org/reports/2009_04/nlts2_report_2009_04_ch2.pdf). While this statistic is an improvement on the Australian statistic, there are, however, still 42% of students with the ASD who do not proceed to post-secondary school pathways.

Poor post-school outcomes prompt an investigation into provision and accommodation of students with HFA, especially in the senior secondary school years. Research reflects that appropriate supports improve academic performance at school and improve post-school success (Stodde & Mruzek, 2010; Fleury et al., 2014). An internal report in one Australian state revealed that adolescents with HFA often refused to attend school as the learning environment provided poor supports and did not accommodate their needs (Bowden, 2012). Many did not receive assistance from their teachers or their peers, resulting in feelings of disconnectedness and alienation (Bowden, 2012). Many in this context reported being bullied, experiencing difficulty in social contexts and keeping up with the workload (Bowden, 2012).

In order to provide better support to adolescents with HFA in the senior secondary school years, educators need to be skilled in how to best accommodate them (Fleury et al., 2014). However, a gap exists between the theory offered to school staff regarding best practice with regard to adolescents with HFA, and subsequent practice (Fleury et al., 2014). The organisation and characteristics of learning environments in the senior secondary school years appear to hinder success for students with HFA. Furthermore, teachers often experience difficulty accommodating students with HFA in the senior secondary school years on account of repetitive behaviours, limited social communication and limited engagement in classroom activities (Estes, Rivera, Bryan, Cali, & Dawson, 2011; Fleury et al., 2014).

5.2 Senior secondary students with HFA

Students with HFA in the senior secondary years may be challenged by certain expectations and elements of learning within these settings. Research reveals that students with HFA have difficulty observing closely, and they appear to lack the ability to learn from others who model appropriate skills (Plavnick & Hume, 2013). Moreover, students with HFA may present with expressive difficulties, behaviour that may be different from the norm and limited social interaction. They are often quiet, non-communicative and may appear reticent, therefore limiting their opportunities to learn from their environments. Skills that often depend on social and verbal interaction may consequently be impeded.

Research in the field also suggests that students with HFA may manage information at different speeds when compared to their peers (Cashin & Barker, 2009). Similar challenges are also evident in their processing of visual stimuli (Cashin & Barker, 2009). Interestingly, scientific endeavours in the field suggest that students with HFA may possess superior abilities as they have the potential to visualise in greater detail (Kunda & Goel, 2011). This apparent strength becomes valuable to students and teachers during problem solving tasks (Kunda & Goel, 2011). In line with this, students with HFA often focus on the details of visual elements associated with a task, i.e., they have a propensity to focus on details and miss the "big" picture (Happe & Frith, 2006). Consequently, students may be more successful with tasks that focus on details, or local processing, but they may be challenged by tasks that require more holistic, globalised thinking (Grinter, Maybery, Pellicano, Badcock, & Badcock, 2010). In addition, students with HFA are likely to find tasks that require multiple steps and those that require considerable planning difficult (Joseph & Tager-Flusberg, 2004). This is on account of their compromised executive brain functioning which comes to bear on the ability to follow chronological steps (Joseph & Tager-Flusberg, 2004).

Research in neuropsychology further points to the phenomenon that compromised executive functioning may increase in adolescence, as the complexity of certain tasks is intensified during secondary school (Rosenthal et al., 2013). As a result, students at this stage, experience challenges with "multi-step" directions, being organised, and initiating complex tasks on their own (Rosenthal et al., 2013). Furthermore, during secondary school more complex conceptualising of ideas are embedded within specific subject areas. Literary concepts such as irony, symbolism and inferences can pose significant hurdles during this period (Hill & Frith, 2003). Students with HFA need support with their organisation, which will have beneficial impact on their academic achievements; therefore, teachers need to be proactive in their own organisation and proactivity (Mckeithan, & Sabornie (2017). The role of the teacher is vital as students with HFA particularly need teachers who work at developing a rapport with them and supporting them (Lindsay, Proulx, Thomson, & Scott, 2013).

This chapter is based on the view that that young people with HFA should be given the opportunity to complete secondary school with a view to entrance into university. In addition, effective support at this level can facilitate authentic learning, leading students to be more successful and achieve goals. The importance of a proactive teacher is crucial to prevent and reduce any stimuli that may negatively impact the student. The teacher must consider the environment and routines. Students with HFA need individualised support from the teacher. Allowing the students with HFA to have an understanding of the content to be studied in the class the next day and providing them with supports in how to best access this content, can enhance their access to the content and potentially avoid anxiety (Lindsay, Proulx, Thomson, & Scott, 2013). It also allows them time to process the information and have a knowledge that their teacher has high expectations of them and wants to help and support them to do their best (Lindsay et al., 2013).

The goal of the current study was to ascertain the views of senior secondary school students with HFA in regard to their accommodation in mainstream classrooms. It offered a forum for students to articulate their views on what they thought their teachers ought to know about them, their preferred teaching and learning methods, and their ability to cope within classrooms. The study employed the qualitative method of case studies and semi-structured interviews. Given the context and dynamics of the current project, case studies were deemed most appropriate. As a data collection method, case studies presented the researchers with an opportunity for more detailed, targeted investigation (Rowley, 2002; Creswell, 2013).

The project further acknowledged the importance of the subjective human experience within context and attempted to enable participants to offer their stories and experiences (Baxter & Jack, 2008). Furthermore, subjects for the project were students with HFA, and as such, the case study would be a more effective way of eliciting their views. Students with HFA often experience difficulty articulating their perspectives and points of view (Ochs, Kremer-Sadlik, Sirota, & Solomon, 2004). Both researchers in this project were classroom teachers of secondary students, and therefore were aware of the underlying issues and the difficulties faced by students. Consequently, the research design for the project utilised an exploratory approach, with multiple case studies. This design allowed for a comparison of similarities and differences between and among selected cases (Baxter & Jack, 2008). Data collected using this method were regarded as more robust and reliable (Baxter & Jack, 2008).

The impetus for this study grew from our personal needs as teachers and teacher educators. We acknowledged that students with HFA embarked on the journey of senior secondary school slightly differently from their peers. Our need was therefore to not only give students a voice, but to provide classroom teachers, including our own students, with a concrete list of suggestions and recommendations arising from what we heard from our respondents. The final years of secondary school can be bewildering and overwhelming for students with HFA. We hoped that by channelling the vision of their teachers to the particular needs of students with HFA, there could potentially be a reduction in the anxiety and stress experienced by both students and teachers in this situation.

While there is an existing body of research on attitudes of teachers to the inclusion of students with diverse needs, studies specifically regarding teachers' attitudes to students with a diagnosis of ASD are a more recent area of study (Segall, 2007; Segall & Campbell, 2012). Teachers are more accepting of the inclusion of students with ASD in mainstream schools, but are still uncertain about practices to support students with ASD (Segall & Campbell, 2012) and this study hopes to provide teachers with specific strategies through the voices of senior secondary students with HFA to ensure their success in a mainstream classroom.

With more students with HFA in mainstream classes, teachers need to be supported to ensure they have an understanding of the unique needs of these students, as the attitude of the teacher is crucial to the success of the inclusive process. Although the education of students with HFA in secondary schools is increasing, it is clear that further specialised training is required for teachers in receiving and integrating these pupils in mainstream schools (Sanahuja Gavalda & Qinyi, 2012).

5.2.1 Theoretical framework

The conceptual framework for this study was drawn from several transformative learning theories, the most pertinent of which is the "Head, Heart and Hands" (HHH) Model. This now popular theoretical base, which has its roots in Dewey's (1934) "Art as Experience" observations, is founded on the premise that teaching and learning are holistic approaches (Singleton, 2015). The HHH Model has come to be regarded as an organising principle that integrates the intellect (head), the emotion (heart) and the physical (hands) (Orr, 1992; Sipos, Battisti, & Grimm, 2008). Within the frame of this model, student engagement during the learning process occupies three domains. The head, the cognitive domain, engages students through academic study and enquiry. The heart taps into an affective domain, which relates to attitudes, motivation and values. The hands refer to the practical enactment of learning involving physical work (Sipos et al., 2008). This study acknowledges that authentic learning has the power to enrich the lives of students with HFA, and that such learning could transform their everyday living experiences, through the head, the heart and the hands. Within this framework, teachers who seek to appropriately accommodate students with HFA, in the senior secondary phase, will consider a "blending" of learning based on the HHH Model. As such, teaching and learning activities will seek to address three elements, perhaps even offering some accent on the element preferred by the student. Active learner engagement in this content will depend on the provision of rich academic experiences (head), will attempt to draw on the student's values (heart) through an appeal to positive attitudes and will apply this knowledge in application tasks (hands). Students with HFA often require logical (head) approaches to learning that can be rationalised and viewed as reasonable. However, teachers will need to incorporate the concept of emotion (heart) by reflecting on learning that inspires and arouses passion and interest in students. Finally, this framework offers the view that learning should also be action-oriented for students (hands), through a practical application that demonstrates learning. The HHH Model addresses three main motivational structures that impact on student learning in this context. It approaches the cognitive, affective and practical domains of learning, therefore ensuring a richer and fuller experience for students with HFA.

5.2.2 Method

The objective of this qualitative study was to offer a voice to students with high-functioning autism through individual case studies. The section following justifies the use of this approach within the Australian context.

5.2.2.1 Experimental design

The use of case studies were deemed appropriate as they allowed the researchers to investigate both specific and general phenomena (Yin, 2014), related to the provision of academic support to students with HFA in the senior secondary school years. The use of the case study further allowed for an investigation of subjects within their real-life contexts (Yin, 2014). Furthermore, the use of multiple case studies offered a degree of external validity of the study, as backgrounds and responses could be compared through thematic matching and through comparable explanation building (Yin, 2014). Both researchers are former secondary school teachers who had accommodated students with HFA in the senior secondary school years. Consequently, both were aware of particular behaviours and therefore adopted a flexible and adaptive approach during contact.

5.2.2.2 Data collection

The case studies derived data from two sources – initial contact by telephone and a follow-up interview lasting around an hour. The initial phone conversation obtained demographic variables and ascertained the most comfortable site for the interview. Semi-structured interviews were conducted with each subject. Such an interview style was considered appropriate for the selected subjects since the interviewer could not accurately predict how subjects would respond and it was more likely to produce richer data (Wengraf, 2001). Interviews were planned loosely around a set of possible questions. However, both researchers who conducted the interviews were aware that they had to be mindful of the student's state of mind, their well-being and their ability to formulate and articulate a response. In order to maintain a degree of homogeneity, the researchers discussed the protocol for each case study prior to implementation. Prior preparation involved the schedule of questions, arrangement of interview times, the actual interviews, and the follow-up contact. The interview adopted the format of a guided conversation, allowing participants to share their experiences more freely.

Both researchers managed the data manually. With research of this nature, data collectionand analysis happen almost simultaneously (Baxter & Jack, 2008). This was possible owing to the small number of cases, and allowed the researchers to utilise inductive data handling procedures where appropriate (Creswell, 2009). Creswell (2009) notes that data analysis, within the context of semi-structured interviews, could be "built" as patterns, themes and categories emerged. The recorded interviews were fully transcribed verbatim. Once transcribed, interviews were subjected to member checks, with transcriptions being sent to respondents via mail, in order for them to establish whether their views had been correctly interpreted. This allowed for more accuracy during analysis. Data were coded, described and explored, guided by the suggestions of Creswell (2009). This was a lengthy manual process conducted by both researchers. An external audit, by other academic staff and the university's ethics committee, allowed for an objective evaluation of the process. Key words, categories and themes were highlighted based on word frequency, similarities and ideas (Creswell, 2009). In addition, there was a need to explore possible patterns and to look at commonalities between and among subjects (Yin, 2003). Similarities and differences in viewpoints were identified with each point being coded for later analysis. In order to establish trustworthiness in the data, the four criteria recommended by Lincoln and Guba (1985) were used to ensure credibility, transferability, dependability and conformability (Lincoln & Guba, 1985). The data have credibility as the collection and analysis utilised rigorous academic procedures.

Transferability was established through thick description, with a comprehensive literature review allowing the research team to determine the extent to which conclusions could be accurately drawn. Dependability was confirmed as the research process was subjected to external audits by the university's ethics committee and by senior academics in the Faculty of Education. The criterion of conformability was met through a careful scrutiny of the data, in relation to the findings of other studies in the field. This is evident in the discussion of the findings of this study.

5.2.2.3 Participants

Recruitment for the project was conducted via two well-known psychologists. Posters and business cards were placed in the waiting rooms of both individuals, with contact details of the researchers. If parents and students were interested, they could voluntarily contact the researchers. Owing to privacy regulations and ethical considerations, the researchers did not actively recruit participants. This method yielded four subjects for participation in the project – three male candidates and one female candidate. Two of the participants had just completed secondary school, with the other two being in their senior secondary school years. Although two of the participants had graduated secondary school, they were still deemed eligible to participate as they had only recently completed their senior secondary school year and stated they wanted to be involved in the research and felt that they had graduated because of the assistance they received from the school. Arrangements were made with regard to times and venues where the interviews would take place.

Megan (pseudonyms are used throughout) was 17 years old, and in Year 11 at a private Christian secondary school. She lived with both her parents, and two younger brothers. Megan was diagnosed with HFA in Grade 6. At the time, she was enrolled at a local state school. She was moved to an independent school as her mother believed that her needs would be better accommodated there. Throughout her school life, Megan felt she was "different". She was home schooled during Grade 3 because she could not cope with being in a classroom with other students. Megan received some assistance from the school's Education Support Program for two periods every week. During this time, she was helped with organisation and with "chunking" challenging tasks. Megan enjoyed mathematics more than any other subject. She found English to be challenging because of the open-ended content of most assessment requirements. Her best subjects were those in which the teacher adopted a structured programme, and she knew what to expect as the lesson unfolded. She loved working on the computer and knows a great deal about the electronic medium. She had few friends at school, and spent most lunch sessions in the library. She found large group conversations to be overwhelming as there were "too many voices" to attend to. Group work in classrooms posed a challenge because she found it difficult to cope with many, varying opinions.

Sam was a 20-year-old male who completed Year 12 at an independent secondary school. Sam was diagnosed with HFA in Year 7. Sam was enrolled at a school that both his parents thought would support Sam's needs. Sam had a small group of friends and received support from the school's Support Services teachers and had the support of a teacher aide for two periods a week in class, who would prompt him to focus on his work, ensure he understood the set task, and scaffolded some of the written tasks with him in detail. As Sam progressed through the year levels, he undertook fewer elective subjects, and was able to spend his non-teaching lessons in small group sessions at the school's Support Services department. Sam was supported with his organisation and with the brainstorming and structuring of his work and also to ensure that he was completing his homework. Sam did not enjoy any classes. He wanted to leave school at the end of Year 11, but his mother insisted that he remains to complete his Victorian Certificate of Education (VCE – final year of secondary school), which Sam did reluctantly.

Dylan was a 19-year-old male who completed Year 12 at an independent secondary school. Dylan was diagnosed with HFA in Grade 5. Dylan was enrolled at a school that his parents believed would support him. Dylan had a wide group of friends and received support from the school's Support Centre and attended specialised support classes there twice a week from Year 7 to Year 10. As Dylan progressed through to VCE, and he undertook fewer elective subjects, he spent his non-teaching lessons in small group sessions at the Support Centre and in the library. Dylan did not want to acknowledge that he needed support and did not like to be perceived as "different", so assistance provided had to be discrete and he had to perceive it as very purposeful. Dylan was supported with his organisation and structuring of tasks as he would become quite anxious and avoid completing them unless given support and prompting. The school also kept contact with Dylan's mother to ensure that there was consistency between home and school in the approach to supporting Dylan and to ensuring that his homework was being completed.

Julian was a 16-year-old male undertaking Year 11 at an independent school. Julian was diagnosed with HFA in Grade 3. Julian is twice exceptional as he is also gifted, but does experience issues with organisation and hubris. Julian had a close group of friends, but did receive assistance from the school's Support Department to support him with his organisation and his motivation. Julian only liked to complete the work that he perceived to be worthy of his consideration and could be quite dismissive and insulting to his peers and teachers. Julian achieved excellent academic results, but did require support with his organisation and to ensure that he was engaged with the content of his classes and completing all work.

5.3 Findings

The objective of this study was to ascertain the views of students with HFA regarding their experiences of completing senior secondary school. The following common themes emerged – visual cues, the role of the teacher, organisation, and general support strategies. Each of these will be discussed in turn.

5.3.1 Visual cues

A key finding to emerge from student interviews was the concept that visual cues are a key learning support for students with HFA. In this regard, Megan noted that: "I like to see the course outline on the wall in a classroom. It helps me to get an idea of what to expect during each lesson. If I have the outline with me, it helps me to prepare for the lesson".

Julian, Sam and Dylan all noted that they liked it when the teacher brainstormed ideas with the class, but then most importantly put the notes from the discussion on the board. The teacher providing visual cues for the student can also enhance their ability to access the information provided and support them in their organisation (Crosland & Dunlap, 2012). Dylan and Sam particularly liked it when a mind map was used. Julian stated that: "Notes on the board are useful for later reference – it's better than verbal instructions' and Sam said that there was 'less writing' which was better".

Sam, Julian and Dylan liked it when the teacher suggested a film version of a novel to provide them with an understanding of the text before the actual reading of it and they also liked to see plays of set texts. Dylan liked to have an audio of an English novel to help and Sam liked it when members of the class completed role-plays or there was a film or theatre production of the text. It helped him gain a visual of the text and the characters and plot. Certain skills, such as adopting a characters' perspective, are often challenging for students with HFA, a skill required for the evaluation of novels studied in schools (Ricketts, Jones, Happe, & Charman, 2013).

Sam and Julian liked to be able to view past exams; so, they had an understanding of the requirements that would be expected of them, which in turn reduced their anxiety levels. Sam also liked to see past essays from English classes and past exams to have an idea of the format and content he may need to know and understand. Norbury and Bishop (2002) found that individuals on the autism spectrum invest a great deal of time processing individual words that comprised a sentence. Consequently, they sometimes missed the meaning of the sentence, thereby influencing their understanding of entire passages (Norbury & Bishop, 2002). By having the information provided in visual format and having prior exposure to the expected format of exams, the student with HFA is permitted more time to process the information as the visual medium is sustained in its presence.

5.3.2 The role of the teacher

Another integral idea that surfaced was the view that teachers are central to the success of students with HFA in the secondary school classroom.

Megan pointed out that:

> I liked my Year 9 teachers best. They were very understanding and did not get impatient when I asked questions.
>
> I like getting the term plan in advance. It helps me to prepare and I know what to expect. I know when the School Assessed Coursework will happen and I can prepare for that. I don't like it when a teacher suddenly changes their mind and moves dates around without telling us.
>
> I like teachers who use clear language. Sometimes I can't understand the instruction, then I don't get it. I have to ask Ms Burton at Ed Support to help me to understand. I think the teacher should speak clearly so that I understand.

Julian, Dylan and Sam emphasised the importance of the teachers' attitude. They liked a teacher who was receptive to their questions and had a positive attitude to supporting them. Sam talked about his teachers *'really listening', 'talking with me rather than at me'* and understanding why he may behave a certain way. Sam also liked it if the teacher worked with him to find a solution – this helped to reduce his anxiety. Dylan said that it helped him *'knowing that I could go to the teachers and that they were helpful.'* Sam liked it when the teacher started the class and then casually wandered over to him to ensure he understood the task and to scaffold his progress. Research reflects that more supportive teachers could ensure better outcomes for students with HFA (Kaweski, 2011). 'The teenager is expected to relate to many teachers, each with his or her own personality and teaching style, and to engage in academic assessment that relies on abstract thinking rather than facts' (Attwood, 2007, p. 20). Teachers of students with disabilities need to be sensitive to the needs of students with HFA (Lawson, 2008; Kaweski, 2011). Research in the field resonates with the view that greater tolerance and patience is required on the part of educators, when providing for the needs of students with HFA (Mayes & Calhoun, 2003; 2008). Students with HFA often experience challenges with drawing inferences or being able to empathise (Hill & Frith, 2003; Norbury & Bishop, 2002). Consequently, teachers may be challenged by the student's inability to comprehend or follow in the same manner as their peers. Effective supports may include, 'priming, prompt delivery, and picture scheduling' (Harrower & Dunlap, 2001, p. 765). Priming involves the teacher reviewing the task to be completed by the students and considering the best interventions to support the student through this. It may involve providing the students with information prior to a class discussion so they have time to prepare and the teacher could even assist them to prepare and then aid in facilitating their involvement in group work or group discussion. Prompt delivery involves providing prompts to the student with HFA that may be in addition to those presented to the rest of the class and picture schedules involve presenting in visual format the structure of the activities to be undertaken during a certain period of time (Harrower & Dunlap, 2001). As researchers, the authors were keen to illuminate details on how the secondary school teacher could offer support and direction to students in his/her classroom. In this regard, the following quote from Hans Asperger, over 60 years ago, is pertinent in context:

> These children often show a surprising sensitivity to the personality of the teacher. However difficult they are, even under optimal conditions, they can be guided and taught, but only by those who give them understanding and genuine affection, people who show kindness towards them and yes, humour. The teacher's underlying emotional attitude influences, involuntarily and unconsciously, the mood and behaviour of the child. Of course, the management and guidance of such children essentially requires a proper knowledge of their peculiarities as well as genuine pedagogic talent and experience. Mere teaching efficiency is not enough (Asperger [1944] 1991, p.48, as cited in Attwood, 2007, p. 246).

5.3.3 Organisation

Organisation proves to be a difficulty for students with HFA, in the senior secondary school years. Megan remarked: "I use my diary often to write down stuff like homework, but sometimes I forget about it. I forget especially when the due date is far off. I have a good memory though".

Dylan liked it when his teachers discretely helped him scaffold his homework; that they worked with him to plan completion dates of longer assignments and that they monitored this to keep him on track.

Julian liked very explicit statements of due dates and a clear outline of the homework task and scaffolding of progression points for longer assignments and very constructive feedback. He also wanted the feedback to be in writing. Some adolescents with HFA can have difficulty 'prioritising which task to concentrate on first and time management. This can be exasperating for parents and teachers who know that the child has the intellectual capacity to complete the work to a high standard, but impaired executive function will contribute to a delay in the submission of the work' (Attwood, 2007, p. 236). There is a need for teachers to assist students with being organised and being aware of task requirements. Sam liked to use the Outlook Calendar application on his IPhone to provide him with reminders to start work on certain tasks. He also preferred teachers monitoring his progress to ensure he was on the right track and to clarify any areas of uncertainty or misunderstanding. This helped reduce his anxiety. He liked it if the teacher was proactive about this. He also liked to talk through the task with the teacher, but he appreciated it when the teacher was able to intuitively understand that he did not understand the task and took the time to non-judgmentally re-explain the task, without annoyance or anger.

Attwood (2007, p.19) notes that

> During adolescence, a teenager with Asperger's syndrome is likely to have increasingly conspicuous difficulties with planning and organisational skills, and completing assignments on time' and that, 'The teenager's intellectual abilities have not deteriorated, but the methods of assessment used by teachers have changed', as has the workload, the expectations and the pressures of undertaking senior school examinations, which may well determine the student's future study and career pathways.

They will require assistance with organisation in an explicit and intentional manner (Kaweski, 2011; Lawson, 2008). Aligned to this concept, students with HFA process information at variable speeds when compared to their peers (Cashin & Barker, 2009). Processing speeds are not necessarily slower. However, teachers need to become aware of the student's need for details, while occasionally missing the "big" picture (Happe & Frith, 2006). Research in the field further points out that students with HFA often become preoccupied with the details (Norbury & Bishop, 2002). These preoccupations have organisational implications as well, and may inhibit progress to the next steps because of students not perceiving the bigger picture. Providing a step-by-step approach could be beneficial as students with HFA often experience difficulties with following chronological steps in task completion (Joseph & Tager-Flusberg, 2004). This becomes especially crucial during the adolescent years for students with HFA, as the complexity of tasks increases, therefore placing additional organisational demands on an already compromised executive brain functioning (Rosenthal et al., 2013).

5.3.4 General support strategies

It became evident through the interviews that students with HFA in the senior secondary years of school would benefit greatly from targeted support strategies. Megan indicated that she preferred a structured, quiet environment:

> I don't like certain classes where the teacher allows lots of talking. I find it very difficult to concentrate. It's impossible for me to finish my work when everyone is disruptive, and then I have to take all the work home. I hate doing stuff at home.

About group work, Megan noted that:

> I don't like working in groups because I become confused by all the opinions. I'm usually very quiet during a group discussion. I find all the background noise to be annoying, and I can't concentrate. I don't know why teachers ask us to work in groups.
> Sometimes I need a bit more time to complete stuff. This happens mostly during English. It would be good if I had a bit more time. I find that I have to think fast and then write fast. This stresses me out sometimes.

Sam, Dylan and Julian all stated that they liked to have a quiet place to go to when they needed help or to '*chill out*'. Julian stated that he liked to have a '*safe place or person*' when he felt he was overwhelmed. All three males liked to have 1:1 support if they experienced any difficulty with a topic. Oral presentations were a source of great anxiety for Sam and Dylan and both preferred to present to a smaller audience, such as the teacher and the Teacher Aide. Sam also liked prior notice about group work and his role in that and any questions that he might be asked so he could have time to think about his potential responses. Sam also liked rest breaks in class for a rest or refresh. Both Dylan and Sam said that they liked extra time to complete tasks.

5.4 Conclusion

Bearing in mind that the views articulated by the four students who formed a part of this study, we recommend the following ideas as researchers to teachers of students with HFA in the senior years of school.

Firstly, we suggest that teachers supplement verbal instructions and discussions with notes on the board. This acts as an external storage and reminder to students, prevents processing overload and minimises the possibility of misunderstanding of what the teacher requires.

Secondly, the teacher should provide very explicit instructions of the task and of the homework. Students are often uncertain how to approach a task. Unambiguous and clear instructions with regard to task completion and homework are essential to the senior secondary school classroom. Teachers should ask the student to explain to them what the task is that they are expected to complete; by asking them to explain their understanding of the task will ensure that they can progress with the task or leave the classroom and know what homework they have to complete. The teacher simply asked the student if they know what they have to do is not enough. Students may reply that they do understand when in fact they do not.

Thirdly, it is important to scaffold a task, progressively for students. Reduced organisational skill often means that a student with HFA will forget about or postpone a task to a later date. Without progressive scaffolding, the task then comes upon them suddenly, and its completion becomes overwhelming. The teachers should therefore provide gradual and ongoing support, with reminders to chunk the task and prompts about how much should have been completed by a set time frame.

Fourthly, students with HFA in the senior years, like any other student, require the support and understanding of an accepting teacher. Students in this category are highly sensitive to teachers who are intolerant or dismissive of their needs. This may discourage or even hinder their progress. Aligned to this, students may require 1:1 help. An understanding and tolerant teacher, who is willing to provide these supports, will be rewarded with a more engaged student and one who is willing to see tasks through to completion. Fifthly, the reminder to use practice examinations as a means of testing content, provides an additional, external means of sustenance. Finally, the provision of a "safe place" to where students can escape when the classroom environment becomes overwhelming is essential to the student with HFA. The student may not utilise this form of assistance frequently but the knowledge that it is available to them acts as another form of care and maintenance.

The original checklist (See the addendum to this chapter) was born out of these recommendations. It yields a set of helpful cues for teachers in the senior secondary years. This offers an element of new information to the field, and responds to the direct need experienced by secondary students in contemporary settings. As researchers and teachers, we understand the time constraints faced by teachers, and hoped to ease the task by honing in on the essential elements of accommodating students with diverse learning needs into regular classroom settings. We believe that the elements contained in the checklist emerging from the case studies summarise the crucial, fundamental factors that would lead to the inclusion of students with HFA in the senior secondary school contexts. As such, we anticipate that this will contribute to the knowledge extant in the field, but more importantly, will offer direct support to both teachers and students with high-functioning autism.

5.4.1 Limitations and future directions

Although this study had only four participants, this research has been able to focus on very specific understandings of the support that students with HFA require of their senior secondary school teacher. The ability of the participants to articulate their desired supports and the consistency of these does shed light on a neglected area of research. Suggestions for future research may include replicating this study with a larger participant group, providing teachers of senior secondary school with the checklist that was developed and determining their perspective on this and any suggestions for improvement. Through the use of qualitative methodology, this study set out to give voice to four senior secondary school students with HFA, regarding the support systems they require at this vital stage of their schooling. The study acknowledged that more students with HFA are entering the senior secondary school years, and as such, it is essential for teachers to accommodate them and to provide for their needs. The use of case studies and semi-structured interviews yielded the following common themes: visual cues, the role of the teacher, organisation, and general support strategies. Adapting and adjusting teaching methods and the learning environment in the senior secondary school years, to suit students with HFA, may result in improved outcomes, better retention rates and enhanced interest and engagement from the point of view of students.

5.4.2 Acknowledgements

We thank all the participants who agreed to be part of this project and who therefore contributed to this research.

References

Australian Bureau of Statistics. (2012). *Autism and Education,* 4428.0, Australian Bureau of Statistics.

Ashby, C. (2011). Whose "voice" is it anyway?: giving voice and qualitative research involving individuals that type to communicate. *Disability Studies Quarterly*: 31(4).

Attwood, T. (2007). T*he Complete Guide to Asperger's Syndrome*. Philadelphia : Jessica Kingsley Publishers.

Baxter, P., & Jack, S. (2008). Qualitative case study methodology: Study design and implementation for novice researchers. *The Qualitative Report*, 13(4): 544-559.

Bowden, J. (2012). Autism Asperger ACT Inc. School Attendance Survey. http://www.autismaspergeract.com.au/assets/Publications/Files/School-Attendance-Survey-Report-2012.pdf.

Boyd, B.A., Conroy, M.A., Asmus, J.M., & McKenney, E.L. (2008). Descriptive analysis of classroom setting events on the social behaviors of children with autism spectrum disorder. *Education and Training in Developmental Disabilities*, 43(2): 186-197.

Bragg, S. (2007). 'Student voice' and governmentality: The production of enterprising subjects? *Discourse: Studies in the Cultural Politics of Education*, 28(3): 343-358.

Cashin, A., & Barker, P. (2009). The triad of impairment in autism revisited. *Journal of Child and Adolescent Psychiatric Nursing*, 22(4): 189-193.

Cefai, C., & Cooper, P. (2009). The narratives of secondary school students with SEBD. In C. Cefai and P. Cooper (Eds.) *Promoting Emotional Education: Engaging Children and Young People with Social, Emotional and Behavioural Difficulties* (pp. 37-56). London: Jessica Kingsley.

Conroy, M.A., Asmus, J.M., Sellers, J.A., & Ladwig, C. (2005). The use of an antecedent-based intervention to decrease stereotypic behavior in a general education classroom: A case study. *Focus on Autism and Other Developmental Disabilities*, 20(4): 223-230.

Creswell, J. (2009). *Research Design: Qualitative, Quantitative and Mixed Methods Approaches*. (3rd ed.).New York: SAGE Publications.

Crosland, K. & Dunlap, G. (2012). Effective strategies for the inclusion of children with autism in general education classrooms. *Behavior Modification*, 36(3): 251-269.

DiGennaro Reed, F.D., Hirst, J. M., & Hyman, S. R. (2012). Assessment and treatment of stereotypic behaviour in children with autism and other developmental disabilities: A thirty year review. *Research in Autism Spectrum Disorders*, 6: 422-430. doi.org/10.1016/j.rasd.2011.07.003

Dixon, R.M., & Tanner, K. (2013). The experience of transitioning two adolescents with Asperger syndrome in academically focused high school. *Australasian Journal of Special Education*, 37: 28-48.

Fielding, M. (2010). The voice of students in an inclusive school. Paper presented at the *International Congress on Inclusive Education*, University of Cantabria. Spain.

Fleury, V.P., Hedges, S., Hume, K., Browder, D.M., Thompson, J.L., Fallin, K., & Vaughn, S. (2014). Addressing the Academic Needs of Adolescents With Autism Spectrum Disorder in Secondary Education. *Remedial and Special Education*, 35(2): 68-79.

Grinter, E.J., Maybery, M., Pellicano, E., Badcock, J., & Badcock, D. (2010). Perception of shapes targeting local and global processes in autism spectrum disorders. *Journal of Child Psychology and Psychiatry*, 51(6): 717-724.

Happe, F., & Frith, U. (2006). The Weak Coherence Account: Detail-focused Cognitive Style in Autism Spectrum Disorders. *Journal of Autism and Developmental Disorders*, 36(1): 5-25.

Harrower, J.K., & Dunlap, G. (2001). Including children with autism in general education classrooms: A review of effective strategies. *Behavior Modification*, 25: 762-784.

Hill, E.L., & Frith, U. (2003). Understanding autism: insights from mind and brain. *Philosophical Transactions of the Royal Society B: Biological Sciences,* 1430: 281-289.

Joseph, R.M., & Tager-Flusberg, H. (2004). The relationship of theory of mind and executive functions to symptom type and severity in children with autism. *Development and Psychopathology*, 16: 137-155.

Kaweski, W. (2011). *Teaching adolescents with autism. Practical strategies for the inclusive classroom.* New York: SAGE Publications.

Klin, A., Danovitch, J.H., Merz, A.B., & Volkmar, F.R. (2004). Circumscribed interests in higher functioning individuals with autism spectrum disorders: An exploratory study. *Research and Practice for Persons with Severe Disabilities*, 32(2): 89-100.

Kunda, M., & Goel, A.K. (2011). Thinking in Pictures as a Cognitive Account of Autism. *Journal of Autism and Developmental Disorders*, 41(9): 1157-1177.

Lawson, W. (2008). Adolescents, autism spectrum disorder and secondary school. *Learning Links News*, 3: 1-6.

Lincoln, Y.S., & Guba, E.G. (1985). *Naturalistic Inquiry*. Newbury Park, California: SAGE Publications.

Lindsay, S., Proulx, M., Thomson, N., & Scott, H. (2013). Educator challenges of including children with autism spectrum disorder in mainstream classrooms. *International Journal of Disability, Development & Education*, 60: 347-362. doi:10.1080/1034912X.2013.846470

Luiselli, J.K., Russo, D.C., Christian, W.P., & Wilczynski, S. M. (2008). *Effective practices for children with Autism: Educational and behavior support interventions that work*. New York: Oxford University Press.

McKeithan, G.K., & Sabornie, E.J. (2017). Interventions for secondary students with high functioning autism in general education settings: A descriptive review. *Exceptionality*, doi: 10.1080/09362835.2017.1359607

Mayes, S., & Calhoun, S.L. (2003). Ability profiles in children with autism. SAGE Publications and the National *Autism Society*, 6(4): 65-80.

Mayes, S., & Calhoun, S. L. (2008). WISC-IV and WIAT-II profiles in children with high functioning autism. *Journal of Autism and Developmental Disabilities* 38(1): 428-439.

Norbury, C.F., & Bishop, D.V.M. (2002). Inferential processing and story recall in children with communication problems: A comparison of specific language impairment, pragmatic language impairment and high-functioning autism. *International Journal of Language & Communication Disorders*, 37(3): 227-251.

Ochs, E., Kremer-Sadlik, T., Sirota, K.G., & Solomon, O. (2004). Autism and the social world: An anthropological perspective. *Discourse Studies*, 6(2): 147-183.

Orr, D. (1992). *Ecological literacy: Education for a post modern world.* New York: State University of New York.

Plavnick, J., & Hume, K. (2013). Observational learning by individuals with autism: A review of teaching strategies. *Autism: International Journal of Research and Practice*. Advance online publication.

Prupas, A., & Reid, G. (2001). Effects of exercise frequency on stereotypic behaviors of children with developmental disabilities. *Education and Training in Mental Retardation and Developmental Disabilities*, 36(2): 196-209.

Rapp, J.T., Patel, M.R., Ghezzi, P.M., O'Flaherty, C.H., & Titterington, C.J. (2009). Establishing stimulus control of vocal stereotypy displayed by young children with Autism. *Behavioural Intervention*, 24(1): 85-105.

Ricketts, J., Jones, C.R., Happe, F., & Charman, T. (2013). Reading comprehension in autism spectrum disorders: the role of oral language and social functioning. *Journal of Autism and Developmental Disorders*, 43(4): 807-816.

Roberts, K. (2010). Topic areas to consider wwhen planning transition from high school to postsecondary education for students with autism spectrum disorders. *Focus on Autism and Other Developmental Disabilities*, 25: 158-162.

Rosenthal, M., Wallace, G.L., Lawson, R., M.C.W., Dixon, E., Yerys, B.E., & Kenworthy, L. (2013). Impairments in real-world executive function increase from childhood to adolescence in autism spectrum disorders. *Neuropsychology*, 27(1): 13-18.

Rowley, J. (2002). Using Case Studies in Research. *Management Research News*, 21(1): 16-27.

Sanahuja Gavalda, J.M., & Qinyi, T. (2012). Improving the process of Inclusive Education in children with ASD in mainstream schools. *Social and Behavioral Sciences*, 46: 4072-4076.

Segall, M. J. (2007). Inclusion of students with autism spectrum disorder: Educator experience, knowledge, and attitudes. Unpublished master's thesis, University of Georgia, Athens, Georgia.

Segall, M.J. & Campbell, J. M. (2012). Factors relating to education professionals' classroom practices for the inclusion of students with autism spectrum disorders. *Research in Autism Spectrum Disorders*, 6(3): 1156-1167.

Singleton, J. (2015). Head, heart and hands model for transformative learning: Place as context for changing sustainability values. *The Journal of Sustainability Education.* http://www.jsedimensions.org/wordpress/march-2015-sustainability-whats-love-got-to-do-with-it/

Sipos, Y., Battisti, B., & Grimm, K. (2008). Achieving transformative sustainability learning: Engaging head, hands and heart. *International Journal of Sustainability in Higher Education*, 9: 68-86.

Stodde, R., & Mruzek, D. (2010). An introduction to postsecondary education and employment of persons with autism and developmental disabilities. *Focus on Autism and Other Developmental Disabilities*, 25: 131–133. doi:10.1177/1088357610371637.

Varney, C. (2015). Education system failing students with autism. *The Age (Newspaper)* http://www.theage.com.au/comment/education-system-failing-students-with-autism-20150405-1mezfn.html.

Volkmar, F.R., Lord, C., Bailey, A., Schultz, R.T., & Klin, A. (2004). Autism and pervasive developmental disorders. *J Child Psychol Psychiatry*, 45(1): 135-170.

Wengraf, T. (2001). *Qualitative research interviewing*. London: SAGE Publications.

Yin, R. K. (2003). *Case study research: Design and methods*. (3rd ed.). Thousand Oaks, California: SAGE Publications.

Yin, R.K. (2014). *Case study research: Design and methods*. (5th ed.). Thousand Oaks, California: SAGE Publications.

Table 5.1: The Senior Secondary Teacher's Checklist: Accommodating Students with High Functioning Autism (An Original Checklist)

	YES	NO	Comment
In Class Support: Have I...			
Presented information visually?			
Provided mind maps of the information, texts and themes covered?			
Noted discussion points on the board?			
Provided templates or graphic organisers of possible structures for each form of assessment?			
Provided past examples of exams and responses?			
Discretely asked the student to retell what the task they are undertaking entails to ensure they understand it?			
Worked with the student to prioritise which tasks to complete first?			
Provided advice/suggestions in writing with very explicit constructive feedback?			
Allowed more time to complete the task?			
Provided audio novels or the text as a film or presented a role play?			
Considered the use of technology to complete a task?			
Academic: Have I...			
Considered the student's attitude/response to group work?			
Provided assistance to the student in terms of problem solving?			
Considered how to support the student with group work – such as providing the questions prior to the group work?			
Gained an awareness of how the student copes in an exam situation?			
Support with homework: Have I...			
Explicitly outlined predetermined due dates that should be adhered to?			
Scaffolded the completion of chunks/sections of assignments that run over a few lessons/days/weeks?			
Emotional: Have I...			
Obtained an awareness of whether the student has a staff member or 'safe' place to go?			
Spoken with support staff, parents, and the student to determine individual needs and controlling factors?			
Gained an awareness of the student's strengths and aspirations?			

6

LEARNERS WITH ASD IN A RURAL CONTEXT

Moyagabo Kate Malahlela

Abstract

There is a challenge in rural areas with regard to identifying and providing support services for children and youth with ASD. Teachers in rural communities are often confronted by various challenges related to learners with ASD, which include impairments of social interaction, communication and thought processes. Owing to lack of knowledge and skills on how to accommodate such learners, teachers ultimately confuse or misconstrue the learning support needs of learners with ASD to be having challenging behaviours, being stubborn, unmotivated, emotionally impaired, undisciplined, severely or intellectually impaired. This may bring about the delays in progressive and relevant intervention strategies that could be established to combat the developmental barriers that young children and youth with ASD may experience. Learners in rural areas who live with ASD, like their counterparts in urban areas, need consistent individual support, structured and adapted curricula to prevent and address learning breakdown.

Since the developmental skills and abilities of learners with ASD are atypical, highly indivualised and do not always develop spontaneously, this chapter will focus on learners with ASD in rural context. I will specifically delve into the causal factors (mainly intrinsic to the learner), how rural environments affect and influence the developmental milestones of learners with ASD, and the intervention strategies, which could provide opportunities for social interaction between learners with ASD and their neuro-typical peers in inclusive settings.

6.1 Introduction

Rural settings present specific discrepancies and actual challenges to families of learners with ASD, which in most cases emanate from limited physical access to resources (Mello, Urbano, Goldman & Hodapp, 2016). This is owing to the geographic distance between families and service providers, inadequate availability of diagnostic treatment and support-services, low reliance on health care professionals and cultural belief systems (Roth, 2017) (see Chapter 4 for more information of belief systems). Moreover, challenges in rural areas are envisaged to be in conjunction with screening, identifying and providing support services for children and youth with ASD. This chapter focuses on the background to ASD in a rural context, the intrinsic etiologic or causal factors, rural environment influence on early identification of learners with ASD, and education intervention strategies which could provide opportunities for social interactions between learners with ASD and their neuro-typical or ordinary peers in inclusive settings (refer to chapter 1 in this book).

6.2 Background on autism in a rural context

ASD is a neurodevelopmental syndrome with growing global health concerns (National Institute of Neurological Disorders and Stroke, 2018). This condition is characterised by deficits in social and communication skills; restricted and repetitive behaviour which adversely impact on learners' and their families' quality of life. A range of behaviour problems common in learners with ASD include self-injury, anxiety, compulsions, withdrawal, uncooperative behaviour, aggression, and destruction of property (Peters-Scheffer, Didden, Korzilius & Sturmey, 2010:2). The United Nations Convention on the Rights of the Child (UNCRC) (1989, see also the chapter on International law in this volume) deliberated on affording all children the right to education in regular schools without discrimination on the basis of disability. It asserts that learners with disabilities are to receive support, according to their educational needs, and that schools should facilitate their effective education within general education (Phasha, 2016:7). Although major global advances in understanding the genetic and developmental aspects of ASD have been made, many aspects of the condition are still poorly understood, especially in rural areas.

Globally, one in every 160 persons is estimated to live with ASD, contributing to 7.6 million disability life adjusted years (Abubakar, Ssewanyana & Newton, 2016). A study conducted in rural Bangladesh (2017) revealed that little is known about ASD in low-income countries, especially in underserved South Asia, where access to health professionals to diagnose and treat child development disorders, like autism, are virtually non-existent. In Saudi Arabia, although not a low-income country, students with autism are still excluded from mainstream schools owing to the lack of knowledge and understanding of autism as a condition and because teachers are unable to adjust classroom environments and their teaching styles to meet the special needs of these students. Students with high functioning autism or Asperger syndrome in Saudi Arabia often remain undiagnosed because teachers are unable to recognise the symptoms of autism (Almasoud, 2010:2). Recent estimated prevalence of ASD in India ranges from 0.15% to 1.01% as recorded in various studies and the prevalence thereof in rural areas has been reported to be 0.90% (Juneja & Sairam, 2018). A study conducted in Bangladesh (Akhter, Hussain, Shefa, Kundu, Rahman & Biswas, 2018) which explored the prevalence of ASD among rural community learners aged 18-36 months, revealed that autism is regarded as a significant burden or disease. In South Africa, most of the barriers to learning were reported to be emanating from the prevalence of poverty in rural areas, which was also associated with the manifestation of ASD in learners (Abubakar, et al., 2016).

Considering rural areas in sub-Saharan Africa, research reports from Africa and among the African diaspora indicate that there is an increased prevalence of ASD in learners from several countries. These include Somali in rural areas of Stockholm, learners of Nigerian origin in Sweden; those whose mothers live in the United Kingdom but are of African origin, and in many African countries (Ruparelia, Abubakar, Badoe, Bakare, Visser, Chugani, Chugani, Donald, Wilmshurst, Shih, Skuse & Newton, 2014; Bakare & Munir, 2011:189). These findings suggest that ASD in African rural contexts may be more common than is recognised. The need for epidemiological research in Africa is therefore urgent.

The findings of many studies in Nigeria (Abubakar, et al., 2016, see also the Introduction of this volume) show a low level of knowledge and awareness about ASD in rural areas of that country. This compromises early identification and intervention to alleviate symptom severity. The findings of the survey revealed a very low level of knowledge and awareness about ASD among the general populace and a low to average level of knowledge and awareness among various categories of health care workers concerning ASD facilities (Bakare & Munir, 2011:189). Studies conducted in sub-Saharan Africa (Bernier, Mao & Yen, 2010) reveal that the perceptions of ASD could be mediated by culture, and screening measures need to consider these rural contextual factors, which are thought to have an influence on characterisation, diagnosis and treatment of ASD. The said contextual factors were revealed in a study conducted in South Africa known as the KwaZulu-Natal-ASD (K-ASD) Project, which indicated that there are disparities across rural South African ethnic groups in diagnosing ASDs and that variations across cultures may account for variations in diagnoses (Wilford, 2013).

A report from the K-ASD Project (Wilford, 2013) further indicated that currently, in South Africa, there are minimal provisions for screening, diagnosis and intervention strategies for ASD learners especially in communal rural settings. It was further reported in this project that many people in South Africa neither have access to services affiliated with ASDs nor the means to have lengthy expensive assessments done on their children. Until about two and half decades ago, ASD in sub-Saharan African rural areas was thought to be exclusively an illness peculiar to western civilisation (Bakare & Munir, 2011:184). The reasons behind this speculation may be attributed to the fact that rural communities face significant challenges regarding the adequate availability of diagnostic, treatment and support-services for individuals with ASD. This may include a variety of factors such as geographic distance between families and service providers, low reliance on health care professionals and cultural characteristics that contribute to the diminished availability and utilisation of services (Antezana, Scarpa, Valdespino, Albright & Richey, 2017).

Rural communities may attach labels to affected individuals either at school or in social settings. For example, learners could be regarded as having challenging behaviours, being stubborn, unmotivated, emotionally impaired or undisciplined. In other words, rural communities including teachers who are not informed about the characteristics of persons with ASD may ultimately conclude that such learners do not have good manners or that they are not well raised. A study conducted in Tanzania by Geraldina (2015) indicates that a number of teachers in rural areas have failed sometimes to recognise and accommodate learners with autism in their regular classes. According to Geraldina (2015), the reasons for such exclusion have been associated with attitudes, knowledge, perceptions and willingness of teachers and other stakeholders including parents towards teaching learners with ASD together with other learners who were regarded as typical for mainstream classrooms. (More information on inclusion of learner diversity in mainstream classrooms can be found in Chapter 12 of this book). This may exacerbate delays in progressive and relevant intervention strategies that could be established to support the developmental milestones in young children and youth who are with ASD.

Cultural variation in rural settings further magnifies potential screening biases suggesting that screening measures may need to be adapted for rural populations to establish reliability (Antezana et al., 2017:3). According to Antezana et al. (2017), very few service providers in rural areas specifically screen for ASD. This puts these communities at a greater risk of not being identified and further contributing to the delay in diagnosing learners with ASD.

Bakare and Munir (2011b) argue that the low level of knowledge and awareness about ASD, as documented by recent studies from Africa, is a call for engaging in activities that can improve the level of knowledge and awareness about ASD among healthcare workers and the general rural population in Africa.

6.3 Rural perspectives of the causes of ASD

The exact cause of ASD is currently unknown. Since this is a complex condition, it may occur because of genetic predisposition (a natural tendency), environmental or unknown factors (Lubin, 2015). Research shows that genetic factors play an important role, but the extent to which it does is unknown. Pre- and perinatal influences have been highlighted as potential risk factors, including infections that may occur in the womb (Murphy, 2013:2). Analysis of data obtained from Maternal and Health Research Database (Lubin, 2015) reveals that "individuals diagnosed within the autism spectrum are more likely to have experienced obstetric difficulties during pregnancy, labour delivery and neonatal period compared with people without an autism diagnosis". Additional research has investigated the possible influence of genetics that five to 20 genes could contribute to the development of autism (Lauritsen & Ewald, 2001; Murphy, 2013:2). Genetic factors are known worldwide to play a significant role in occurrence of ASD (Muhle, Trentacoste & Rapin, 2004:472). Although the hereditary acquisition of autism has been estimated to be as high as 90%, the genetic factors are heterogeneous, complex, and for the most part, poorly understood. The precise mechanisms of genetic inheritance of autism are presently being explored through methods of genome-wide screening, cytogenetic studies and evaluation of candidate genes whereby multiple genetic markers of autism have been susceptibility identified (Strathearn, 2009).

Although strong genetic association in etiology of ASD has been established, the specific model of inheritance is still unclear. Autoimmune factors (Bakare & Munir, 2011:188) also play a role. In rural contexts, the causes of ASD vary across cultures. Studies conducted in African countries such as Kenya (Gona, et al., 2016) revealed that the participants made mention of preternatural causes of ASD such as evil spirits, witchcraft and curses. The same studies in Kenya (Gona, et al., 2016) further reveal bio-medical cause of ASD such as infections, drug abuse, birth complications, malnutrition and genetic related problems. Treatment varied from traditional and spiritual healing to modern treatment in health facilities, and included consultations with traditional healers, offering prayers to God, and visits to hospitals. However, Bakare and Munir (2011) in their study conducted in Nigeria maintained that many of the cases that are often less severe are likely to seek help from prayer houses, spiritualists and traditional healers.

6.4 Rural environmental influences on early identification of learners with ASD

"Environment" includes any influence – physical or social – that might change or be changed by one's behaviour (Autism Response Team, 2017). Owing to environmental factors, learners with ASD in rural Africa are diagnosed relatively late compared to those in high-income countries (Bakare & Munir, 2011). One of the major practical and ethical difficulties in identifying learners with ASD in rural Africa lies in the general lack of appropriate services and inadequate standard of available educational and medical infrastructure. Antezana et al. (2017) attest that there is an increased dependence on the school system for access to services and screening for learners with ASD in rurally situated families, and comparatively less reliance on health care providers as compared to urban families. Within the community, there are notable rural and urban disparities regarding early identification of learners with autism because an urban setting may differ with rural environments, as urban families have exposure to more media, for example, radio and television advertisements as well as billboards (Abubakar, Bakare, Wilmshurst & Newton, 2016).

Another environmental influence comes to the surface through a common pathway adopted in rural African rural communities for a child with a neurodevelopmental disorder to be taken first to a traditional healer, before a parent seeks mainstream medical assistance (for more information, see Chapter 4 of this book). Seeking out help or other services is often perceived as a weakness in rural areas where individuals believe that problems should be taken care of within the home (Murphy, 2013:25). Although rural African communities appear to be self-sufficient by depending on their indigenous knowledge regarding ASD, the possibility is that their affected children may end up not having been given the necessary support. The potential delay in seeking mainstream medical assistance may contribute to a late diagnosis and could be a further exacerbating factor in the more severe cognitive and expressive language outcomes reported in children with ASD (Abubakar et al., 2016:2). This delay in diagnosis may also partly contribute to the lack of appropriate language skills in many of the learners with ASD because they did not have access to early interventions.

6.4.1 ASD and supernatural etiological factors

In a survey conducted by Bakare and Munir (2011), psychiatrists and paediatricians in Nigeria were asked about the causes of autism and many regarded ASD as having supernatural causes precipitated by angered ancestral spirits, sinful wrongdoing, predominantly by the mother or the action of the devil. Some members of rural communities may even go to an extent of misinterpreting manifestations of ASD in children and youth to be an outcome of a family curse from the ancestors. The preternatural and supernatural etiological explanation for ASD further corroborates the inseparable spiritual beliefs of Africans as it relates to etiological explanations for neuro-psychiatric disorders (Bakare & Munir, 2011:187). Similar findings were reported in a study conducted in Kenya (Gona, et al., 2015) where it was pointed out that preternatural causes that involve external forces were believed to have been the result of witchcraft, evil spirits and curses.

Teachers in rural communities are often confronted by various challenges related to learners with ASD. Owing to limited knowledge and cultural influences, teachers and the community at large become confined to misconceptions and stigmatisation of the affected learners, children and youth with ASD. A study conducted in Pakistan and India (Minhas, Vajaratkar, Divan, Hamdani, Leadbitter & Taylor, 2015) revealed that there is considerable stigma and discrimination affecting children with autism and their rural families. Pathways to care for children with ASD in the African setting are often different to their counterparts in well-resourced environments (Abubakar, et al., 2016:3).

6.5 Education intervention strategies to improve social interaction

Facilities for children with autism remain scarce, particularly in rural areas. People with autism can be fully incorporated into the social order or society and lead independent lives, especially when provided with the appropriate support (Geraldina, 2015). The idea of providing support to learners with ASD resonates with an African philosophy of Ubuntu which upholds the values of respect, collectivism, social cohesion, consideration for others and respect for life (Phasha, 2016, see also the Introduction to this volume). Similarly, Masondo (2015) attests that Ubuntu summarises moral norms and values such as "altruism, kindness, generosity, compassion, benevolence, courtesy, respect and concern for others". While educational services are often considered a universal service available to learners with disabilities, research suggests that access to these important services may be complicated for individuals living in rural areas. This may be owing to limited availability of highly trained educational professionals, limited choices for specific services, or disability-specific specialists such as developmental paediatricians, paediatric neurologists, speech therapists and physical therapists (Murphy, 2013:1).

Learners in rural areas who live with ASD, like their counterparts in urban areas, need high levels of consistent and professional support, structured and adapted curriculum or programmes to prevent and address their learning breakdowns (Murphy, 2013). Intervention strategies that can be applied to improve social interactions between learners with ASD and their neuro-typical peers in Inclusive Education setups are intended, not to cure autism, but to support learners with ASD, depending on their level of support need (Murphy, 2013:10; Lekgetho, 2016).

Despite the observation that parents of children with ASD who live in rural areas report a high reliance on schools for referrals and support, it is also known that learners who are first identified through the school system are the least likely to receive services. The school system plays a pivotal role in initiating pathways to services and diagnosis for rural communities. However, it is likely that learners who are first flagged for ASD in schools are less likely to be properly linked to support entities for diagnosis and services owing to increased geographic distances between practitioners and affected individuals in rural areas (Antezana et al., 2017:2).

The outcomes of the study conducted in rural Pakistan and India indicated that strategies for intervention should include building community and family support networks to provide respite to the main carer. In the absence of specialists, community members such as community health workers, traditional herbal practitioners and even motivated family members could be trained in recognising and providing evidence-based interventions. Such task-shifting strategies should be accompanied by campaigns to raise awareness so greater inclusivity can be achieved (Minhas et al., 2015). Other coping strategies include accessing information, working towards inclusion and greater acceptance of the child, community-based rehabilitation, equalisation of opportunities, poverty reduction, and social integration of persons with disabilities and their families (Gona, et al., 2015:3).

There are many intervention approaches including, diets and vitamins, floor time, holding, medication, Picture Exchange Communication System, sensory integration, speech and music therapy, special education and visual schedules. However, there is little empirical evidence for the effectiveness of many of these approaches and available evidence shows mixed results (Peters-Scheffer et al., 2010). The goal often is to provide accommodations and services to help children with ASD lead an adapted life that allows them to function successfully in society (Peters-Scheffer et al., 2010). The study conducted in Northeast Ohio by Geib (2011:128) suggests a successful education programme for students with ASD, which include among others, highly individualised programming delivered by highly skilled and trained staff to address the core deficit areas related to communication and behaviour through methodology-based interventions. These could include Applied Behaviour Analysis (ABA), Early Intensive Behavioural Intervention (EIBI) as well as some structural components of Teaching Education to children with Autism and Communication Handicaps (TEACCH). However, in a study conducted by Mello et al. (2016) it was reported that only a minority of families can successfully implement different services such as ABA, sleep evaluations and genetic testing.

In rural settings, the most common services that are mostly recommended but sometimes not implemented include behaviour support services and parent support groups (Mello et al., 2016). ASDs were thought to be caused by supernatural realm, precipitated by angered ancestral spirits, sinful wrongdoing (predominantly by the mother), or the action of the devil in rural communities. Therefore, the common pathway for these communities for a child with a neurodevelopmental disorder is to first take their child to a traditional healer before they seek mainstream medical assistance (Ruparelia et al., 2016). According to Murphy (2013), cultural influences on rural communities in the USA who occupy 83% of the rural land outside urban areas may adversely affect the level of active participation of parents of learners with ASD in their children's educational needs and the types of services they seek outside of the school system.

6.5.1 Applied Behaviour Analysis (ABA)

Currently, there are several promising and well-established intervention strategies for learners with ASD which include among others, ABA. This strategy involves applying learning principles to the acquisition of new skills (skill-based instruction) such as social, emotional and language skills. ABA is an approach to behaviour modification rooted in the experimental analysis of behaviour, in which operant conditioning and other learning principles are used to change problematic behaviour (Geib, 2011:32). In particular, ABA principles and techniques can foster basic skills such as looking, listening and imitating, as well as complex skills such as reading, conversing and understanding another person's perspective (Autism Response Team, 2017). The ABA interventions also highlight the importance of the integration of learners with ASD with their typical peers to generalise newly acquired skills to different, more realistic settings (Murphy, 2013:10). Core facets of this methodology include early intervention, parental involvement and intensive, comprehensive treatment that is tailored to the individual's needs and strengths. ABA can be broken down into specific types of behaviour interventions applicable to learners with ASD. Furthermore, learners with ASD are taught behaviours that build upon one another in a non-distracting environment and are consistently rewarded for completing the smaller unit of behaviour until it is mastered. Such intervention strategies include among others, Natural Environment Training (NET) and Discrete Trial Training (DTT) (Sundberg & Partington, 1999; Lovaas, 2003). Natural Environment Training is similar to the Natural Language Paradigm (NLP) and to Pivotal Response Training, which both emphasised the use of intrinsically motivating materials, teaching in natural contexts and focusing on the child's immediate interests to guide language instruction (Weiss, 2001).

6.5.2 Early Intensive Behavioural Intervention (EIBI)

Early and Intensive Behavioural Intervention (EIBI) is an evidence-based intervention using principles and procedures from ABA to teach adaptive behaviours to young children with ASD (Klintwall, 2014). For EIBI to be successful, children are provided with 20 to 40 hours of one-on-one therapy and families are also incorporated into the process so that young children get as much exposure as possible. EIBI uses the principles of behaviour analysis to increase positive and useful behaviours and decrease unwanted behaviours such as tantrums, aggression and self-injury. EIBI sessions are customised for each child's skill level. A certified behavioural therapist works with the child and family to address specific behaviours that are carefully defined in observable terms, measured and recorded to track the child's development in learning, communication, self-care, and social competence. Tasks that are more complex are broken down into easy to achieve units of behaviour as the child develops skills (Stebbins, 2015). Building on research from the 1960s, EIBI is the most often studied type of intervention for children with ASD (Matson & Smith, 2008). The treatment is carried out by parents and teachers under supervision by a professional and consists of identifying the skills that the child lacks, breaking these down into components and teaching those component behaviours separately. The child is provided with guidance to learn novel behaviours and this help is then phased out until the child can perform the target skills independently. The complexity of tasks is gradually increased as the child progresses so that the child can master each consecutive step. Much emphasis is placed on generalisation of taught skills, meaning that skills taught in an EIBI programme must be functional for the child in everyday life. EIBI consists of both one-to-one discrete trial teaching for basic skills such as imitation (verbal and motor), expressive and receptive language, and matching, and less structured teaching such as naturalistic and incidental teaching working on all areas of functioning, such as communication, self-help skills and independent functioning (Klintwall & Eikeseth, 2014).

6.5.3 Teaching Education to learners with Autism and Communication Handicaps (TEACCH)

TEACCH is a university-based project founded at the University of North Carolina at Chapel Hill in 1970 and has become one of the frequently used intervention programmes for learners with autism in educational settings (Geib, 2011). TEACCH programme focuses on maximising the skills of learners with ASD while emphasising their strengths, as opposed to attempting to cure them and it is designed to provide a structured learning environment in which learners with ASDs can develop skills including vocational ones (Geib, 2011:29). This kind of approach is also referred to as structured teaching which is aimed at making teaching methods and environment autism friendly by considering a student's cognitive ability, needs and interests and modifying the environment accordingly (Almasoud, 2010). Structured teaching involves four components, namely:

- differentiating the physical environment which involves the way of arranging furniture, materials and general surrounding to add meaning and context to the environment and to provide an interesting, clear and manageable environment for students with autism;
- daily schedules to establish a consistent routine, which encourages students to be organised and less dependent on adult prompting and direction;
- work system which refers to organising a student's activities by indicating what work should the student work on, how much work is required, how his or her progress is evaluated, when the work is finished and what will happened after it is completed; and
- visual cues and instruction which involve organising and structuring tasks visually in order to add meaning and increase student understanding and interest (Almasoud, 2010:8).

In a TEACCH classroom, each student has an individual workstation where they engage in completing various tasks. For example, activities could include visual-motor activities completing an assembly task, sorting objects by colour, shape, and sise, as well as completing basic academic tasks.

6.6 Conclusion

ASD, visible in poor social interactions, communication and thought processes on children and youth, poses a major challenge specifically in rural areas owing to their geographical positions away from resources and in many instances, professional or expert services. This chapter addressed ASD in a rural context, specifically focusing on background information concerning rural communities in different countries of the world including sub-Saharan African countries. The chapter also discussed rural perspectives of the causes of ASDs, rural environments and their influence on early identification of learners with ASD. Cultural beliefs about the preternatural world as being related to the onset of ASD, as well as the intervention strategies including the African philosophy of Ubuntu that can be established to ensure that children and youth with ASD function productively and independently in the society are also addressed. The rural communities' preternatural interpretations of ASD as revealed by several studies in this chapter elucidate the influences they have on their judgment of the child and the effect the child has on the family. The discussion about rural context of ASD in this chapter further revealed the feelings of stigmatisation of families affected and their frustrations with regard to assistance and service provisions owing to lack of knowledge and facilities in rural areas. However, a few intervention strategies that could be put in place for persons with ASD were also discussed.

References

Abubakar, A., Bakare, M.O., Wilmshurst, J.M. & Newton, C. (2016). Autism Spectrum Disorders in Africa: Current challenges in identification, assessment, and treatment: A Report on the International Child Neurology Association Meeting on ASD in Africa, Ghana, April 3-5, 2014. *Journal of Child Neurology*, ResearchGate, 1(1):1-9.

Abubakar, A., Ssewanyana, D. & Newton, C.R. (2016). A Systematic Review of Research on Autism Spectrum Disorders in Sub-Saharan Africa. *Behavioural Neurology*, 2016 (2016):1-14.

Akhter, S., Hussain, E.H., Shefa, J., Kundu, G.K., Rahman, F. & Biswas, A. (2018). Prevalence of Autism Spectrum Disorder (ASD) among the children aged 18-36 months in a rural community of Bangladesh: A cross sectional study, Bangladesh. https://orcid.org/0000-0003-2496-0818

Almasoud, H. (2010). The education of children with autism in Saudi Arabia: A teaching guide. Lecturer, Special Education Department, College of Education King Saud University.

Antezana, L., Scarpa, A., Valdespino, A., Albright, J. & Richey, J.A. (2017). Rural trends in diagnosis and services for Autism Spectrum Disorder. *Front. Psychol.* 8:590. doi: 10.3389/fpsyg.2017.00590

Arieff, Z., Kaur, M., Gameeldien, H., Merwe, L.V. & Bajic, V.B. (2010). 5-HTTLPR polymorphism: analysis in South African autistic individuals. *Hum Biol*, 82(3): 291-300.

ASHA. 2017. Autism. American Speech-Language Hearing Association (ASHA). ASHA Corporate Partners.

Autism Response Team. (2017). Applied Behavior Analysis (ABA). Autism Speaks.

Bakare, M.O. & Munir, K.M. (2011_a). Autism Spectrum Disorders in Africa. Department of Psychiatry, Harvard Medical School Nigeria and USA. Researchgate. www.intechopen.com

Bakare, M.O. & Munir, K.M. (2011_b). Autism spectrum disorders (ASD) in Africa: a perspective. *African Journal of Psychiatry* July 2011. https://www.researchgate.net/publication/51591801

Bernier, R., Mao, A. & Yen, J. (2010). Psychopathology, Families and Culture: Autism. *Child Adolesc Psychiatr Clin N Am*, 19(4): 855-867.

Duker, P., Didden, R. & Sigafoos, J. (2004). *One to one training: Instructional procedures for learners with developmental disabilities*. Austin, TX: Pro-Ed.

Geib, J.M. (2011). The Public Education of Students with Autism Spectrum Disorders in North-East Ohio: The Examination and Comparison of Current Practices to the Perspective of Parents and Professionals. Cleveland State University.

Gona, J.K., Newton, C.R., Rimba, K., Mapenzi, R., Kihara, M., Van de Vijver, F.J.R. & Abubakar, A. (2015). Parents' and Professionals' Perceptions on Causes and Treatment Options for Autism Spectrum Disorders (ASD) in a Multicultural Context on the Kenyan Coast. *PLoS ONE* 10(8): e0132729. https://doi.org/10.1371/journal.pone.0132729

Gona, J.K., Newton, C.R., Rimba, K., Mapenzi, R., Kihara, M., Van de Vijver, F.J.R. & Abubakar, A. (2016). Challenges and coping strategies of parents of children with autism on the Kenyan coast. *The International Electronic Journal of Rural and Remote Health Research, Education Practice and Policy*, James Cook University 2016, http://www.jcu.edu.au

Juneja, M. & Sairam, S. (2018). *Autism Spectrum Disorder: An Indian Perspective*. Child Development Centre, Department of Pediatrics, Maulana Azad Medical College, India: SM Group.

Klintwall, L. & Eikeseth, S. (2014). *Early and Intensive Behavioral Intervention (EIBI) in Autism. Comprehensive Guide to Autism*. New York: Springer 1(1): 117-137.

Lauritsen, M.B. & Ewald, H. (2001). The genetics of autism. *Acta Psychiatr Scand* 2001: 103: 411-427.

Lovaas, O.I. (2003). *Teaching individuals with developmental delays: Basic intervention techniques*. Austin, TX: Pro-Ed.

Lubin, J. (2015). *Etiology of Autism Spectrum Disorder (ASD): Familial Perceptions versus Empirically Validated Data*. Los Angeles County.

Majoko, T. (2017). *Practices That Support the Inclusion of Children with Autism Spectrum Disorder in Mainstream Early Childhood Education in Zimbabwe*. SAGE Open.

Masondo, C.N. (2015). Enhancing the Effectiveness of Principals in Implementing Inclusive Education using Ubuntu Approach. Bloemfontein, University of the Free State.

Matson, J.L., & Smith, KR. (2008). Current status of intensive behavioral interventions for young children with autism and PDD-NOS. *Research in Autism Spectrum Disorders*, 2: 60-74.

Mello, M.P, Urbano, R.C, Goldman, S.E. & Hodapp, R.M. (2016). Services for Children with Autism Spectrum Disorder: Comparing Rural and Non-Rural Communities. *Education and Training in Autism and Developmental Disabilities*, 51(4):355-365.

Minhas, A., Vajaratkar, V., Divan, G., Hamdani, S.U., Leadbitter, K. & Taylor, C. (2015). Parents' perspectives on care of children with autistic spectrum disorder in South Asia – Views from Pakistan and India. *International Review of Psychiatry*, 27(1): 247-256.

Mostafa, G.A. & Shehab, A.A. (2010). The link of C4B null allele to autism and to a family history of autoimmunity in Egyptian autistic children. *J Neuroimmunol* 223(1-2): 115-119.

Muhle, R., Trentacoste, S.V. & Rapin, I. (2004). The Genetics of Autism. *Pediatrics*, 113(5): 472-486.

Murphy, M.A. (2013). An Examination of Education Services for Children with Autism Spectrum Disorders in Rural Areas. University of Kentucky, UKnowledge.

National Institute of Neurological Disorders and Stroke. (2018). Autism Spectrum Disorder Fact Sheet. NIH.

Peters-Scheffer, N., Didden, R., Korzilius, H. & Sturmey, P. (2010). A meta-analytic study on the effectiveness of comprehensive ABA-based early intervention programs for children with Autism Spectrum Disorders. *Research in Autism Spectrum Disorders*, doi:10.1016/j.rasd.2010.03.011

Phasha, N. & Condy, J. (2016). *Inclusive Education: An African Perspective*. Cape Town: Oxford University Press, South Africa.

Phasha, N. (2016). Understanding Inclusive Education from an Afrocentric Perspective. In N. Phasha & J. Condy (Eds.). *Inclusive Education: An African Perspective*. Cape Town: Oxford University Press.

Roth, I. (2017). Autism: a cross-cultural perspective on service provision and capacity building.The Northern Ireland Assembly KESS seminar 'Addressing Autism', The Open University.

Ruparelia, K., Abubakar, A., Badoe, E., Bakare, M., Visser, K., Chugani, D., Chugani, H.T., Donald, K.A., PhD, Wilmshurst, J.M., Shih, A., Skuse, D. & Newton, C.R. (2016). Autism Spectrum Disorders in Africa: Current Challenges in Identification, Assessment, and Treatment: A Report on the International Child Neurology Association Meeting on ASD in Africa, Ghana, April 3-5, 2014. *Journal of Child Neurology*, 31(8): 1018-1026.

Stebbins, L. (2015). *A Closer Look: Early Intensive Behavioral Intervention* (EIBI). Harvard Graduate School of Education.

Strathearn, L. (2009). The Elusive Etiology of Autism: Nature and Nurture? USA. Front Behaviour Neuroscience.

Sturmey, P., & Fitzer, A. (2007). (Eds.), *Autism spectrum disorders: Applied behavior analysis, evidence and practice*. Austin, TX: Pro-Ed.

Sundberg, M. L. & Partington, J. W. (1999). The need for both DT and NE language training for children with autism. In P.M. Ghezzi, W. L. Williams, & J. E. Carr (Eds.). *Autism: Behavior analytic approaches*. Reno, NV: Context Press.

Weiss, M.J. (2001). *Teaching social skills to people with autism*. Rutgers, State University of New Jersey, USA.

Wilford, A. (2013). *Cultural variations in behaviours related to ASD in South African Children*. Human Sciences Research Council (HSRC), Human and Social Development, School of Applied Human Sciences, College of Humanities, University of KwaZulu-Natal.

7

TECHNOLOGY OPENING NEW WORLDS FOR THOSE WITH AUTISM – AN OVERVIEW

Leila Goosen

Abstract

Using information and communication technologies (ICTs) has transformative effects on people with ASD. Technologies open worlds for those on the spectrum. The research question addressed is: How can technology be used to help students with ASD to be active participants in school, at home and in the community? Theoretical and conceptual frameworks and/or strategies as lenses for understanding this research include augmentative and alternative communication (AAC), technology-aided interventions and instruction for students with ASD and how technology can be used to facilitate personal, social and vocational skills in youth with ASD. A literature review e.g. compares direct and technology-based praise statements to increase physical activity for students with ASD. This section looks at portable video modelling technology to increase compliment behaviours, collaborative virtual environment technology, and the acceptance, challenges and application of wearable technology to support people with ASDs. Sections illustrate methodologies and designs used and research undertaken. Discussion of findings detail samples implemented. The value of findings is illustrated regarding filling gaps identified, with a summary concluding the chapter regarding how technology is used to advance autism research and treatment.

7.1 Introduction

Against the background of the vast changes in Information and Communication Technologies (ICTs) over especially the past ten years, the use of such technologies has been having profoundly "transformative effects on the lives of people" with ASD (Chandler, 2016, p. 43).

Since the introduction of smart phones and tablet devices, like the iPad and the subsequent explosion of such devices with specialised applications for communication and related skills (Chandler, 2016), the proliferation of such relatively inexpensive mobile technologies have dramatically changed how education and behavioural services are provided and/or delivered to individuals with ASD (Lofland, 2016).

Students these days are frequently referred to as digital natives in terms of technology. According to Lofland (2016), this is often also true for students on the autism spectrum. In fact, many individuals with ASD are more comfortable when interacting with inanimate objects like a computer or an iPad rather than communicate face-to-face with other humans.

It has been established that mobile technology, that, for most people, serve as only entertainment or convenience (Chandler, 2016), can be also be used effectively for assisting in learning academic areas. These include fine motor to social, functional life and organisational skills, video modelling, reinforcement, speech-language therapy, visual support and increasing independence (Lofland, 2016).

Personal computers (PCs) and standard operating systems first became an early option, and now, technology is opening new worlds and creating great new possibilities, not only for developers, but also for those on every part of the autism spectrum (Chandler, 2016; Lofland, 2016). Since they came along, multiple-use technologies have been offering opportunities to consumers and/or students, which extend far beyond the capacities of earlier mobile computing devices, which have never been less expensive, more user-friendly and/or more universally available.

ICTs, including affective computing, multi-touch interfaces, robotics and virtual reality have been developed for supporting people with ASD (Chen, 2012). Innovative technologies, from touch screen telephones to tablets, on their own or in conjunction with others, could be used positively in several critical areas, which affect individuals with ASD, their families and the professionals who support them. As also mentioned in the book by Tustin (2018) on autism and childhood psychosis, this chapter will therefore attempt to highlight various treatment possibilities and techniques, especially those related to technology.

7.2 Theoretical and conceptual frameworks

Persons with ASD are a heterogeneous group with pervasive and complex neuro-developmental disabilities (Acab & Muotri, 2015). Symptoms could include qualitative impairment regarding social interaction skills, language or communication challenges (Nkabinde, 2014). For example, students with ASD show significant challenges with social skills such as to initiate a conversation and respond appropriately in social situations (Reed, Hyman & Hirst, 2011).

Other aspects in the triad of impairments/deficits could involve difficulties with reciprocal social interactions, cognitive dysfunction, that may also have co-occurring developmental or medical conditions (Rubenstein, et al., 2018) accompanied by restricted and unusual patterns of stereotyped repetitive behaviours, interests and activities (Fountain, et al., 2015).

According to Tseng and Do (2010, p. 464), ASD represents "one of the Pervasive Developmental Disorders" (PDDs). Although Nkabinde (2014, citing Putman and Chong) indicated that the effects of autism vary between students, ASD is usually diagnosed by age three. Nkabinde (2014, p. 977) goes on to indicate that, according "to the Diagnostic and Statistical Manual of Mental Disorders", Fourth Edition, Text Revision (DSM-IV-TR), within the autism spectrum, "several classifications of disorders exist: Rett's Disorder, Asperger's Disorder, Pervasive Developmental Delay Not Otherwise Specified (PDD-NOS), Autistic Disorder and Disintegrative Disorder". According to these authors, each of these has its own particular attributes. In 2013, the American Psychiatric Association (APA) published the Diagnostic and Statistical Manual of Mental Disorders, Fifth Edition (DSM-V).

The genetic basis of ASD is known as consisting "of contributions from de novo mutations in variant-intolerant genes". Brandler, et al. (2018, p. 327) hypothesised that rare paternally inherited Cis-Regulatory Element Structural Variants (CRE-SVs) of such genes could also contribute to an association with autism.

In the paper by Odom, et al. (2015), these authors proposed theoretical and conceptual frameworks to examine using technology by and for students and/or adolescents with ASD in their schools, homes and community settings. Their framework was then used for describing research literature on the efficacy of interventions and instruction, which utilised technology.

The technology program designed by Diener, Wright, Wright and Anderson (2016) was built on the interests and strengths of youth with autism, as well as positive youth development frameworks for creating and promoting social engagement, software skill development, and vocational exploration, and was grounded in a participatory community-based research model.

7.3 Augmentative and Alternative Communication (AAC) strategies

When individual students experience severe barriers to learning in terms of speech and/or language, AAC strategies can provide them with opportunities for expressing themselves, enabling them to have a 'voice' (Lofland, 2016). According to Shane, et al. (2012), the burgeoning role of applying technologies in society had provided us with opportunities for developing new means to visually support language and communication for individuals with ASDs. The paper by Shane et al. (2012) also offered an organisational framework to describe traditional and emerging AAC technologies and highlighted how tools within their framework could support a visual approach for everyday communication and improving language instruction. Increased adoption of handheld devices, together with applications, which were acquired via consumer-oriented delivery models, suggested potential paradigm shifts in AAC for people with ASD.

Many students with ASD and/or developmental disabilities are not able to meet the daily communication needs they have with speech alone (Alzrayer, Banda, & Koul, 2017). Such individual students are considered to be potential candidates for Speech-Generating Devices (SGDs), for teaching them to perform multistep requesting using an iPad.

The study by Thirumanickam, Raghavendra, McMillan and van Steenbrugge (2018) compared and evaluated the effectiveness of packaged Video-based Modelling (VM) and Video Self-Modelling (VSM) interventions for developing the conversational turn taking behaviours of four adolescent students with ASD, who used AAC.

Comprehensive interventions for students with ASD often incorporate AAC. However, variability in outcomes exists even among students who access similar interventions (Rose, Paynter, Vivanti, Keen, & Trembath, 2020). The latter authors therefore endeavoured to find predictors of expressive language change for children with ASD receiving AAC-infused comprehensive interventions.

An earlier article by Mirenda (2001) provided a review of the empirical published literature through 1999 on topics relating to AAC and assistive technologies as these were used for supporting communication and learning in individual students with autism and/or PDD-NOS. Please note that although recommendations for future research provided by

Mirenda (2001) will be discussed in the applicable section (7.7) of this chapter, the latter article did not offer any findings.

Typically, using technology applications (apps for short) to develop the social skills of students with ASD, which are critical to success later in school and their adult lives, can supplement interaction with caregivers and their peers (Withey, 2017). The purpose of the study by Caron, Light, Holyfield and McNaughton (2018) was to investigate the effects of software features in an AAC app on the sight word reading for individuals with ASD.

Logan, Iacono and Trembath (2017) conducted a systematic review of research into aided AAC interventions, which have been shown as effective to support students with ASD towards communication, particularly for requesting preferred items and activities, as well as to increase social-communication functions in students with ASD.

The growing diffusion of ICT-based innovative learning technologies raised the need for methodologically being able to effectively guide interdisciplinary Research and Development (R&D) teams' activities (Di Mascio & Tarantino, 2020). In the literature, the problems related to exploiting such ICTs are often underlined. The latter authors therefore proposed the structured methodological framework 'Deejay' as foundation and its application to the design of an ASD-oriented AAC technology.

Some students with ASD are facing considerable challenges with understanding, which include difficulties following spoken directives that involve prepositional relations (Schlosser, et al., 2013). The latter authors therefore provided a comparison of spoken cues with the use of two types of augmented input through visual modalities, which might be effective for supplementation purposes.

According to Abidoğlu, Ertuğruloğlu and Büyükeğilmez (2017), educational technologies such as computers and tablets, which were being used in educating 'normally developing' students starting from pre-school, were also being used in educating special needs students, albeit inadequately. The importance of computer-aided education for students with ASD has therefore recieved significant attention.

7.4 Review of the literature

The use of various technologies in intervention and instruction, as well as the therapeutic support of, students and adolescents with ASD has increased at a remarkable tempo. The purpose of the paper by Odom, et al. (2015) was to examine literature, which underlie the use of such technologies in interventions and instruction, related to high school students with ASD. These authors' literature review from 1990 through to end 2013 identified 30 studies which documented the efficacy of different technology forms and the impact of these on academics, adaptive and/or challenging behaviour, independence, communication, social competence as well as vocational skills. The current chapter will extend the review of literature to also include 2014 through 2020.

The chapter by Stasolla, Boccasini and Perilli (2017) provided readers with a literature overview regarding empirical evidence available in literature within the decade 2005 through 2015, which concern the use of assistive technology-based programs to support adaptive behaviours by students with ASDs. According to the inclusion and exclusion criteria, 36 studies were grouped and retained into four main categories, relating to communication, adaptive, life and/or social skills, and challenge behaviours. The chapter outlined the strengths and weaknesses of these studies and emphasised practical application of assistive technology-based programs. Please note that the main results (7.6), as well as guidelines for future research and the implications of these (7.7), provided by Stasolla et al. (2017), will be discussed in the applicable sections of this chapter.

The purpose of the paper by Goldsmith and LeBlanc (2004) was to review the growing number of studies, which have investigated and provided empirical support towards the efficacy of diversely applying technology-based interventions related to students with autism and for recommending future directions for research. Their review focused on five examples of technologies introduced as temporary instructional aids to be removed as soon as the goal of behavioural change has been met in terms of auditory and tactile prompting devices, computer-aided instruction, robotics, video-based instruction and feedback, and virtual reality. Goldsmith and LeBlanc (2004) further pointed out that a growing number of studies investigated a diversity of applications related to technology-based interventions with students with autism. Please note that although recommendations regarding future directions for research from Goldsmith and LeBlanc (2004) are referred to in the applicable section (7.7) of this chapter, no implications from their study for autism therapy were made available.

Studies conducted in the field in recent years showed that the use of Socially Assistive Robotics (SARs) was a promising method to improve the social skills of students with ASD (Syriopoulou-Delli & Gkiolnta, 2020). As the use of such robots as collaborators may positively affect the the training of children with ASD, the latter authors provided a review of these as assistive technologies.

An article by Grynszpan, Weiss, Perez-Diaz and Gal (2014) reported on these authors having conducted a systematic research review, which used a pre–post design for assessing innovative technology-based interventions, which included computer programs, robotics and virtual reality, resulting in a meta-analysis of innovative technology-based intervention research studies for students with ASDs. Please note that limitations related to the findings of the meta-analysis and recommendations from the study by Grynszpan, et al. (2014) will be presented in in the applicable section (7.7) of this chapter.

Recently, the chapter by Newbutt, Sung, Kuo and Leahy (2017, p. 221) provided a brief review of the acceptance, challenges and future applications of wearable technology and how Virtual Reality Technologies (VRTs) had been used within research contexts for supporting students "on the autism spectrum." One area ofresearch and innovation, which had evolved since the mid-1990s for aiding people with an ASD was that of using Virtual Reality Technology (VRT). Research, such as reported on in the chapter by Diener, et al. (2016), has focused on using technology to help facilitate the development of functional, personal, social, and pre-vocational/vocational skills in youth with ASD (Newbutt, et al., 2017). The chapter by the latter authors provided a review of literature of these and related fields; additionally, distilling the key affordances, challenges and issues identified in these evolving areas of research. The latter authors' review focused on potentially useful applications of virtual reality technologies for training and supporting people with an ASD to develop life-skills (that is, independent living skills, job skills, social skills) and where these had been successfully implemented in applied contexts. As increasingly accessible and affordable wearable devices, such as Oculus Rift™ become commercially available. Newbutt, et al. (2017) described a project they undertook, which sought to answer questions surrounding acceptability and practicality, which quickly needed to be addressed if sustainable lines of inquiry surrounding the role of Head-Mounted Displays (HMDs) and VRTs, as well as the impact these might have had for this specific population, is to be developed. Please note that main aspects related to the research methodologies (7.5) used in the chapter by Newbutt, et al. (2017), as well as their suggestions in terms of guidance for future scholars in this field (7.7) and the conclusions they came to (7.8), will be presented in the applicable sections of this chapter.

For individuals with ASDs, using technology for providing interventions, which particularly target "the core social–communication deficits of the disorder, is promising." The literature review provided by Wainer and Ingersoll (2011, p. 96) examined studies, which "have used innovative technology, such as interactive computer programs and virtual reality," for delivering direct interventions focused on developing communication and social skills to individual students with an ASD. "Given that the study and using such programs was "still relatively new, the majority of the published literature" had a descriptive or exploratory nature. As such, the review by the latter authors provided a summary of some of these initial studies. Please note that although the main aspects of the study by these authors were briefly discussed here, their preliminary findings (7.6) and recommendation (7.7) are presented in the applicable sections of this chapter.

A review of the literature, in the paper by Chen (2012) considered and reflected on existing research on multi-touch tabletop technology for ASD and identified challenges and opportunities with designing and applying multi-touch table-top applications for people with ASD. These technologies provided improved opportunities to flexibly collaborate, compared with traditional "Window, Icon, Menu and Pointer" (WIMP) interfaces by allowing face-to-face interactions "and multiple simultaneous inputs from several users" (Chen, 2012, p. 199). This same author (Chen, 2012), however, also warned that there were some technical challenges, which needed to be tackled before it could impact larger special needs populations.

In Reed et al. (2011, p. 1003), the deficits shown in students with ASD were targeted through the application of technology to teach social skills – some of these used "a technology-based approach as a resource-efficient alternative to common forms of instruction." Their literature review aimed to "determine the number of empirical studies using a technology-based social skills intervention," explored "the features of social skills targeted in these studies, and analysed "the number of studies reporting reliability of the dependent and independent variables." Please note that although the main findings reported by these authors, and what we can learn from these, are provided in the applicable section (7.6) of this chapter, they did not offer any recommendations in their article.

The increased accessibility and utilisation of mobile phone technologies have "greatly enhanced the lives of many" individual students, "including those with disabilities such as ASDs." In their article, Asaro-Saddler and Akhmedjanova (2015, p. 1514) provided a comprehensive literature review on using mobile phone technologies for delivering interventions supporting the communication, socialisation and academic skills of individual students with ASDs. Please note that although the main findings reported by these authors are provided in the applicable section (7.6) of this chapter, recommendations could not be accessed.

Using assistive technologies for enhancing skill development among students "with autism continues to expand" (Andersen, Levenson & Blumberg, 2014, p. 1). Such technologies have been used primarily for remediating deficits in social skills, language, and, to a lesser extent, academic skills. Despite the growing body of literature, which have examined using such "technologies among students with autism, the success of these interventions" had been mixed. Andersen, et al. (2014, p. 1) reviewed results concerning the promise and limitations of "available forms of assistive technology" used among students with autism and the factors, which impact their efficacy among students with autism, such as severity of impairments and developmental level.

Although participation in out-of-school activities is related to improved "outcomes for neuro-typical youth in a number of domains," which include "higher school functioning and psycho-social development", parents of youth with ASD often report that their students have difficulty in these (Diener, et al., 2016, p. 97). Another growing concern for all individual students with ASD was "employment and having skills to live independently" (Lofland, 2016, p. 28). A program was therefore designed by Diener, et al. (2016, p. 97) to tap into technical talent and use technology to facilitate personal and social skills, as well as "address gaps in vocational preparation for adolescents and young adults on the autism spectrum." These authors therefore "developed a technology-based summer and after-school program", which teaches students with ASD software skills, which enabled "them to create 3D designs." The preliminary results produced by Diener, et al. (2016, p. 97) indicated "that by focusing on the talents, strengths, and interests of youth with ASD, rather than on remediating deficits", a difference can be made in three domains: "enhanced social engagement with peers and family members,increased self-esteem and confidence for youth, and vocational exploration and aspirations."

There are many benefits to engaging in regular physical activity such as increased quality of life and decreased levels of obesity (Savage, 2016, p. ix). Individuals with ASD, however, "often do not engage in healthy levels of physical activity. Low motivation, poor motor skills, and behavioural challenges combine to make engaging in regular physical activity a challenge". The purpose of the study by Savage (2016, p. ix) "was to determine whether direct (i.e., in-person) praise statements or technology-based praise statements were more effective in increasing engagement in physical activity for secondary" students with ASD. Participants engaged in aerobic activity while receiving praise statements either directly or through technology. Lofland (2016, p. 28) pointed out that like "all technologies and techniques, certain things work for certain people": Two of the three participants performed better and preferred the technology-based condition, and they "were able to maintain performance levels during the fading conditions and" generalise "their performance to a new setting" (Savage, 2016, p. ix). The other participant, who exceled and performed better in, and preferred, the direct condition, however, "was unable to maintain performance levels during fading conditions or" generalise performance to new settings.

The study by Rivera, Mason, Jabeen and Johnson (2015, p. 101) "investigated the effects of using mobile technology as an intervention to increase the amount of praise delivered by teachers to low-performing students with autism." In addition, the study also investigated the impact, which praise would have on the on-task behaviours of these students. Participants included five elementary students with autism, two teachers, and two paraprofessionals. Results indicated that prompts from the mobile devices were effective in increasing the amount of praise provided by each of these teachers. The extent, however, "to which teachers' contingent praise impacted" student on-task behaviours was less clear.

Collaborative Virtual Environments (CVEs) "hold great potential for people with autism" (Moore, Cheng, McGrath & Powell, 2005, p. 231). As one such example, Cramer, Hirano, Tentori, Yeganyan and Hayes (2011, p. 1) indicated that "vSked is an interactive and collaborative assistive technology for students with autism, combining interactive visual schedules, choice boards, and a token-based reward system into an integrated classroom system", used collectively. According to Cobb, Parsons, Millen, Eastgate and Glover (2010, p. 4374), "COSPATIAL is a 3-year international project funded by the European Commission exploring the design, development and use of innovative technologies for supporting collaborative interaction and development of social competence" for students on the autism spectrum as well as their typically developing peers.

According to Green (2001, p. 72), numerous behaviour "analytic methods developed since the early 1960s have been" proven as effective to develop wide-ranging skills in students with autism. Advances "in stimulus control technology, in particular, offer effective methods for teaching many important skills and for promoting independent", generalised performances.

Citing Kimball and Smith, Goodwin (2008, p. 125) pointed to the former authors as having articulated the advantages and disadvantages of the creation of computer technologies for supporting individuals with autism. The latter authors also provided a well-devised three-point plan for stimulating and supporting progress in technology development for such a population.

For many decades, eye-tracking has been used to investigate gaze behaviour in the normal population (Boraston & Blakemore, 2007, p. 893). Recent studies have extended its use to individual students with disorders on the autism spectrum. Such studies typically focus on the processing of socially salient stimuli.

The article by Sohl, Mazurek Brown (2017, p. 510) asked what "if there was a way to share subspecialty knowledge" about using technology and mentorship to bridge gaps, increase access to care, and bring best-practice autism care to primary care? The answer provided by the latter authors (Sohl, et al., 2017, p. 510) is that if Primary Care Providers (PCPs) could be supported in the "screening and management of autism, the referral process would be improved, services would be expedited and medical and psychiatric comorbidities would be better managed."

According to Broder Fingert, et al. (2018), the US National Institute of Mental Health, in 2013, funded five trials of unique, multi-component, systems-based innovations, which were designed to improve access to the early screening and diagnosis, as well as treatment services, for students with ASD.

The study by Sacrey, et al. (2018, p. 322s) examined whether "the Autism Parent Screen for Infants", a novel parent-report questionnaire based on behaviour observed at between six months and two years of age, could differentiate such infants subsequently diagnosed with ASD from a high-risk cohort, represented by siblings of students, who had been diagnosed with ASD.

In their conference paper Crane-Mitchell and Stafford (2017) indicated that the number of students with ASD continues to increase. Both the latter authors (Crane-Mitchell &

Stafford, 2017, p. 2225) and Fountain, et al. (2015) cited 2012 statistics from the Autism Society of America, to demonstrate that surveillance efforts estimate that in one in every 68 United States (US) students aged eight years are diagnosed with ASD, "with rapid increases in identified incidence over the past decade". Nkabinde (2014, p. 977) cited slightly earlier statistics by the National Institute of Mental Health, which reported that 3.4 of every 1, 000 students 3-10 years old had autism. ASDs affect one in 88 students, with a higher prevalence in boys (1 in 54), than girls (1 in 252) (The Center for Disease Control and Prevention as cited in Rigo (2013). Results reported by Baio et al. (2018, p. 2) for 2014 showed that the overall prevalence of ASD among 11 sites were 16.8 per 1,000 (one in 59) students aged eight years. The latter authors (Baio, et al., 2018, p. 3) also indicated that in order to reduce the influence of various factors on prevalence estimates, th Autism and Developmental Disabilities Monitoring (ADDM) Network has consistently tracked ASD. This was done through the application of a surveillance case definition of ASD, as well as using the same record-review methodology and behaviourally defined case inclusion criteria since 2000.

Using assistive technologies was widely recommended by the Division of Early Childhood of the Council for Exceptional Children as appropriate intervention strategies for using especially with students who have ASD (Fountain, et al., 2015).

Demonstrating comprehension of text is a complex skill, which is an area of difficulty for many students with ASD. Technology-based shared story readingfor students with autism, who are English-language students, is an intervention which has a history of effectiveness in teaching literacy skills to students with extensive support needs. The study by Alison, Root, Browder and Wood (2017, p. 91) used a multiple probe across participants design to evaluate the effects of shared story reading using e-texts and embedded prompting on vocabulary and reading comprehension of grade-aligned narrative texts by elementary students with ASD who were also English-language students. Outcomes indicated that shared story reading with the embedded technological supports was effective for teaching comprehension of questions, as well as the identification of rules and definitions. According to Alison, et al. (2017, p. 91), comprehension requires the simultaneous application of many subskills including accessing text, understanding what is being asked, and constructing a response. A student in the study reported by Alison, et al. (2017, p. 99) was therefore "learning how to apply emerging English skills to the task of comprehension".

Towards a technology of treatment individualisation of young students with ASDASD, Stahmer, Schreibman and Cunningham (2011, p. 229) indicated that research in the field of autism has heavily emphasised the importance of early intervention (i.e. treatment before the age of 4 years). At the time, several methods have been demonstrated to be efficacious with some students. However, no treatment completely ameliorates the symptoms of ASD or works for all students with the disorder. The heterogeneity and developmental nature of the disorder makes it unlikely that one specific treatment will be best for all students or will work for anyone throughout her or his educational career. Therefore, the paper by Stahmer, et al. (2011, p. 229) examined early research validating different technologies for individualising treatment. A discussion of current research on pre-treatment characteristics associated with differential outcomes in treatment, including student, family, and practitioner variables; and how specific intervention techniques address each of those pre-treatment characteristics was provided. The ultimate goal of the line of research described by Stahmer, et al. (2011, p. 229) was enabling practitioners to prospectively tailor treatments to specific students and increase the overall rate of positives outcomes for students on the autism spectrum. Research, which furthers understanding of how to match clients with efficacious treatments could decrease the outcome variability, which presently characterises early intervention research, as well as providing for the most efficient allocation of resources during the critical early intervention time-period. The type of research described by Stahmer, et al. (2011, p. 229) was in its infancy, but it is imperative if we are to determine a priori which treatment method would be most effective for specific students.

Tseng and Do (2010, p. 464) indicate that there is currently no cure for autism; however, with appropriate aid, autistic students could learn progressively and maintain a good quality of life with their disorder. Therefore, the market demands ICT applications to facilitate students dealing with ASD in their lifetime. Although many ICT designs have been developed and used already in early intervention and treatment, they are not common in long-term training of students with ASD. The work by Tseng and Do (2010, p. 464) present a novel design prototype, Facial Expression Wonderland (FEW), to train students with ASD, based on progressive levels of training for a given background context. The prototype was designed to improve the abilities of students with ASD in facial expression recognition. The work also discussed how ICTs could further facilitate life for youngsters with ASD.

According to Vélez-Coto et al. (2017, p. 25), people with low-functioning ASD and other disabilities often find it difficult to understand the symbols traditionally used in educational materials during the learning process. Technology-based interventions, especially for low-functioning autism, are becoming increasingly common, helping students with cognitive disabilities to perform academic tasks, train skills to work with visual signifiers and concepts and improve their abilities and knowledge in this regard.

In a book on autism imaging and devices, the chapter by Arriaga (2017, p. 419), on using an ecological systems approach to target technology development for autism research and beyond, introduced the role of design in Human-Computer Interface (HCI) and psychology research, together with theory and practice related to building a new bridge between psychology and HCI. The chapter by Arriaga (2017, p. 419) considered "the role of theory in design and how it can be used to better support technology to improve quality of life for individual students with autism and their caregivers". It also provides a review of how theory has been used by HCI researchers from the inception of the discipline until now. Finally, Ecological Systems Theory is proposed as another theory, which could be used by HCI researchers. A set of examples were provided, which showed how this theory could be used to aid design.

The chapter by Lierheimer, Murray, Wooldridge and Smith (2014, p. 34) describe how Bowling Green State University (BGSU) partnered with the Ohio Center for Autism and Low Incidence (OCALI), a quasi-governmental agency, to use technology and community partnerships to improve educator preparation. This changing of the landscape for individuals with ASD was carried out to meet the training needs of the local, state, national, and international community by providing an online ASDs certificate programme. The curriculum incorporated and built on numerous OCALI online learning modules specifically focused on ASD, which were developed by experts in the field of autism.

At the time, over 100 students from eight states and three countries have completed the comprehensive certificate ASD programme through BGSU. The program was one example of how technology has broadened the outreach of educational preparation in ASD from local to national and international audiences.

The goal of the chapter by Nkabinde (2014, p. 976) was to explore the effective use of ICTs to assist individual students with autism. In 1985, the Picture Communication System (PECS), was developed for students who had limited abilities to express themselves verbally. The idea was that by pointing to a picture, the student could communicate what (s)he wanted. PECS has been modernised with the development of applications for the iPad. A student could choose from a wide variety of communication choices simply by touching a screen, which would facilitate the process and provide a wide variety of choices never before available. The chapter could help parents and teachers to understand how ICTs could improve communication for students with autism. In addition, the use of iPad and how it improves communication for students with autism were discussed.

Over the years, students with autism have often been portrayed in the professional literature and the popular media as asocial creatures bereft of words and subjective worldviews. Alternatively, Sirota (2010, p. 93) examined the lived contexts in which students with ASDs actively engaged with family members in co-constructed narrative recounting of personal life events, and are apprenticed into culturally consonant genres of life narrative as a technology of the self in the relational worlds of these students. Sirota (2010, p. 93) employed naturalistic video- and audio-taped data documenting the everyday lives of 17 US students diagnosed with high functioning autism and Asperger's syndrome. He demonstrates how everyday narratives of personal experience offer a vehicle for expression of the students subjective life worlds and a venue for self-presentation and intersubjective attunement in which social and moral distinctions of normativity and difference are at stake. These deeply interactive self-fashioning processes highlighted and made visible the dynamic intersubjective practices, which contributed to human subjectivity.

Major trends show that mobile devices have gained popularity among the special needs community (Yee, 2012, p. 1). These devices are the new and cool gadgets to be seen with, unlike issues regarding the 'old', complex and 'I-am-not-normal-looking' assistive devices. These mobile devices were said to serve as a communication device in the pocket, a learning device on the go and even a lifesaver for some. Among the features are its flexible multimedia content and storage, portability, mobility and affordability. The touch screen interface makes it appealing and simple to use, particularly for those who have weak fine motor skills. It offers practical communication solutions for persons with autism in relating to their families and others in the community. Several anecdotal reports gave an early indication of the immense possibilities of how these devices could play a significant role in enhancing the quality of life of the students with ASD and their families.

Reporting on the promise and the perils of using entertainment technology in autism research, Munson and Pasqual (2012, p. 89) postulate that it could play a significant role in developing computing-based assessment tools, which lead to improvements in the treatment of students with autism.

Tang and Flatla (2016, p. 1) reported on the good, the bad and the challenging in terms of autism awareness and technology-based intervention research in China. The latter authors indicated that impressive advances have been made to further our understanding of the psychological and neurobiological processes, which underlie ASD since it was first reported by Kanner in 1943. Research on assistive technologies for ASD has also substantially increased in both quality and quantity for aspects pertinent to individual students with ASD (including their family members, caregivers and special education teachers).

Gentry, Kriner, Sima, McDonough and Wehman (2015, p. 669) assert that Personal Digital Assistants (PDAs) are versatile task organisers, which hold promise as assistive technologies for people with cognitive behavioural challenges. This delayed randomised controlled trial compared two groups of adult workers with ASD to determine whether the use of an Apple iPod Touch PDA as a vocational support improves work performance, reducing the need for personal support on the job.

Campbell, et al. (2018) demonstrate the computer vision analysis capability for detecting atypical orienting and attention behaviours in 104 toddlers of between 16 and 31 months old with ASD, who participated in their study.

Social media use holds promise as technologies for facilitating social engagement and improving friendship quality, while playing a moderating role in the anxiety of adolescent students with ASD (van Schalkwyk, et al., 2017), who are well suited to benefit from the unique features with regard to it requiring reduced decoding.

According to Sutton, Webster and Westerveld (2018), technologies such as those discussed in this chapter are valuable resources, which are increasingly being used in classrooms are motivating for students, and have flexibility towards promoting social communication behaviours. The latter authors (Sutton, et al., 2018, p. 283) provide a systematic review of intervention studies based in mainstream elementary schools, which targeted such behaviours, reporting on intervention outcomes, and found it interesting that none of the studies. They considered using technology-based interventions because the availability of such technologies in classrooms had prompted researchers, such as Lofland (2016), to suggest using technology towards supporting the communication goals of students with autism.

7.5 Research methodologies

As one example of the research methodologies and designs, which had been used previously in this and related fields, Fountain, et al. (2015) report on the performance of an observational cohort study, which used linked records from California.

Porayska-Pomsta, et al. (2012) present an interdisciplinary methodology towards the design of interactive multi-modal technologies for young students with ASDs. Like many other researchers in this field, the latter authors (Porayska-Pomsta, et al., 2012) believed that the key to the development of technologies in contexts like these was embracing perspectives from a variety of disciplines, and therefore arriving at a methodology, which delivered outcomes satisfying all stakeholders.

According to Picard (2009, p. 3575), people with ASD often experience states of emotional or cognitive overload, which posed challenges to their interests in learning and communicating. Measurements taken from home and school environments show that extreme overload experienced internally, measured as Autonomic Nervous System (ANS) activation may not be visible externally. A person can have a resting heart rate twice the level of non-autistic peers while outwardly appearing calm and relaxed.

In the study reported on by Macpherson, Charlop and Miltenberger (2015, p. 3836), a multiple baseline design across participants was used for examining the effects of a portable video modelling. The intervention delivered in the natural environment on the verbal compliments and compliment gestures was demonstrated by five students with autism during athletic group play. Participants were observed playing kickball with peers and adults. In the baseline study, participants demonstrated few compliment behaviours. During the intervention, an iPad was used to implement the video modelling treatment during the course of the athletic game. Viewing the video rapidly increased the verbal compliments participants gave to peers. Participants also demonstrated more response variation after watching the videos. Some generalisation to an untrained activity occurred and compliment gestures also occurred (Macpherson, et al., 2015, p. 3836).

Moore, et al. (2005, p. 231) conducted an exploratory empirical study to determine if students and youth with autism could understand basic emotions as represented by a humanoid avatar.

More than a decade earlier, the study by Sherer, et al. (2001, p. 140) was designed to compare the efficacy of 'self' versus 'other' video-modelling interventions as a model in terms of enhancing the conversation skills of five students with autism, ranging in age from 4 to 11. They were taught to answer a series of conversation questions in both self and other video-modelled conditions. Results reported on in Sherer, et al. (2001, p. 140) were evaluated using a combination of a multiple baseline and alternating treatments design.

In terms of methods, Vélez-Coto et al. (2017, p. 25) implemented a pre-test/post-test design to test SIGUEME. Seventy-four students with low-functioning ASD were trained with SIGUEME over 25 sessions and compared with 25 students, who had not received any intervention.

In the study reported on by Bereznak, Ayres, Mechling and Alexander (2012, p. 269), a multiple probe design across behaviours replicated across participants was used to evaluate the effectiveness of the intervention. Three male high school students with ASDs participated in the study reported on by Bereznak et al. (2012, p. 269). To increase daily living and vocational independence, skills were taught using video, self-prompting and mobile technology via an iPhone, where using a washing machine, making noodles and using a copy machine were taught. The study introduced a novel approach to using instructional video, in that two of the three students were able to learn how to self-prompt with the iPhone and ultimately teach themselves the target skills. Maintenance probes were also conducted and the iPhone had to be returned to all three participants for two out of three behaviours for a return to criterion levels. Please note that results obtained in this study are reported in the applicable section of this chapter (6.6), as are limitations and implications (6.7).

The study by Wright, Diener, Dunn and Wright (2011, p. 135) used a qualitative design to examine intergenerational family relationships facilitated by an intervention employing Google SketchUp™, a freeware 3D design program. Seven high-functioning boys (ages 8–17) with ASDs participated in computer workshops. The investigators capitalised on the boys' strengths in visual-spatial skills. The interdisciplinary team structured the workshops to facilitate computer skill development and social interaction. Qualitative analysis involved thematic analysis of transcripts from focus groups with parents and grandparents.

Active engagement is critical to promote learning for students with autism. Although evidence-based strategies exist for promoting engagement for individual students with autism, there are few strategies designed for use with small groups. The study by Carnahan, Basham and Musti-Rao (2009, p. 76) used an ABCAC design to assess the effects of a low-technology use strategy, namely interactive books with and without music on the engagement levels of six students with autism and significant learning needs in kindergarten through fourth grades. The results indicated that the use of interactive books paired with music showed increased levels of engagement during small group instruction. Implications related to research-based instruction, teacher education, instructional design, and future research were discussed.

In a recent study, Schafer, et al. (2019) looked at the verification and validation of remote-microphone technology on children and college-age adults who have ASD. The goal of their earlier study (Schafer et al., 2016, p. 1) was to conduct assistive technology evaluations on twelve students diagnosed with ASD for evaluating the potential advantages of Remote-Microphone (RM) technologies. A single group, within-subjects research design was used for exploring "individual and group data from functional questionnaires", together with behavioural test measures administered, which had been designed for assessing "school- and home-based listening abilities, once with and once without RM technology". Because some of the students were unable to complete the behavioural test measures, particular focus was given to the functional questionnaires completed by primary teachers, participants, and parents. Behavioural test measures with and without the RM technology included speech recognition in noise, auditory comprehension and acceptable noise levels. The individual and group teacher (n = 8–9), parent (n = 8–9), and participant (n = 9) questionnaire ratings revealed substantially less listening difficulty when RM technology was used compared to the no-device ratings. On the behavioural measures, individual data revealed varied results that were discussed in detail in their results section. However, on average, the use of the RM technology resulted in improvements in speech recognition in noise (4.6 dB improvement) in eight students, higher auditory working memory and comprehension scores (12–13 point improvement) in seven students, and acceptance of poorer signal-to-noise ratios (8.6 dB improvement) in five students. The individual and group data from this study suggested that RM technology may improve auditory function in students with ASD in the classroom, at home and in social situations. However, variability in the data and the inability of some students to complete the behavioural measures indicates that individualised assistive technology evaluations including functional questionnaires will be necessary to determine if the RM technology will be of benefit to a particular student who has ASD.

Newbutt, et al. (2017, p. 221) report in a rich, descriptive and illustrative manner, the process that was engaged in, to work with a range of participants with ASD (here range refers to low-high functioning ASD with a wide range of IQ). They assessed and measured the acceptability of experiences within, head-mounted display virtual reality technologies (immersion, presence, ecological validity, and any negative effects). These authors discussed, in some detail, the ethical approaches the research team took in using HMDs with this population (as this is sometimes a neglected aspect of this type of research).

Roelfsema, et al. (2012, p. 734) requested schools to provide the number of students enrolled, the number having a clinical diagnosis of Autism Spectrum Conditions (ASC) and/or 2 control neurodevelopmental conditions. Prevalence was evaluated by negative binomial regression and adjustments were made for non-response and size of the schools.

Many first-hand accounts from persons diagnosed with an ASD highlighted the challenges inherent in processing high-speed, complex, and unpredictable social information such as facial expressions in real-time. In their paper, Madsen, El Kaliouby, Goodwin and Picard (2008, p. 19) describe a new technology aimed at helping people capture, analyse and reflect on a set of social-emotional signals communicated by facial and head movements in live social interaction, which occured with their everyday social companions. In addition, Madsen et al. (2008) describe their development of a new combination of hardware using a miniature camera connected to an ultra-mobile PC together with custom software developed to track, capture, interpret, and intuitively present various interpretations of the facial-head movements (e.g., presenting that there is a high probability the person looks 'confused').

In a description of autism and family interventions through technology, Ferdig, et al. (2010, p. 232) indicate that most research on family interventions of students with autism has focused on the role of the mother, and little is known about the effects of training fathers. Through a series of National Institutes of Health–funded studies, Ferdig, et al. (2010) demonstrated treatment success by focusing on fathers who are trained at home. Although the research by Ferdig, et al. (2010) had been successful, their work also introduced questions related to how best to train fathers when on-site, in-home training is not a viable option owing to the geographical distance or a variety of other logistical constraints. Ferdig, et al. (2010) describe the development and initial use of an Internet-based tool to offer training more broadly. These same authors (Ferdig, et al., 2010) also briefly discuss past research, and the need for the implementation of an Internet-based tool. They then described the system, documented early indicators of success and discussed metrics they were using with 'their' fathers.

There has been developing interest in the potential for the use of mobile technology in schools to achieve educational objectives, particularly for students with ASD (Mintz, 2013, p. 294). The Helping Autism-diagnosed teenagers Navigate and Develop Socially (HANDS) project had developed a software application for mobile phones that helps students with ASD to develop social and self-management skills. Two successive prototypes of the application have been implemented and tested with 15 teachers and 27 students with ASD at four special schools in the UK, Demark, Hungary, and Sweden. Mintz (2013, p. 294) reports on issues involved with introducing a mobile technology innovation at one of the schools. Interviews were undertaken with teachers on the project during the introduction of the technology. The extent to which teachers identify themselves as teachers of social skills development that is often considered an expression of informal learning was identified as one of the key factors in the determination of the extent to which successful engagement with these technologies solutions occurred: teacher attitude made all the difference.

According to Chao, Chang, Chin, Li and Chen (2018), a descriptive phenomenological analysis showed that an ASD could result in considerable stress and confusion for Taiwanese parents of students, as they attempt to understand their student's problems and experience the process of obtaining a diagnosis, with few studies having explored the parental experience in the context of Chinese culture.

Boraston and Blakemore (2007) indicated that it is important for researchers to ensure that the participatory methods that they use embrace authenticity, credibility and transferability in terms of application and dissemination.

7.6 Results

The results obtained by Vélez-Coto et al. (2017) showed an improvement, which was statistically significant in the experimental group in terms of their attention as well as a significant change in association and categorisation and interaction. Sherer, et al. (2001, p. 140) indicate that three out of the five students performed at levels of 100% post-treatment. The results further showed no indication in terms of overall differences in rate of task acquisition between the two conditions, implying that participants, who were successful in learning from video in general, learned equally as well via both treatment approaches. Anecdotal evidence suggested that students who were successful with video treatment had higher visual learning skills than participants who were unsuccessful with this approach.

The two key themes, which emerged in the study reported on by Wright, et al. (2011, p. 135) were reframing expectations in terms of parental efficacy and creating a safe environment, and building intergenerational bridges among parents, students, siblings, and grandparents. These results indicated that technology could build on the strengths of students with ASD and promote social engagement of these students with their families.

The study reported on by Roelfsema, et al. (2012, p. 734) found that the prevalence estimates of autism spectrum conditions in Eindhoven was 229 per 10,000, which was significantly higher than in Haarlem (84 per 10,000) and Utrecht (57 per 10,000), while the prevalence for the control conditions were similar in all regions.

The main findings reported by Reed et al. (2011, p. 1003) indicate that a majority of the studies relied on a video or DVD to deliver the intervention (modelling or feedback), were conducted in school settings, and targeted more than one social skill. The most common social skill addressed was initiating conversation followed by play skills. All but one study included standardised assessment before treatment. However, none of the studies used a published social skills assessment. Like previous research, reliability of the dependent variables was common. However, reliability of the independent variables was infrequent.

In the study reported on by Bereznak, et al. (2012, p. 269), the results indicated that the three participants increased performance across all behaviours by increasing the percent of steps performed independently. Although some failures occurred, the results discussed in the chapter by Stasolla et al. (2017) were fairly positive.

The paper by Madsen et al. (2008, p. 19) describes the new technology together with the results of a series of pilot studies conducted with adolescents diagnosed with ASD who used the technology in their peer-group setting and contributed to its development via their feedback.

In their paper, Cramer, et al. (2011, p. 1) portrayed the results of a study of three deployments of vSked over the course of one year in 2 autism classrooms. The results of their study demonstrated that vSked could encourage consistency and predictability, promote student independence, as well as reducing both the quantity of teacher-initiated prompts and the time required to transition from one activity to another.

Weiss, et al. (2011, p. 1) presented the results of two usability studies, which evaluated using collaborative technologies designed to support students with ASCs' learning "social competence skills through technology-delivered" Cognitive-Behavioural Therapy (CBT), while Asaro-Saddler and Akhmedjanova (2015) indicate that the main findings were not surprising, as people with ASDs preferred visual stimuli and Wainer and Ingersoll (2011) provided a summary of some of the preliminary findings from their study.

7.7 Future directions for research

Newbutt, et al. (2017) suggest some guidelines for future scholars and/or practitioners who work in fields related to VRTs. The paper by Goldsmith and LeBlanc (2004) also recommended future directions for research. The results from the study by Cramer, et al. (2011, p. 1) revealed practices which surrounded using assistive technologies in classrooms, as well as highlighting important considerations for both the design and the evaluation of assistive technologies in the future, especially those destined for classroom use.

Mirenda (2001) provided several recommendations for further research, some of which were quite general, while others were more specific – these were made based on a review. Recommendations related to aided AAC were presented, followed by ones related to assistive technologies.

Banire, Khowaja, Mansoor, Qaraqe and Al Thani (2020) made a recommendation with regard to a food intake intervention using reality-based technologies for children with ASD.

The flexibility and the advanced capabilities of mobile technologies have been opening new opportunities for future research in areas related to computer-based interventions for students with ASD. There was definitely a lack of published research studies on the use of mobile technologies for students with ASD (Yee, 2012, p. 1). Owing to the growing popularity towards the adoption of mobile devices as assistive devices, this same author therefore indicated that more in-depth research was warranted.

Wainer and Ingersoll (2011, p. 96) suggest developing and evaluating programmes similar to those they examined. Because of the complexities, which arouse when interpreting the effects of intervention programmes and comparing efficacy across programmes, the creation of guidelines or recommendations for treatment research methodology was critical (Wainer & Ingersoll, 2011, p. 106).

Implications for practitioners and researchers, along with potential areas for further research, were also discussed in the article by Asaro-Saddler and Akhmedjanova (2015, p. 1514). Although the majority of the studies reviewed in the article by Asaro-Saddler and Akhmedjanova (2015, p. 1514) indicated the potential effectiveness of mobile technology as a medium to deliver interventions, additional research in these emerging fields was warranted.

The chapter by Stasolla et al. (2017) pointed out useful guidelines for futher research, as well as educational, rehabilitative, clinical and psychological implications were also discussed.

The implications for practice of video self-prompting were discussed in the study reported on by Bereznak et al. (2012, p. 269), in addition to study limitations.

In terms of future implications, Acab and Muotri (2015, p. 542) indicate that the most useful applications of models like the Induced Pluripotent Stem Cells (iPSC) disease modelling strategy were for identifying "cellular phenotypes, the elucidation of affected molecular pathways, and for the generation of new therapeutic strategies.

With regard to implications for practice, Bereznak, et al. (2012, p. 283) specified that as with any relatively new commercial technology, future research was needed for investigating applying, and the advantages of using an iPhone with students with ASD.

The purpose of the paper by Brosnan, Holt, Yuill, Good and Parsons (2017, p. 43) was reporting on the sixth seminar in a series of seven, entitled 'Innovative Technologies for Autism: Critical Reflections on Digital Bubbles', funded by the United Kingdom (UK) Economic and Social Research Council (ESRC). The aim of the seminar reported on in the paper by Brosnan, et al. (2017) was to reflect on the implications from neuro-diverse communities to develop technologies for autism.

Previous studies of global–local information processing in ASDs indicated mixed results, with some evidence of a local processing bias, or preference for detail-level information, and other results suggesting typical global advantage, or preference for the whole or gestalt (Johnson, Blaha, Houpt & Townsend, 2010, p. 53). The results from this paradigm have been used to argue for or against a detail focused processing bias in autism spectrum disorders, and therefore have important theoretical implications. Systems factorial technology also provided new insights.

Roelfsema, et al. (2012) planned a second phase for validating school-reported cases that use standardised diagnostic methods and for exploring the possible causes of these differences.

Limitations related to "range of IQ, age, and duration of treatment should be taken into account when" generalising the findings of the meta-analysis presented by Grynszpan, et al. (2014, p. 357). According to these same authors (Grynszpan, et al., 2014, p. 358), it is imperative that such interventions be accessible for parents and teachers, as it is highly recommended that such tools should be used in practice rather than being mainly a research-based field. They also recommend that studies be more rigorous about randomisation and evaluator blindness and use standardised measurement instruments, which would ensure that the type and quality of measures be equivalent across studies. Finally, it is of high importance to address the impact of technology on the functional aspects of those with ASD, and therefore, Grynszpan, et al. (2014) recommend that more studies assessed the maintenance of effectsand generalisation towards everyday life.

7.8 Conclusion

Vélez-Coto, et al. (2017) concluded that SIGUEME was an effective instrument to improve attention, categorisation and interaction in low-functioning students with ASD. It is also a powerful and useful tool for teachers and parent-educators to increase students' motivation and autonomy.

Finally, based on their preliminary study, their chapter concluded with how Newbutt, et al. (2017) thought head-mounted displays and virtual reality technologies might be used in future studies for helping to enable ASD populations for addressing some of the challenges that they face on a daily basis. These authors were primarily concerned with these challenges, as well as the contexts in which VRT could be applied, specifically focusing on moving research from laboratories towards real-life, potentially beneficial contexts.

References

Abidoğlu, Ü. P., Ertuğruloğlu, O., & Büyükeğilmez, N. (2017). Importance of computer-aided education for children with autism spectrum disorder (ASD). *Eurasia Journal of Mathematics, Science and Technology Education*, 13(8): 4957-4964. https://doi.org/10.12973/eurasia.2017.00975a

Acab, A. & Muotri, A. R., (2015). The use of induced pluripotent stem cell technology to advance autism research and treatment. *Neurotherapeutics*, 1 July, 12(3): 534-545.

Alison, C., Root, J. R., Browder, D. M. & Wood, L., (2017). Technology-Based Shared Story Reading for Students With Autism Who Are English-Language Learners. *Journal of Special Education Technology*, 32(2): 91-101.

Alzrayer, N. M., Banda, D. R., & Koul, R. (2017). Teaching children with autism spectrum disorder and other developmental disabilities to perform multistep requesting using an iPad. *Augmentative and Alternative Communication*, 33(2): 65-76. doi:10.1080/07434618.2017.1306881

Andersen, K., Levenson, L. & Blumberg, F. C., (2014). The Promise and Limitations of Assistive Technology Use among Children with Autism. In N.R. Silton (Ed.), *Innovative Technologies to Benefit Children on the Autism Spectrum*. (pp. 1-19). Hershey(PA): IGI Global.

Arriaga, R. I., (2017). Using an ecological systems approach to target technology development for autism research and beyond. In M.F. Casanova, A. El-Baz & J.S. Suri (Ed.), *Autism Imaging and Devices*. (pp. 419-436). London: SAGE.

Asaro-Saddler, K. & Akhmedjanova, D., (2015). The Use of Mobile Phone Technology to Support People with Autism Spectrum Disorders (ASD). In Z. Yan, *Encyclopedia of Mobile Phone Behavior*. (pp. 1514-1530). Hershey (PA): IGI Global.

Baio, J., Wiggins, L., Christensen, D.L., Maenner, M.J., Daniels, J., Warren, Z., Kurzius-Spencer, M., Zahorodny, W., Rosenberg, C.R., White, T. & Durkin, M.S., (2018). Prevalence of autism spectrum disorder among children aged 8 years—Autism and Developmental Disabilities Monitoring Network, 11 Sites, United States, 2014. *MMWR Surveillance Summaries*, 67(6): 1.

Banire, B., Khowaja, K., Mansoor, B., Qaraqe, M., & Al Thani, D. (2020). Reality-Based Technologies for Children with Autism Spectrum Disorder: A Recommendation for Food Intake Intervention. In *Personalized Food Intervention and Therapy for Autism Spectrum Disorder Management* (pp. 679-693). Cham: Springer.

Bereznak, S., Ayres, K. M., Mechling, L. C. & Alexander, J. L., (2012). Video self-prompting and mobile technology to increase daily living and vocational independence for students with autism spectrum disorders. *Journal of Developmental and Physical Disabilities*, 24(3): 269-285.

Boraston, Z. & Blakemore, S., (2007). The application of eye-tracking technology in the study of autism. *The Journal of Physiology*, 581(3): 893-898.

Brandler, W.M., Antaki, D., Gujral, M., Kleiber, M.L., Whitney, J., Maile, M.S., Hong, O., Chapman, T.R., Tan, S., Tandon, P. & Pang, T., (2018). Paternally inherited cis-regulatory structural variants are associated with autism. *Science*, 360(6386): 327-331.

Broder Fingert, S., Carter, A., Pierce, K., Stone, W.L., Wetherby, A., Scheldrick, C., Smith, C., Bacon, E., James, S.N., Ibañez, L. & Feinberg, E., (2018). Implementing systems-based innovations to improve access to early screening, diagnosis, and treatment services for children with autism spectrum disorder: An Autism Spectrum Disorder Pediatric, Early Detection, Engagement, and Services network study. *Autism*. http://journals.sagepub.com/doi/abs/10.1177/1362361318766238

Brosnan, M., Holt, S., Yuill, N. Good, J. & Parsons, S., (2017). Beyond autism and technology: lessons from neurodiverse populations. *Journal of Enabling Technologies*, 11(2), 43-48.

Campbell, K., Carpenter, K.L., Hashemi, J., Espinosa, S., Marsan, S., Borg, J.S., Chang, Z., Qiu, Q., Vermeer, S., Adler, E. & Tepper, M., (2018). Computer vision analysis captures atypical attention in toddlers with autism. *Autism.* http://journals.sagepub.com/doi/abs/10.1177/1362361318766247

Carnahan, C., Basham, J. & Musti-Rao, S., (2009). A low-technology strategy for increasing engagement of students with autism and significant learning needs. *Exceptionality*, 13 April, 17(2): 76-87.

Caron, J., Light, J., Holyfield, C., & McNaughton, D. (2018). Effects of dynamic text in an AAC app on sight word reading for individuals with autism spectrum disorder. *Augmentative and Alternative Communication,* 34(2): 143-154. doi:10.1080/07434618.2018.1457715

Chandler, D. L., (2016). Opening New Worlds for Those with Autism: Technology Is Creating Great New Possibilities for Those on Every Part of the Spectrum. *Institute of Electrical and Electronics Engineers (IEEE) pulse*, July/August, 74: 43-46.

Chao, K. Y., Chang, H. L., Chin, W. C., Li, H. M., & Chen, S. H., (2018). How Taiwanese parents of children with autism spectrum disorder experience the process of obtaining a diagnosis: A descriptive phenomenological analysis. *Autism*, 22(4): 388-400.

Chen, W., (2012). Multitouch tabletop technology for people with autism spectrum disorder: A review of the literature. *Procedia Computer Science*, 14: 198-207.

Cobb, S., Parsons, S., Millen, L., Eastgate, R. & Glover, T., (2010). *Design and development of collaborative technology for children with autism: COSPATIAL.* Valencia, International Academy of Technology, Education and Development.

Cramer, M., Hirano, S. H., Tentori, M., Yeganyan, M. T., & Hayes, G. R., (2011). *Classroom-based assistive technology: collective use of interactive visual schedules by students with autism.* Vancouver, Association for Computing Machinery (ACM).

Crane-Mitchell, L. & Stafford, L., (2017). *Enhancing Learning Outcomes for Students with Autism through the Use of Assistive Technology: Effect of Parent-Teacher Collaboration.* Chesapeake, Association for the Advancement of Computing in Education.

Di Mascio, T., & Tarantino, L. (2020). The Structured Methodological Framework "Deejay": Foundation and Its Application to the Design of an ASD-Oriented AAC Tool. In *Project and Design Literacy as Cornerstones of Smart Education.* (pp. 247-259). Singapore: Springer.

Diener, M. L., Wright, C. A., Wright, S. D. & Anderson, L. L., (2016). Tapping into Technical Talent: Using Technology to Facilitate Personal, Social, and Vocational Skills in Youth with Autism Spectrum Disorder (ASD). In T. A. Cardon, (Ed.) *Technology and the Treatment of Children with Autism Spectrum Disorder*. (pp. 97-112). Heidelberg: Springer.

Ferdig, R.E., Amberg, H.G., Elder, J.H., Donaldson, S.A., Valcante, G. & Bendixen, R., (2010). Autism and Family Interventions through Technology: A Description of a Web-based Tool to Educate Fathers of Children with Autism. In E.M.W. Ng, N. Karacapilidis & M. Raisinghani (Eds). *Dynamic Advancements in Teaching and Learning Based Technologies: New Concepts.* (pp. 232-246). Hershey(PA): IGI Global.

Fountain, C., Zhang, Y., Kissin, D. M., Schieve, L. A., Jamieson, D. J., Rice, C. & Bearman, P., (2015). Association between assisted reproductive technology conception and autism in California, 1997–2007. *American Journal of Public Health*, May, 105(5): 963-971.

Gentry, T., Kriner, R., Sima, A., McDonough, J. & Wehman, P., (2015). Reducing the need for personal supports among workers with autism using an iPod touch as an assistive technology: delayed randomized control trial. *Journal of Autism and Developmental Disorders*, 1 March, 45(3): 669-684.

Goldsmith, T. R. & LeBlanc, L. A., (2004). Use of technology in interventions for children with autism. *Journal of Early and Intensive Behavior Intervention*, 1(2): 166-178.

Goodwin, M. S., (2008). Enhancing and accelerating the pace of autism research and treatment: The promise of developing innovative technology. *Focus on Autism and Other Developmental Disabilities*, 23(2): 125-128.

Green, G., (2001). Behavior analytic instruction for learners with autism: Advances in stimulus control technology. *Focus on Autism and Other Developmental Disabilities*, 16(2): 72-85.

Grynszpan, O., Weiss, P. L., Perez-Diaz, F. & Gal, E., (2014). Innovative technology-based interventions for autism spectrum disorders: a meta-analysis. *Autism*, 18(4): 346-361.

Johnson, S. A., Blaha, L. M., Houpt, J. W. & Townsend, J. T., (2010). Systems factorial technology provides new insights on global–local information processing in autism spectrum disorders. *Journal of Mathematical Psychology*, February, 54(1): 53-72.

Lierheimer, K. S., Murray, M. M., Wooldridge, D. G. & Smith, S., (2014). Using Technology and Community Partnerships to Improve Educator Preparation: Changing the Landscape for Individuals with Autism Spectrum Disorder. *International Journal of Adult Vocational Education and Technology (IJAVET)*, 15 August, 5(3): 34-44.

Lofland, K. B., (2016). The use of technology in the treatment of autism. In T.A. Cardon, (Ed.). *Technology and the Treatment of Children with Autism Spectrum Disorder*. (pp. 27-35). Heidelberg: Springer International Publishing .

Logan, K., Iacono, T., & Trembath, D. (2017). A systematic review of research into aided AAC to increase social-communication functions in children with autism spectrum disorder. *Augmentative and Alternative Communication,* 33(1): 51-64. doi:10.1080/07434618.2016.12 67795

Macpherson, K., Charlop, M. H. & Miltenberger, C. A., (2015). Using portable video modeling technology to increase the compliment behaviors of children with autism during athletic group play. *Journal of Autism and Developmental Disorders*, 45(12): 3836-3845.

Madsen, M., El Kaliouby, R., Goodwin, M. & Picard, R., (2008). *Technology for just-in-time in-situ learning of facial affect for persons diagnosed with an autism spectrum disorder*. New York, ACM.

Mintz, J., (2013). Using Mobile Technology in Schools to Develop Social Skills in Children with Autism: Teacher Attitude Makes All the Difference. In H.H. Yang & S. Wang (Eds.), *Cases on E-Learning Management: Development and Implementation*. (pp. 294-317). Hershey (PA): IGI Global.

Mirenda, P., (2001). Autism, augmentative communication, and assistive technology what do we really know? *Focus on Autism and Other Developmental Disabilities*, 16(3): 141-151.

Moore, D., Cheng, Y., McGrath, P. & Powell, N. J., (2005). Collaborative virtual environment technology for people with autism. *Focus on Autism and Other Developmental Disabilities*, November, 20(4): 231-243.

Munson, J. & Pasqual, P., (2012). Using Technology in Autism Research: The Promise and the Perils. *Computer*, 45(6): 89-91.

Newbutt, N., Sung, C., Kuo, H. J. & Leahy, M. J., (2017). The acceptance, challenges, and future applications of wearable technology and virtual reality to support people with autism spectrum disorders. In A.L. Brooks, S. Brahnam, B. Kapralos & L. C. Jain (Eds.). *Recent Advances in Technologies for Inclusive Well-Being*. (pp. 221-241). Cham: Springer.

Nkabinde, Z. P., (2014). Information and Computer Technology for Individuals with Autism. In N.R. Silton, (Ed.) *Innovative Technologies to Benefit Children on the Autism*. (pp. 71-85). Hershey (PA): IGI Global.

Odom, S.L., Thompson, J.L., Hedges, S., Boyd, B.A., Dykstra, J.R., Duda, M.A., Szidon, K.L., Smith, L E. & Bord, A., (2015). Technology-aided interventions and instruction for adolescents with autism spectrum disorder. *Journal of Autism and Developmental Disorders*, 45(12): 3805-3819.

Picard, R.W., (2009). Future affective technology for autism and emotion communication. Philosophical Transactions of the Royal Society of London B. *Biological Sciences*, 364(1535): 3575-3584.

Porayska-Pomsta, K., Frauenberger, C., Pain, H., Rajendran, G., Smith, T., Menzies, R., Foster, M.E., Alcorn, A., Wass, S., Bernadini, S., Avramides, K., Keay-Bright, W., Chen, J., Waller, A., Guldberg, K., Good, J. & Lemon, O., (2012). Developing technology for autism: an interdisciplinary approach. *Personal and Ubiquitous Computing*, 16(2): 117-127.

Reed, F. D. D. G., Hyman, S. R. & Hirst, J. M., (2011). Applications of technology to teach social skills to children with autism. *Research in Autism Spectrum Disorders*, 5(3): 1003-1010.

Rivera, C. J., Mason, L. L., Jabeen, I. & Johnson, J., (2015). Increasing Teacher Praise and on Task Behavior for Students with Autism Using Mobile Technology. *Journal of Special Education Technology*, 30(2): 101-111.

Roelfsema, M.T., Hoekstra, R.A., Allison, C., Wheelwright, S., Brayne, C., Matthews, F.E. & Baron-Cohen, S., (2012). Are autism spectrum conditions more prevalent in an information-technology region? A school-based study of three regions in the Netherlands. *Journal of Autism and Developmental Disorders*, 42(5): 734-739.

Rose, V., Paynter, J., Vivanti, G., Keen, D., & Trembath, D. (2020). Predictors of Expressive Language Change for Children with Autism Spectrum Disorder Receiving AAC-Infused Comprehensive Intervention. *Journal of Autism and Developmental Disorders*, 50(1): 278-291.

Rubenstein, E., Wiggins, L. D., Schieve, L. A., Bradley, C., DiGuiseppi, C., Moody, E., Pandey, J., Pretzel, R. E., Howard, A. G., Olshan, A. F. & Pence, B. W., (2018). Associations between parental broader autism phenotype and child autism spectrum disorder phenotype in the Study to Explore Early Development. *Autism*, 29 January. https://doi.org/10.1177%2F1362361317753563

Sacrey, L.A.R., Bryson, S., Zwaigenbaum, L., Brian, J., Smith, I.M., Roberts, W., Szatmari, P., Vaillancourt, T., Roncadin, C. & Garon, N., (2018). The Autism Parent Screen for Infants: Predicting risk of autism spectrum disorder based on parent-reported behavior observed at 6–24 months of age. *Autism*, 22(3): 322-334.

Savage, M.N., (2016). *Comparing direct and technology-based praise statements to increase physical activity for students with autism spectrum disorder*. West Lafayette (Indiana): Purdue University.

Schafer, E. C., Gopal, K. V., Mathews, L., Kaiser, K., Canale, E., & Creech, A. (2019). Verification and Validation of Remote-Microphone Technology on Children and College-Age Adults Who Have Autism Spectrum Disorder. *Journal of Educational, Pediatric & (Re)Habilitative Audiology*, 24. http://www.edaud.org/journal/2019/3-article-19.pdf

Schafer, E.C., Wright, S., Anderson, C., Jones, J., Pitts, K., Bryant, D., Watson, M., Box, J., Neve, M., Mathews, L. & Reed, M.P., (2016). Assistive technology evaluations: Remote-microphone technology for children with Autism Spectrum Disorder. *Journal of Communication Disorders*, 64: 1-17.

Schlosser, R. W., Laubscher, E., Sorce, J., Koul, R., Flynn, S., Hotz, L., Abramson, J., Fadie, H., & Shane, H. (2013). Implementing directives that involve prepositions with children with autism: A comparison of spoken cues with two types of augmented input. *Augmentative and Alternative Communication,* 29(2): 132-145. doi:10.3109/07434618.2013.784928

Shane, H.C., Laubscher, E.H., Schlosser, R.W., Flynn, S., Sorce, J.F. & Abramson, J., (2012). Applying technology to visually support language and communication in individuals with autism spectrum disorders. *Journal of Autism and Developmental Disorders*, 42(6): 1228-1235.

Sherer, M., Pierce, K. L., Paredes, S., Kisacky, K. L., Ingersoll, B., & Schreibman, L., (2001). Enhancing conversation skills in children with autism via video technology: Which is better, "self" or "other" as a model? *Behavior Modification*, 25(1): 140-158.

Sirota, K. G., (2010). Narratives of distinction: Personal life narrative as a technology of the self in the everyday lives and relational worlds of children with autism. *Ethos*, 38(1): 93-115.

Sohl, K., Mazurek, M. O. & Brown, R., (2017). ECHO Autism: Using Technology and Mentorship to Bridge Gaps, Increase Access to Care, and Bring Best Practice Autism Care to Primary Care. *Clinical Pediatrics*, 56(6): 509-511.

Stahmer, A. C., Schreibman, L. & Cunningham, A. B., (2011). Toward a technology of treatment individualization for young children with autism spectrum disorders. *Brain Research*, 1380: 229-239.

Stasolla, F., Boccasini, A. & Perilli, V., (2017). Assistive Technology-Based Programs to Support Adaptive Behaviors by Children with Autism Spectrum Disorders: A Literature Overview. In Y. Kats *Supporting the Education of Children with Autism Spectrum Disorders*. (pp. 140-159). Hershey (PA): IGI Global,

Sutton, B. M., Webster, A. A. & Westerveld, M. F., (2018). A systematic review of school-based interventions targeting social communication behaviors for students with autism. *Autism*. Retrieved July 13, 2018, from http://journals.sagepub.com/doi/abs/10.1177/1362361317753564

Syriopoulou-Delli, C. K., & Gkiolnta, E. (2020). Review of assistive technology in the training of children with autism spectrum disorders. *International Journal of Developmental Disabilities*, 1-13. doi:https://doi.org/10.1080/20473869.2019.1706333

Tang, T. Y. & Flatla, D. R., (2016). *Autism Awareness and Technology-Based Intervention Research in China: The Good, the Bad, and the Challenging*. San Jose, ACM, pp. 1-6.

Thirumanickam, A., Raghavendra, P., McMillan, J. M., & van Steenbrugge, W. (2018). Effectiveness of video-based modelling to facilitate conversational turn taking of adolescents with autism spectrum disorder who use AAC. *Augmentative and Alternative Communication,* 34(4): 311-322. doi:10.1080/07434618.2018.1523948

Tseng, R.-Y. & Do, E. Y.-L., (2010). *Facial Expression Wonderland (FEW): a novel design prototype of Information and Computer Technology (ICT) for children with Autism Spectrum Disorder (ASD)*. New York: ACM.

Tustin, F., (2018). *Autism and Childhood Psychosis*. London: Routledge.

van Schalkwyk, G. I., Marin, C. E., Ortiz, M., Rolison, M., Qayyum, Z., McPartland, J. C., Lebowitz, E. R., Volkmar, F. R. & Silverman, W. K. (2017). Social media use, friendship quality, and the moderating role of anxiety in adolescents with autism spectrum disorder. *Journal of Autism and Developmental Disorders*, 47(9): 2805-2813.

Vélez-Coto, M., Rodríguez-Fórtiz, M.J., Rodriguez-Almendros, M.L., Cabrera-Cuevas, M., Rodríguez-Domínguez, C., Ruiz-López, T., Burgos-Pulido, Á., Garrido-Jiménez, I. & Martos-Pérez, J., (2017). SIGUEME: Technology-based intervention for low-functioning autism to train skills to work with visual signifiers and concepts. *Research in Developmental Disabilities*, 64: 25-36.

Wainer, A. L. & Ingersoll, B. R., (2011). The use of innovative computer technology for teaching social communication to individuals with autism spectrum disorders. *Research in Autism Spectrum Disorders*, 5(1), 96-107.

Weiss, P.L., Gal, E., Zancanaro, M., Giusti, L., Cobb, S., Millen, L., Hawkins, T., Glover, T., Sanassy, D. & Eden, S., (2011). Usability of technology supported social competence training for children on the autism spectrum. Zurich, *IEEE*, pp. 1-8.

Withey, K. L. (2017). Using apps to develop social skills in children with autism spectrum disorder. *Intervention in School and Clinic,* 52(4): 250-255. doi: https://doi.org/10.1177/1053451216659475

Wright, C., Diener, M. L., Dunn, L. & Wright, S. D., (2011). SketchUp™: A technology tool to facilitate intergenerational family relationships for children with autism spectrum disorders (ASD). *Family and Consumer Sciences Research Journal*, December, 40(2), 135-149.

Yee, H. S. S., (2012). Mobile technology for children with Autism Spectrum Disorder: Major trends and issues. Kuala Lumpur, *IEEE*, pp. 1-5.

8

PARTNERSHIPS FOR AUTISM IN THE ZIMBABWEAN INCLUSIVE EDUCATION SYSTEM

Jabulani Mpofu

Abstract

Partnerships in Inclusive Education span a range of options, supports and activities including with special populations. An increasing prevalent population is learners with ASD. This chapter will address issues around partnerships in the identification of learners with ASD in the Zimbabwean education system, inclusive support options for them, their families and communities. Early identification of learners with ASD is crucial as it facilitates the process of early intervention such as curriculum adaptation. Learners with ASD who experience friendly learning environments perform better as their environments will be responding to their educational needs. Levels of support for which partnerships are needed and the prospects for their availability and implementation in the Zimbabwean Inclusive Education system will be discussed. The chapter will also address challenges that are being met by inclusive community partners in the Zimbabwean education system in their endeavour to create conducive learning spaces of learners with ASD.

8.1 Theoretical framework

This chapter adopts the systems theory to explain autism and issues related to partnerships for ASD in the Zimbabwean Inclusive Education system. The systems theory was adopted for two main reasons:

- It looks at an individual with ASD from a community point of view, which is consistent with the philosophy of Inclusive Education practices worldwide. The theory does not view poor learning outcome in learners with ASD as the problem of their condition, but rather as the symptom of a problem in the education system as a whole (Shora, 2004).
- It views ASD from a social model perspective, which is again in line with globally accepted trends of disability and health (Mpofu & Oakland, 2010; WHO, 2004).

The next section provides an overview of the systems theory.

8.1.1 Systems theory

Systems theory was proposed in the 1940s by the biologist Ludwig von Bertalanffy, and further developed by Ross Ashby (1950). Von Bertalanffy was both reacting against reductionism and attempting to revive the unity of science. He emphasised that real systems (Makore-Rukuni, 2003) are open to, and interact with their environments, and that they can acquire qualitatively new properties through experiences, resulting in continual evolution (Makore-Rukuni, 2003).

Systems theory also alludes that a system consists of subsystems and these constitute a hierarchical order of systems (Makore-Rukuni, 2003). For instance, the individual in a subsystem is made up of the nervous, digestive, respiratory and other systems. In turn, the individual is a subsystem of a larger system: the nuclear family, the family subsystem of the extended family, and the extended family subsystem in the community, which is the supra-system of the subsystems and systems mentioned above. The different parts of the system are not to be viewed in isolation from each other. The best way to understand the parts is to look at them as functioning parts of the total system.

In the next section, the focus is on the key concepts of systems theory and how they could be applied to enhancing our understanding of issues related to partnerships for Autism in Zimbabwean Inclusive Education system.

8.1.2 Systems theory and its applicability to partnerships for autism in the Zimbabwean Inclusive Education system

This section provides a detailed discussion of the key concepts of systems theory. The key concepts of system theory will allow us to understand experiences of learners living with ASD learning in an inclusive setting (see chapter on autism and inclusion). The discussion will focus on the major components of systems theory: equifinality, homeostasis, hierarchy, boundaries and feedback (Makore-Rukuni, 2003).

8.1.2.1 Equifinality

Equifinality when applied to systems theory refers to the ability of a system to arrive at the same destination from different paths or conditions. The concept explains that similar outcomes may stem from different early experiences (Guttman, 1991; Shora, 2004). The principle of equifinality explains that in any closed setting the final state is determined by the initial state (Makore-Rukuni, 2003; Shora, 2004). In Inclusive Education, it refers to how negative early experiences in life (e.g. having ASD, negative attitudes towards people with ASD) can lead to similar negative outcomes (e.g. limited participation in inclusive learning activities) (Mpofu, 2003). In other words, if people develop negative attitudes towards learners with ASD in early stages those early negative experiences by ASD learners may lead to learning limitations outcomes (Shora, 2004).

In the context of this chapter, the concept of equifinality supports development of positive attitudes towards people with ASD by community members (e.g. parents, peers, teachers, para professionals, doctors, nurses, counsellors) to achieve positive learning outcomes among learners with ASD in regular schools. What it means then is that learners with ASD need to be exposed to different pro-inclusive support subsystems in their communities simultaneously, e.g. teachers, psychologists, social welfare officers, and others with a view to creating conducive learning spaces for them. These subsystems will expose them to different levels of power and different skills (Shora 2004). Participation in these various subsystems will assist learners with ASD to navigate different adverse environments, and this may assist them in developing enhanced learning outcomes.

The next component of systems theory is homeostasis.

8.1.2.2 Homeostasis

Homeostasis is the tendency of a system toward maintenance of a relatively stable internal environment through a series of interacting processes (Makore-Rukuni, 2003; Shora, 2004). This concept in the context of this chapter suggests that all members in a human living system (with or without disabilities) tend to follow organised ways of behaving towards one another (Shora, 2004). A preferred pattern for relating to one another evolves over time. As the needs of an Inclusive Education system change, a healthy system will also work towards changing its preferred patterns of behaving (Mpofu, 2012). For instance, the current trend in Inclusive Education involves the use of preferred terms to refer to people with ASD (ICF, 2001; WHO, 2004). A healthy Inclusive Education system will always work to develop positive terms for referring to its people with ASD such as differently abled persons. Another example of a homeostatic situation in ASD context is using time out procedures for a learner with ASD who exhibits difficulties that interfere with his/her learning. In this situation, the school may attempt to interrupt this pattern of restriction and help the learner with ASD family to search for a supportive learning environment that is adapted to meet learning needs of the learner with ASD. Example of such includes learning environments that make use of assistive technologies. This action will not only modify preferred patterns of interaction but also contribute to changing the system.

The next important aspect of systems theory involves feedback.

8.1.2.3 Feedback

Feedback (Makore-Rukuni, 2003; Shora, 2004) is the process by which the input of each community member leads to a more complex, systems-oriented output. The output of the community system is therefore no longer individually determined and analysed. The concept of feedback in the context of this chapter assumes that the poor learning outcomes in learners with ASD is caused not by a breakdown in the intrapsychic machinery (biological factors), but by the failure of the Inclusive Education partners as community systems fail to operate properly (Makore-Rukuni, 2003; Shora, 2004). There are both negative and positive feedbacks. Negative feedback is an attempt that is made to correct a system in trouble and to re-establish its previous state of equilibrium (Makore-Rukuni, 2003). This becomes relevant to those with ASD emanating from a combination of genetic and environmental factors and idiopathic autism (autisim whose origin is not known). For example, a learner who acquired ASD as a result of combination of genetic and environmental factors and has been side-lined to special schools must be re-enrolled in an Inclusive Education setting in order to re-establish harmony at his or her school. In this case, negative feedback is used to keep the status quo or maintain homeostasis. Positive feedback, on the other hand, forces someone into new ways of behaving by making old behaviour patterns unattainable. It is often used to counteract negative feedback.

In the context of this chapter, systems theory views a mainstream school as an inclusive entity that is made up of people with different abilities rather than of the characteristics of each part, such as people with specific abilities and disabilities (Mpofu, 2003). It focuses on how the school functions inclusively, instead of on the problems of individuals in the school. Systems theory does not view poor learning outcome in learners with ASD as the problem of their condition, but rather as the symptom of a problem in the education system as a whole (Shora, 2004). It suggests that the elimination of behaviour problems such as negative and poor socialisation (as is the case with most learners with ASD) is only attainable by changing the structure of the education system rather than by trying to change the behaviour problem directly (Loreman, Deppeler & Harvey 2005). Thus the systems theory, like the social model of disability, emphasises the role of collaboration in Inclusive Education partners in addressing the learning needs of learners with ASD (Fox, Prilleltensky, & Austin, 2009).

Until relatively recently, the education of people with ASD has been viewed to consist of associations between two individuals – such as the parent and the individual with ASD – independent of any other partners within the greater community (Fox et al., 2009). However, an Inclusive Education system posutulates that relationships among Inclusive Education partners are interdependent and that the community is more than the sum of its individual members (Makore-Rukuni & Maunganidze, 2001). Individuals exert influence on community members and are in turn influenced by other community members and by the contexts in which all community members interact (Mpofu, 2003). Relationships are therefore described as a 'system', operating so that all members are affected in some way by experiences of any one individual in the system, in much the same way that a machine's function 'emerges' from the mutually dependent actions of its various parts (see chapter on Autism and Inclusion) (Makore-Rukuni & Maunganidze,2001).

8.2 Partnerships for autism in Zimbabwean Inclusive Education system

The increased prevalence of children identified with ASD in Zimbabwean education system coupled with the paradigm shift from exclusive to Inclusive Education resulted in students with ASD being placed more frequently in Inclusive Education classrooms (Chakuchichi & Mutamiswa, 2003). As a result, a number of Inclusive Education partners are becoming more visible in the teaching and learning of children with ASD in Zimbabwe (Chimhonyo et al., 2012). The partners are working in a collaborative way to provide early identification and intervention, development of local training facilities, procurement of equipment, provision of support and monitoring services and teaching and learning to children with ASD in Zimbabwean Inclusive Education settings (Chakuchichi & Mutamiswa, 2003; Chimhonyo et al., 2012). This section addresses issues around partnerships in supporting/enhancing learning for learners with ASD in the Zimbabwean education system. I provide an overview of inclusive supports options available for learners with ASD, their families and Zimbabwean communities at large.

8.3 Early identification of learners with ASD

The Zimbabwean Inclusive Education system provides opportunities for early identification of learners with ASD at the earliest possible time (Mpofu, 2003). This can be done through the following: general observation and as in most cases with the administration of standardised tests (Chimhonyo et al., 2012). This is done to identify the individual's conditions to provide appropriate Inclusive Education support. This type of assessment is biopsychosocial in nature. It incorporates useful aspects of the medical and social model. It integrates both medical and social perspective of disability into contemporary conceptualisations of disability and functioning.

8.4 Development of local training facilities

Partners for Autism in Zimbabwean Inclusive Education system (e.g. Lenard Cheshire Trust. FJ Kennedy Trust, Ministry of Primary and Secondary Education, Ministry of Health Child and Social Welfare) assist in developing institutions where those who work with learners with ASD are trained. They also assist in human resource development by training and in-servicing staff that work with learners with autism in the country (Mutamiswa & Chakuchichi, 2003).

Partners for Autism in Zimbabwean Inclusive Education system also provide various learning equipment that make learning supportive for learners with ASD in Zimbabwean inclusive learning settings. Through the buying of adapted Inclusive Education equipment individuals with ASD are assisted to experience the supportive learning life (Mutamiswa & Chakuchichi, 2003). Examples of such (e.g. Occupational therapy equipment) and other forms of assistive devices for various types of ASD are used.

8.5 Types of partners in the learning of ASD learners in Zimbabwean Inclusive Education system

There are generally two types of partners in teaching and learning of learners with ASD in Zimbabwe. These are natural and formal support partners. These partners are essential for enabling learners with ASD to learn in the supportive environments within Zimbabwean Inclusive Education settings. Natural support partners are located in the community and are provided by peers, parents and other community members (Mpofu et al., 2012). Formal support refers to support coming from professionals such as doctors, teachers and physiotherapists.

8.5.1 Natural support partners

Zimbabwean learners with ASD in the Inclusive Education system receive support from natural support partners (Chakuchichi & Mutamiswa, 2003). Natural support partners provide help, which is obtained naturally at home. This support is obtained from the parents, siblings and friends of learners with ASD Chakuchichi *et al.*, 2003). The Zimbabwean Education Act of 1987 and the revised version of 2006 acknowledge the application of parental involvement in teaching and learning of learners with ASD (Zimbabwean Education Act 1987; Zimbabwean Education Act 2006). The Zimbabwean Education Act of 1987 and the revised version of 2006 clearly explain that parents must be involved to promote and provide the necessary equipment, facilities and materials for the successful implementation of inclusive environment for learners with special needs including learners with ASD (Zimbabwean Education Act, 1987; Zimbabwean Education Act,2006). The revised Education Act (2006) supports parents' participation and management of Inclusive Education schools (UNESCO, 2002).

In most Zimbabwean communities, the majority of members in the natural support partnership group for learners with ASD (e.g. parents) are functionally illiterate and vulnerable, but they contribute vital information about their children (Florian, 2015, Mpofu, et al., 2011, Mpofu et al., 2010). Parents of children with ASD work together and collaborate with teachers by providing information on the strengths and challenges, the likes and dislikes, and the developmental history of their children with ASD. They provide reports (both written and nonverbal), notes and homework diaries to other stakeholders in the partnership (Chakuchichi & Mutamiswa, 2003, Florian & Beaton 2017, Seekins, Ipsen & Arnold, 2007). They also create a physical environment and emotional space for performing various Inclusive Education activities such as school tasks (Engelbrecht, 2007). Parents also attend meetings, both formal and informal, and engage with teachers and other staff members. Parents provide classroom aides, assist in maintaining classrooms, and help to raise funds for the school. They are also useful in Inclusive Education policy formulation by being active in disability advocacy meetings (Mckenzie & Loebenstein, 2007).

8.5.2 Learners with ASD

Learners with ASD are also major partners in Zimbabwean Inclusive Education activities. Like their parents, they may be functionally illiterate and vulnerable, but they contribute vital information about their own condition (ASAN, 2018; Chakuchichi & Mutamiswa, 2003), their abilities and weaknesses, their likes and dislikes, and their developmental history. They can provide written and non-verbal report or notes, do homework, and take part in Inclusive Education tasks (ASAN, 2018, Mckenzie & Loebenstein, 2007). At the collaboration level, learners with ASD in Zimbabwean Inclusive Education settings cooperate and participate in various Inclusive Education activities. As their parents, learners with ASD are also able to attend formal and informal meetings at school, and engage with staff members (Mpofu *et al*., 2012). Although they are young, they are useful in Inclusive Education policy formulation because they are active in disability advocacy meetings, they take part in disability related demonstrations and they attend partnership conferences (ASAN, 2018, Chakuchichi & Mutamiswa, 2003).

8.5.3 Formal support partners

Besides natural support partners in teaching and learning of learners with and learning of learners with ASD in Zimbabwean Inclusive Education system, the country also makes use of formal support partners. Formal support partners involve support that is funded by the Zimbabwean government via the general community (Chakuchichi & Mutamiswa, 2003). Some of the formal support partners include qualified teachers, para-professionals, doctors, nurses and physiotherapists, as well as appropriate curriculum materials and technological assistive device systems relevant to teaching and learning of children with ASD (Mpofu, 2003).

8.5.4 The philanthropic community

The philanthropic community is also a major partner in the education of learners with ASD in Zimbabwe. The philanthropic community is the donor community (Ndawi, 2000). In most cases, donors assist the Zimbabwean government in funding Inclusive Education activities targeting the education of learners with special needs which includes those with ASD. They provide training to both natural and formal support players in Inclusive Education activities. In some cases, donors run the programmes themselves under the supervision of the government (Ndawi, 2000).

8.6 Challenges that are being met by inclusive community partners

There has been an increasing trend to promote partnerships for teaching and learning of learners with ASD in Zimbabwe Inclusive Education settings. Partnerships that share responsibility for teachers' and students' learning, yet the complexities of collaborating across institutions and professions as well as the identity work that goes with it has been under-theorised in Inclusive Education partnerships. Drawing from the Zimbabwean Inclusive Education system partnership in the education of ASD learners is not without challenges. Among the challenges confronted by ASD learning partnerships, are issues related to negative attitudes towards learners with ASD from the greater community, including some of the partners (Mpofu et al., 2012). Further challenges include poor teacher preparation (Chakuchichi & Mutamiswa, 2003), the absence of an inclusive curriculum, the absence of specific legislation pertaining to the education of learners with ASD and under reporting of ASD cases in Zimbabwean ordinary schools (Chimhonyo et al., 2012).

8.6.1 Attitudinal challenges

Although the introduction of Inclusive Education in Zimbabwe helped in creating learning spaces for learners with ASD in the Zimbabwean public school system, some partners involved in the teaching and learning of learners with ASD (professionals such as teachers, nurses, psychologist, parent's peers, and others) still display negative attitudes towards these learners (Mpofu, 2003; Mpofu, 2017). The attitudes and behaviours of these partners toward the inclusion of learners with ASD in regular educational programmes are critical since "non-disabled" students often model the attitudes and behaviours of significant others. Partners in the inclusion of learners with ASD, such as heads of schools, teachers and others need to demonstrate appropriate attitudes and behaviours regarding the inclusion of learners with ASD as the instructional leaders in the school (Chimhonyo et al., 2012). As schools become more inclusive, there is a strong need for heads of schools and teachers who are able to clearly define and articulate a mission, which incorporates the values of acceptance (Chakuchichi & Mutamiswa, 2003, Molosiwa & Mpofu, 2017). For inclusion to be successful, the partners in the inclusion of learners with ASD need to foster a climate in which the school embraces the success and achievement of all students (Florian, 2017; Majoko, 2015). Key partners such as school heads must manage and coordinate resources for curriculum and instruction in ways that support the inclusion of learners with ASD;

monitor and support individual learner's progress; and supervise teaching to continually encourage and strengthen that culture (Florian & Beaton, 2017). Placement decisions are made based on beliefs and experience (Chakuchichi & Mutamiswa, 2003). Therefore, if learners with ASD are given equal opportunity to be placed in regular education classes, students with autism in Zimbabwe are likely to be recommended for inclusion by education professionals (Mpofu, 2017). In order to assure that inclusive practices and reflect more fundamental change in schools, it is necessary to overcome attitudinal and knowledge barriers that can impact on the success of the inclusion of learners with barriers to learning such as autism, in ordinary schools (Avissar *et al.*, 2003; Praisner, 2003).

8.6.2 Teacher preparation

Although there is evidence that Zimbabwean educationists are moving towards a broader view of Inclusive Education, the majority of these teachers are not adequately trained to provide educational services to learners with ASD. As a result, they do not have the capacity to address the educational needs of learners with autism (Chakuchichi & Mutamiswa, 2003; Mo,losiwa & Mpofu 2017). The few who received training related to special needs education from teachers' colleges and universities are also not able to handle learners with ASD as this group is not covered in most of these teacher preparation course (Mpofu, 2003). If partners in the teaching and learning of ASD learners in Inclusive Education settings lack appropriate training to work with children with ASD, then it cannot be expected that the learning outcomes of these children will show much improvement. This inefficacy affects socialisation of ASD learners. Socialisation is a critical consideration since it is a deficit area in autism and an essential element in successful inclusion at any level (Marks et al., 2003).

8.6.3 Curriculum

The inclusion of students with ASD in Zimbabwean Inclusive Education has received support from several professional organisations (Chimhonyo *et al.*, 2012). However, one of the most problematic and stressful challenges facing Zimbabwean schools and Inclusive Education partner's officials today is to provide an appropriate curriculum for the increasing number of students with ASD, alongside their "non-disabled" peers, in general education inclusive classrooms (Florian, & Spratt, 2013; Mpofu *et al.*, 2012). Education in Zimbabwean public schools is mainly geared towards the majority of learners who find themselves in mainstream schools. It is apparent that the development and learning needs of learners with ASD in the country is not catered for adequately by the national curriculum (Choruma, 2006; Florian, & Black-Hawkins, 2011). This issue of curriculum that does not adequately cater for learners with autism is not only unique to Zimbabwean Education system but it is a global challenge (Florian 2010). The pace at which the learners are expected to master learning material does not consider either the temporary or the permanent needs of learners with ASD. This situation leaves partners in the teaching and learning of learners with ASD designing individual educational programmes for ASD learners, which may be inconsistent with their ecological needs (Florian & Linklater, 2010). The situation becomes worse when the teachers are not trained to teach ASD learners which is the case in most schools in the country.

8.6.4 Policies

The absence of one Inclusive Education policy poses a great challenge to partners that seek to support the inclusion of ASD learners in Zimbabwean Inclusive Education system (Black-Hawkins, & Florian, 2012; Mpofu et al., 2008). The country has several legislations and departmental policies targeting vulnerable children including those with ASD (Black-Hawkins, & Florian, 2012; Chimhonyo et al., 2012). Example of such scenario is the country has operational guidelines targeting children with ASD from the ministry of health, social welfare, education and others. These policies and legislations must be integrated to form one comprehensive legislation to cover all children in Inclusive Education settings not only children at risk. This will avoid duplication of effort from Inclusive Education partners and live up to the real intent of Inclusive Education. A comprehensive law and teachers with adequate knowledge, skills and attitudes to translate policy in their daily practice would assist in effective collaboration among Inclusive Education partners (Black-Hawkins, Florian, & Rouse, 2007).

8.6.5 Funding

Zimbabwe is a signatory of the United Nations Convention of Rights for Persons with Disabilities (Mpofu, 2017). Consistent with this, it is committed to providing adequate human and financial resources when offering Inclusive Education services to all its people including those with ASD. To live up to this commitment, the Zimbabwean government put a significant portion of its fragile national budgetary allocation to education (Choruma, 2006). Despite this, the education system in general is still faced with lack of adequate teachers trained to teach learners with ASD (Mpofu & Molosiwa, 2017; Mpofu et al. 2017). This hinders the effective implementation of a coherent Inclusive Education programme. Inclusive education programmes that cater for special learners such as those with ASD needs, with adequate human and material resources.

8.6.6 Under-reporting of cases of ASD learners

The other challenge being met by partners in the inclusion of learners with ASD in Zimbabwean Inclusive Education system is the issue of late diagnosis (Mpofu & Oakland, 2010) of ASD in Zimbabwean communities. Late diagnosis of ASD and other neurodevelopmental disorders is common among Zimbabwean children in spite of early parental concerns about development (Choruma, 2006, Majoko, 2016). Possible factors identified as being responsible for late diagnosis of ASD include poor knowledge/awareness about ASD (Florian 2016); Igwe et al., 2011); negative cultural beliefs and practices (Dymond, Gilson, & Myran, 2007); inadequate number of trained personnel (Bakare et al., 2009a); and inadequate healthcare and intervention facilities (Bakare et al., 2009).

8.7 Conclusion

While partnerships (Majoko, 2016) are considered to be the most effective way of creating learning spaces (Florian, 2015) for learners with ASD in Zimbabwean public schools, the implementation of this partnership is facing serious challenges that pose limitations to the learning of learners with ASD in Inclusive Education settings (Mpofu et al., 2017). They face challenges related to poor teacher preparation (Mpofu, 2017), absence of an inclusive curriculum (Mpofu & Oakland, 2010), absence of specific legislation (Mpofu & Molosiwa, 2017) on the education ASD learners and under reporting of ASD cases in Zimbabwean mainstream schools. However, the lessons learnt from these challenges to date provide evidence that there is a wide range of benefits to be gained if these challenges are addressed. This gives cause for optimism about the future of learners with ASD learners in Zimbabwean mainstream schools.

References

ASAN (2018). ASAN Letter to ASHA on the right to communicate. http://autisticadvocacy.org/

Black-Hawkins, K. Florian, L. & Rouse, M. (2007). *Achievement and Inclusion in Schools.* London: Routledge Falmer.

Bakare, M. O.& Munir, K. M. (2011). Excess of non-verbal cases of autism spectrum disorders presenting to orthodox practice in Africa – a trend possibly resulting from late diagnosis and intervention. *South African Journal of Psychiatry*, 17(4): 118-120.

Campbell, J., Gilmore, L. & Cuskelly, M. (2003). Changing student teachers' attitudes towards disability and inclusion. *Journal of Intellectual and Developmental Disability*, 28(4): 369-379.

Carter, E.W. & Hughes, C.H. (2006_a). Promoting Access to the General Curriculum Using Peer Support Strategies. *Research & Practice for Persons with Severe Disabilities*, 31(4): 284-292.

Carter, E.W. & Hughes, C. (2006_b). Including high school students with severe disabilities in general education classes: Perspectives of general and special educators, paraprofessionals, and administrators. *Research & Practice for Persons with Severe Disabilities*, 31(9): 174-185.

Chakuchichi, D. D., Chimedza, R. M. & Chiinze, M. M. (2003). *Including the Excluded: Issues in Disability and Inclusion.* Harare: Zimbabwe Open University.

Chakuchichi, D.D. & Mutamiswa, H. B. (2003). *(Re)Habilitation for Students with Physical and Motor Disabilities.* Harare: Zimbabwe Open University.

Choruma, T. (2006). *The forgotten tribe.* London: Progresso.

Chimhonyo, I., Kaputa, T. M., Mamvura, E. K., Hlatwayo, L., Munemo, E. T., Nyatsanza, T. D. & Mutandwa, E. (2011). *Breaking Down Barriers to Inclusive Education in Zimbabwe.* Harare: Zimbabwe Ministry of Primary and Secondary Education.

Dymond, S. K. Gilson, C. L. & Myran, S.P. (2007). Services for children with autism spectrum disorders: What needs to change? *Journal of Disability Policy Studies*, 18(3): 133-147.

Engelbrecht, P. & Green, L. (2007). Responding to the challenges of Inclusive Education: An introduction. In P. Engelbrecht & L. Green. *Responding to the challenges of Inclusive Education in Southern Africa.* (pp.82-88). Pretoria: Van Schaik.

Florian. L. (2010). The concept of inclusive pedagogy. In G. Hallett & F. Hallett (Eds.). *Transforming the role of the SENCO.* (pp 61-72). Buckingham: Open University Press

Florian, L (2015). Conceptualising Inclusive Pedagogy: The Inclusive Pedagogical Approach in Action. In F. Kiuppis & R. S. Hausstätter (Eds.). *Inclusive education twenty years after Salamanca*. (pp. 219-230). New York: Peter Lan.

Florian, L. (2017). The heart of Inclusive Education is collaboration. *Pedagogika* 126(2): 248-253

Florian, L. & Beaton, M. (2017). Inclusive pedagogy in action: getting it right for every child. *International Journal of Inclusive Education*: 870-889.

Florian, L., & Black-Hawkins, K. (2011). Exploring Inclusive Pedagogy. *British Educational Research Journal*, 37(5): 813 -828.

Florian, L. & Kershner, R. (2009) Inclusive Pedagogy. In H. Daniels, H. Lauder and J. Porter (Eds.) *Knowledge, Values and Educational Policy: A Critical Perspective.* (pp.173 -183). London: Routledge.

Florian, L., & Linklater, H. (2010). Preparing Teachers for Inclusive Education: Using Inclusive Pedagogy to Enhance Teaching and Learning for All. *Cambridge Journal of Education*, 40(4): 369-386.

Florian, L. & Spratt, J. (2013). Enacting inclusion: A framework for interrogating inclusive practice. *European Journal of Special Needs Education*, 28(2): 119-135.

Fox, D., Prilleltensky, I. & Austin, S. (2009). *Critical Psychology: An Introduction*. London: Sage.

Goodman, G. & Williams, C.M. (2007). Interventions for increasing the academic engagement of students with autism spectrum disorders in inclusive classrooms. *Teaching Exceptional Children*, 39(6), 53-61.

Guttman, H. A. (1991). Systems theory, cybernetics and epistemology. In A. S. Gurman and D.P. Kniskern(eds.). *Handbook of Family Therapy.* (pp.287-301). New York: Brunner/Mazel.

Igwe, M.N., Ahanotu, A.C., Bakare, M.O., Achor, J.U.& Igwe, C. (2011). Assessment of knowledge about childhood autism among pediatric and psychiatric nurses in Ebonyi State, Nigeria. *Child Adolescents Psychiatry Mental Health*, 5(1): 1-10.

Loreman, T., Deppeler, J. & Harvey, D. (2005). *Inclusive Education. A practical guide to supporting diversity in the classroom.* Sydney: Allen & Unwin.

Makore-Rukuni, M. (2000). *Counselling of students with disabilities and their families*. Harare: Zimbabwe Open University.

Majoko, T. (2016). Inclusion of Children with Autism Spectrum Disorders: Listening and Hearing to Voices from the Grassroots. *Autism Dev Disorder*, 46(4):1429-40.

McKenzie, J. & Loebenstein, H. (2007). Increasing parent recognition and involvement. In P. Engelbrecht & L. Green (Eds.), *Responding to the challenges of Inclusive Education in southern Africa*. (pp.186-202). Pretoria: Van Schaik.

Molosiwa, S.M. & Mpofu, J. (2017). Practice and Opportunities of Inclusive Education in Botswana. In G.J. Sefa Dei, N. Phasha and D. Mahlo (Eds.). *Inclusive Education in African Contexts: Anti-Colonial Educational Perspective for Transformative Change.* (pp.65-84). Boston: Sense Publishers.

Mpofu, E, Ukasonya, G, Mupawose, A., Harley, D.A, Charema, J. & Ntinda K. (2011). Counselling people with disabilities. In E. Mpofu and T. Oakland (Eds.). *Counselling people of African Ancestry.* (pp. 295-309). Cambridge.

Mpofu, E. & Oakland, T. (2010). Trends in rehabilitation and health assessments. In E. Mpofu and T. Oakland (Eds.). *Rehabilitation and Health Assessment: Applying ICF Guidelines*. (pp.1-10). New York: Springer.

Mpofu, E. (2003). *Educational considerations for students who are mentally challenged/retarded.* Harare: Zimbabwe Open University.

Mpofu, J. (2017). Psychological wellbeing of adolescents with physical disabilities living in inclusive community settings. Unpublished PhD thesis. Pretoria: University of Pretoria.

Mpofu, J., Gasva, D., Mubika, A.K. & Gwembire, J. (2012). *Introduction to Disabilities and Special Needs Education.* Harare: Zimbabwe Open University.

Mpofu, J and Serefete, M. (2017). Disability and Inclusive Education in Zimbabwe. In G.J. Sefa Dei, N. Phasha and D. Mahlo (Eds.). *Inclusive Education in African Contexts: Anti – Colonial Educational Perspective for Transformative Change.* (pp.49-65). Boston: Sense Publishers.

Mutamiswa, H.H. & Chakuchichi, D.D. (2003). *Rehabilitation of people with disabilities*. Harare: Zimbabwe Open University.

Ndawi, O.P. (2000). The role of legislation in facilitating CBR in Zimbabwe. In S. Hartley (Ed). *CBR: A participatory strategy in Africa.* (pp. 46-47). University College of London.

Praisner, C. L.(2003). Attitudes of Elementary School Principals toward the Inclusion of Students with Disabilities. *Exceptional Children*, 69(2): 135-145.

Seekins, T, Ipsen, C & Arnold, N. L (2007) Using ecological momentary assessment to measure participation: a preliminary study. *Rehabilitation Psychology*, 52: 319-330.

Shora, R.M. (2004). *Training and Development*. Harare: Zimbabwe Open University.

The Government of Zimbabwe. (1987). *Zimbabwean Education Act of 1987*. Harare: Government Printers.

The Government of Zimbabwe. (2006). *Zimbabwean Education Act of 2006*. Harare: Government Printers.

UNESCO. (2003). *Overcoming Exclusion through Inclusive Approaches in Education: Conceptual Paper.* Paris: UNESCO.

World Health Organization. (2004). *ICF: International Classification of Functioning, Disability and Health*. Geneva: WHO.

9

PARENTS AND COMMUNITY PARTNERSHIPS IN EDUCATING CHILDREN WITH ASD AS AN INCLUSIVE EDUCATION STRATEGY

Mahlapahlapana J Themane

Abstract

The ancient African adage that 'it takes a village to raise a child' has special relevance for this chapter. My discussion highlights parent and community partnerships as essential for educating children with ASD. In traditional African communities, children belong to the communities in which they are born and raised. Parents are responsible for participating in their children's development, especially in terms of moral development. Drawing on community partnerships may therefore be a viable strategy for providing access to quality education for children with ASD as well as Inclusive Inclusive Education For All children. My systematic evaluation of community outreach programmes leads me to suggest that failure to involve parents and community members would undermine the meaningful implementation of Inclusive Education. Furthermore, I provide suggestions that could strengthen relationships and result in more meaningful and effective partnerships. In particular, I consider how community and school-based management capacity could be enhanced through committees, parent-teacher-associations and school governing bodies. These structures should play an active role in establishing, implementing and monitoring programmes that promote quality Education For All children, including children with ASD. This approach advocates for valuing the social capital of parents and the community, since Inclusive Education is fundamental to social justice. The approach further acknowledges the complexity of providing support to children with ASD and recommends a multi-pronged strategy that is affordable and sustainable. When teachers feel supported by parents and the community, their confidence and commitment increase.

9.1 Introduction

Most teachers experience challenges in educating learners with additional needs, including those with ASD because they have not received any training to teach such children. They are often not able to cope with children with any perceived social, emotional, cultural, intellectual or linguistic difference or disability (Florian, Young & Rouse, 2010). As a result, they often feel overwhelmed by the challenges that learners with additional needs bring into their classrooms. This feeling of despondency affects their social agency for social justice. Therefore, there is a need for concerted efforts from the ′tripartite alliance′ of parents, community members and teachers to teach children with additional needs. Otherwise, the task of educating these children may be overwhelming (Goudie, Havercamp, Ranbom & Jamieson, 2011). According to the existing scholarship, where such partnerships exist, parents and teachers experience social and emotional benefits of inclusion as well as positive educational outcomes (Murray, Ackerman-Spain, Williams & Ryley, 2011; Rodríguez, Saldaña & Moreno, 2012). Both parents and teachers have acknowledged the need for a shared commitment among all involved parties. Parents reported that positive attitudes toward persons with disabilities were essential to successful inclusion while teachers focused on the need for enhanced support and resources.

However, despite empirical evidence from a few studies, especially those related to ASD, previous research has not focused on the practical application of this relationship. Parents and community members continue to be marginalised in the promotion of an inclusive society. In countries where policy makers have attempted to add a dimension of parents' perceptions on the inclusion of all learners, there has been marked progress. Studies reveal that parents tend to support the concept of inclusion from a legal and philosophical standpoint (Nes, Demo & Ianes, 2017). Researchers have further identified social and emotional outcomes among the benefits of Inclusive Education. The problem of side lining parents and community members in the education of children with additional needs is not limited to developing countries. Instead, the marginalisation of parents is common in many educational systems in both developing and developed countries (Booth & Ainscow, 2002).

The findings of existing studies suggest that the problem calls for in-service training in various areas, accompanied by increased support to promote inclusion (Buell, Hallam, Gamel-Mccormick, 2010). Whereas this might be true to a certain extent, there is also a need to tap into the collective resource that parents and community members might provide in the teaching and learning situation. In particular, some studies highlight the benefits that could accrue from partnering with parents and communities in promoting Inclusive Education (Leyser & Kirk, 2007). More specifically, these studies fall short of exploring inclusive pedagogy (Florian & Black-Hawkins, 2011) to enhance teachers' craft knowledge of their practice of inclusion that leverages parents and community linkages and partnerships. Teachers' display positive attitudes towards inclusion when they receive external support (Norwich & Avramidis, 2002). This calls for a broadened conceptual understanding of Inclusive Education as a key principle to attain and sustain quality EFA (UNESCO, 2009). If this ideal can be achieved by building an inclusive society, where children can live together without any fear, such a culture should be inculcated at school. The purpose of education is to prepare for life, so inclusion in education prepares for inclusion in society. It is therefore essential that all children should be taught to participate freely in school without any fear. In the following section, I reflect on theoretical frameworks that could provide a lens for understanding social models of inclusion.

9.2 Social theories underpinning pedagogic responsiveness for ASD children

Limited progress in strengthening partnerships between parents, communities and teachers, in teaching children with ASD could be attributed to the description and explanation of such relationships based on the medical model, rather than the social model of inclusion. Contrary to the medical model, the social model places emphasis on valuing and understanding the complexities, multiplicity and intersectionality in which children with ASD and teachers find themselves. Furthermore, the social model affords teachers to understand how diversity (such as ASD) hierarchies and institutionalised oppressive pedagogical practices are constructed and sustained by the powerful.

The social model allows an understanding that social class relationships shape the manner in which we approach communication with parents, teachers and community members. For example, Bernstein's (1971) model of the two types of schools, namely, instrumental and expressive provides a useful analysis for understanding schools as simultaneously concerned with the transmission of (i) formal knowledge and skills , and (ii) values and norms in order to develop particular kinds of conduct and character traits. This understanding of how schools function gives us insight into schools as potentially divisive, since they consciously construct patterns of success and failure. For example, children with ASD could be designated lower societal positions, consciously or unconsciously because of their disability or differences.

Therefore, this chapter explores the importance of parents and community partnerships in educating a child with ASD as a possible pedagogy that elevates the importance of parents and the community in educating children. I begin by arguing that parental and community partnerships are the key building blocks in realising Inclusive EFA children. Then I present arguments in favour of partnerships, since the scholarship suggests that failure to involve parents and community members hampers Inclusive Education for children with ASD. In addition, I provide suggestions that could make these types of relationships more meaningful and effective. For example, how to build community capacity of school-based management through committee, parent-teacher-associations, school governing bodies, which could establish and monitor programmes that promote quality education for children with ASD and other differences.

9.3 Parents and school partnerships

A plethora of studies such as those conducted by Ames (1999) and Sharpe, Swee and Heng (1995) on the relationship between parents, community and teachers have identified multiple benefits associated with positive working relations among these three groups of stakeholders. For example, Ames (1999) reports that when parents are provided with information about classroom work and practices, information about their own children's work and progress, and receive assistance to work with their children on schoolwork at home, parents' sense of efficacy improves and they feel comfortable with the school. I therefore argue as others do (cf. Hill, 2001; Goudie, Havercamp, Ranbom & Jamieson, 2011) that this relationship has not fully been leveraged to assist teachers who are faced with children with ASD in their classrooms. Inclusion and parent involvement are considered best practice in early childhood education. Yet few empirical studies have focused on the practical application of these concepts. Most parents reported that they felt a high degree of involvement in the team. Teachers generally indicated positive attitudes toward parent involvement.

There are several ways in which parents and community members could help the school to cope with the challenges associated with the implementation of inclusion, especially since children with ASD rank among the most likely to be excluded. They could for example, help improve equitable access to and enrolment in schools regardless of children's backgrounds or abilities. For example, a community could ensure equality among children by providing equal conditions to participate in the teaching and the learning process, regardless of backgrounds and their abilities. They could do this for example, by reaching out to all children, especially those marginalised and vulnerable to exclusion. This will mitigate against children with ASD from being excluded from the education system.

School should priortise communication and keep parents and community members informed about their children's school attendance. This is especially important for children from diverse backgrounds and those with diverse abilities. Armed with such information, parents and community members could offer valuable assistance to the school and teachers by providing resources and ideas that could assist the Inclusive Education agenda. For example, schools should initiate partnerships with parents and other communities organisations such as churches, NGOs and traditional leaders.

To make this ideal possible, teachers should understand the roles and responsibilities of parents and teachers in educating children irrespective of which section of the community they come from. In addition, teachers could also be taught to value and respect the role of parents in teaching children with ASD. This could be possible if they are trained to develop and build relationships and partnerships with them (Corman, 2009). Where such ties exist, parents have reported positive attitudes toward inclusion and resources.

9.4 Community and school partnerships in teaching children with autism

Besides parent relationships, teachers of children with autism could benefit significantly from partnering with diverse community organisations such as faith-based groups, including churches and other religious organisations, NGOs, traditional leaders and the others in tackling the problem jointly. This model has been applied in communities where problems of poverty, crime and bereavement were overcome through a collective effort. For example, where communities are vulnerable and experience stress over a period of time, such communities have come together to overcome their challenges (Ebersöhn, 2012). They use their problem to unite them like buffalos joining together to fight a lion. Recently, South Africa has experienced numerous cases of mass mobilisation where people act collectively to protest against poor service delivery by government.

Just as South African communities and schools have in the past galvanised to confront chronic and cumulative adversity (poverty childhood adversity, elevated health problems), systematic inequalities and prejudices (racism, sexism, ethnocentrism, historical oppression), the same model could be adopted by teachers to accommodate the complex learning needs of learners with autism. It is the community's responsibility to ensure that learners with autism have access to quality education. This can happen if there is a political will to do so A correct mind-set could be created to see autism as a form of diversity rather than an abnormality or disability (Clasquin-Johnson & Clasquin-Johnson, 2018).

In South Africa and elsewhere in the world, the establishment of community and school partnerships are possible given the legislative and policy environment. This enabling environment has been made possible by the Salamanca Statement (1994), United Nations Convention on the Rights of People With Disabilities (2006), Constitution of the Republic of South Africa (1996), White Paper 6 on Special Needs Education (2001) and the Screening Identification Assessment and Support Strategy (SIASS) (2014), affords every child equitable access to quality education. These policy documents envision the provision of quality EFA children in an education and training system that respects and responds effectively to the diverse learning needs of every child (Dreyer, 2015).

Some schools already implement the logic of these policy and legislative frameworks as guides to creative enabling environments that accommodate children in their pedagogical practices. However, there are others that are still lagging behind, by resisting the call for inclusivity by ratcheting up externally imposed discipline, enforced by police and security personnel.

While some schools implemented the logic of these enabling environments and leveraged their schools programmes on them, others have responded by resisting change. This reactive approach reflect three factors:

- a punitive mind-set that rejects research demonstrating the ineffectiveness of reactive and punitive approaches (Osher, Bear, Sprague & Doyle, 2010);
- the lack of willingness and readiness staff and school capacity to address the needs of learners with diversity, especially those who have experienced the adversities of poverty and trauma; and
- implicit discrimination like children with autism, which created disparities in terms of who experienced exclusionary practices.

Where these policies have been implemented positively, they have managed to enable schools to create developmentally appropriate, innovative teaching methods (pedagogies) to meet the needs of learners with autism. Unfortunately, these practices are seldom shared with other schools in the neighbourhood. This chapter aims to highlight and promote these good practices.

Partnering with communities can be a problem in most African communities where individualism is frowned upon and collective support is valued (Gunnsted, 2006; Phasha, 2010; Theron & Phasha, 2015). The concept of Ubuntu as an African philosophy (see also the Introduction to this volume) can be described as the elevation and promotion of the values and principles that promote human rights, social justice and inclusivity, which underlay humanness and the value of community. In this philosophy, no one is supposed to suffer or struggle alone when others in the surroundings have the means to help. It is here where the expression: *motho ke motho ka batho* (a person is a person because of others) finds its place.

Teachers as mobilisers of schools (as an organisational structure) and community could leverage upon such cosmologies to build a Relationship-Resourced Resilience (RRR) they could turn schools to be enabling environments. A view of curriculum as a cultural construct could be used to foster partnerships and ownership of the school.

9.5 Partnerships with other professionals in teaching children with autism

Another area where schools or teachers could collaborate to maximise their capacity to teach children with autism is with professional specialists. These could include medical practitioners (doctors, nurses and psychiatrists), social workers, and other related specialists such as speech and occupational therapists. These professional services are often expensive to acquire and are only afforded by private schools, which are inaccessible to public schools. It is here where schools or teachers should be responsive enough to foster relations or linkages where they could partner with business or other community organisations such as business and non-governmental organisations to source funding for creating effective schools. There are a few examples of good practice where schools partner with the business community (such as mines and banks) to alleviate the adversity of poverty.

Other than relying on donations that might not be sustainable, these specialists could be encouraged to donate some of their time as part of their community engagement at schools by offering their services. For example, doctors, nurses, educational psychologists, therapists and pastors rendering much-needed services that my assist teachers cope with the burden of things that are not trained to do.

9.6 Partnerships with other stakeholder in the school in teaching children with autism

Much assistance could be harnessed from fellow teachers and other related structures including School Based Support Teams (SBSTs) and District Based Support Teams (DBSTs). These department of education support structures within the school environment are often not maximised to their full potential because they are often misconstrued as a burden by teachers who are overladen with barrage of policies and much paper work to contend with. However, where they are used correctly and not just for compliance, they can yield much fruit. Studies such as those conducted by Modipane and Themane (2014) have demonstrated that where the social capital of teachers is leveraged for curriculum development, teachers feel more empowered and resilient to face adverse conditions. Similarly, Thobejane (2017) found that where teachers collaborate with other stakeholders (SBSTs and DBSTs) and school governing bodies (SGBs) in the implementation of full-service schools, there is remarkable success.

Teachers could form teams and communities of practice with other senior teachers in a number of ways. For example, in the use for ICT in meeting the needs of diverse children, working together with other teachers to monitor Individual Support Plans (ISP) of learners as a strategy to include diverse learners.

9.7 Conclusion

This chapter has considered how partnerships with parents and communities offer an alternative strategy for facilitating access to quality education for children with autism. I have argued against individualistic models which isolate teachers in teaching children with autism. A collaborative approach to teaching these children could afford them improved protection, health, nutrition and care compared to a reliance on individualistic approaches.

References

Ames, C. K., Hoju, M., & Watkins, T. (1993). *Teacher's school-to-home communication and parent involvement: The role of parent perceptions and beliefs (Report #15)*. Baltimore. MD: Center on Families, Communities, Schools, and Children's Learning.

Ames, C. (1995). Teachers' School-to-Home Communications and Parent Involvement: The Role of Parent Perceptions and Beliefs. Report No. 28.

Barbour, C., Barbour, N., & Scully, P. A. (2008). *Families, schools, and communities: Building partnerships for educating children.* Prentice Hall.

Bennett, T., Deluca, D. & Bruns, D. (1997). Putting inclusion into practice: Perspectives of teachers and parents. *Exceptional Children*, 64(1): 115-131.

Booth, T. & Ainscow, M. (2002). *Index for inclusion: Developing learning and participation in schools*. Centre for Studies on Inclusive Education (CSIE), Rm 2S203 S Block, Frenchay Campus, Coldharbour Lane, Bristol BS16 1QU, United Kingdom, England.

Butler, J. M. (1992). Effective Parent Involvement Strategies as Identified by Parents, Administrators, and Teachers. https://eric.ed.gov/?id=ED355027

Clasquin-Johnson, M.G. & Clasquin-Johnson, M. (2018). How deep are your pockets? Autoethnographic reflections on the cost of raising a child with autism. *African Journal of Disability*, 7(1).

Corman, M. (2009). The positives of caregiving: Mothers' experiences caregiving for a child with autism. *Families in Society: The Journal of Contemporary Social Services*, 90(4): 439-445.

Davies, D. (1996b). *Partnerships for student success*. Baltimore, MD: Center on Families, Communities, Schools, and Children's Learning.

Davies, D. (1997). Crossing boundaries: How to create successful partnership with families and communities. *Early Childhood Education Journal*, 25(1): 73-77.

Dreyer, L. M. (2015). Experiences of parents with children diagnosed with reading difficulties. *Southern African Review of Education with Education with Production*, 21(1): 94-111.

Ebersöhn, L. & Loots, T. (2017). Teacher agency in challenging contexts as a consequence of social support and resource management. *International Journal of Educational Development*, 53: 80-91.

Epstein, J. L. & Dauber, S. L. (1991). School programs and teacher practices of parent involvement in inner-city elementary and middle schools. *The Elementary School Journal*, 91(3): 289-305.

Goudie, A., Havercamp, S., Ranbom, L. & Jamieson, B. (2011). Caring for children with disabilities in Ohio: the impact on families. Unpublished Manuscript.

Gunnestad, A. (2006). Resilience in a Cross-Cultural Perspective: How resilience is generated in different cultures. *Journal of Intercultural Communication* 11 (2006).

Kagan, S. L., Neville, P. & Rustic, J. (1993). *Family education and training: From research to practice (Report #14).* Baltimore, MD: Center on Families, Communities, Schools, and Children's Learning.

Malcolm-Smith, S., Hoogenhout, M., Ing, N., Thomas, K. G. & de Vries, P. (2013). Autism spectrum disorders—Global challenges and local opportunities. *Journal of Child & Adolescent Mental Health*, 25(1): 1-5.

Modipane, M. & Themane, M. (2014). Teachers' social capital as a resource for curriculum development: Lessons learnt in the implementation of a Child-Friendly Schools programme. *South African Journal of Education*, 34(4): 1-8.

Murray, M. M., Ackerman-Spain, K., Williams, E. U. & Ryley, A. T. (2011). Knowledge is power: Empowering the autism community through parent-professional training. *School Community Journal*, 21(1): 19.

Nes, K., Demo, H. & Ianes, D. (2017). Inclusion at risk? Push-and pull-out phenomena in inclusive school systems: The Italian and Norwegian experiences. *International Journal of Inclusive Education*, 1-19.

Phasha, T.N. (2010). Educational resilience among African survivors of child sexual abuse in South Africa. *Journal of Black Studies*, 40(6): 1234-1253.

Osher, D., Bear, G. G., Sprague, J. R. & Doyle, W. (2010). How can we improve school discipline? *Educational Researcher*, 39(1): 48-58.

Seely, D. S. (1981). *Education through partnership*. Washington, DC: American Enterprise Institute.

Shirvani, H. (2007). Effects of teacher communication on parents 'attitudes and their children's behaviours at schools. *Education*, 128(1): 34.

Sibiya, S.N.K. (2011). Teachers' and parents' perceptions of their relationship: a case study of two secondary schools in Ubombo circuit, KwaZulu-Natal (Doctoral dissertation).

Swart, E. & Phasha, T. (2005). *Family and community partnerships. Addressing barriers to learning: a South African perspective*. Pretoria: Van Schaik.

Tatto, M. T., Rodriguez, A., Gonzalez-Lantz, D., Miller, C., Busscher, M., Trumble, D. & Woo, A. (2001). The challenges and tensions in reconstructing teacher-parent relations in the context of school reform: A case study. *Teachers and Teaching*, 7(3): 315-333.

Theron, L. C. & Phasha, N. (2015). Cultural pathways to resilience: Opportunities and obstacles as recalled by black South African students. In *Youth resilience and culture* (pp. 51-65). Springer Netherlands.

Thobejane, H. R. (2017). Towards an inclusive model for teacher education on the implementation of Inclusive Education in full service schools of Limpopo Province. University of Limpopo, PhD thesis. Polokwane. University of Limpopo.

Watkins, T. J. (1997). Teacher communications, child achievement, and parent traits in parent involvement models. *The Journal of Educational Research*, 91(1): 3-14.

Zaidman-Zait, A. & Curle, D. (2016). Complexity: An interpretative phenomenological analysis of the experiences of mothers of deaf children with cochlear implants and autism. *Journal of Health Psychology*, 23(9):1173-1184.

10

ASD: ADOLESCENTS AND SEXUAL EXPERIENCES IN RURAL MPUMALANGA

Joyce Mcgogo

Abstract

Adolescence is viewed as a critical period of sexual scouting and experimenting between fantasies and realities. Experiences of adolescents with ASD of coping with demands of growing-up, and sexual puberty issues are scarce. Sexuality education is an important developmental task during adolescents influenced by hormonal puberty body changes. As a result, adolescents with autism develop sexually in the same way as their peer age group, but may require extra help to build the social skills and maturity that go along with sexual development of puberty. The sexuality education needs of adolescence with ASD are unique; and are not adequately addressed in the existing curriculum on sexuality education programmes. An issue of sexuality education is only implemented when behaviour is demonstrated that is considered deviant or problematic. Adolescent learners with ASD are often viewed as innocent and the need for sexuality education may be overlooked and ignored by both parents and teachers. Parents and teachers fear engaging discussions on sexuality issues; that it will increase sexual experimentation with ASD adolescents. Adolescents with ASD have sexual needs but may not understand their physical and emotional development experience if not guided.

Keywords: Autism Spectrum Disorder; sexuality education and parents

10.1 Introduction

This chapter aims to provide understanding and explore existing knowledge and experiences on sexuality-related issues among adolescents with ASD in the South African context. ASD is a complex disorder with varying presentations of cognitive, social and behaviour denial school (Hayward & Saunders, 2010). Existing literature focuses more on people with intellectual disabilities than on people with ASD. This chapter therefore emphasises the importance and right to education and adequate information on sexuality-related issues for people with ASD.

There is a growing consensus on the importance of thinking about comprehensive sexuality education (CSE) as a normative and positive aspect of child and adolescent development (International Technical Guideline on Sexuality Education, 2018). This requires understanding of interaction between ASD and the development domain of comprehensive sexuality education. The role of comprehensive sexuality education in development and daily functionality of adolescents' including ASDs has been recognised as an important component of adolescent health intervention (World Health Organization (WHO), 2017). Skills on these domains are important for sexual development as normative and positive aspect of adolescent developmental experiences which includes pleasure, safety, respect, privacy, and rights. The absence of these domains leads to acquisition of diseases such as HIV and AIDS, sexually transmitted infections, coerhion and discrimination (UNESCO, 2018). A study conducted in Netherlands among adolescent boys with ASD (Dewinter, Vermeiren, Vanwesenbeeck, van Nieuwenhuizen, 2016) report that parents of children with ASD were less inclined to discuss issues of sexuality with their children if they believed that their child's condition involved a sexual relationship. Parents expressed concern of uncertainty about, what, how and when to start talking to their children about sexuality issues (Ballan, 2012). This uncertainty may be owing to a combination of lack of knowledge about sexual development in adolescents with ASD, lack of awareness or underestimation of their adolescent child's sexual experience.

The right of all children to formal education is asserted by numerous international organisations. UNESCO (2014) affirms an obligation to respect, protect and fulfil the right and needs of all learners in education irrespective of gender, race and disability. The Sustainable Development Goal 3 (SDG), (UN, 2015) on health promotion calls for access to sexual and reproductive health-care services, information and education, including family planning and integration of family health programmes into national strategies. SDG is aligned to SDG 4 on education and calls for inclusive and equitable quality education and lifelong learning opportunities for all by 2030. It emphasises inclusion as a foundation for quality education and learning, and being sensitive to the developmental needs of learners and adolescents with multiple developmental disabilities – including autistic children with ASD. The Education For All initiative (UNESCO, 1990) marked a global movement towards providing basic education to all children, young and adults including learners with multiple developmental disabilities such as autistic children. This initiative proposed six specific goals which include the provision of learning and life skills programmes for young and adults and improvement of all aspects of education in order to provide quality EFA. South Africa, as a signatory to this mandate, ensured that policies were established for implementation purposes.

The National Adolescent Sexual and Reproductive Health and Right Framework Strategy, (2014-2019) is a response to SDG3 (UN, 2015). It serves as an action guide to create and support a responsive policy and planning environment to meet the sexual reproductive health and right of adolescents especially taking cognisance of those with different sexual orientations and those with multiple developmental disabilities. This requires understanding learners' diverse needs including their sexualities as a right to human development. However, sexuality has been neglected in policies and fails to address the needs of young adolescents with multiple developmental disabilities such as ASD.

10.2 Sexuality education and ASD

Few young adolescents receive adequate preparation for their sexual lives. This leaves them potentially vulnerable to coercion, abuse and exploitation, unintended pregnancy and sexually transmitted infections (STIs) including HIV. These young people including those with ASD are faced with conflicting messages about their sexualities (UNESCO, 2014). This is exacerbated by embarrassment, silence and unwillingness to discuss sexual issues with adults including teachers at the very same time when it is highly desired and needed in their lives.

South African adolescents, like the youth from elsewhere in the world, are undergoing a developmental transition in a rapidly changing social, economic, political and emotional climate (Reddy, James & Sewpaul, 2013). Adolescents are constantly exposed to risky sexual behaviours which promote early sexual initiation, sexual experimentation, promiscuity, exploration resulting in unplanned pregnancy and substance abuse including adolescents with ASD. This is a period of complex transition and difficult time for all adolescents; it is especially tough for teens who struggle to understand ever changing social and physical expectations in their environment. Adolescents with ASD have unique challenges that are often hard for parents and teachers as well as peers to understand, particularly on sexuality related issues. The problems of adolescents' sexual behaviour including adolescents with developmental disabilities (ASD) are sensitive. Many people believe that it is inappropriate to talk about sexual issues with young adolescents and fear that it will encourage risky sexual behaviour as reported in the Youth Risk Behaviour Survey conducted in the nine provinces (Reddy, James & Sewpaul, 2013). Therefore, in attempting to address these emerging risk sexual behaviours comprehensively, the National Adolescent Sexual and Reproductive Health and Rights Framework Strategy (2014-2019) provides priority guidelines for adolescents with ASD.

10.3 Why is sexuality education important?

Sexuality education is a fundamental aspect of human life. It has physical, spiritual, social, economic, political and cultural dimensions. Too many young people receive confusing and conflicting information about sexual related issues as they make transition from childhood to adolescence. This has led to increasing demand from young people for reliable information which prepares them for safe productive and fulfilling life for all adolescents when taught well in schools. Sexuality education is a critical part of prevention against early unintended pregnancies, gender based violence, HIV and STIs, which pose serious risks to the well-being of adolescents (UNESCO, 2014). Lack of quality, age and developmentally appropriate sexuality education may lead adolescents ASD vulnerable to harmful sexual behaviours and sexual exploitation. According to UNESCO (2018), sexuality education programmes have several mutual reinforcing objectives and emphasise that:

- Sexuality education has positive effects including increasing adolescents' knowledge and improving their attitude related to sexual reproductive health and behaviour.
- Gender programmes are substantially more effective at achieving health outcomes such as reducing unintended pregnancies and STIs.
- Sexuality education has the most impact when school-based programmes are complemented with involvement of parents and linked to youth friendly services.

The White Paper on the Right of Persons with Disabilities (2016) further reinforces all children should access age appropriate quality education including sexuality issues to adolescent boys and girls with developmental disabilities. Adolescents with ASD experience considerable scrutiny from their parents, teachers and peers who are non-disabled concerning their perceived differences of their functionality. Adolescents with disabilities are viewed as inferior with no sexual desires and intimacy feelings. Their expression of sexual behaviour is frowned, pitied and protected from being harmed. Such practices violate international conventions and national policies designed for all South Africans to access quality education regardless of gender or disability. If adolescents ASD are discriminated, the results can have serious consequences; STI including HIV transmission and unintended pregnancy. Most often, these adolescents may have limitation in advocating for themselves and ensuring that their best interests on sexualities issues are prioritised.

Traditionally, the sexual lives of people with disabilities including autism have been actively disregarded and socially stigmatised. Robison, Smith and Davies (2016) ascertained that children's and adolescent's sexuality in school and families is plagued with tension and controversies. These stem largely from cultural practices that perpetuate that sexuality education is irrelevant, developmentally inappropriate, risky and dangerous for the adolescents. Consequently, adolescent access to sexuality is severely compromised in terms of age and content taught. Today's society is secret-less with children finding out about things from many sources, not all reliable. Consequently, they need help in learning how to process the many messages about sexuality they may receive each day from many sources such media and cell phones. The topic was constantly avoided because of its taboo and it was difficult to address. Esmail, Darry, Walter and Knupp, (2009) suggest that sexuality as form of pleasure and expression of love is still not recognised for adolescents with ASD. It is considered a private and personal matter that no one should invade. These problems have stemmed from many aspects of society and misconception surrounding ASD and the teaching of sexuality education programmes.

Sexuality education is viewed as a developmental task for all children and adolescents including ASD. Research studies, according to Adams, Edelson, Grandin, Rumland and Jones (2012), have ascertained that ASDs affect young adolescents differently. In less severe cases on the spectrum, these children may even be intellectually gifted but have social interaction and behaviour problems with delayed language/speech development extending into sexual development skills and risk sexual behaviours. These adolescents become aware of their autism and how it affects their lives and the gap between their developing peers. They can even struggle with minor changes in their bodies.

Nevertheless, the display of such characteristics does not mean that all autistic young adolescents present such characteristics. Each adolescent is unique and differ according to their level of functionality. Core functionality of skills in these domains are important for sexual development and health. There is growing consensus on the importance of thinking about adolescent and sexual behaviour of the autistic young adolescent (UNESCO, 2018; Tolman & McClelland, 2011).

10.4 Autism in the South African context

It is a grave concern that children with multiple developmental disabilities on the African continent face barriers to learning for a multitude of reasons (Dalton, McKenzie &

Kahonde 2011). In the South African context, this has resulted in a massive exclusion of disabled children including ASD from education and sexuality-related issues (Department of Education [DoE], 2001). However, the provision of EFA learners including those with ASD is enshrined in the Constitution of the Republic of South Africa, Act No. 108 of 1996 (Parliament, 1996). In Section 29 (Bill of Rights), it is stated that everyone has a right to basic education. The adoption of an Inclusive Education system is laid out in Education White Paper 6 Policy (DoE, 2001) that attempts to address the diverse needs of all learners experiencing barriers in the education system. However, despite the development of an Inclusive Education policy to address this exclusion, one of the issues that hamper progress is the lack of teachers' skills in adapting the curriculum to meet the range of learning needs of all learners including sexual development of the young adolescent with ASD. The inclusive framework is based on a premise of belonging which spells out the agenda to facilitate quality EFA learners irrespective of characteristics or background. The policy further stipulates that all children, youth and adults have a potential to learn given the necessary support. Phasha, Mahlo & Maseko (2013) revealed that most teachers are not sufficiently trained and unable to appropriately respond to diverse needs of Inclusive Education. These teachers need support and reorientation as a fundamental shift in their mind-sets and attitudes towards teaching of sexuality education in an inclusive class.

The Screening, Identification, Assessment Support (SIAS) strategy (Department of Education, 2008) provides guidelines for responding to diverse needs of all learners by defining the process of identification and assessment of learners to determine the nature of support required for individual learners including ASD learners and their sexual needs. Hence, the Curriculum Assessment Policy Statement (CAPS) (Department of Basic Education, 2011) has been re-drafted to incorporate curriculum changes to accommodate gaps identified on the teaching of sexuality education in South African Schools. Kirby (2011) recommends scripted lessons as a practical guideline for responding to sexuality education of all learners. Glover and Macleod (2016) report that sexual development normally focuses chiefly on negative consequences messages aspects of young people engaging in sex, namely, the possibility of sexually transmitted diseases and HIV, sexual violence and pregnancy. According to Glover and Macleod (2016), sex is characterised as something that is harmful, risky and dangerous.

Arguably, little attention is paid to positive sexual messages that provide pleasurable aspects of sexualities including desire, fulfilment and warmth. Ideally, sexually education needs to start before puberty and continue throughout adolescence. Sexuality cannot be separated from the emotional and social development of the adolescent. This requires understanding of ASD's sexual developmental aspect of sexuality which includes different themes such as privacy, privaty body parts and personal hygiene, masturbation, relationsships, sexual relationships, HIV and STI's.

10.5 Ubuntu theoretical framework

Sexuality education is confined to the home and family; social and cultural norms create an environment of Ubuntu. Ubuntu is a South African concept which claims its origin from 'Bantu' and embraces mutual understanding and the value of human dignity that include values such as love, respect, acceptance, tolerance and compassion.

In South Africa Lefa (2015) describes Ubuntu as a value of humanness towards others, acceptance and mutual caring with compassion and proving age appropriate information including sexuality education. Ubuntu plays a significant role in building communities and societies that reflect diversity and inclusivity during puberty stage of cultural initiation periods and sexulity matters among the adolescence. Teaching of comprehensive sexuality education is part humanness that is cultural and traditional fibre of Ubuntu. Letseka (2013) contends that Ubuntu prevails as moral theory in the society and it brings Africans in touch with awareness of their traditional realities and identity of sexuality education practices from birth through adulthood.

This concept of Ubuntu has been widely theorised in different practices of cultural and traditional values across communities (Berghs, 2017; Letsteka, 2013; Metz, 20 11; Mahlo, 2016; Phasha & Moichela, 2011; Shanyanana & Waghid, 2016). The concept of Ubuntu is found in almost in all African languages under various names. Shanyanan and Waghid (2016) affirm that Ubuntu is used in several Bantu languageses. In West Africa, 'Sankofa' means reclaiming powers of social practices and indigenous knowledge from colonial powers. It turns to historical traditions and takes the African cultural perspective of teaching sexuality with reference to adolescence on developmental disabilities. Sankofa and Ubuntu are similar in that they are both founded in indigenous thought and practise African lifestyle (Gbewonyo, 2017). This is an approach of reclaiming back the contours of sexuality education and re-assessing seclusion practices that narrowed oportunities of equipping young ASD adolescents with sexuality education as a basic human right of all children regardless of race and disability. Adolescents with ASD are often discriminated to participate on community dialogues and discussions on sexuality education issues such as HIV, STI and contraceptives because of cultural attitudes, beliefs and practices which has been doctrinated by the West.

Ubuntu in the context of comprehensive sexuality involves creating a climate where adolescent boys and girls are free from any form of abuse, where teachers are viewed as trusted and accessible sources of information and advice on individual problems related to sexual issues such as HIV, STI and abuse.

The White Paper 6 policy, building an Inclusive Education and training system (2001), requires that all learners irrespective of race, gender, class, religion, disability, HIV/AIDS status or culture have a right to access education and acknowledges that all children can learn with support. In the same vein, the National Curriculum Statement (NCS), (2002) and CAPS (2011) have the general aims and principles that reveal Ubuntu. Similarly, Lefa (2015) asserts that principles stated by policy documents; equality, kindness, and human rights, inclusivity environment, infusing principles and practices of human rights and these values of Ubuntu and inclusivity are contained in White Paper 6 which supports practices of humanness.

Case study 1

Thabi, a learner support agent, has been contracted to work in the full service school in mixed ability class of learners with ASD between the ages of 10-15 years to provide life skills activity. Teacher Thabi was excited on the new task but soon realised that the class was experiencing challenges of growing up. Big boys were chasing, squeezing and touching girls quite often during play time. She then conducted an activity on puberty. This was to promote body awareness and responsible behaviour. Learners were divided according to their age group and the following items were used appropriately. She showed the young person pictures of different rooms. Asked them to match the rooms with different activities such as eating, washing and watching TV. Teacher Thabi stressed that if a boy and a girl are washing taking off their clothes and or touching their private parts, they need to be in a private place or room and shut the door. They should not allow others to touch them and should report uncomfortable situations to their parents and teachers. After the lesson, Vuyiswa a 14 year old girl reported to Teacher Thabi that some boys were touching her breast in the bus when they go home and mentioned Thabo a 15 year boy. She went on to say, he shows me things I don't know on the cell phone and she started sobbing. This was not surprising on teacher Thabi's side because she had already observed Thabo's frequent touch and pushing girls' inappropriately. Vuyiswa went on to say she now come to school by public transport because she afraid of Thabo. The teacher was not aware of this development. Vuyiswa's mother was invited to school and told teacher Thabi that she knows that her daughter is innocent and young and to protect her from boys put her in a public transport while arranging with a relative to stay near the school. She said, 'I want to move Vuyiswa away from Thabo because that boy is pushy and always walking together'. It transpired that the parent has not spoken anything about growing up with her adolescent girl. On engaging with Vuyiswa's parent it was clear that Vuyiswa's association with boys was viewed with innocent attitude. The mother had mixed feelings about her daughter because she's different from the other adolescent girls in the classroom and she doesn't fit well with other girls. She is more of a loner; so, she makes friends with Thabo which can be dangerous for her age. Both parents were invited to assist their young adolescents to cope with the body transition to adolescence. Each parent had a story about her/his child. Parents started engaging with their children on dangers of touching girls walking with boys. The talk was more of a warning to their children. Vuyiswa went back to the scholar transport and Thabo was distant and respected her. Now they are in the nearby secondary school. They know their boundaries, like they know there are things they should not do until they are adults.

All children have rights and needs relating to their sexuality – the right to privacy, the right to access age appropriate information, the right to dignity, the need to express sexual feelings with dignity and the right to be free from sexual exploitation. Both boys and girls need to be guided like all growing into adulthood.

10.6 Understanding human sexuality in the African context

From an African perspective, human sexuality would mean the attitudes, values and relationships that Africans attach to human interactions according to their cultural understanding. African indigenous culture had no hang-ups with sexuality. However, Bayer (2011) contends that owing to the development of society, sexual practices have become a complex issue. Norms and values regarding sexual behaviour change with time, creating confusion in those who want to conform to them. In this regard, we are all shaped by our culture and life experience and our behaviour is determined by what we are taught. Although sexuality is traditionally associated with pleasure, it is contrasted with realities and dangers in society, such as sexually transmitted diseases, HIV and rape. This contrast could cause adolescents with autism to find it difficult to experience sexuality in a positive way. Okeke, Van Wyk and Phasha (2014) assert that indigenous knowledge is an important concept in the African practice that sustains knowledge and skills possessed by a particular community and enables them to get on with their lives within a particular geographical set up. Issues of education including sexuality-related matters were Africanised as a philosophy of Ubuntu that was characterised by people supporting one another within their communities.

In the South African context, Buthelezi (2004) argues that the Zulu nation had a holistic understanding of sexuality. Sexuality begins at birth with every child and is marked by distinct phases of development impacted by the cultural practices, customs and traditions of the society. Hence society has a responsibility to ensure that the social context supports the regulatory system and assists adolescents and individuals to understand the stages of growth in relation to their human sexuality. With regard to sexuality, the Zulu culture has many public ritual ceremonies and discourses that discuss sexuality issues relating to stages of development such as puberty for boys and girls. During this period, the community openly addresses sexuality through educational dances, songs, talks and offering advice on adolescence. This cultural practice includes the young adolescent with developmental disabilities like ASD.

Therefore, throughout a young person's life, sexual conduct is addressed and the youth are strictly observed and guided on sexual behaviour. Reddy, James and Sewpaul (2013) contend that sexuality issues among the Zulu culture are appreciated and recognise the physical needs of the growing body and the changes that occur in young people's bodies during adolescence. In this regard, human sexuality and relationships among young people are allowed but kept within well-defined social control. However, the issue of sexuality education has become an exceptionally controversial one. The mere mention of sexuality education gives rise to many questions, but before one can ask questions there needs to be clarification and definition. The discourse on value in sexuality education is firmly grounded on the South African Constitution and the Bill of Rights that provide the rationale for Curriculum diversity emphasising the value for human difference. Arguably, Francis (2013) indicates that the inclusion of social and moral value hygiene practices in traditional cultures focussed on prevention of diseases. Such practices of teaching moral values encouraged teachers to be selective on sexuality topics (McGogo, 2016). Francis (2013) further asserted that such practices compromised and undermined comprehensive sexuality education which is right based for all children and adolescents irrespect of race, gender and disability.

Sexuality encompasses many things: the right to knowledge, love, identity, positive and adaptive behaviours, increase of self-understanding, self-esteem and self-determination. Hence, there is a need for adequate response to the rights, and proper sexuality education is very important to the wellbeing of youth and adolescents including those with ASD. In this regard, Dewinter, Vermeiren, Vanwesenbeeck and Nieuwehuizen (2013) recognise sexual development as part of life for with ASD of all developmental levels and the need for sexual expression regardless of ability. Travers and Tincani (2010) recognise the needs of persons with autism and other disabilities to understand and explore their sexual bodies, build and maintain relationships and engage in sexual behaviours. However, individuals with ASD are frequently excluded from sexual education.

10.7 Adolescents and sexual experiences and ASD

From the African context, the period of puberty and adolescence is a clear affirmation of sexuality that is good and welcomed with smiles of appreciation. This confirms the normality of human sexuality. Adolescence has long been characterised as a unique developmental period during which changes in physical, cognitive, social and emotional development occur rapidly. For adolescents with ASD, the normal challenges of adolescence are compounded by social and communication deficits that characterise the disorder (Loftin & Hartlage, 2015). Adolescents with ASD enter puberty at much the same time as their peers but this physical development is often not accompanied by concomitant cognitive and social maturation (Corona, Fox, Christodoulou & Wanock, 2016). As adolescents with ASD begin to explore sexuality and romantic relationships, challenges in social ability and communication can hinder the development of a comprehensive knowledge and understanding of physical body changes. Notably, Corona et al. (2016) further indicate that lack of knowledge and ability to develop meaningful social and romantic relationships can cause harm, risky sexual behaviour and embarrassment. Kalyva (2010) reports that young people and adolescents face difficulties in expressing their sexual interests and such inadequacy results in a socially inappropriate approach that is presented in the figure below:

Discrimination where to and frequency of certain sexual behaviours, public or private Having suitable personal hygine	→	Self-protection and preservation in relation to sexual exploitation	→	Difficulties experienced by individuals with ASD include sexual issues of masturbation and menstruation	→	Repetition of sexuality terms in appropriate contexts

Figure 10.1 Adolescent sexuality challenges. Adapted from Hayward and Saunders (2010)

People with ASD lack knowledge and understanding of functionality about their sexuality, and many of these above could be prevented if these adolescents are better educated about their bodies, sexuality and law (Hatton & Tector, 2010). Schools and institutions for children and adolescents with ASD focus mainly on academic progression but areas of sexuality education including teaching social behaviours and personal care must be specifically taught and learned early in life as preparation for puberty in order to ensure holistic maturation and progress towards adult life (Kalyva, 2010).

The South African inclusion initiative seeks learning models that allow for inclusive classroom differentiation, supporting the philosophy that all children and youth have the potential to learn within all bands of education and they all require support (DoE, 2001).

10.8 Sexual education

From the international perspective, WHO (2014; 2017), sexuality is defined as:

> A central aspect of being human throughout life and encompasses sex, gender identities and roles, sexual orientation, eroticism, intimacy and reproduction. Sexuality is experienced and expressed in thoughts, fantasies, desires, pleasure, beliefs, attitude, values, behaviours, practice, roles and relationships. While sexuality can include all of these dimensions, not all of them are always experienced or expressed particular by adolescents with autism. Sexuality is influenced by the interaction of biological, psychological, social, economic, political, cultural, ethical, legal, historical, religious and spiritual factors.

According to WHO (2014), sexuality is perceived as an important component of quality of life. Hence, young adolescents with ASD have a right to learn about relationships, parenthood and sexuality.

Sexuality development is an important phase of adolescence with hormonal changes at the start of puberty, body growth and sexual reproductive maturity, accompanied by a series of emotional, cognitive and behavioural transformations that mark the period of adolescence of a person's life (WHO, 2011). Human sexuality among the adolescents is often misperceived as referring to certain individuals without developmental disabilities (Kirby, 2009). However, individuals with ASD mature physically and sexually according to normal developmental stages but can have difficulties in developing social and emotional understanding (Hayward & Saunders, 2010). Hence, individuals with ASD present unique needs regarding sexuality-related issues. Experts such as Beddows and Brooks (2016) recognise that the persons with ASD need to explore their own bodies, build relationships, appreciate and engage in sexual behaviour. Such practices should not be viewed as taboo. However, individuals with ASD are frequently regarded as non-sexual.

In the same vein, UNESCO, (2018) further maintains that sexuality is the exploration of our bodies, images and relations with others. It is one of the most basic human instincts regardless of the level of ability; it is human to discover functionality of our bodies. Young adolescents with ASD are often taken for granted that they know or it is less important for them because of the nature of their condition. When working with individuals with multiple developmental disabilities, in particular with ASD, several methods of teaching and learning can be applied to accommodate diversity in the classroom. The following is an example of such an intervention.

Activity: This is me

Introducing them to the differences in bodies and correct names will help them better understand themselves when reaching or on puberty. List names to be learned:

Group 1. Head, Arms, Leg, Stomach, Feet, Hands, Fingers, Lips, Eyes, Nose, Hips, Breasts, Penis, Testicles, Pubic Area etc.

Group 2. They will paint and draw or create presentation of a boy or girl.

Group 3. Will create a body image of him/her or give the opportunity of learning through various times via magazines.

Different methods of learning assist the learner to understand and appreciate her/his body. This is the time she/he may open up and talk about sexual experiences, feelings and abuse or even ask questions about whatever she/he is going through. It is important to use different learning techniques to ensure that individuals with ASD are provided with expanded opportunities to understand and clearly define and enjoy the importance of the lesson. According to the Canada-South Africa Teacher Development Project (2005), it is the educator's role to adapt the curriculum and be sensitive to the content taught and its relevance to all learners including those individuals with ASD. This requires differentiation of teaching and learning instruction in order to meet the diverse learning needs of the individual learners. Teaching towards inclusion ensures effective participation, social interaction and communication at all levels.

10.10 Sexual behaviour and individuals with ASD

The influence of the characteristics of individuals with ASD on sexual development and relationships has been discussed and researched in different contexts (Dewinter, 2016;

Toman & McClelland, 2011). Travers and Tincani (2010) maintain that many problems among individuals with ASD can be linked to poor understanding of sexuality and an inability to appropriately express feelings of sexual desire. These individuals often lack the ability to learn in unstructured social situations regardless of the setting. The inability to learn social interaction skills is often misperceived by professionals and family members (Stokes & Kaur, 2005). Consequently, young adolescents with ASD may be viewed as sexually immature and no sexual orientation and desires. Chan and John (2012) assert that studies on sexuality education and awareness of ASD indicate negative experiences of sexuality education with issues of vulnerability, social anxiety and confused sexuality being predominant. The report suggests that mainstream sexual education is not sufficient for young adolescents with ASD and that specific methods and curriculum are necessary to meet their needs. Individuals with ASD require specific instruction with regards to sexual related issues and social skills education.

Case Study 2

Senzo is 12 years old and stays at Tjakastad with his mother, father and three siblings in a small mud shack. Senzo was once admitted to Marietjie Special School but owing behavioural problems he was expelled and admitted to Fr. Charles Full Service School. At Fr. Charles, they also found that Senzo was experiencing behavioural problems. Mrs Mkhonza who was Senzo's class teacher reported this to the Head of Department and some learners reported that, in the school bus, Senzo wanted to undress the girls and sleep with them.

Mrs Mkhonza completed a Support Needs Analysis 1 (SNA1) form and discovered that Senzo had been expelled from his previous school for the same problem. Mrs Mkhonza asked the Learner Support Agent (LSA) to visit Senzo's home. The LSA found that Senzo was staying in one small shack where there was no privacy. Notably, Senzo's behaviour of kissing and touching girls' breasts could have been observed in his home environment that had no privacy. His behaviour was multi-challenged, and he thought it was the correct thing to do to undress a girl and want to sleep with her. Mrs Mkhonza referred this case to School Based Support Team (SBST) for further intervention; SBST interviewed him and found that Senzo needs to be referred to the District Based Support Team (DBST). The results from the DBST indicated that such behaviours were associated with autism. The team debated the problem and decided that Senzo should not be placed in a special school as he was high-functioning and special schools were not appropriate to his needs. One official argued that all learners can learn provided differentiated support strategies are implemented after assessment. Senzo's report was sent back to the school and the class teacher was supported to provide expanded learning opportunities in order to support Senzo in his sexual behaviour through Curriculum Differentiation.

The class was taken through a body awareness lesson from the Life Skills Grade 6 text books on "Knowing your body". This provided all learners with an opportunity to talk about emotions and experiences in relation to their bodies. Senzo was able to share his sexual experiences and how he has been sexual abused by other boys during break in the toilet. To him, it was normal until this lesson was presented.

The provision of individualised education about caring for the human body is an important component for sexuality education. Travers and Ticani (2010) suggest topics of instruction that include body parts, desires, relationships, dating and reproductive health. Owing to language deficits, children with ASD may lack body awareness and its function. Therefore, it is important that children with ASD should be taught about the importance of their body parts and their functions. They should also be taught skills of protecting themselves from sexual exploitation: a) learning about what touch is acceptable and not acceptable in public; and b) how and when to report sexual abuse. Hayward and Saunders (2010) suggest that before teaching sexuality and social skills, individuals' preferences, strengths of communication should be assessed.

Sexuality education has influenced behaviours such as delaying sexual initiation, identifying risky sexual behaviour and increasing knowledge to make informed decisions on sexual related issues (UNAIDS, 2011). The case study below assists to understand the inclusion of young adolescents with ASD.

Case study 3

Njabulo is 16 years. He comes from Chief KJ Nkosi. He started coming to school at the age of 13. He was born after his mother had had three miscarriages which occurred at a mature pregnancy stage between five and six months. The birth of Njabulo restored joy and hopes in the family. However, it was short lived.

Birth History

From five months pregnancy, the mother was sick, resulting in her being in and out of hospital. Finally, she was given bed rest until delivery. She reported that "the birth was a breach delivery. He was born after three days of labour. At birth, he did not cry and from there I knew there was something wrong. Like a mother, I was concerned and moved from hospital to local traditional healers. I never had a promising word. Doctors told me that he will never walk or talk and I should just accept that he is one of those children who are unfortunate. I left the doctor's room more frustrated and discouraged than before. From traditional aspect, I was told that I needed to sacrifice with a white goat and let the child drink and bathe with goat's blood and told that he would walk, talk and would go to school. Njabulo started babbling with limited body movements and his speech was delayed but that alone gave hope.

10.11 School life

In a community advocacy initiative, the mother came to know that Njabulo could attend the local full-service school. It was a moment of great relief. However, the mother had mixed feelings about whether the boy would cope. Njabulo came from a struggling family but the mother was able to make ends meet and could afford to buy school uniform and shoes. Njabulo who never smiled nor communicated his needs learnt to smile and stutter a few words. Early in the morning he was taken to the school and the principal welcomed this adolescent young boy who appeared very reserved and took him through an informal assessment tool which would help to understand his level of functionality and class placement. (This informal instrument shown below was designed by the official to assist teachers to get their own insight about the child).

Table 10.1: Assessment tool

Particulars of the learner
• Name and age • Name of parent/guardian • Home address
Birth history
• Was pregnancy normal? • Was it a normal birth? • Did he cry at birth? • When did he start crawling/talking/walking?
Academic/previous school life?
• Has he/she ever been to school? • If so up to what grade? • Can he write his name? • Were you referred to the school? • Tell us about his social behaviour and communication level. • Can he communicate his needs? • What else would you like the school to know?

During the assessment, the mother was very emotional and broke down in tears many times. Reminiscing about the pregnancy evoked memories of loss and difficult labour at birth. Njabulo had never been to school; this was his first experience, he could not make eye contact and spent his time behind the chicken shed and was aggressive to girls if they teased him. The mother reported that neighbours always accused him of beating their girls but "I have not observed that. How do I know because Njabulo cannot express himself?"

Njabulo was finally placed in the reception class for beginners. The class teacher reported that the boy was naughty and too old for the class. He was petting and touching the girls on their private parts. Boys reported that during break he was exposing his penis and showing the girls and calling them. The mother was informed of this behaviour but denied any knowledge of such behaviour at home. Parents started flocking to the school to complain about a boy who was touching their children in the bus and girls did not want to take the school transport any more. Teachers were concerned and started complaining and even suggested that he should stay at home, as he was not fit to be in the school. The SBST coordinator advised the teachers about making schools inclusive, managing the teaching and learning environment for all learners, providing an enabling environment for Njabulo, involving family in his education as a right to learn and instilling the responsibility to behave appropriately with the support of school and family.

10.12 Parental involvement and sexuality

Research suggests that parents be the primary source of sexuality education for adolescents including ASD from which children obtain norms and values for daily living and be tailored to child's developmental level (Holmes & Himle, 2014; Lukola & Van Dyk, 2015). Notably, children and adolescent on ASD display difficulties in the areas of social and communicative behaviour. Beddows and Brooks (2016) ascertain that parents and family members are the main communication partners of children with ASD and they must take a lead with sexuality education as they know the adolescent. However, talking about sexuality has never been easy in most South African cultures. Moreover, parents feel uncomfortable and embarrassed to talk openly with their children about sexuality. Earlier research (Dewinter, Vermeiren, Vanwesenbeeck & Van Niewenhuizen, 2016) suggest that parents do not know what to expert when it comes to the sexual development of adolescent children with ASD and hesitate to discuss issues related to sexuality when they are unsure whether the adolescent has a sexual interest. This indicated that parents of ASD were less inclined and uncertain to discuss issues of sexuality with their children. This uncertainity may be a combination of lack of knowledge about sexual development in adolescents with ASD, and lack of awareness of their adolescent's sexual experience. Certainly, all children and adolescents with ASD will experience, physical, emotional and sexual development. This may not be at the same time as their peer but teachers and parents should not deter from teaching children and adolescents with ASD the necessary skills and self understanding of their growing changing bodies that promote positive relationships of sexual experience (Loftin & Hatlage, 2015). Parental involvement is widely acknowledged to be a critical best practice in the education of young adolescents with ASD. Parents of young adolescents with autism play multiple roles in their children's lives.

According to Holmes and Himle (2014), communication between parents and children that starts in early years is more effective and delays sexual initiation. However, parents are not convinced; they fear that if they start talking about sexual related issues to their adolescents with ASD, it will create desire and promote sexual activity. In fact, Ballan's (2012) research conducted in Malaysia on parents' attitude towards inclusion of sexuality education in schools (Makol-Abdul et al., 2009) found that parental involvement in supporting schools on sexuality education is important in order for children to be better informed about sexually sensitive issues and how to protect themselves against sexual exploitation, abuse, unintended pregnancy, sexually transmitted infection and HIV/AIDS. Rambiyana and Kok (2002) assert that the South African Schools Act (SASA) allows for parental participation in education mainly through representation in SGBs to enable parental involvement in their children's education as well to create a supportive environment of modalities through which learners can demonstrate to the teacher what they have learned from the curriculum. Such modalities include written work, projects, models and oral presentation (Marishane, 2013). Products are ways for students to demonstrate what they have come to know, understand and be able to do after an extended period of learning (Tomlinsons & Imbeau, 2010).

Research has shown that one of the most effective ways to increase parent to child communication is to provide homework assignments to discuss selected topics with parents or trusted adults (Kirby, 2010). A UNAIDS (2010) study reported on the evaluation of the parental involvement programme, 'Families Matter', which was developed to improve HIV-prevention knowledge and communication skills of parents in the USA and adapted culturally for use in Kenya. Results yielded increased parenting behaviours, better parent-child communication around sexuality and sexual risk reduction, and positive effects on parents' attitudes towards sexuality education.

It is recommended that programmes such as 'Families Matter' are implemented to develop parenting skills on sexuality-related issues with the objective of delaying early sexual debut, reducing risky sexual behaviours and keeping learners in school.

10.13 Community involvement and stakeholders

Working towards Inclusive Education can never be the sole responsibility of the school or teacher alone (Phasha, Mahlo & Maseko, 2013). The community also sets norms for acceptable behaviour and the tone of discussion around issues of sexuality. For effective teaching of sexuality education, Rambiyana and Kok (2002) recommend the establishment of school-community partnerships. This would make it possible, among other things, to deal with issues relating to sexuality education through public engagement and enrichment with stakeholders. Phasha et al. (2013) further assert that families and community stakeholders have a major responsibility in supporting, teaching and learning and realisation of Inclusive Education. Sexuality issues are very sensitive of modalities through which learners can demonstrate to the teacher what they have learned from the curriculum. Such modalities include written work, projects, models and oral presentation. Products are ways for students to demonstrate what they have come to know, understand and be able to do after an extended period of learning (Tomlinsons & Imbeau, 2010).

The Department of Education (2011b: 22) emphasises that the minimum requirements for achieving grades may not be compromised. The product refers to the manner in which the learner will be evaluated in the form of tests, projects, written work or oral presentation to see whether the learner has mastered the content or not. Marishane (2013) views continuous instruction-linked assessment and adjustment as involving an on-going formal and informal assessment of learners' work to identify differences in learners' learning weaknesses and strengths. Knowledge gained from such assessment enables the teacher to adjust and teachers form part of a wider community; taking sexuality education into the classroom is, therefore, not easy.

All children come to school with family and community knowledge, experiences and skills and values. Their sexual education and experiences are community school-based issues. Therefore, parents should become equal partners with their community schools in order to overcome cultural difficulty on communicating with their children about sexuality issues. Notably, McGogo (2016) observed that teachers struggled with their emotions and conscious to balance community norms and practices with sexuality-related issues and expectations of the employer in terms of policy practice as mandated in the Manifesto on Values Education and Democracy of South Africa The Manifesto served as an example of a set of human right values constructed socially as means of supporting texts in specific educational setting of the curriculum in order to address social ills and cultural intolerance and the teaching of sexuality related issues in South African schools. For effective teaching of sexuality education, Rambiyana and Kok (2002) recommend the establishment of school-community partnerships. This would make it possible, among other things, to deal with issues relating to sexuality education through public engagement and enrichment with stakeholders. Kirby, Laris and Rolleri (2005) in extensive work with curriculum-based interventions on sexuality education identified that community involvement contributes to programme success but that community needs should be assessed prior to designing a programme. It is, therefore, necessary to find out the community's cultural norms and practices that shape their sexual landscape including language and appropriate messages commonly used. A needs assessment can be the first step in a broader scheme of community involvement.

UNESCO (2018) asserts that teachers alone cannot address many of the lessons on sexuality-related issues, such as HIV and early sexual initiation practices, sexual abuse because the root cause is in the community practices, with their confusing and contradictory beliefs. The RNCS (DoE, 2002; CAPS, 2011) encourages full participation of community and faith-based organisations to implement sexuality education that will assist community and parents in fulfilling their responsibilities and supporting the DoE's educational programmes and objectives. Equally, Kirby (2011) reports on a broader need for involvement and commitment of community and stakeholders in matters involving gender equality, STIs and HIV infections. This requires all stakeholders to engage with teachers and learners. Schools should develop a sexuality education policy involving all stakeholders and incorporate all existing policies that relate to inclusion in terms of the White Paper 6 (DoE, 2001).

10.14 Conclusion

Adolescents with ASD have similar sexual needs as the general population and mature sexually, both physical and emotional via the normal developmental stages. Sexuality as development domain appears as typical normative development for the adolescent which is part of life for people with ASD. The factors underlying sexuality development for the ASD adolescent boy aand girl remain under researched despite of the relevance for comprehensive sexuality education in school. Parents and teachers need specific support in dealing with adolescent's sexual experiences in the aspect of growing up and body changes. Sexuality education needs to be reinforced and repeated with varying details as the adolescents develop, and keeping in mind age appropriateness of information.

The area of privacy must be delivered in a manner that the adolescent understands the need for visual representation to support verbal interaction and sexual development and intimacy. Other key areas of instruction should include HIV, STIs, sexual abuse and hygiene, health services for contraceptives and it should be delivered in a range of friendly formats.

References

Adams, J.B, Edelson,S.M., Grandinz, R.B & Jones, J. (2012). *Understanding Autism: Advice for Parents*. Autism Research Institute. San Diego, California.

Ballan, M.S. (2012). Parental Perspectives of Communication about Sexuality in Families of Children with ASDs. *Journal of Autism Spectrum Disorders*, 42: 676-684.

Baxley, D.L. & Zendell, A. (2005). *Sexuality education for children and adolescents with developmental disabilities: An instructional manual for parents or care givers of individuals with disabilities.* Sexuality Across the Lifespan. Florida Developmental Disabilities Council, Inc.

Beyers, C. (2011). Sexuality education in South Africa: a sociocultural perspective. *South African Journal*, 33 (4): 192-209.

Buthelezi, T. (2004). The HIV/AIDS epidemic and teacher development: Defining 'Positional' Perspectives. In Balfour. R., Buthelezi, T. and Mitchell, C. (Eds.). *Pre-service teachers' professional learning experiences during rural teaching practice in Acornhoek, Mpumalanga Province*. Pietermaritzburg: Teacher Education at Centre of Change. Intrepid. https://www.researchgate.net/publication/319616439_Pre-service_teachers›_professional_learning_experiences_during_rural_teaching_practice_in_Acornhoek_Mpumalanga_Province [accessed Sep 08 2020].

Canada-South Africa Teacher Development Project. (2005). *Towards Inclusive Education*. Pretoria: Government Printers.

Carona, L.L., Fox, S.A., Christodulu,K.V. & Worlock, J.A. (2016). Providing education on sexuality and relationships to adolescents with autism spectrum disorder. *Sexuality and Disability*, 34 (2): 199-214.

Constitution of the Republic of South Africa. (1996). *Chapter 2, Bill of Rights, section 12. Freedom and security of person*. Pretoria: Government Printer.

Dalton, E.M., McKenzie, J.A. & Kahonde, C. (2012). The implementation of Inclusive Education in South Africa: Reflections arising from a workshop for teachers and therapists to introduce Universal Design for Learning. *African Journal of Disability*, (1)1.

Department of Basic Education. (2015). *National Adolescent Sexual and Reproductive Health and Rights Framework Strategy:2014-2019*. Pretoria: Government Printers.

Department of Basic Education. (2011). *Curriculum assessment policy statement*. Pretoria: Government Printer.

Department of Education. (2001). *Education White Paper 6, Special Needs Education: Building an Inclusive Education and Training system*. Pretoria: Government Printer.

Department of Education. (2002). *Revised National Curriculum Statement*. Pretoria: Government Printer.

Department of Education. (2008). *National strategy on screening, identification, assessment and support: School pack*. Pretoria: Government Printer.

Department of Education. (2001). *Education White Paper 6, Special Needs Education: Building an Inclusive Education and Training System*. Pretoria: Government Printer.

Department of Social Development. (2016). *White Paper on the Right of Persons with Disabilities*. Pretoria: Government Printer.

Dewinter, J., Vermiren, R., van Wesenbeeck & van Niewenhuizen, C. (2016). Sexuality in adolescent boys. *Journal of Autism and Development*, 46: 713-719.

Dewinter, J., Vermiren, R., van Wesenbeeck & van Niewenhuizen, C. (2013). Autism and normative sexual development: a narrative review. *Journal of Clinical Nursing*, 22: 3476-3483.

Dewinter, J., Vermiren, R., van Wesenbeeck & van Niewenhuizen, C. (2013). Autism and normative sexual development. A narrative review. *Journal of Clinical Nursing*, 22: 3467-3483.

Esmail, S., Darry, K., Walter, A. & Knupp, H. (2010). Attitudes and perceptions towards disability and sexuality. *Disability and Rehabilitation*, 32 (14): 1148-1155.

Francis, D.2013. Sexuality education in South Africa: Whose values are we teaching? *Journal of Human Sexuality*, 22 (2).

Gbewonyo, Y.A. (2017). Parents and special educators' persective on the Sexuality Educational Needs of Learners with Intellectual Developmental Disabilities in Ghanian Special Schools. Unpublished MA Thesis. Queens' University, Canada.

Glover, J. & Macleod, C. (2016). Rolling out comprehensive sexuality education in South Africa. An overview of research conducted on Life Orientation sexuality education. Unpublished policy brief document, Critical studies in sexualities and reproduction research programme. Rhodes University, Grahamstown.

Hatton, S. & Tector, A. (2010). Sexuality and relationship education for young people with Autistic Spectrum Disorder: Curriculum change and staff support. *British Journal of Special Education*, 37 (2): 69-76.

Hayward, B. & Saunder, K. (2010). Sexual Behaviours of Concern in Young People with Autism Specrum Disorders. *Disability Support Worker Conference*. Melbourne.

Holmes, LG. & Himle, MB. (2014). Parent Child sexuality communication and ASD. *Journal Autism Development* 44 (1): 64-70.

Kalyva, E. (2010). Teacher Perspective of sexuality of children with autism spectrum disorders. *Research in Autism Spectrum Disorders*, 4: 433-437.

Kirby, D., Laris, B.A & Rolleri,L. (2005). *Impact of sex and HIV education programs on sexual behaviours youth in developing and developed countries*. Family Health International- Research Triangle Park.

Kirby, D. & Laris, B.A. (2009). Effective curriculum and comprehensive sex and STI/HIV education programmes for adolescents. *Child Development Perspectives,* 3 (1): 21-29.

Kirby, D. (2011). *A way forward: Recommendation to the South African DBE to design and implement an effective HIV education curriculum that reduces sexual risks for HIV*. Scotts Valley, CA: ETR Associates.

Kirby, D., Laris, B.A. & Rolleri, L. (2005). Impact of sex and HIV education programme on sexual behaviours of youth in development and developed countries. Family Health International, Youth Research Working Paper 2.

Lefa, B.J. 2015. *Ubuntu in South African Education*. Cape Peninsula University of Technology. Cape Town.

Letseka, M. (2013). Educating for Ubuntu/Botho: Lessons from Basotho indigenous Education. *Open Journal of Philosophy*, 3 (2): 337-344.

Loftin, R.L. & Hartlage, S.A. (2015). Sex education, sexual health and autism spectrum disorder. *Chicago Paediatric Care Journal*.

Magezi, V. (2016). A proposing for an integrated and community intervention to adolescents and youth sexual reproductive health challenges. *HTS Teologiese Studies/ Theological Studies* 72 (2): 93-83.

Mahlo, F.D. (2016). Ubuntu and Inclusivity. Unpublished. University of South Africa.

Metz, T. (2011). Ubuntu as a moral theory and human rights in South Africa. *African Human Rights Law Journal*, 11(2): 532-559.

Mcgogo, J.B. (2016). Teaching sexuality education in rural secondary schools: Mpumalanga Province. PHD: Inclusive Education. Unpublished Thesis. UNISA.

Nichols, S. & Blakeley-Smith. (2010). 'I'm not sure we're ready for this', working with families toward facilitating healthy sexuality for individuals with autism spectrum disorders. *Social Work in Mental Health*, 08: 72-91.

Okeke, C., van Wyk, M. & Phasha, N. (2014). *Schooling, society, and Inclusive Education: An Afrocentric perspective*. Cape Town: Oxford University Press.

Phasha, N., Mahlo, D. & Maseko, N. (2013). Developing inclusive Grade R classrooms. In R. Davin (Ed.) *Handbook for Grade R Teaching*. New York: Pearson.

Phasha, T.N. & Moichela, K.Z. (2011). Inclusive Education in South Africa. In AB Nsamenang and Tchombe, T.M.S. (Eds.). *Handbook of African Educational Theories and Practices*. A Generative Teacher Education Curriculum. SAIF, 2009.

Rambiyana, N.G. & Kok, J.C. (2002). Parents expectations of public schooling in the Northern Province of South Africa. *South African Journal of Education*, 22(1): 14-15.

Reddy, P.S., James, S. & Sewpaul, R. (2013). *Umthente uhlaba usamila*. 3rd South African Youth Risk Behavior Survey 2011. South African Research Council, Cape Town.

Robinson, K.H., Smith, E. & Davies, C. (2016). Responsibility, tensions and way forward: Parents perspective on children's sexuality education. *Sex Education*, 17 (3): 333-347.

Tolman, D.L. & McClelland, S.L. (2011). Normative sexuality development in adolescence. A decade review, 2000-2009. *Journal of Research*, 21, 241-255.

Travers, J. &Tincani, M. (2010). Sexuality Education for individuals with autism spectrum disorders. Critical issues and decision making guidelines. *Education and Training in Autism and Developmental Disabilities*, 45(2): 284-293.

UNAIDS. (2010). *Towards universal access. Scaling up priority HIV/AIDS interventions*. Geneva, Switzerland: UNAIDS.

UNESCO. (2016). *Sustainable Development Goals: A guide for ensuring inclusion and equity in education – 2030*. Geneva: UNESCO.

UNESCO. (2018). *International Guidelines on Sexuality Education. An evidence informed approach to effective comprehensive sexuality education*. Geneva: UNESCO.

UNESCO. (2014). *Comprehensive sexuality education: The challenges and opportunities of scaling-up*. Geneva: UNESCO.

UNESCO. (2009). *International Guidelines on Sexuality Education. An evidence informed approach to effective sex , relationships and HIV/STI education*. Geneva

UNESCO. (1990). *World Declaration on EFA*. Jomtien, Thailand.

UN. (2014). *Transforming our world: the 2030 Agenda for Sustainable Development*. Geneva, Switzerland. UNESCO.

World Health Organization. (2017). *Defining sexual health. Report of technical consultant on sexual health*. Geneva: WHO.

World Health Organization. (2014). *Sexual and reproductive health: Gender and human rights*. Geneva: WHO.

World Health Organization. (2011). *Youth and health risks*. Geneva: WHO.

11

CLASSROOM ASSESSMENT OF LEARNERS WITH AUTISM – IMPLICATIONS FOR EDUCATORS

Serefete M Molosiwa

Abstract

In the age of outcome-based reforms, where accountability and high-stakes testing are at the core of educational practices, it is important that ALL learners including those with ASD benefit from educational assessment in the general education classroom. Underlying such inclusion is a three-pronged practice that is critical for learners with autism to benefit from classroom assessment; the teachers should (i) believe in diversity, (ii) provide academic supports, and (iii) ensure continued behavioural supports. Because of the predominant use of pen and paper-assessments in education, this chapter aims to empower teachers in Inclusive Educational settings to understand that learners with autism though non-verbal or minimally verbal, can access conventional educational assessments with appropriate supports. However, some learners with autism may require alternate assessments. This chapter therefore recommends that teachers should adopt tiers for assessment of learners falling within the autism spectrum within inclusive classrooms so that the learning products and assessment tasks are fair and appropriate for their abilities. Such inclusive assessments should be varied and inclusive to accommodate the diverse and highly individual needs of learners with autism. Moreover, assessments should include portfolios, reports, presentations, practical tasks, created products, performances, non-verbal assessments, as well as written and oral tests. To ensure that alternate assessment practices are credible and effective, classroom teaching needs to become more innovative by employing approaches such as universal design for learning (UDL) that accommodates diverse learning needs and styles.

11.1 Introduction

Accountability in education is critical and teachers need to be accountable for all learners including those with autism. This particular group of learners present with challenges in some core areas like social, communication and behavioural (Abubakar, Ssewanyana, & Newton, 2016; Wong et al., 2015). A large number of non-verbal autistic spectrum disorder (ASD) children (50–71%) and over 60% comorbid intellectual disability is reported among African children (Abubakar et al., 2016). Nevertheless, in some African countries such as in South Africa, successful teaching and learning in schools is influenced by too many factors including the distinctive social, economic, political and educational spaces within which the young African learner grows and develops (Molosiwa & Monyatsi, 2016). Such factors may interfere with providing adequate support for inclusion of young children with autism and may as a result compromise teacher-accountability. In addition, those assessing autistic learners such as in the African context should be cognisant of the linguistic and cultural background of the families. It is recommended therefore that class teachers and others assessing and providing services to such learners should consider how cultural and linguistic variations which may affect learner-attainment and their ability to access the assessment itself are addressed (West et al., 2016).

With such a wide difference in young learners' backgrounds, teachers are forced to rethink and reformulate their assessment practices, especially when young learners with developmental delays like autism are taught alongside others who also experience barriers to learning. Nonetheless, though being in an inclusive classroom for autistic learners is one of the goals of education, it is not the premise because young learners with disabilities have a right to equal early childhood educational (ECE) opportunities including being assessed (Downing, 2008). Thinking and planning for classroom assessment of diverse learners of nine years of age and below in ECE programmes with some falling within the autism spectrum can be a daunting task.

Classroom assessment during early learning is a complex undertaking that keeps educators wondering about the unpredictable, and it becomes even more challenging in an inclusive and democratic classroom where equality of learning opportunities is emphasised (Hudson, 2016). This uncertainty is owing to the variability in the young learners linguistic, emotional, cognitive, motor, and physical developments that take place fast and are influenced by different factors in the environment (Carr, 2002; Leonard & Hill, 2014). Such developments make the assessment of young children a difficult task indeed. The National Council for Curriculum and Assessment (2008) contends that because of the complexity of children's learning during the early childhood period, it can be made visible through careful and well thought-out assessment. Nonetheless, for children with the autism, classroom assessment covers both their academic learning and their behaviours. Some reasons for emphasising on their behaviours include their inability or limited ability to socialise and their limited or absence of communication skills (Abubakar, Ssewanyana, & Newton, 2016). It is recommended therefore that assessment of autistic children should consider their ability to imitate, the gestures they habitually make, as well as other behaviours they use to complement their linguistic resources' needs (Abubakar, et al., 2016; Hayes, O'Toole & Halpenny, 2017). Also noteworthy are the autistic children's strengths (Oakley, Howitt, Garwood, & Durack, 2013), which must be recognised in the teaching and learning environment. While children with ASD differ greatly as individuals, they have been generally identified as having relative strengths in visuospatial skills and in detail-focused processing, with relative weaknesses in abstraction and concept formation (Kuschner, Bennetto & Yost, 2007).

Teachers of young learners with autism must also understand that it is essential to assess the learner's level of adaptive behaviors. It is from such an understanding that the assessment of skills such as communication, cooperation, self-determination, independence, as well as basic literacy and numeracy is determined. Assessment of adaptive functioning is critical in facilitating comprehensive evaluations for children who fall within the High Functioning Autistic Spectrum Disorder (HFA SD) and those with Asperger syndrome as it provides important information that helps with proper diagnosis, attainment of services and treatment/educational programming (Lopata, Smith, Volker, Thomeer, Lee, & McDonald 2013). As children are classified for assessment purposes, it should be noted that the concept of HFA SD remains controversial; this is partly because a definitive model for how cognition functions—or fails to function—in autism has not been established (Silverman, 2011). Furthermore, it is worth noting that HFA is not a recognised diagnosis in the DSM-5 or the ICD-10, and that the degree of overlap between HFA and Asperger syndrome continues to be disputed (de Giambattista, Ventura, Trerotoli, Margari, Palumbi, & Margari 2018).

The nature of assessment of young autistic learners is varied and could be unconventional as well as symbolic. It is varied and unconventional in the sense that it may include verbal as well as non-verbal such as in the use of photographs, pictures and/or drawings for those who are non-verbal. Furthermore, learners may be assessed using alternate forms of assessment such as portfolios (Hayes, et al., 2017).

This chapter is arranged starting with the some theoretical lenses which guide the teaching and learning as well as the classroom assessment of young autistic learners. This is followed by the rationalising on why early childhood assessment of young autistic learners is important. Then, ethical issues, family-partnerships, and learner-challenges are discussed to validate the assessment of learners with ASD. The types of classroom assessment suited for young learners with autism are presented as well as their functions and/or purpose. Finally, further assistance to guide the users of this book is given from explaining some important terms in the glossary at the end of the chapter.

11.2 Theoretical beliefs that support early childhood assessment

Theoretical foundations have been persuasive in influencing new and emerging assessment practices. Four such theories are adopted for this chapter in relation to their implications for the assessment of early learning and development. These are the socio-cultural, the ecological perspective, the activity-based intervention and the developmental theories.

11.2.1 The ecological and socio-cultural theories

These two theories are renowned for influencing young children's growth and development as well as how they are assessed; for example, theories such as the ecological (Bronfenbrenner 1979) and the bio-ecological (Bronfenbrenner & Morris, 1998) models of human development. These models place the child at the centre of their learning and development (Hayes et al., 2017). Explanations of how these theories fit in the development, and in the learning and assessment of the young autistic learner are provided.

11.2.1.1 The socio-cultural theory

As one of the adopted conceptual framework for this chapter, the socio-cultural theory draws upon the individual, the interpersonal, the cultural as well as the societal processes which are all interlocked while demonstrating the young learner's competencies in the various existing contexts (Mercer & Howe, 2012); inside classrooms and within the school. The individual and the class mates have a symbiotic relationship as part of the classroom which is the cultural space that provides certain opportunities of development. As such, young autistic learners' achievements do not merely depend on individual efforts or discoveries, but they are a product of culturally-situated forms of social interaction (Mercer & Howe, 2012). These authors further argue that while knowledge can be individualistic, it is also "the creation and shared property of members of communities, who use 'cultural tools' (including spoken and written language), relationships and institutions (such as schools)", (p. 12). Young autistic learners are exposed to several social situations and in the process interact with their peers which in itself is a learning experience (Watkins, O'Reilly, Kuhn, Gevarter, Lancioni, Sigafoos, & Lang 2015). During assessment in the ECE classrooms, the teacher or other learners may guide the autistic learners on how to locate answers as they work in a team. Watkins et al. (2015) conclude that peer-mediated instruction (PMI) has the potential to increase social interaction in young children with ASD in inclusive settings, as it promotes positive generalisation, maintenance and social validity outcomes.

11.2.1.2 The ecological-theory outlook

In terms of the ecological understanding, this entails direct contextual influences, such as parents, school, and peers (microsystem), and the effects they have through interactions between these contexts, such as parent-teacher associations and relationships (the mesosystem). More external factors also affect children's experiences, including other services like psychological and clinical systems (the exosystem), and broader, societal factors (e.g., policies and Education Acts) that govern service provision (the macrosystem) (Bush, Cohen, Eisenhower & Blacher, 2017). Bronfenbrenner (1979) describes how the learner can take part in more multifaceted learning situations and in doing so take increasingly greater responsibility in their own learning. The ecological theory is appropriate for unpacking classroom practices because of the following tenets which guide its major contributions in early childhood education:

- its recognition of the factors within the immediate environment which include the home and the classroom;
- the partnership between the teacher and the parent(s) or caregivers and how they influence the young learner's participation in various settings through their ongoing communication; and
- the influences of the wider ecology which involves the state policies, as well as the cultural values (Odom & Wolery, 2003; McConachie, 2016).

Teachers should understand that learners' educational attainment improves when the school and the parents/caretakers communicate and collaborate; and that a poor relationship between the school and the home is often detrimental to the welfare of the young learner (Brofenbrenner in Aubrey and Riley, 2016), especially if they also have a special need.

Classroom assessment of young learners with autism therefore is not to be solitary and individualistic as is the practice of classroom instructional assessment in most schools in Africa. It should be noted that many learners with ASD especially those who are high functioning are capable intellectually and should as a result receive their education in general education classrooms (de Bruin et al. 2013; Fleury et al. 2014). This suggests that such learners qualify to be taught alongside their peers without ASD and should in fact benefit from general classroom instruction, provided they receive appropriate individualised support. Furthermore, Brofennbrenner argues that classroom teachers should embrace group assessment as an option particularly as the young autistic learner begins to demonstrate the development of both physical and cognitive traits and has regular interactions with classmates (Brofennbrenner, 1979; Kamps et al., 2016). Classroom teachers should note that peer-mediated interventions are more effective while providing opportunities for social learning opportunities through peer interaction, peer modeling and peer reinforcing (Crossland and Dunlap, 2012). For example, class wide-peer tutoring which involves the pairing of all children in the class has resulted in gains in reading fluency, reading comprehension and social interactions between students with autism and their typically-developing peers (Harrower & Dunlap, 2001; Kamps et al., 2016). Furthermore, these authors commend peer-mediated interventions for promoting the educational inclusion of children with autism and more importantly those having high social validity.

The assessment of young learners with autism in inclusive classrooms is also affected by many other social systems. For instance, Brofennbrenner asserts that there are concentric circles that include the *microsystem, the mesosystem and the macrosystem.* The microsystem is the immediate setting around the child. Such environments include the child's family and the home. For any child, this support system is extremely critical in the early years of their education (Maconachie et al., 2018) as it promotes consistent learning and positive developmental outcomes for children. Furthermore, research attests to improved literacy outcomes when there is family involvement in the child's education at a very young age (Mackey & Mackey, 2009). For young learners in the spectrum, the importance of continuity between the formal learning setting and the home cannot be overemphasised (Agur, et al., 2018). Evidence also exists which underscores the importance of adult supervision on a one-on-one for learners with autism during their learning and their classroom assessment (Rhoad-Drogalis, Sawyer, Justice & O'Connell, 2018). The *mesosystem* refers to the interactions between two or more microsystems which could in this case be the school and the home. There is need for close collaboration between the two systems (Agur, et al., 2018; Mackey & Mackey, 2009) so that they are both involved in whatever activity that takes place in the child's learning and in-class assessment. Chances of success for the young autistic learner are increased when the school and the home are in meaningful and effective partnership (Agur, et al., 2018). In addition, the macrosystem influences the learning and development of the young learner in the sense that it is the overarching level because it includes all the other levels of Brofenbrenner's ecological model.

11.3 Activity-based intervention theory (ABI)

This theory is used in most early childhood programmes that serve to address the special needs of young children and their families (McConachie, Livingstone, Morris, Beresford, Le Couteur, Gringras, & Parr, 2018). The activity-based intervention (ABI) theory has eight perspectives that explain its relevance in education. For this book-chapter, the author will select only those that are relevant to young children with autism learning and assessment and those that have not already been discussed. These include (i) the cognitive and the (ii) developmental.

- **Cognitive** – the cognitive stems from Piaget's theory which postulates that children will usually explore their environment as a way of developing and constructing knowledge. It is imperative that classroom teachers in South Africa ensure that the assessment environment in which the autistic learners are tested must be least-restrictive and enabling. Once the classroom setting is least-restrictive and enabling, it would be friendly and increase opportunities for the young autistic learner to perform optimally. It is also important that the classroom teacher considers the learner with autism lead (i.e. cues and level of motivation) during assessment to increase chances of success (Macy, 2007).

- **Developmental** – A developmental theory is relevant as it can assist in describing the learner's functioning from typical to atypical development. This theory has implications for the activity-based intervention as it covers both the developmental and educational goals of young children by soliciting their participation in meaningful daily activities through employing behavioural learning principles (Macy, 2007). Based on such an understanding, Macy recommends that class-assessment for the young autistic learner should be comprehensive and should also address multiple developmental domains. Furthermore, it helps in the understanding of any risks, adaptation, maladaptation and disability patterns from a young age (Grills, & King, 2001; Ungar, 2015). Such an approach promotes some level of resilience from a young age. According to Ungar (2015), the autistic learner needs a strategy for survival as they may face social marginalisation during learning. Such information is important for teachers in making decisions about the most appropriate ways of assessing learners with autism in the classroom.

Activity-based assessment involves creating an activity circumstance that closely resembles the real thing. Such an approach assists the autistic young learner to relate what they learn to real life-situations and to generalise to other similar situations, therefore promoting lifelong learning (Glofcheski, 2017). This next section of the chapter tries to unravel the importance of early-childhood classroom assessment, particularly for the young autistic learner.

11.4 Why is early childhood classroom-assessment of autistic learners essential?

Autism may have a dramatic impact on a young child's ability to learn. It is nonetheless mandatory that teachers appreciate the conditions surrounding autism and know how to accommodate such learners from an early age both in classroom instruction /intervention in class assessment. Early childhood is a critical time in the growth and academic development of young learners which often challenges educators to determine the appropriateness and effectiveness of programmes offered to young children with developmental disorders, including those with ASD (Black , Walker, Fernald, Andersen, DiGirolamo, Lu, & Devercelli , 2017; Hurtb, Shaw, Izeman, Izeman & Rogers, 1999). Moreover, for countries to meet Sustainable Development Goals (SDGs) equitable early childhood policies and programmes are crucial, particularly for children with disabilities for them to develop the intellectual skills, creativity, and wellbeing needed to become productive citizens (Black et al., 2017). Furthermore, autism is not widely studied in Africa. Therefore, much as learners with autism are found in general education and special schools, prevalence is not known

(Elsabbagh et al., 2012). There is also scant information about planning for effective intervention strategies for children with ASD in Africa in general (Abubakar, Ssewanyana & Newton, 2016). Early intervention therefore is a strategy that could be used to provide equitable services early to such learners and reduce or eliminate the onset of secondary disabilities, which could complicate service provision priorities.

Early intervention is important no doubt, especially when the young learner also has a developmental delay that interferes with his/her ability to achieve the set learning outcomes much like their peers. Though the Education 2030 Framework for Action promotes inclusive and equitable quality education and lifelong learning opportunities for all, issues of equitable access to the school curriculum and assessment affect most learners with various special needs including those with autism (International Disability and Development Consortium (IDDC, 2013). It is therefore not surprising that concerns about equitable access to educational assessment remain a critical issue in the teaching and learning of young children, particularly when living with a disability such as autism. Learner assessment, nonetheless, is the core of many educational improvement reforms (Shepard, 2000; Suskie, 2018), and must be conducted to monitor learner progress. However, providing early intervention could be faced with some difficulties.

Several key matters must be considered during the assessment of young children within the autistic spectrum. These include ethical concerns, family-partnership, learner-unique challenges (academic and behavioural), as well as the type of classroom assessment suited to young autistic learners and functions of assessment at that early age. Notably, as teachers assess young autistic learners, they need to be aware of some ethical issues. Such issues are discussed in the next section of the chapter.

11.5 Ethical considerations

Ethical concerns that are likely to be faced by a young autistic learner and their family members include the dominance by the school authorities including the teacher which may lead to disempowerment. If family members feel threatened by the school authorities and the teacher owing to their illiteracy or semi-literacy, this could lead to entire dependence on the professionals. Such a situation may lead to the parent feeling totally powerless and dependent on the teacher/school personnel (Bush et al., 2017; Iadarola, 2015). This could lead to their rights as well as those of the young learner being violated. Teachers of young learners may also be faced with power-relations and confidentiality issues particularly if the learners also have a disability (Einarsdóttir, 2007). These learners may be taken advantage of and information about their test performance released without their consent (Salvia, Ysseldyke & Witmer, 2013), or the consent of the legal guardian if the learners are unable to speak for themselves. It is therefore critical that class teachers of young autistic learners in South Africa empower the family-members of the young learner and treat them as important team-players with an irreplaceable role. Such as approach would entice the family members to be committed to value the partnership and to ensure the success of the team effort for the benefit of the young learner (Cox & John, 2016).

11.6 Family-partnerships during classroom assessment

Families play a significant role in the education of young learners since they are often times their children's voice, mentors and advocates (Bush et al., 2017). Fundamentally, parents and caretakers of children with autism should be involved in their education from the very young age as well and specifically in their classroom assessments. Parents of very young children have rich information that may not be obvious to the school until the learner would have spent a longer time with the school personnel and some level of trust is built. The experiences and perspectives of the parents and the family-members of children with a disability are critical in understanding their children's needs (Brett, 2002; Zanello, 2015). Brett further declares, "Parents often hold the key in accessing their child's experiences and provide essential insight into their child's world", p. 827. For this reason, family members' involvement especially their physical presence is crucial in the overall performance of their child/sibling.

11.7 Types of classroom assessment suited to young autistic learners

Inclusive assessment of learners who fall within the autistic spectrum requires the use of varying tools and approaches at different times to obtain a wide-ranging picture of their learning and development (Dunphy, 2008). Such assessment practice resonates with how Suskie (2018) defines the term assessment in early childhood education (ECE) and care as referring to the provision of a detailed picture of the manner in which children act, think and learn (Clark, 2017). Such a picture centres on the individual's learning that is progressive and gives evidence of learning in a number of different contexts.

Children who are autistic like any other category of special needs learn in different ways. It is therefore important for teachers to be sensitive to the multimodal, non-verbal competencies demonstrated by learners with autism as described in p. 46-47. For example, these include imitation, facial and non-facial gesture, hands-flapping, or jumping around on one foot as complementing linguistic skills of autistic learners (Dunphy, 2008). Assessment in this regard as a result focuses on processes and not necessarily on the product, and is therefore developmental (National Council for Curriculum and Assessment (NCCA, 2008; Overton, 2012). The NCCA (1999) asserts that even in Ireland the assessment of the product received much recognition over the assessment of the affective domain of the student. For the autistic learner, sometimes affective development assessment is more meaningful and relevant. It is also evident that meaningful educational assessment for young autistic learners is mainly the formative type. With this type of assessment, teachers do not focus on assessing quantity and presentation of work, but rather they must concentrate on the *quality of learning.*

Classroom assessment of children with autism must be varied as widely as those pupils' individual needs, hence the different teaching, learning and assessment tiers (Lerner, 2012). It should therefore include both the conventional assessment for those young autistic learners who are not cognitively challenged and alternate assessments methods for those who would not be able to participate in standard tests and exams. Furthermore, there should be assessment accommodations effected for young autistic learners. This would promote participation and fairness in the assessment. Some recommended accommodations include but are not limited to:

11.7.1 Testing Adaptations and /or accommodations

Classroom testing can be confusing and stressful when proper supports are not offered (Bayat, 2017). Some suggestions of techniques that the classroom teacher could adopt for children with autism include:

- Allowing breaks during the assessment;
- Being flexible enough to allow them to bring a cheat sheet;
- Reading the test to them;
- Drawing pictures to prompt them;
- Practicing paired or small-group tests; and
- Taking into consideration the learner's preference for the test-mode (Bayat, 2017).

In addition to this list of accommodations during classroom assessment, teachers may also incorporate using various types of alternate assessments. Authors come up with different lists: for example Bayat (2017) identified the following assessments; learning logs, anecdotal reports, observations, daily journals, puzzles and games, photographic essays, collages, interviews and drama/performance. A discussion of alternate assessment that teachers could use in classrooms in Southern Africa is given and a few examples are described.

11.8 Alternate assessment

Alternate assessment allows young autistic learners to have individualised opportunities for determining their progress towards learning objectives in their educational plan (Wong, Odom, Hume, Cox, Fettig, Kucharczyk, Brock, Plavnick, Fleury, Schultz, 2015). Some of the types of alternative assessment are discussed below.

The portfolio, play-based, checklists rating scales, practical tasks, created products, performance-assessment, non-verbal assessments, written and oral tests, where feasible among others, are assessment procedures suited for use with learners falling in the ASD continuum (Odom, 2014; Wong et al., 2015). While adopting these assessment approaches, young autistic learners may require prompting by using priming. Priming is a technique that allows the learner to be privy to assessment information before engaging in the actual assessment activity. Priming is recommended as it facilitates the inclusion of autistic learners by relating individual instruction to the larger general education classroom activities, which is a feature of the latter (Crosland & Dunlap, 2012). Prompting through priming and other means as complementary strategies to the general education classroom instructional routine and assessment enhances learners with autism's responses to academic and/or behavioural activities. Because learners with autism do better in predictable and routine environments, priming and prompting are therefore techniques that are recommended for them during teaching and classroom assessment (Kodak, Clements, & LeBlanc, 2013; Overton, 2012).

Owing to the limited language proficiency among learners who are autistic, the language used in classroom assessment by teachers or in other assessments should to be both explicit and literal so as not to confuse the young learners (Kodak et al., 2013). Moreover, complex and figurative language would throw learners with autism off balance and should be avoided. For instance, while multiple choice questions can be confusing to most learners, they are even more so for autistic learners; therefore, using alternate/alternative assessment modes may be the ideal (UK National Autistic Society, nd.). This chapter discusses some alternate assessment techniques that are responsive to the South African context and to other African countries. Two such assessment practices are the learner-portfolio and play-based assessment.

11.8.1 The learner-portfolio

A portfolio is a type of alternate assessment that is individualised and helps track the progress of learners with disabilities. It gives young learners with autism the opportunity to demonstrate their skills, strengths and interests (Downing, 2008).

Learner-portfolio is described as "a systematic collection of student work and related material that depicts a student's activities, accomplishments and achievements in one or more school subjects". It aims at helping young learners to be practically involved in assembling products that also show the processes that were involved. It therefore captures their talents, their functional academic literacy skills and their capabilities. Overall, it tells the young autistic learners' stories of school experiences and achievement (Venn, 2000, pp. 530-531). Contents of the learner-portfolio may include photographs showing performances, created products, processes towards achieving some skill, etc. Because of the comprehensive nature of the portfolio assessment, it is regarded as a useful tool that documents the autistic learner's learning and progress while helping the teacher understand the effect of the intervention used (Bayat, 2017). For a country like Botswana where resources may be a challenge, portfolio assessment is amenable to most classroom conditions as it requires nothing sophisticated but the learners' progress in some processes and products. The National Curriculum Assessment Framework (2015) asserts that assessments should be as inclusive as possible to address the diverse needs of learners including those living with a disability such as autism. Notwithstanding, there are electronic portfolios and those class teachers and learners with autism who have the facilities could use those for assessment, but not every teacher has the knowledge and skills to use them.

11.8.2 Play-based classroom assessment

One huge benefit of play-based assessment is the fact that it is child-centred. The teacher prepares activities that are interesting to a particular learner that would promote positive experiences for the child. However, play-based assessment gives the learner with autism opportunities to show-case their abilities, strengths and needs as they play. The teacher then conducts a systematic observation of the play and how the child accomplishes the different play-activities during class-assessment. Such an assessment incorporates activities that are adaptable to the autistic learner's physical and cognitive aptitudes (Bayat, 2017). Such play as recommended by this author is indoors with colourful and sophisticated toys that some schools may not have in our context. Bearing in mind that autistic learners do not do well with surprises and sudden changes, and sometimes bright colours, teachers may have to be innovative and introduce indigenous play materials with which the learner is familiar. In addition, they may have to find some quieter space where such play has to take place for the young autistic learner to pay attention and to benefit from such instruction and assessment. While preparing the play activities, teachers should also bear in mind that children have different priorities, inclinations and approaches to learning and therefore have varied needs for support (Beetham, 2007; Wong et al., 2015). To give this chapter more relevance it is of necessity to determine the functions of assessment during early childhood for autistic learners.

11.8.3 Functions of classroom assessment for autistic learners during early childhood

It is important for educators to understand and appreciate why young autistic learners need to be assessed using educational measures (Wong et al., 2015). Learners with autism are taught literacy, functional, social and independence skills among others. It is therefore important that the class-teacher has information about the learners' levels of competency in the different skill-areas through class assessment. Such class assessment of young autistic learners also helps the teacher to be accountable as he/she attempts to understand why certain learners have difficulties in some area of learning. The teacher will therefore evaluate the intervention strategy. This is the correct step to take because assessment must be linked to intervention. The results of a class assessment should therefore inform the teacher on whether the intervention has had any effect or not. It is an opportunity for the teacher to determine if the teaching techniques, materials used and other issues could have affected the learner's performance and influenced their responses.

Assessment in early childhood supports the extension and enrichment of children's early learning and development (NCCA, 2008). It provides a kind of tracking system that assists all stakeholders to monitor growth and development by looking at performance before and after intervention (MacDonald, Parry-Cruwys, Dupere, & Ahearn, 2014). Some authors contend that assessment in ECE facilitates meeting children's needs and supporting their cognitive development (Coogle, Floyd, Hanline, & Kellner-Hiczewski (2013). Earlier, Wood and Attfield (2005) identified several functions of assessment in ECE as ipsative, diagnostic, summative, evaluative and informative. The NCCA (2008) suggests that the final aim of assessment in early childhood is to make learning more fascinating, gratifying and effective for children.

The ipsative function involves the use of a forced-choice scale, which is basically a personality checklist (Overton, 2012). It assesses an individual's personality traits or behaviour, and ensures that the problems of normative items, such as social desirability bias are included. For example, ipsative assessment tool gives the applicant a choice of 2-4 equally positive statements, and they must give their preference or agreement to one of them. An example being to choose from: "I enjoy social events" or "I like to keep organised". Because of the way the items are structured, the assessed is forced to think more about their answer, and hopefully answer more genuinely, as there is not one obviously desirable option to pick from. Ipsative assessments would therefore be more preferred for use with young autistic children because they are also criterion-referenced and provide an objective evaluation of an individual's adaptive behaviours.

Assessment facilitates score interpretation for the learners. Scores from classroom assessment of young learners with autism found in inclusive settings are used for accountability just like for anyone else. However, classroom teachers need to be aware of the individual differences among autistic learners. These differences between ASD learners must be considered during scores mean interpretation as some particularly with Asperger may score far above average while their peers with pervasive developmental disorders (PDD) may score far below average as they may not even complete the activity given (Whalon, Otaiba, & Delano, 2009). Such variances will skew the class performance positively with a considerable number of learners getting low scores in areas like reading or oral comprehension (Whalon et al. 2009). In essence, when class teachers of young autistic learners report on learner-attainment, quantitative scores should not be given more recognition over effort.

In spite of the invaluable benefits that classroom assessment information gives to the classroom teacher and the school in general, the parent and the learner, there are issues that the autistic learner experiences which cause some difficulties (McLeskey, Waldron & Redd, 2014). The next section of this chapter will therefore present possible barriers to successful classroom assessment for the learner.

11.8.4 Learner-challenges during classroom assessment: Implications for educators

There are many challenges that teachers of autistic learners should be aware of during classroom assessment. This chapter only focuses on two that are deemed appropriate: the academic and the behavioural. It is necessary that young autistic learners like each and every learner make adequate progress on academic achievement standards, while being included in the general education classroom settings whenever possible. Nevertheless, only a limited number of schools have been successful in meeting these, sometimes competing demands for excellence and equity for this special group of learners (McLeskey, et al., 2014).

In instances where general education teachers are faced with teaching young autistic learners, the children may be expected to engage with the academic content just like everyone else because the teacher is not trained on methods of teaching and assessing such learners. This calls for collaboration or co-teaching between the general and special education educators' collaboration. The general education teacher will be responsible for teaching to the whole class and assessing all the learners. The special educator would be in charge of teaching and supporting the autistic learner during class activities and assessment (Strogilos & Avramidis, 2016).

One of the most common concerns for young children with developmental disabilities, such as autism is the risk of pervasive problem behaviours (Horner, Carr, Starin, Todd & Reed, 2002). Autistic learners have behaviours that form part of their behavioural repertoire that could be distracting to other learners and themselves during class assessment and during their own assessment of learning. They may flap their hands; jump about in circular movements or rock on their seats at a time when class activities are ongoing. Should such a situation arise, it would require the class teacher to be familiar with behaviour interventions such as procedures for functional behavioural assessment (FBA), applied behaviour analysis (ABA) and other behaviour interventions. At the centre of these interventions is to identify the relationship between the environmental activities and occurrences of certain behaviours (Honner et al. 2002) so that during class assessment, opportunities for the autistic learner to focus are increased. The teacher must identify the function that the behaviour serves as well as the antecedents that trigger such behaviours. Understanding the behaviour function and the antecedents places the class teacher in a better position to manage the undesirable behaviours. He/she could remove the stimuli or avoid it if it triggers the behaviours or avoid situations that would reinforce the inappropriate behaviours (Wong et al., 2015).

11.9 Conclusion

For inclusive class assessment to work for the South African learner, the educator and the community at large, there is the need to retool teachers in certain ethical assessment practices that are suited for the young autistic learner. The different theoretical frameworks that directly fit the South African education environment must inform their assessment practices. The importance of partnership with the family for successful teaching and assessment of young learners who are autistic is emphasised in this chapter and should be treated cautiously and professionally for it to function. Teacher-preparation in South Africa and within the region must therefore emphasise assessment practices that are inclined towards indigenous approaches and practices where suitable for the autistic learner to relate easily with the content and the world around him/her.

References

Abubakar, A., Ssewanyana, D., & Newton, C. R. (2016). A systematic review of research on autism spectrum disorders in sub-Saharan Africa. *Behavioural Neurology*. https://www.hindawi.com/journals/bn/contents/year/2016/

Agur, M., Hallam, R., Barber, J., Meagher, J., Roberts, L., Ross, P., & King, E. (2018). *A Rapid Evidence Assessment of the Effectiveness of Educational Interventions to Support Children and Young People with Autistic Spectrum Disorder.* Conwy: Welsh Government.

Beetham, H. & Sharpe, R. (2007). An introduction to rethinking pedagogy for a digital age. In Beetham & R. Sharpe (Eds.). *Rethinking Pedagogy for a Digital Age. Designing and Delivering e-Learning*. (pp. 1–11). London: Routledge.

Black, M. M., Walker, S. P., Fernald, L. C., Andersen, C. T., DiGirolamo, A. M., Lu, C., & Devercelli, A. E. (2017). Early childhood development coming of age: science through the life course. *The Lancet*, 389(10064): 77-90.

Botswana Government (2015). *National Curriculum and Assessment Framework (NCAF)*. Gaborone: Government Printers.

Brett, J. (2002). The Experience of disability from the perspective of parents of children with profound impairment: Is it time for an alternative model of disability? *Disability & Society* 17(7): 825-843, DOI: 10.1080/0968759022000039109.

Bronfenbrenner, U. (1994). Ecological models of human development. *International Encyclopedia of Education*, 3(2): 37-43.

Bronfenbrenner, U. (1979). *The ecology of human development: Experiments by nature and design.* Cambridge, MA: Harvard University Press.

Bronfenbrenner, U. (1977). Toward an experimental ecology of human development. *American Psychologist,* 32(7): 513.

Bush, H. H., Cohen, S. R., Eisenhower, A. S., & Blacher, J. (2017). Parents' Educational Expectations for Young Children with Autism Spectrum Disorder. *Education and Training in Autism and Developmental Disabilities*, 52(4): 357-368.

Chan, J. M., Lang, R., Rispoli, M., O'Reilly, M., Sigafoos, J., & Cole, H. (2009). Use of peer-mediated interventions in the treatment of autism spectrum disorders: A systematic review. *Research in Autism Spectrum Disorders*, 3(4): 876-889.

Clark, A. (2017). *Listening to Young Children: A Guide to Understanding and Using the Mosaic Approach.* (Expanded Third Edition) Jessica Kingsley Publishers.

Coogle, C. G., Floyd, K., Hanline, M. F., & Kellner-Hiczewski, J. (2013). Strategies used in natural environments to promote communication development in young children at risk for autism spectrum disorder. *Young Exceptional Children*, 16(3): 11-23.

Cox, A. J., & John, V. M. (2016). Transformative learning in post-apartheid South Africa: Disruption, dilemma, and direction. *Adult Education Quarterly*, 66(4): 303-318.

Crosland, K. & Dunlap, J. (2012). Effective strategies for the inclusion of children with autism in general education classrooms. *Behavior Modification*, 36(3): 251-269.

de Bruin, C. L., Deppeler, J. M., Moore, D. W., & Diamond, N. T. (2013). Public school-based interventions for adolescents and young adults with an autism spectrum disorder: A meta-analysis. *Review of Educational Research*, 83(4): 521-550.

de Giambattista, C., Ventura, P., Trerotoli, P., Margari, M., Palumbi, R., & Margari, L. (2018). Subtyping the Autism Spectrum Disorder: Comparison of Children with High Functioning Autism and Asperger Syndrome. *Journal of Autism and Developmental Disorders*, 1-13.

Downing, J. E. (2008). Including students with severe and multiple disabilities in typical classrooms: Practical strategies for teachers (3rd edition). Baltimore: Paul H. Brookes Publishing Co.

Dunphy, E. (2008). *Supporting early learning and development through formative assessment: A research paper.* Dublin: National Council for Curriculum and Assessment, NCCA.

Einarsdóttir, J. (2007). Research with children: Methodological and ethical challenges. *European Early Childhood Education Research Journal*, 15(2): 197-211.

Fleury, V. P., Hedges, S., Hume, K., Browder, D. M., Thompson, J. L., Fallin, K., Vaughn, S. (2014). Addressing the academic needs of adolescents with autism spectrum disorder in secondary education. *Remedial and Special Education*, 35(2): 68-79.

Glofcheski, R. (2017). Making Assessment for Learning Happen Through Assessment Task Design in the Law Curriculum. In *Scaling up Assessment for Learning in Higher Education* (pp. 67-80). Singapore: Springer.

Harrower, J. K., & Dunlap, G. (2001). Including children with autism in general education classrooms: A review of effective strategies. *Behavior Modification*, 25(5): 762-784.

Hayes, N., O'Toole, L., & Halpenny, M. (2017). *Introducing Brofenbrenner: A guide for practitioners and students in early years education.* Routledge: London.

Hudson, K. D. (2016). With equality and opportunity for all? Emerging scholars define social justice for social work. *British Journal of Social Work*, 47(7): 1959-1978.

Hurtb, J., Shaw, E., Izeman, S. G., Whaley, K., & Rogers, S.ally J. (2009). Infants & young children: Areas of agreement about effective practices among programs serving young children with autism spectrum disorders. *Infants & Young Children* 17-26.

International Disability and Development Consortium (IDDC, 2013). https://www.iddcconsortium.net/resources-tools/quality-inclusive-education-SDGs

Kamps, D. M., Leonard, B., Potucek, J., & Garrison-Harrell, L. (1995). Cooperative learning groups in reading: An integration strategy for students with autism and general classroom peers. *Behavioral Disorders*, 21(1): 89-109.

Kamps, D., Heitzman-Powell, L., Rosenberg, N., Mason, R., Schwartz, I., & Romine, R. S. (2016). Effects of reading mastery as a small group intervention for young children with ASD. *Journal of Developmental and Physical Disabilities*, 28(5): 703-722.

Kodak, T., Clements, A,. & LeBlanc, B. (2013). A rapid assessment of instructional strategies to teach auditory-visual conditional discriminations to children with autism. *Research in Autism Spectrum Disorders* 7, 801-807.

Kuschner, E.S., Bennetto, L. & Yost, K. J. (2007). Patterns of nonverbal cognitive functioning in young children with autism spectrum disorders. *Autism Dev Disord* 37: 795-807. https://doi.org/10.1007/s10803-006-0209-8

Iadarola, S., Hetherington, S., Clinton, C., Dean, M., Reisinger, E., Huynh, L., & Harwood, R. (2015). Services for children with autism spectrum disorder in three, large urban school districts: Perspectives of parents and educators. *Autism*, 19(6): 694-703.

Leonard, H. C., & Hill, E. L. (2014). The impact of motor development on typical and atypical social cognition and language: A systematic review. *Child and Adolescent Mental Health*, 19(3): 163-170.

Lerner, W. J. & Johns, B. (2012). *Learning disabilities and related mild disabilities: Characteristics, teaching strategies, and new directions* (12th ed.). Wadsworth: Cengage Learning.

Lopata, C., Smith, R.A., Volker, M.A., Thomeer, M.L., Lee, G. K., & McDonald, C.A. (2013). Comparison of adaptive behavior measures for children with HFASDs. *Autism Research and Treatment*, Article ID 415989, 10 pages, 2013. doi:10.1155/2013/415989

MacDonald, R., Parry-Cruwys, D., Dupere, S., & Ahearn, W. (2014). Assessing progress and outcome of early intensive behavioral intervention for toddlers with autism. *Research in Developmental Disabilities*, 35(12): 3632-3644.

Mackey, B. W., & Mackey, W. C. (2009). The presence of the US father as an enhancement for his children's reading achievement: masculine influence or a second parent?. *Reading Improvement*, 46(2): 99-108.

Macy, M. (2007). Theory and theory-driven practices of Activity Based Intervention. *Journal of Early and Intensive Behavior Intervention*, 4(3): 561.

McConachie, H. (2016). *Parents and young mentally handicapped children: A review of research issues*. Abingdon-on-Thames: Routledge.

McConachie, H., Livingstone, N., Morris, C., Beresford, B., Le Couteur, A., Gringras, P., & Parr, J. R. (2018). Parents suggest which indicators of progress and outcomes should be measured in young children with autism spectrum disorder. *Journal of Autism and Developmental Disorders*, 48(4): 1041-1051.

McLeskey, J., Waldron, N. L., & Redd, L. (2014). A case study of a highly effective, inclusive elementary school. *The Journal of Special Education*, 48(1): 59-70.

National Council for Curriculum Assessment, NCCA (2008). Accessed August 30th 2017 at http://ncca.ie/en/About_Us/Annual_Report/Annual_Report_2008.pdf

National Council for Curriculum Assessment, NCCA (1999). Special educational needs: Curriculum issues discussion paper.

Odom, S. L., & Wolery, M. (2003). A unified theory of practice in early intervention/early childhood special education: Evidence-based practices. *The Journal of Special Education*, 37(3): 164-173.

Odom, S. L., Boyd, B., Hall, L., & Hume, K. (2014). Comprehensive treatment models for children and youth with autism spectrum disorders. In Volkmar, S. Rogers, K. Pelphrey, & R. Paul (Eds.), *Handbook of autism and pervasive developmental disorders* (Vol. 2, pp. 770-778). Hoboken, NJ: Wiley.

Oakley, G., Howitt, C., Garwood, R., & Durack, A. R. (2013). Becoming multimodal authors: Pre-service teachers' interventions to support young children with autism. *Australasian Journal of Early Childhood*, 38(3): 86.

Overton, T. (2012). *Assessing children with special needs: An applied approach* (7th ed.). New Saddle, New Jersey: Pearson Education, Inc.

Rhoad-Drogalis, A., Sawyer, B. E., Justice, L. M., & O'Connell, A. A. (2018). Assessing Learning Behaviors in Early Childhood Special Education Classrooms. *Early Education and Development*, 29(4): 450-466.

Salvia, J., Ysseldyke, J., & Witmer, S. (2013). *Assessment in special and Inclusive Education.* Wadsworth: Cencage Learning.

Silverman, C. (2011). *Understanding autism: Parents, doctors, and the history of a disorder.* Princeton University Press.

Suskie, L. (2018). *Assessing student learning: A common sense guide.* John Wiley & Sons.

UK National Autistic Society, (nd.). Teaching & assessment strategies for students with autism spectrum disorder. Accessed 28th August 2017 https://www.plu.edu/dss/wp-content/uploads/sites/159/2014/10/teaching-and-assessment-strategies.pdf

Ungar, M. (2015). Practitioner review: diagnosing childhood resilience–a systemic approach to the diagnosis of adaptation in adverse social and physical ecologies. *Journal of Child Psychology and Psychiatry*, 56(1): 4-17.

Venn, J. J. (2000). *Assessing students with special needs* (2nd ed). Upper Saddle River, NJ: Merrill.

Watkins, L., O'Reilly, M., Kuhn, M., Gevarter, C., Lancioni, G. E., Sigafoos, J., & Lang, R. (2015). A review of peer-mediated social interaction interventions for students with autism in inclusive settings. *Journal of Autism and Developmental Disorders*, 45(4): 1070-1083.

West, E. A., Travers, J. C., Kemper, T. D., Liberty, L. M., Cote, D. L., McCollow, M. M., & Stansberry Brusnahan, L. L. (2016). Racial and ethnic diversity of participants in research supporting evidence-based practices for learners with autism spectrum disorder. *The Journal of Special Education*, 50(3): 151-163.

Whalon, K. J., Al Otaiba, S., & Delano, M. E. (2009). Evidence-based reading instruction for individuals with autism spectrum disorders. *Focus on Autism and Other Developmental Disabilities*, 24(1): 3-16.

Wong, C., Odom, S. L., Hume, K. A., Cox, A. W., Fettig, A., Kucharczyk, S., & Schultz, T. R. (2015). Evidence-based practices for children, youth, and young adults with autism spectrum disorder: A comprehensive review. *Journal of Autism and Developmental Disorders*, 45(7): 1951-1966.

Zanello, E., Calugi, S., Rucci, P., Pieri, G., Vandini, S., Faldella, G., & Fantini, M. P. (2015). Continuity of care in children with special healthcare needs: a qualitative study of family's perspectives. *Italian Journal of Pediatrics*, 41(1): 7.

12

AUTISM AND INCLUSION

Tawanda Majoko

Abstract

This chapter will focus on strategies for inclusion of learners with autism in mainstream education in accord with human rights policies and legislation. These strategies will be addressed by being entrenched in the inclusive pedagogy. The teaching strategies for inclusion of learners with autism addressed will be grounded in ensuring equity and equitable access, acceptance, participation and success of these learners mainstream classes in the community of their typically developing peers. This will include understanding inclusion, autism and how teachers can meet the needs of learners with and without autism in mainstream classes simultaneously. Teachers will be guided on applying their knowledge of inclusion, curriculum adaptation, classroom support, psycho-social support, emotional support, communication support and positive behaviour management in collaboration and discourse with other stakeholders. They will also be motivated to reflect on the success and effectiveness of adoption and adaptation of inclusion strategies in response to the needs of individual learners with autism and their contexts. Furthermore, practical considerations with respect to the process, content, environment and product of teaching and learning in mainstream classes will be discussed in a bid to bridge the theory and practice gap in inclusion of learners with autism in mainstream school classrooms. Teachers will be sensitised on how to support the social, behavioural and communication development of learners with autism in mainstream classrooms. The provision of interventions/support that meet the needs of learners with autism in the context of the mainstream classes will be discussed.

12.1 Introduction

Embedded within international research findings, this chapter presents challenges and 'best practices' in inclusion of learners with autism in mainstream education using Afrocentric lens particularly Ubuntu philosophy. Globally, autism is the most prevalent neurological disorder among children (Chandler-Olcott & Kluth, 2009). Autism is diagnosed in about 1:68 children (Centres for Disease Control and Prevention, 2014). This is higher than 1:88 that was revealed in 2012 (Centres for Disease Control and Prevention, 2014). Autism is characterised by deficits in language development (communication), lack of peer relationships, impaired non-verbal behaviour (social development), ritualistic behaviour and resistance to change (American Psychiatric Association, 2013; Humphrey 2008; Lynch & Irvine, 2009; Mandell, Ittenbach, Levy & Pinto-Martin, 2007). Autism is perceived as the ultimate learning disability because of its associated social and language difficulties (Jones & Frederickson, 2010). Several countries have passed policies and legislation on inclusion of learners with autism and other disabilities. These include Zimbabwe, the Education Act of 1986 as revised in 2006 (Majoko, 2017), the United Kingdom, No Child Left Behind (Humphrey & Symes, 2008), the USA, the Individuals with Disabilities Act

(Forbes, 2007) and South Africa, Education White Paper 6 (Naicker, 2009). These policies and legislation can be viewed as being in alignment with Ubuntu values and principles including compassion, dignity, humanity and mutuality that are grounded in building and maintaining communities through mutual caring and justice (Khoza, 2006, see also the Introduction to this volume). In the same vein, Inclusive Education is founded on respect for human rights and social justice (Pantic & Florian, 2010).

Since the Salamanca Statement and Framework for Action on Special Needs Education (UNESCO, 1994) endorsed the international practice of inclusion, the number of learners with autism educated in mainstream classrooms is significantly increasing across countries (Segall & Campbell, 2012; Symes & Humphrey, 2010). This can be attributed to the compliance of several countries with the policy of inclusion and its institutionalisation. Internationally, inclusion is the model option of service delivery in education of passion, inspiration and contention the world over (Appl & Spenciner, 2008; Allday et al., 2013; Sze, 2009). This is because of its entrenchment in realisation of human rights and social justice for learners with unique needs including autism whose marginalisation and exclusion in education are as old as humanity. Similarly, group solidarity, which is core to the existence of African communities underpins the Ubuntu philosophy (Mbigi & Maree, 2005). An African is not a rugged entity, but a person surviving within a community. It is only through such community that any challenges can be survived through brotherly and sisterly concern, cooperation, sharing and caring of the community (Luhabe, 2006). This includes the challenges in the inclusion of learners with autism in mainstream education which require collaboration and discourse of stakeholder individuals, organisations and institutions including parents, professionals, para-professionals, teachers, the government and communities.

Despite the global pursuit of inclusion since 1994, a single universally accepted definition of the philosophy is still illusive because of conceptual difficulties in defining it including what counts as evidence of its practice and model practice (Ainscow, 2005; Black-Hawkins & Florian, 2012; Dyson & Gallannaugh, 2007; Florian & Spratt, 2013). Inclusion is also complex because of the embedment of the philosophy in competing discourses coupled with its openness to multiple interpretations and understandings (Ballard, 2012; Donnelly & Watkins, 2011; Graham & Slee, 2008; Pantic & Florian, 2015). There are divergent understandings and practices of inclusion across continents, countries, states, provinces and districts. However, inclusion can be viewed as a process which entails the transformation of mainstream schools so as to ensure that all learners are supported to meet their full range of needs and the elimination of barriers in education (Florian, 2012; Friend & Bursuck, 2012; Kisanji & Saanane, 2009; Rouse, 2008). In the same vein, the premise that "a person is a person because of, or through others" (Moloketi, 2009), underpins the Ubuntu philosophy.

Inclusion includes a far wider range of learners vulnerable to marginalisation and exclusion in education than those with special educational needs (Ainscow, 2005; Berry, 2010; Blanton, Pugach & Florian, 2011; Florian & Black-Hawkins, 2011). The provision of quality EFA learners propels Inclusive Education. Access, participation, achievement and acceptance of all learners in mainstream education, irrespective of their individual differences and circumstances including disability, religion, race, ability, ethnicity, culture, gender, social and economic status, ability and health through the use of learner-centred pedagogy underpin inclusion (Agbenyega, 2007; Naicker, 2009; Donnelly & Watkins, 2011; EADSNE, 2011; Florian, 2009; Forbes, 2007). Central in inclusion is successful and effective pedagogy of all learners with unique needs and those vulnerable to marginalisation and exclusion in education in their neighbourhood mainstream schools in the community of their counterparts without developmental challenges (Ballard, 2012; Berry, 2010; Chhabra, Srivastava & Srivastava, 2010; Flecha & Soler, 2013; Florian, 2012). Inclusion is, therefore, a broad human rights and social justice agenda that contradicts with the values and principles of special education. The provision of education to those with unique needs, including autism in special settings is perceived as segregatory and violating the dignity of these learners let alone violating their fundamental right to inclusion in all domains of life, including education. Similarly, the African philosophy of Ubuntu is grounded in individuals' expression of compassion, reciprocity, dignity, humanity and mutuality in establishment and sustenance of communities with communalities and justice (Poovan, Du Toit & Engelbrecht, 2006).

African societies are humanist, community-based and socialist in orientation (Nussbaum, 2003). Underpinning inclusion In African society we see not only physical integration, but also social, cultural and emotional integration of all learners in mainstream schools regardless of their individual differences and circumstances (Chireshe, 2013; Deluca, Tramonta & Kett, 2013; Majoko, 2016; Mandina, 2012). Inclusion entails identification and reduction of barriers to learners' access to mainstream settings including educational institutions, communities and families and maximising support practices to enhance achievement (Chireshe, 2013; Majoko, 2013). Such barriers can stem from individual and systemic factors including individuality of learners and environmental variables. The successful and effective practice of inclusion embodies participation of all learners and their families in the activities of the mainstream school communities while meeting their unique needs, as well as contributing to the advancement of these institutions (Chakuchichi, 2013; Deluca, Tramonta & Kett, 2013; Mushoriwa & Gasva, 2008).

The inclusion of learners with autism is an international challenge to teachers (Emam & Farrell, 2009; Falkmer, Anderson, Joosten & Falkmer, 2015). Nevertheless, inclusion benefits both learners with and without autism (Chandler-Olcott & Kluth, 2009). Inclusive classes provide conducive settings for growth and education of learners with autism alongside their peers without developmental delays (De Boer & Simpson, 2009; Chandler-Olcott & Kluth, 2009; Vakil, Welton, O'Connor & Kline, 2009). Similarly, Ubuntu philosophy advances that Africans are social beings who are in constant communion with one another in a setting where a human being is considered a human being through her or his relationships to other human beings (Van den Heuvel, Mangaliso & Van de Bunt, 2006). Inclusive classes can also be stimulants for learning, development and feelings of acceptance for learners with autism (Emam & Farrell, 2009; Leblanc, Richardson & Burns, 2009; Lindsay, Proulx, Scott & Thompson, 2014). Inclusive classes are, therefore, catalytic in equalisation of opportunities in social and educational domains.

Learners with autism who are fully included in mainstream classes have more social networks, social support and better educational targets compared to their peer counterparts in special classes (Leach & Duffy, 2009; Lindsay et al., 2014). Learners with autism who are included in mainstream classes also develop a realisation and accommodation of individual differences (De Boer & Simpson, 2009; Symes & Humphrey, 2010). This is because of their exposition to counterparts with a diversity of talents and temperaments (Falkmer, Granlund, Nilholm & Falkmer, 2012; Leach & Duffy, 2009; Lindsay et al., 2014). Inclusion in mainstream school classes further increases educational expectations for learners with autism and their typically developing peers (Emam & Farrell, 2009; Finke, McNaughton & Drager, 2009; Horrocks, White & Roberts, 2008). Inclusion can facilitate social cohesion and the provision of quality education to all learners irrespective of their differences. Similarly, the tenet that the survival of an individual is dependent on other people – the society and the community, underpins the Africa philosophy of Ubuntu (Mangaliso, 2001).

Limited systemic change in educational institutions in several countries has resulted in negligible progress toward inclusion for learners with autism in the entire mainstream education curricula and contexts (Leach & Duffy, 2009; Maich & Belcher, 2012). This can be attributed to the complexity of practising the philosophy because of the lack of a universally accepted understanding of it. Attempts to support inclusion and access to the mainstream school curriculum have culminated in the shift primarily from where learners receive their educational programmes, to what and how the learners are taught (Ballard, 2012; Berry, 2010; Black-Hawkins & Florian, 2012). This is because unlike special education, inclusion goes beyond physical access of learners to mainstream schools. The present assumption for teaching learners with autism is to consider the access of these learners to the mainstream classes focusing on the quality of learning in progress (Humphrey & Lewis, 2008). As a result, the presence of learners with autism in mainstream settings alone will not guarantee better outcomes for them (Bitterman, Daley, Misra, Carlson & Markowitz, 2008; Falkmer, Ochlers, Granlund & Falkmer, 2015). This is because inclusion is a fundamental educational change which requires individual and systemic change, including changing of stakeholders' attitudes and the processes and physical infrastructure of educational institutions (Ballard, 2012). Similarly, Ubuntu pivots on humanness, a spirit of caring within the community wherein people in the community love one another (Mangaliso, 2001). Successful and effective support for access, learning, acceptance, participation and success of these learners should be considered (Chandler-Olcott & Kluth, 2009; Jones & Frederickson, 2010; Pellecchia, Connell, Beidas, Xie, Marcus & Mandell, 2015). These are complex considerations since they necessitate the active participation and involvement of all stakeholders who may lack the expertise, positive attitudes and resources such as assistant teachers.

Several studies have examined strategies for including learners with autism in mainstream settings. These include Humphrey and Symes (2013), Jones and Frederickson (2010), Maich and Belcher (2012), and Leblanc et al. (2009). Tailored teaching methods, essential training, teamwork, establishing collaborative cultures with families, nurturing a welcoming class climate and pooling resources are common features of these studies. Similarly, Ubuntu is in contrast to individualism, unilateral decision-making and insensitive competitiveness (Eze, 2006). Although these are currently perceived as model practices, this chapter shows how they are implemented in inclusion of learners with autism in mainstream settings. While several researchers reveal numerous benefits of inclusion in mainstream education, they report that strategies for inclusion of learners with autism in mainstream settings are a fundamental international gap with regards to the knowledge base (Emam & Farrell, 2009; Humphrey & Symes, 2013; Vakil et al., 2009).

12.2 Challenges in inclusion of learners with autism

Several studies have explored challenges related to the inclusion of learners with disabilities. There are individual differences among learners with autism (Hess, Morrier, Heflin & Ivey, 2008; Beaston, 2008; Dingfelder & Mandell, 2011; Humphrey & Symes, 2013). Consequently, the challenges revealed in literature may not apply to all of them. Autism is characterised by significant deficits in interacting and repetitive behaviour, interests, activities and communication (American Psychiatric Association, 2013; Humphrey, 2008; Park, Chitiyo & Choi, 2010). This curtails social cohesion of these learners with their typically developing peers. Because of the corresponding difficulties in social and language development of learners with autism (Chandler-Olcott & Kluth, 2009; Humphrey & Lewis, 2008; Lynch & Irvine, 2009), their navigation of the social world is often a challenge (Pellecchia et al., 2015; Jones & Frederickson, 2010; Mandell, Stahmer, Shin, Xie, Reisinger & Marcus, 2013). Therefore, language deficits interfere with the communication of learners with autism with their counterparts without developmental delays. Resultantly, learners with autism are approximately 20 times more vulnerable to social exclusion in educational institutions compared to their typically developing peers (Humphrey, 2008). Interventions are therefore needed to eliminate the marginalisation and exclusion of learners with autism in mainstream schools.

Processing of sensory input, creative play, social interaction and verbal and non-verbal communication are among the essential aspects of development, which are usually challenging in educating learners with autism (Brewin et al., 2008; Beaston, 2008; Emam & Farrell, 2009; Wilmshurst & Brue, 2010). In particular, sensory overload, may interfere with the inclusion of learners with autism in mainstream classes. Understanding and conveying personal needs to peers and teachers is often a challenge for learners with autism (Kasari, Locke, Gulsrud & Rotheram-Fuller, 2011; Maich & Belcher, 2012). This can lead to frustration and ultimately, outbursts. Reading the verbal and body expressions of their teachers and following class instructions may also challenge learners with autism (Chandler-Olcott & Kluth, 2009; Segall & Campbell, 2012; Wilmshurst & Bruce, 2010). Learners with autism have further complications in sustaining noisy settings, touches of others and maintaining eye contact owing to sensory issues (Lindsay et al., 2014; Leblanc et al., 2009; Symes & Humphrey, 2010). However, school settings are busy, loud and crowded (Farrell, Alborz, Howes & Pearson, 2010). This complicates the inclusion of learners with autism in mainstream settings. The difficulties of grasping the social domain for learners with autism can restrict the establishment and reinforcement of relationships with their counterparts (Brewin et al., 2008; Bitterman et al., 2008; Vakil et al., 2009). This can invoke anxiety and stress in them. Because of difficulties in social and emotional comprehension of learners with autism (American Psychiatric Association, 2012; Pellecchia et al., 2015; Lynch & Irvine, 2009), strategies are needed to include them in mainstream settings.

Despite the challenges, the inclusion of learners with unique needs including autism in education is an international priority (Chandler-Olcott & Kluth, 2009; Falkmer et al., 2012; Humphrey & Lewis, 2008). Resultantly, several countries are including these learners in mainstream classes in high numbers. As a notable proportion of learners with autism are educated in mainstream classes globally (Lynch & Irvine, 2009; Symes & Humphrey, 2010), teachers and families confront the challenge of realising successful inclusion despite the lack of clear policies and adequate teacher preparation (Segall & Campbell, 2012; Vakil et al., 2009). Although autism is a life-long condition, the impairments may be mitigated through intervention (Dingfelder & Mandell, 2011; Hinton, Sofronoff & Sheffield., 2008). The knowledge base for medicine and education demonstrate that using inclusive pedagogy is among the best practices for delivery of services to learners with autism (Chandler-Olcott & Kluth, 2009; Falkmer, Anderson, Joosten & Falkmer, 2015; Horrocks et al., 2008). This is because it facilitates the holistic development of these learners and their typically developing peers. However, research reveals that the inclusion of learners with special needs in mainstream classes is a complicated and ill-conceptualised domain of education (Emam & Farrell, 2009; Humphrey & Lewis, 2008). Worldwide, schools struggle to meet to the needs of learners with autism (Falkmer et al., 2015; De Boer & Simpson, 2009). Therefore, identification of strategies for inclusion of these learners in mainstream school education is imperative.

Stakeholders, including parents of learners with autism, usually express dissatisfaction with educational programmes and services and advocate for programmes and services that meet the unique needs of these learners (Lynch & Irvine, 2009). More effort is, therefore, required to nurture and sustain classes that are friendly to learners with autism (Emam & Farrell, 2009; Hinton et al., 2008; Jones & Frederickson, 2010). Typically, developing learners often emulate the behaviour and attitudes of adults, attitudes of teachers towards the teaching and learning of learners with autism in mainstream classes are integral with respect to nurturing an inclusive educational setting (Barnes, 2009; Falkmer et al., 2015; Horrocks et al., 2008). Consequently, meeting the needs of learners with autism is essential, as these learners are vulnerable to social exclusion and bullying (Finke et al., 2009; Jones & Frederickson, 2010; Kasari et al., 2011).

Research on strategies for successful and effective inclusion is needed (Park et al., 2010; Segall & Campbell, 2012). However, many studies have examined teachers' attitudes, beliefs and perceptions about the inclusion of learners with special needs, educational processes and supports in mainstream classes (Berry, 2010; Donnelly & Watkins, 2011; Florian & Black-Hawkins, 2011). This chapter, therefore, presents strategies for inclusion of learners with autism in mainstream classes in order to add to the limited literature base and to glean practices to enhance access, acceptance, participation, achievement, equity, equality and achievement of these learners in education in compliance with the global priority.

12.3 Inclusion strategies for learners with autism

Worldwide, the placement of learners with autism in mainstream classes is a common practice (Leach & Duffy, 2009). Nevertheless, the presence of learners with autism in mainstream classes is not a guarantee of learning and their counterparts' welcoming of them (Brewin et al., 2008; Finke et al., 2009; Humphrey, 2008) creating a challenge for teachers (Pellecchia et al., 2015; Lindsay et al., 2014). Inclusion in education is integral in social, educational and career development, sense of belonging and full participation of learners with autism in mainstream families, communities and schools (Maich & Belcher,

2012). Nurturance of conducive teaching and learning process, content, environment and assessment is integral in successful inclusion of learners with autism in mainstream classes.

Strategies for inclusion of learners with autism in mainstream classes presented in this chapter are international research evidence based. Teachers need to entrench individualised instruction in a whole-class educational context to include learners with autism in mainstream classes (Barnes, 2009; Boyle et al., 2013). Moreover, the individuality of learners with and without autism need to underpin teaching and learning in mainstream classes (Emam & Farrell, 2009). Teachers who successfully manage inclusive pedagogy in mainstream classes, respond to the needs of all learners and optimise their educational achievement and full participation (Hess et al., 2008; Horrocks et al, 2008; Kasari et al., 2011). Similarly, inclusion entails access and success of all learners in mainstream classes including those with special needs who require teaching and learning support (Black-Hawkins & Florian, 2012; Boyle, Topping & Jindal-Snape, 2013; Florian & Black-Hawkins, 2011; Florian & Linklater, 2010). To realise inclusion, the individuality of both learners with autism and their peers without the condition takes centre stage in pedagogy (Locke et al., 2010). The understanding of teachers that every learner with or without autism is a unique individual and not defining learners by their diagnosis, supports inclusion in mainstream classes (Lindsay et al., 2013; Segall & Campbell, 2012). Teachers need to look beyond the label in order to challenge stereotypes and their expectations about the potentialities of learners with autism (Wilmshurst & Bruce, 2010).

Teachers' strategic management of structured routines to nurture rich educational communities for learners with autism and their typically developing peers facilitates inclusion in mainstream classes (Barnes, 2008; Boyle et al., 2013). Such includes the use of visual schedules and reinforcement for both learners with and without autism in mainstream classes (De Boer & Simpson, 2009). Similarly, inclusive pedagogy requires teachers to extend what is ordinarily availed to all learners and the creation of a community of practice rather than use of pedagogy that is appropriate for most alongside something "additional" or "different" with respect to learners with disabilities (Black-Hawkins & Florian, 2012; Donnelly & Watkins, 2011). It is fundamental for teachers to manage pedagogy of learners with autism in the community of their typically developing counterparts (Emam & Farrell, 2009; Falkmer et al., 2015), as inclusion entails the equal valuation of every learner as a member of the school culture (Flecha & Soler, 2013; Florian & Linklater, 2010; Slee, 2011).

The focus of teachers on abilities instead of limitations of individual learners with and without autism supports inclusion in mainstream classes (Flecha & Soler, 2013). Similarly, inclusive pedagogy rejects rigid perceptions about capability and the premise that the inclusion of learners with special needs interferes with the achievement of their typically developing peers (Deluca et al., 2013; Forlin & Chambers, 2011). The use of reinforcements in developing and maintaining the behaviour and educational success of individual learners with and without autism promotes inclusion in mainstream classes (Jones & Frederickson, 2010; Leach & Duffy, 2009). "Learning for all" which curtails differences can underpin teachers' management of behaviour and pedagogy to realise the inclusion of learners with autism in mainstream classes (Boyle et al., 2013; Falkmer et al., 2015). Research, similarly, reveals that inclusive educational settings support learners with autism to learn in the community of their peers without developmental delays (De Boer

& Simpson, 2009; Chandler-Olcott & Kluth, 2009; Vakil et al., 2009). The use of positive reinforcements based on the interests of individual learners with autism and their typically developing peers is support in inclusion in mainstream classes (Humphrey, 2008).

In order to realise inclusion and academic success of both learners with and without autism in mainstream classes, teachers can use academic modifications (Hinton et al., 2008; Kasari et al., 2011; Leblanc et al., 2009) including task analysis, reduction of assignment items, alternate response modes in question answering and peer and para-professional support (Lynch & Irvine, 2009; Majoko, 2017). The premise of inclusive pedagogy that all learners can progress with support needs to underpin teachers' practices in mainstream classes (Kisanji & Saanane, 2009; Mandina, 2012; Slee, 2011). Similarly, research demonstrates that inclusion in education entails co-existence and achievement of both learners with disabilities and their typically developing counterparts (Ballard, 2012; Deluca et al., 2013; Slee, 2011). Support from peer teachers and para-professionals and teachers' utilisation of learning and assessment strategies and techniques that meets the individual needs of learners with autism supports the inclusion of these learners in mainstream classes (Park et al., 2010; Vakil et al., 2009).

Teacher modification of the educational environments can include learners with autism in mainstream classes (Barnes, 2009; Brewin et al., 2008). Similarly, inclusive pedagogy requires teachers to research and adopt innovative strategies in order to facilitate teaching and learning of learners with and without special needs (Chakuchichi, 2013; Chhabra et al., 2010; Chireshe, 2013; Flecha & Soler, 2013). Teacher modifications of the educational environment including strategic sitting arrangements of both learners with and without autism and reducing the noise levels facilitates inclusion in mainstream classes (Humphrey, 2008; Lindsay et al., 2014). Nurturing "autism friendly" classes promotes inclusion in mainstream classes (Barnes, 2009; Falkmer et al., 2015; Hinton et al., 2008). Teacher exploration of strategies for establishing and reinforcing educational environments that supports learning of learners can support inclusion in mainstream classes (Mpofu & Shumba, 2012; Mugweni & Dakwa, 2013; Segall & Campbell, 2012). Similarly, inclusive pedagogy requires teachers to view complexities with respect to teaching and learning as barriers to education (Ballard, 2012; Slee, 2011). Teacher modification of mainstream classes through creating structured environment can include learners with autism in these settings (De Boer & Simpson, 2009).

Teachers' socialisation of learners with autism and their typically developing peers is integral in inclusion in mainstream classes (Emam & Farrell, 2009). Furthermore, teachers' socialisation of learners with autism and their typically developing peers can facilitate social interaction in mainstream classes (Majoko, 2017; Kasari et al., 2011). Similarly, studies show that learners with autism who are fully included socially interact (Hess et al., 2008; Kasari et al., 2011; Locke et al., 2010). Teachers need to socialise both learners with autism and their peers without developmental delays utilising in-class disability awareness information sessions and peer models to facilitate inclusion in mainstream classes (Jones & Fredrickson, 2010; Kasari et al., 2011). Such strategies can support the full involvement and participation of learners with and without autism in mainstream classes (Majoko, 2017; Lindsay et al., 2014). Similarly, the premise that "all" learners can succeed underpins inclusive pedagogy (Chireshe, 2013; Flecha &b Soler, 2013). Inclusion embodies equal valuation of every learner as an integral part of the culture of the school system (Ballard, 2012; Chhabra et al., 2010; Donnelly & Watkins, 2011) which involves access and achievement (Falkmer et al., 2012; Forlin & Chambers, 2011; Flecha & Soler, 2013). Similarly, respecting the self-worth of individual learners as equal partners in the class informs inclusive pedagogy (Florian & Black-Hawkins, 2011). Teaching of social skills entrenched in home and school contexts supports the social development of learners with autism and ultimately facilitates their inclusion in mainstream classes (Humphrey, 2008; Lynch & Irvine, 2009).

Teachers' support of communication of learners with autism promotes the inclusion of these learners in mainstream classes (Segall & Campbell, 2012). In such support, teachers can use sign language, paired gestures with speech in communication, total communication, concrete language and reinforce positive communication and capitalise on the strengths/ abilities of learners with autism. Inclusive pedagogy, similarly, requires teachers to focus teaching and learning on what learners are able to do rather than on what they are not able to do. In the same vein, previous research reveals that preparation of teachers for autism (Falkmer et al., 2015; Hinton et al., 2008; Park et al., 2010) is indispensable in the inclusion of learners with the condition in mainstream classes. Learner diversity needs to underpin teaching and learning in mainstream classes in order to realise inclusion of learners with autism in these settings (Barnes, 2009). Inclusive pedagogy requires teachers to account for differences as an essential component of the development of learners in any conceptualising of teaching and learning (Florian & Linklater, 2010). Teaching communication to learners with autism and the use of augumentative techniques of communication based on their communication abilities support the inclusion of these learners in mainstream classes (Emam & Farrell, 2009).

Teachers are required to strategically manage obsessions and compulsion to include learners with autism in mainstream classes (De Boer & Simpson, 2009; Falkmer et al., 2015). This aligns with inclusive pedagogy which is embedded in learning for all – the idea of everybody ("not some or most") instead of exclusively learners diagnosed with "additional needs" (Florian & Black-Hawkins, 2011). Teachers need to explain changes regarding daily routines and use reinforcement focused on learners with autism and their counterparts without the condition. Teacher application of a universal approach to the management of obsessions and compulsions assists in eliminating typically developing learners' stigmatisation of their counterparts with autism (Horrocks et al., 2008; Humphrey & Lewis, 2010). Previous research demonstrates that social justice and human rights principles need to underpin inclusive teachers' management of learners with disabilities and their typically developing peers (Ballard, 2012; Donnelly & Watkins, 2011; Vakil et al., 2009). Teacher creation of a schedule that informs learners with autism on the daily routine and make them aware in advance of events taking place supports the inclusion of these learners in mainstream classes (Kasari et al., 2011).

Engagement of teachers with other stakeholders can support inclusion of learners with autism in mainstream classes (Hinton et al., 2008). This can entail their consultation and partnership with para-professionals, professionals, parents and typically developing learners. Similarly, inclusive pedagogy is grounded in collaboration of teachers with other stakeholders who respect the dignity of learners (Black-Hawkins & Florian, 2012). Previous studies, similarly, reveal that teacher collaboration with other stakeholders in implementing Inclusive Education is foundational in pooling inclusive resources (Boyle et al., 2013; Chireshe, 2013), including personnel, materials, finance and technology.

Strategies for inclusion of learners with autism presented in this chapter primarily focused on the classroom. However, the inclusion of these learners extends beyond the classroom. The inclusion of learners with autism in mainstream classes need to be embedded in the development of inclusive policies, communities, structures and cultures. This requires consultation and partnership of schools with their neighbourhood stakeholder individuals, organisations and institutions. Respect for diversity, commitment to quality teaching for all and the premise that inclusion is a process instead of an event are integral in inclusion of learners with autism in mainstream classes.

References

American Psychiatric Association. (2013). *Diagnostic and statistical manual of mental disorders* (5th ed.). Arlington, VA: American Psychiatric Publishing.

Ballard, K. (2012). Inclusion and social justice: Teachers as agents of change. In *Teaching in Inclusive School Communities.* (pp. 65- 87). Hoboken, NJ: John Wiley & Sons.

Barnes, K. (2009). The attitudes of regular education teachers regarding inclusion of students with Autism. *Dissertation Abstracts International*, 69 (10): 3905.

Beaston, J. E. (2008). Walk a mile in their shoes: Implementing family centred care in serving children and families affected by autism spectrum disorder. *Topics in Language Disorders*, 28(4): 309-322.

Berry, R. W. (2010). Pre-service and early career teachers' attitudes toward inclusion, instructional accommodations and fairness. Three profiles. *The Teacher Educator*, 45(2): 75 -95.

Bitterman, A., Daley, T.C., Misra, S., Carlson, E., & Markowitz, J. (2008). A national sample of pre-schoolers with autism spectrum disorders: Special education services and parent satisfaction. *Journal of Autism and Developmental Disorders*, 38: 1509-1517.

Black-Hawkins, K. & Florian, L. (2012). Classroom teachers' craft knowledge of their inclusive practice. *Teachers and Teaching Practice*, 18(5): 567-584.

Boyle, C., Topping, K., & Jindal-Snape, D. (2013). Teachers' attitudes towards inclusion in high schools. *Teachers and Teaching*, 19: 527-542.

Brewin, B.J., Renwick, R., & Fudge Schormans, A. (2008). Parental perspectives of the quality of life in school environment for children with Asperger Syndrome. *Focus on Autism and Other Developmental Disabilities*, 23(4): 242-252.

Centre for Disease Control and Prevention (2014). Prevalence of autism spectrum disorders aged 8 to 10 years. Autism and developmental disabilities monitoring network, 11 sites, United States, 2010. *MMWR Surveillance Summary* 63: 1-21.

Centres for Disease Control and Prevention (2012). Prevalence of autism spectrum disorders. Autism and developmental disabilities monitoring network, 14 sites, United States, 2010. *MMWR Surveillance Summaries*, 61(3): 1-19.

Chakuchichi, D. (2013). Inclusive education in Zimbabwe: Mashonaland West Province. Unpublished Report, Leonard Cheshire Disability Zimbabwe Trust.

Chandler-Olcott, K., & Kluth, P. (2009). With everyone benefits from including students with autism in literacy classrooms. *The Reading Teacher* 6(7): 548-557.

Chhabra, S., Srivastava, R., & Srivastava, I. (2010). Inclusive education in Botswana: The perceptions of school teachers. *Journal of Disability Policy Studies*, 20: 219-228.

Chireshe, R. (2011). Special needs education in-service teacher trainees' views on Inclusive Education in Zimbabwe. *Journal of Social Science* 27(3): 157-164.

Chireshe, R. (2013). The state of Inclusive Education in Zimbabwe: Bachelor of Education (Special Needs Education) students' perceptions. *Journal of Social Science* 34(3): 223-228.

De Boer, S., & Simpson, R. (2009). *Successful inclusion for students with autism: Creating a complete, effective ASD inclusion program*. San Francisco, CA: Jossey-Bass.

Deluca, M., Tramonta, C., & Kett, M. (2013). Including children with disability in primary school: The case of Mashonaland, Zimbabwe. Unpublished report.

Dingfelder, H. E., & Mandel, D. S. (2011). Bridging the research-to-practice gap in autism intervention: An application of diffusion of innovation theory. *Journal of Autism and Developmental Disorders*, 41: 597-609.

Donnelly, V. & Watkins, A. (2011). Teacher education for inclusion in Europe. *Prospects*, 41(3): 341-353.

Emam, M., M., & Farrell, P. (2009). Tensions experienced by teachers and their views of support for pupils with autism spectrum disorders in mainstream schools. *European Journal of Special Needs Education*, 24(4): 407-422.

Falkmer, M., Anderson, K., Joosten, A., & Falkmer, T. (2015). Parents' perspectives on inclusive schools for children with Autism Spectrum Conditions. *International Journal of Disability, Development and Education*, 62 (1): 1-23.

Falkmer, M., Granlund, M., Nilholm, C., & Falkmer, T. (2012). From my perspective-Perceived participation in mainstream schools in students with autism spectrum conditions. *Developmental Neurorehabilitation*, 15: 191-201.

Falkmer, M., Ochlers, K., Granlund, M., & Falkmer, T. (2015). Can you see it too? Observed and self-rated participation in mainstream schools in students with and without autism spectrum disorders. *Developmental Neurorehabilitation*, 18: 365-374.

Farrell, P., Alborz, A., Howes, A., & Pearson, D. (2010). The impact of teaching assistants on improving pupils' academic achievement in mainstream schools. A review of the literature. *Educational Review*, 62: 435-448.

Finke, E., McNaughton & Drager, K. (2009). All children can and should have the opportunity to learn. *Augmentative and Alternative Communication*, 25 (2): 110-22.

Flecha, R. & Soler, M. (2013). Turning difficulties into possibilities: engaging Roma families and students in school through dialogic learning. *Cambridge Journal of Education*, 43(4): 451-465.

Florian, C., & Linklater, H. (2010). Preparing teachers for Inclusive Education: Using inclusive pedagogy to enhance teaching and learning for all. *Cambridge Journal of Education*, 40: 369-386.

Florian, L. & Black-Hawkins, K. (2011). Exploring inclusive pedagogy. *British Educational Research Journal*, 37(5): 813-828.

Forlin, C., & Chambers, D. (2011). Teacher preparation for Inclusive Education: Increasing knowledge but raising concerns. *Asia-Pacific Journal of Teacher Education*, 39: 17-32.

Hess, K., Morrier, M., Heflin, L., & Ivey, M. (2008). Autism treatment survey: Services received by children with autism spectrum disorders in public school classrooms. *Journal of Autism and Developmental Disorders*, 38 (5): 961-971.

Hinton, S., Sofronoff, K, & Sheffield, J. (2008). Training teachers to manage students with Asperger's syndrome in an inclusive classroom setting. *The Australian Educational and Developmental Psychologist*, 25 (2): 34-48.

Horrocks, J., White, G. & Roberts, L. (2008). Principals' attitudes regarding inclusion of children with autism in Pennsylvania public schools. *Journal of Autism and Developmental Disorders*, 38: 1462-1473.

Humphrey, N. & Symes, W. (2013). Inclusive education of pupils with autistic spectrum disorders in secondary mainstream schools: teacher attitudes, experience and knowledge. *International Journal of Inclusive Education*, 17 (1): 32-46.

Humphrey, N. (2008). Including pupils with autistic spectrum disorders in mainstream schools. *Support for Learning*, 23(1): 41-47.

Humphrey, N., & Lewis, S. (2008). Make me normal: The views and experiences of pupils on the autistic spectrum. *Journal of Research in Special Educational Needs* 6: 76-86.

Jones, A., & Frederickson, N. (2010). Multi-informant predictors of social inclusion of students with autism spectrum disorders attending mainstream school. *Journal of Autism and Developmental Disorders* 40(9): 1094-103.

Kasari, L., Locke, J., Gulsrud, A., & Rotheram-Fuller, E. (2011). Social networks and friendships at school: Comparing children with and without ASD. *Journal of Autism and Developmental Disorders*, 41: 533-554.

Kisanji, J., & Saanane, C. B. (2009). *Responding to marginalization and exclusion in education in Tanzania. Chapter prepared for the Research Forum*. Institute for Inclusive Education: State University of Arizona.

Leach, D., & Duffy, M., L. (2009). Supporting students with autism spectrum disorders in inclusive settings. *Intervention in School and Clinic*, 45(1): 31-37.

Leblanc, L., Richardson, W., & Burns, K.,A. (2009). Autism spectrum disorder and the inclusive classroom. *Teacher Education and Special Education: The Journal of the Teacher Education Division of the Council for Exceptional Children*, 32(2): 166-179.

Lindsay, S., Proulx, M., Scott, H., & Thompson, N. (2014). Exploring teachers' strategies for including children with autism spectrum disorder in mainstream classrooms. *International Journal of Inclusive Education*, 18(2): 101-122.

Locke, J., Ishijima, E. H., Kasari, C., & London, N. (2010). Loneliness, friendship quality and the social networks of adolescents with high-functioning autism in an inclusive school setting. *Journal of Research in Special Educational Needs*, 10: 74-81.

Lynch, S., & Irvine, A. (2009). Inclusive education and best practice for children with autism spectrum disorder: An integrated approach. *International Journal of Inclusive Education*, 13(8): 845-849.

Maich, K., & Belcher E. C. (2012). Using picture books to create peer awareness about autism spectrum disorders in the inclusive classroom. *Intervention in School and Clinic*, 47(4): 206-213.

Majoko, T. (2013). Challenges in School Guidance and Counselling (SGC) services provisions for children with disabilities in Zimbabwean inclusive primary schools. D.Ed. Unpublished University of South Africa.

Majoko, T. (2016). Inclusion of children with autism spectrum disorders: Listening and hearing to voices from the grassroots. *Journal of Autism and Developmental Disorders*, 46(4): 1429-1140.

Mandell, D. S., Stahmer, A.C., Shin, S., Xie, M., Reisinger, E., & Marcus, S.C. (2013). The role of treatment fidelity on outcomes during a randomized field trial of an autism intervention. *Autism*, 17(3): 281-295.

Mandina, S. (2012). Bachelor of education in-service teacher trainees' perceptions and attitudes on Inclusive Education in Zimbabwe. *Asian Social Science*, 8(13): 227- 232.

Mandipa, E. & Manyatera, G. (2014). *African Disability Rights Yearbook Volume 2.* Pretoria: Pretoria University Law Press.

Mpofu, J., & Shumba, A. (2012). Challenges faced by students with special educational needs in early childhood development centres in Zimbabwe as perceived by ECD trainers and parents. *Anthropologist*, 14(4): 327-338.

Mugweni, R. M., & Dakwa F.E. (2013). Exploring the implementation of 'EFA' in Early Childhood Development in Zimbabwe: Successes and challenges. *Case Studies Journal*. 1: 1-9.

Musengi, M., & Chireshe, R. (2012). Inclusion of deaf students in mainstream primary schools in Zimbabwe: Challenges and opportunities. *Stud Tribals*, 10(2): 107-116.

Mushoriwa, T., & Gasva, O. 2008. Attitudes of secondary school pupils towards inclusion of educably mentally challenged pupils in Harare. *Zimbabwe Bulletin of Teacher Education* 15 (1).

Naicker, S. (2009). From policy to practice: A South African perspective on implementing Inclusive Education policy. *International Journal of Whole Schooling*, 3(1): 7.

Park, M., Chitiyo, M., & Choi, Y. (2010). Examining pre-service teachers' attitudes towards children with autism in the USA. *Journal of Research in Special Educational Needs* 10 (2): 107-14.

Pellecchia, M., Connell, J. E., Beidas, R.S., Xie, M., Marcus, S.C., & Mandell, D.S. (2015). Dismantling the active ingredients of an intervention for children with autism. *Journal of Autism and Developmental Disorders*, 45: 2917-2927.

Segall, M. J., & Campbell, J. M. (2012). Factors relating to education professionals' classroom practices for the inclusion of students with autism spectrum disorders. *Research in Autism Spectrum Disorders*, 6: 1156-1167.

Slee, R. (2011). *The irregular school: Exclusion, schooling and Inclusive Education*. Oxon: Routledge.

Symes, W. & Humphrey, N. (2010). Peer indicator of social inclusion among pupils with autistic spectrum disorders (ASD) in mainstream secondary schools. *School Psychology*, 31 (5): 478-494.

Vakil, S., Welton, E. O'Connor, B., & Kline, L. (2009). Inclusion means everyone! The role of the early childhood educator when including young children with autism. *Early Childhood Educational Journal*, 36: 321-126.

Wilmshurst, L. & Brue, A. (2010). *The complete guide to special education*. San Francisco: Jossey-Bass.

13

AUTISM AND THE LAW

Thersia Du Toit-Smit

Abstract

When a child is diagnosed with ASD, his or her parents embark on a journey into the world of autism. However, most often parents have to navigate this journey without a road map. Many authors worldwide and in Africa have lamented that diagnosis is not accompanied by clear guidelines for intervention and support. Stress arises owing to a myriad of questions. For example:

What are my child's rights to education, to services and how do I enforce these rights?

- Where do I find information to assist my child?
- What therapies do my child need?
- Will my child be able to go to school and how will my child be accommodated?
- Will my child be able to cope in this world without me?
- Will I be able to manage parenting my child with my work commitments
- What are my rights as a parent of a special needs child?
- How will I be able to afford all the costs involved in raising my child?

There are no clear answers to these questions. International studies reveal that parents of children with autism experience more stress compared to parents of children with other disabilities. In the absence of clarity, parents are driven to become advocates for their children's rights. As a parent of (i) a child with autism and (ii) a child with ADHD and sensory integration difficulties, I am intrinsically motivated by my need to understand my role as a partner in my children's education and ultimately to be able to advocate for their rights. This propelled me into the world of parenting a child with autism. In this chapter, I share my knowledge of some of the legislation that governs the rights of children with autism. I am a mother advocating for her son and an advocate with many years of legal expertise. I will endeavour to motivate practical solutions within the scope of the current legislation and examine the vast body of literature on the rights of children with autism. Specific focus will be given to access to justice for children and families living with autism, educational rights, children's rights and the balance of work-life.

13.1 Introduction

Children, whatever the colour of their skin or the condition of their birth, bless us by their mere existence on this earth. The great unanswered question of our age is whether our society plans to bless them in return (Kozel in Wilder, Dyches, Obiakor & Algozzine, 2004).

In an in-depth report on persons with disabilities, using the data of the 2011 census, Stats SA reported that the national disability prevalence rate is 7.5 % in South Africa. Provincial variations show that Free State and Northern Cape provinces had the highest proportion of persons with disabilities (11%), followed by the North West and Eastern Cape (10% and 9.6% respectively). Western Cape and Gauteng provinces have the lowest percentage of persons with disabilities (5%) (Stats SA, Report-03-01-592011).

People with disabilities in South Africa face barriers that prevent them from enjoying their full civil, political, economic, social, cultural and development rights. This is to a large extent owing to the ignorance and prejudice in our society. It is also because some legislation fail to protect the rights of persons with disabilities, and to meet the standards and principles of international human rights (SAHRC, 2002). The extent of the prevalence of children with ASD is unknown in South Africa (Bateman, 2013). In the Western Cape, approximately 10 children are diagnosed each week between Red Cross Children's Hospital, Lentegeur and Tygerberg Hospitals (Bateman supra).

The population of South Africa in 2012 was approximately 50 590 000; with 19.48 babies being born to every group of 1000, it would suggest that, in the year 2012, an average of 985 493 children were born in South Africa, of whom 11 198 were likely to be on the Autistic Spectrum (Autism South Africa, 2012). On estimate, this indicates that 933 new cases of children will be diagnosed each month, 216 cases per week and 31 cases per day, therefore, one can conclude that every 45 minutes in South Africa a child is born with ASD (Autism South Africa, 2012, see also the chapter on Framing Autism in this volume). No full census has been conducted since 2011, but these estimates can only have grown since then. Autism South Africa recently (2018) alluded that 1 million South African children and adults are living with autism. Accurate statistics for South Africa are hard to find. The statistics available internationally and in South Africa clearly conclude that a very large population of parents are searching for answers regarding their child's diagnoses and needing to know what their children's rights are.

13.2 Autism and the Constitution

The Constitution of South Africa, Act No. 108 of 1996 ("the Constitution of SA") was first a bill in 1994 and brought hope, pride and huge expectations to all South Africans. However, for millions of people with disabilities inequality, discrimination, torture, abuse, segregation, exclusion and deprivation are still a reality. Much has been achieved in making human rights central to our democracy, but we still have a long way to go to make the rights real to all of our people.

The Constitution applies to natural and juristic persons, as well as all law. It binds the legislature, the executive, the judiciary and all organs of state. Section 2 of the Constitution of South Africa states that this Constitution is the supreme law of the Republic, law or conduct inconsistent with it is invalid and the obligations imposed by it must be fulfilled. The South African Human Rights Council (SAHRC) is faced with challenges to ensure that the rights entrenched in our Constitution are enjoyed and that redress is sought is they are transgressed. Therefore, it is the SAHRC's mandate to monitor organs of state in the execution of their constitutional obligations, as well as to educate people about their rights.

As indicated earlier, my focus areas include children diagnosed with Autism and their families, what barriers prevent them from enjoying their full civil, economic, social, cultural and development rights. Human rights can be defined as 'those entitlements which are basic to being human and not connected to the accident of being born in a certain country or with skin of a particular colour' (Norma Tarrow, Human Rights Education: Alternative Conceptions, p22 taken from Values and Human Rights in the Curriculum, Department of Education).

- Human rights are inherent; they are your rights because you are born human.
- Human rights are universal; they belong to all people.
- Human rights are inalienable; they can not be taken away.
- Human rights are indivisible; all human rights are inter-related with each other.

Social justice can be defined as the challenge of injustice, respecting diversity and encouraging an unbiased society. Individuals are not discriminated against their welfare and well-being is not constrained or prejudiced in terms of sexuality, religion, age, race, belief, social class, socioeconomic circumstances, location or disability (Nussbaum, 2009). Social justice is based on the concepts of human rights and equality.

Sect 7 (2) of the Constitution of SA demands that the State must respect, protect, promote and fulfil the rights in the Bill of Rights which is defined in Chapter 2 of the Constitution.

> The Bill of Rights is a cornerstone of democracy in South Africa. It enshrines the rights of all people in our country and affirms the democratic values of human dignity, equality and freedom.

This section means that the rights of *all* people are included. The South African Constitution compels the state in section 7(2), to respect, promote and fulfil the rights contained in the Bill of Rights. According to Currie and De Waal (Currie & De Waal, 2013), this section compels the state by means of four obligations, through positive and negative duties, to adhere to their responsibilities under the Bill of Rights.

Positive actions may include preventing the violation of human rights contained in Chapter 2 of the Constitution by a third party, it may also include enacting legislation which serves to enhance the protection of the vulnerable member of society, such as children with autism. The obligation created by section 7(2) indicates that should the state fail to uphold these instructions, it may be seen as acting unlawfully and unconstitutionally (Currie & De Waal, 2013).

In Christiaan Education South Africa v Minister of Education, the Constitutional Court reiterated that along with the state's specific duty towards children, the obligations contained in section 7(2) represent a powerful responsibility on the state to act. According to Glenister v President of the Republic of South Africa, the South African Constitution leaves the choice to the state of ways to fulfil these responsibilities. The Court held that the steps the state takes to respect, protect, promote and fulfil constitutional rights must be reasonable and effective.

The following was stated in the Constitutional Court Case, Mazibuko v City of Johannesburg:

> Ordinarily it is institutionally inappropriate for a court to determine precisely what the achievement of any particular social and economic right entails and what steps government should take to ensure the progressive realisation of the right. This is a matter in the first place for the legislature and executive ... Indeed it is desirable as a matter of democratic accountability that they should do so for it is their programs and promises that are subjected to democratic popular choice.

Section 7(2) linked to section 237, which determines that all constitutional obligations must be adhered to thoroughly and devoid of any delay, becomes a tool for holding the state to account in respect of protecting the rights of children with autism, and doing so in a reasonable and effective manner. Rautenbach (2004) argues that section 7(2) is a constitutional command. This means that where the state may have failed to properly put in place reasonable measures, for example proper and responsive legislation to address the duties prescribed under the Constitution, the state may fail to adhere to section 7(2) of the Constitution. Section 8 (1) binds the legislature in its law making, the executive in its resource allocation and initiation of legislation and the judiciary in its decision-making.

Legislation, whether it is stand-alone or whether it forms part of other legislation, must be based on the principles enshrined in the Constitution. It must ensure equality, non- discrimination and protection for individuals with autism. Existing legislation must be scrutinised for compliance with the constitutional principles. It is essential to include individuals with autism in policy, planning and decision-making processes. The ways in which individuals with autism are denied access to information, physical environments, opportunities and rights are not always obvious to typical people. The needs of individuals with autism cannot and must not be interpreted by people whose knowledge and awareness of autism is limited (See also Chapter 5, Voices and Views of students with Autism).

Section 8(2) provides for the protection of individuals against rights abuses from each other. Therefore, the Courts must remedy these rights violations between individuals. Cockrell (2013) expresses the opinion that this is a stipulation that certain constitutional rights are to apply directly against private agencies. For example, providing for free legal representation in civil matters to a child with autism (a disability) if substantial injustice would result otherwise, would constitute a vertical responsibility whereas refraining from calling such child derogatory names can be enforceable horizontally (Carter, 2015).

The Bill of Rights (Chapter 2) specifically prohibits direct and indirect discrimination, by the state of an individual, against anyone on the basis of disability. Therefore, the denial of any other constitutional right on the basis of disability constitutes a violation of a person with disability's right. Discrimination against a person on the basis of that individual's disability is automatically unfair unless a case can be proved by the body or individual concerned that the discrimination was fair. The onus to prove unfair discrimination does not lie with the person with disability.

This brings me to discuss the right to equality and dignity and the access to justice as it relates to individuals with autism.

13.2.1 Equality and dignity

Holnes and Rule (2014) argue that the rights to equality and access to justice are often not realisable without accessibility being provided to a person with disabilities (autism).

Discrimination means any act or omission, including policy, law, rule, practice, condition or situation which:

- Imposes burdens, obligations or disadvantages on; or
- Withholds benefits, opportunities or disadvantages from any person on one or more of the prohibited grounds, which include disability and any other ground that might disadvantage a person, undermines human dignity and affects a person's rights and freedoms.

To ensure equality, the development of anti-discriminatory legislation must seek to address past inequalities by equalising opportunities and control any tendency towards further discrimination. The aim of any legislation must end discrimination faced by persons with autism and promote their fundamental rights enshrined in the Constitution.

The right to equality, Sect 9 of the Constitution of South Africa, stipulates that everyone is equal before the law and the right to equal protection and benefit of the law. It states further that this right includes the full and equal enjoyment of all rights and freedoms. Moreover, the state may not unfairly discriminate directly or indirectly against anyone on one or more grounds, which grounds include discrimination against individuals with autism. Individuals with autism are in need of protection because of their vulnerability and historic disposition for being discriminated against. This protection must not rid the person of his identity and autonomy to make his own decisions.

Against this background, it is apparent that children with autism, in having to face the challenges experienced by both children, as well as individuals with a disability, may consequently experience the compounded effect of being denied their equal rights assertion as a result of their two-tier vulnerability (Carter, 2015). They may face inequality on both levels, from the state as well as other individuals. Matshedisho (2007) argues that for rights to be effective, it must be recognised by someone other than the right-bearer. Rights such as the right to equality must therefore be recognised and respected by, for instance a court, or prosecutor as well as a family member or friend. This implies that the law must determine that children with autism are not denied an integral right such as equality.

Section 9 is viewed as one of the founding provisions of the South African Constitution and takes centre stage in addressing the above-mentioned challenge. This anti-discrimination clause in the Constitution specifically mentions disability, but we have yet to make the letter and spirit of our Constitution concrete realities for our children with autism. If we understand the ways in which people with disabilities are denied their rights, then attitudes and practices can change, and barriers can fall (SAHC, November 2002).

Various statutes aim to give effect to the constitutional right to equality. The promotion of Equality and Prevention of Unfair Discrimination Act, Act No. 4 of 2000 has met the provision of section 9 of the Constitution; it expands on the constitutional provisions prohibiting unfair discrimination and guarantees equality before the law. Chapter 5 of the Act, dealing with the promotion of equality, rules that it is the general duty of the state to promote equality. This Act also rules that the promotion of equality is the responsibility of persons operating in the public and private domains.

This has far-reaching implications and means that members of the public and all government officials must be equipped with the appropriate skills and knowledge to ensure the rights of children with autism, and to remove the barriers that deny them their rights. What is essential and of utmost importance is that we must also remember that older children, young adults and adults with autism have the right to represent themselves in all matters concerning them. Including the voices of persons with autism in developing law, case law and removing barriers would mean that the public awareness of their rights are raised, it challenges stereotypes and removes false perceptions of autism.

Within the realms of the interconnectedness of the rights contained in Chapter 2 of the Constitution, section 9 may therefore provide the benchmark of rights assertion: equal enjoyment of rights for children with autism despite their age and disability. There exists a duty to accommodate difference, which underscores a paradigm shift from considering age and disability as subordinate statuses pleading for welfare and pity, to elements merely informing diverse approaches and responses (Carter, 2015). The value of human dignity is safeguarded and promoted by the Bill of Rights section 10 of the Constitution which highlights that everyone has the right to have their dignity respected and protected. Ackermann (2013) argues that the close linkage between equality and dignity makes it impossible to discuss equality without some reference to dignity, and vice versa (see also Chapter 5, Voices and Views of students with Autism, Chapter 1, Framing Autism, Chapter 4, Religion and Autism, Chapter 6 Autism in a Rural Context)

The right to life and dignity was described by the Constitutional Court as the most important human rights as "human beings are entitled to be treated as worthy of respect and concern" (in S v Makwanyane). Human dignity is also explicitly protected by art 1 of the Universal Declaration of Human Rights, and by art 5 of the African Charter on Human and People's Rights and very difficult to define.

In a commentary on the South African Bill of Rights (1999), dignity is reflected as the moral premise and the essential ingredient of constitutionalism. Woolman (2006) asserts that human dignity is the respect for the "unique set of ends that an individual pursues". Everyone has inherent dignity and the right to have their dignity respected and protected. Dignity is a concept which talks about a person's intrinsic worth and self-respect. It is concerned with physical and psychological integrity and empowerment.

In the South African Constitutional Court decision of S v Makwanyane 1995 (6) BCLR 665 (CC) at par 328 the honourable Judge O'Regan expressed the following view.

> Recognising a right to dignity is an acknowledgement of the intrinsic worth of human beings: human beings are entitled to be treated as worthy of respect and concern. This right therefore is the foundation of many of the other rights that are specifically entrenched in … [the Bill of Rights].

This implies that human dignity, together with the right to life, was the source of all other rights. Dignity is a value that informs the understanding of many and possibly all other rights.

Human dignity and the determination of an individual's self-worth are in turn central to equality. In MEC of Education Kwazulu-Natal and Others v Pillay, the honourable Judge Langa stated the following:

> Our society which values dignity, equality, and freedom must therefore require people to act positively to accommodate diversity. Those steps might be as simple as granting and

regulating an exemption from the general rule or they may require that the rules or practices be changed or even that buildings be altered or monetary loss incurred.

Honourable Judge Langa links a respect for dignity, to the recognition of difference and diversity. He argues that the South African Constitution determines that international law must be consulted for purposes of interpreting rights contained in the South African Constitution (Section 39).

Section 233 of the Constitution further provides that when interpreting domestic legislation, which gives life to the principles contained the South African Constitution, every court must prefer any reasonable interpretation which is consistent with international law over another interpretation that is inconsistent with international law. International law can therefore play an important role in providing content to the rights of children with autism, and further to their rights of access to justice (Carter, 2015). They include:

- The White Paper on Disability, namely the Integrated National Disability Strategy (INDS, 1997);
- The World Programme of Action concerning persons with disability, the United Nations Standard Rules on the Equalisation of Opportunities for People with Disabilities;
- The Disability Rights Charter of South Africa;
- The African Decade for People with Disabilities and the United Nations Convention of the Rights of Persons with Disabilities (UNCRPD);
- United Nations Convention on the Right of a Child (UNCRC, 2012) and the principles and policy objectives of the White Paper on Social Welfare (1997); and
- White Paper on the Rights of Persons with Disabilities all focus on addressing disability within a social model framework (White Paper on the Rights of Persons with Disabilities, 2015).

The two most significant international agreements which was ratified by the South African Government, relating to the rights of children and the rights of individuals with autism will be examined. South Africa has indicated that it will abide by the rules, standards and regulations of such. These agreements can assist in interpreting sections 9, 10, 28, 34 and 35 of the South African Constitution and ensure the provision of access to justice for children with autism.

In M v the Constitutional Court indicated that since its introduction, the UNCRC has become the international benchmark against which to evaluate relevant legislation in South Africa. The Court also reiterated that certain principles included in the UNCRC have become "international currency" and by themselves guide all policy in South Africa in relation to children.

In DPP, Transvaal v Minister of Justice and Constitutional Development, placing emphasis on the importance of the UNCRC, the court pointed out that South Africa, as a state party to this instrument, is obliged to give effect to these instruments and to take all appropriate legislative and other measures to give effect to the articles contained in the UNCRC. In addition to the above-mentioned Constitutional Court matters, the UNCRC has also been cited in Kirsch v Kirsch, Bhe and others v Magistrate, Khayelitsha and others,

Centre for Child Law and others v Minister of Home Affairs, Grootboom v Oostenberg Municipality and Others, Jooste v Bohma, DPP, Kwazulu-Natal v P.

Articles 2, 3, 6 and 12 of the UNCRC are seen as the four pillars of the UNCRC. With regard to the rights of a child with autism specifically, Article 23 may be seen as the fifth pillar as this article describes the rights of a child with a disability in particular. Article 13 of the UNCRPD provide a further element of access to justice for these vulnerable children.

The question that comes to mind is *"How must the provisions of the UNCRC and the UNCRPD be interpreted"?*

Article 31 of The Vienna Convention on the Law of Treaties provides for emphasis to be placed on the ordinary text of a convention, that conventions such as the UNCRC and the UNCRPD shall be interpreted in "good faith" in accordance with the "ordinary meaning to be given to the terms of the treaty in their context and in the light of its object and purpose" (http://www.refworld.org/docid/3ae6b3a10.html).

The purpose of the UNCRC was to recognise the vulnerability of children and the previous lack of provision for and protection of children's rights in general (Van der Walt, 2010). South Africa ratified the UNCRC on 16 June 1995. In its preamble, the UNCRC states that childhood is entitled to special care and assistance. The child, by reason of his or her physical and mental immaturity, needs special safeguards and care (Carter, 2015).

The child's vulnerability is emphasised throughout the UNCRC. Article 3 of the UNCRC describes the "best interest of the child" principle. This principle binds both private and public institutions, and that every legislative, judicial and executive body must apply this principle by considering how their decisions may affect the rights of children. The UNCRC therefore places a direct obligation on states parties to implement this principle and follow and active approach in doing so. The United Nations Committee on the Rights of the Child (CORC) which is established by Article 43 of the UNCRC, plays a key role in the purpose of examining the progress made by states parties in achieving the realisation of the obligations undertaken in the UNCRC. This committee comprises ten independent human rights experts elected by governments that have ratified the UNCRC.

This committee issues General Comments on rights contained in the UNCRC. In its ninth General Comment, the CORC stated that, in general, state parties in their endeavours to prevent and eliminate all forms of discrimination against children with disabilities must include disability explicitly as a ground for unfair discrimination.

Awareness-raising campaigns must be conducted to eliminate discrimination and … provide for effective remedies in case of violations of the rights of children with disabilities, and ensure that those remedies are easily accessible to children with disabilities and their parents and/or others caring for the child.

This means that the states parties must have accessible recourse and remedies available for children with autism, not only in seeking redress for discrimination, but "in case of violations of the rights of children with autism" in general. These remedies must be available when any of the rights of children with autism are violated (Carter, 2015).

Article 4 stipulates that parties shall undertake such measures to the maximum extent of their available resources for the implementation of the rights contained in the UNCRC. According to the General Comment No 9, the CORC views article 4 as insisting that children with disabilities be a priority in budget allocation, by stating the following:

> However, it should not be forgotten that it is the state parties ultimate responsibility to oversee that adequate funds are allocated to children with disabilities along with strict guidelines for service delivery.

Sufficient funds must therefore be earmarked for programmes promoting the equal rights of children with autism and their inclusion in society. This means that proper resources must be allocated to achieve equal access to justice for children with autism and provide them with effective remedies in the event that their rights are being violated.

South Africa submitted its first country report within two years of ratification of the UNCRC. In February 2000 the CORC issued its concluding observations and comments on South Africa's first report. The CORC expressed its concern that insufficient measures have been adopted to ensure that all children are guaranteed access to various social services. The CORC was particularly concerned with the access of children with disabilities and recommended that South Africa increased its efforts in this regard.

The disability rights movement in South Africa emerged during the 1980s. Disabled People South Africa (DPSA) negotiated with the Government of South Africa during the early 1990s for the right of disabled people to speak for themselves. They conceptualised this popular phrase: "Nothing about us without us".

The "social model" approach to addressing disability was introduced to the post 1994 democratic government. The social model is encapsulated in a number of government policies and legislation as indicated above. This makes the application of the approach mandatory. The Constitution protects the rights and dignity of individuals with disabilities (autism) and promotes equalisation of opportunities of these individuals. Language reflects the values and attitudes of the social context in which it is used. It is important to understand the effect of words we use and choose if we are to break down barriers and participate in building a better society for all (SAHC, November 2002).

People with autism are particularly vulnerable to the misuse of language and terminology that labels and stereotypes them. Negative terminology ultimately creates a culture of non-acceptance of diversity. It is therefore needed to respect the wishes of individuals with autism to be referred to as they would prefer, be it a person with autism, an autistic person or neurodivergent individual.

The social model of disability recognises that people's activities are limited because of the way society is organised. Using the social model means that all disabled people have the right to belong to and be valued in the communities, their strengths are recognised and the physical and social barriers that obstruct them at school, work, home and anywhere else is the focus.

The diagram below reflects the disablement faced by individuals with autism and which should be considered when forming policy and legislation. The author engaged with parents and adults with autism to adapt this diagram. These are only some of the issues highlighted by them.

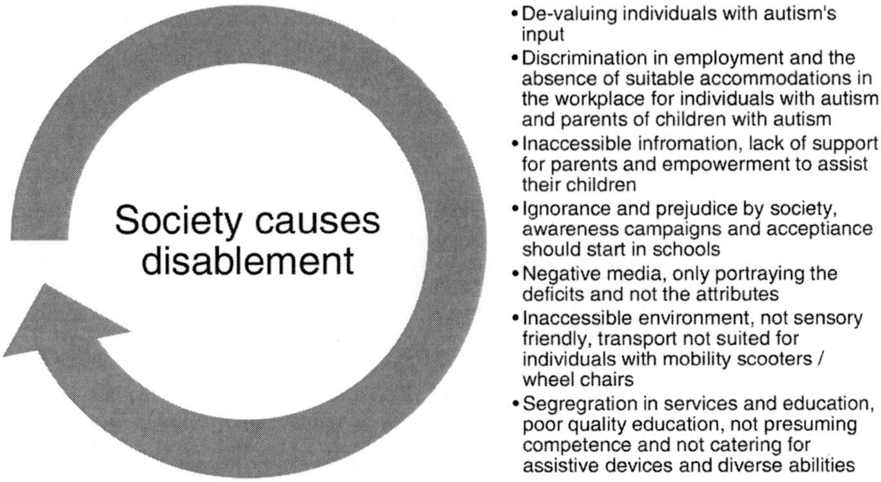

Figure 13.1 The social model for disability adapted to be autism-specific (duToit-Smit, 2020)

The social model defines 'impairment' and 'disability' as very different things:

> Impairment is the loss or limitation of physical, mental or sensory function on a long-term of permanent basis. Disablement is the loss or limitation of opportunities to take part in the normal life of the community on an equal level with others due to physical and social barriers (Disabled People's International, 1981).

Society has a responsibility towards individuals to include and accept rather than exclude them. A person with autism is disabled if the world at large will not take into account their physical, sensory or mental differences. The social model of thinking has important implications for the education system and particularly in primary and secondary schools. Prejudiced attitudes towards disabled people are learned through contact with the prejudice and ignorance of others. Society disables individuals with autism by failing to consider their rights and needs, as groups or individuals. Acceptance, equality and the respect for dignity of individuals with autism should begin in schools. The primary task of the Department of Education is the establishment of a just and equitable education and training system, which provides a relevant, high quality education to all learners.

The Inclusive Education policy of the Department of Education (2001) and the Curriculum and Assessment Policy Statements (2011) stress the role that constitutional values can play in the development of active citizens in a united, caring and economically developed South Africa. Making human rights a central theme of the curriculum acknowledges the critical role that education can play in transformation and the elimination of prejudice. Universal access for people with disabilities is the ultimate goal of the disability rights movement (SAHC, 2002).

Universal access means the removal of cultural, social and other barriers that prevent children with autism from entering, using or benefiting from the various systems of society that are available to other children. Furthermore, universal access is the only way children with autism can enjoy equal opportunities and benefits, and to mainstream with their families and friends into society. When buildings, facilities, services and built spaces are inaccessible to children with autism, it means these children are denied opportunities, services and normal community life.

When government officials, employers, architects, property developers and other members of the public are not sensitive to what the sensory and special needs are of children with autism, discrimination against them are perpetuated, often overtly, perhaps unintentionally. Inaccessible environments deny these children their rights to equality, dignity and freedom, amongst other fundamental human rights. Society disables these children by failing to take into account their rights and needs, as groups or individuals. As a member country of the United Nations, South Africa is a signatory to The United Nations Standard Rules on the Equalisation of Opportunities for People with Disabilities (1993). The SAHRC, South African Law-and policy-makers, and organisations of people with disabilities are guided by these rules outlining the minimum requirements United Nations member states need to meet in fulfilling their responsibilities to persons with disability. The political and moral foundations of the Rules lie in the following human rights instruments:

- The International Bill of Rights, comprising the Universal Declaration of Human Rights (1948);
- The International Covenant of Economic, Social and Cultural Rights (1966);
- The International Covenant on Civil and Political Rights (1966);
- The Convention on the Rights of the Child (1989); and
- The World Programme of Action Concerning Disabled Persons (adopted for the UN Decade of Disabled Persons 1983 – 1993).

The Rules state in their introduction the following framework for action to create equal opportunities:

> The purpose of the Rules is to ensure that girls, boys, woman and men with disabilities, as members of their societies, may exercise the same rights and obligations as others. In all societies … there are still obstacles preventing persons with disabilities from exercising their rights and freedoms and making it difficult for them to participate fully in the activities of their societies. It is the responsibility of States to take appropriate action to remove such obstacles. Persons with disabilities and their organisations should play an active role as partners in this process. The equalisation of opportunities for persons with disabilities is an essential contribution in the general and worldwide effort to mobilise human resources…

The other international human rights treaty discussed earlier addressing the rights of people with disabilities serves as the second important international instruments promoting the rights of the child with autism. It does not create new rights, but rather sets out measures to ensure that people with disabilities are afforded access to basic rights already entrenched in other international instruments and in the Constitution of South Africa.

Section 38 of the Constitution empowers courts to "grant appropriate relief, including a declaration of rights". Section 39(2) of the Constitution provides that in interpreting any legislation, courts must promote the spirit and objects of the Bill of Rights. Section 172(1)(b), afford courts the powers to make an order that is "just and equitable", including an order "limiting the retrospective effect of the declaration of invalidity". An order may also suspend the declaration of invalidity "for any period and on any conditions to allow the competent authority to correct the defect".

As per Ngwena in Western Cape forum for disability v Government of the Republic of South Africa: A case study of contradictions in Inclusive Education (2013), the motivation behind the UNCRPD is inclusive equality. States parties are obliged to implement these measures at national level and agree to promote, protect and ensure the full and equal enjoyment of all human rights and fundamental freedoms by all persons with disabilities, including the promotion of their intrinsic dignity.

Article 7 of the UNCRPD refers expressly to the best interest of the child principle. Article 7(2) states that in all actions concerning a child with a disability, the best interests of the child shall be a primary consideration. This text is almost exactly the same as Article 3(1) of the UNCRC.

The rights of the child to survival and development is also reflected in the UNCRPD. Article 24(1)(a) stipulates that states parties, with the focus on education, shall ensure the full development of human potential and the development of the personalities', talents and creativity of individuals with disabilities to their fullest potential (Carter, 2015).

As indicated above, when considering policy, legislation and any issue where children with autism or individuals with autism is concerned, the views of these individuals must be considered. Article 7(3) of the UNCRPD stipulates that states parties shall ensure that children with disabilities have the right to express their views freely on all matters affecting them.

Article 12(1) of the UNCRC supports this and indicate that due weight in accordance with the child's age and maturity must be given to children with disabilities views. This section also again obliges state parties to provide a child with a disability assistance to realise the right to express their views.

The implication of Article 12 of the UNCRPD read with Article 12 of the UNCRC is that it determines that children with autism, who are capable of forming their own views, must be provided with measures to allow for their participation. Their disability may not exclude them from partaking in the decision-making process.

The very important concept that is addressed by Article 12(3) of the UNCRPD is that states parties must take steps to provide people with disabilities with the necessary support they need in order to exercise their legal capacity, and that these measures must be tailored to the person's preferences and circumstances. The implications of the above for individuals with autism is that the support implied in Article 12(3) may take on the form of a legal representative, a family member or an interpreter (Carter, 2015).

It was not until the UNCRPD that the phrase "access to justice" was stipulated in an international treaty as a standalone, substantive right (Kanter, 2015). Article 13 explicitly explains how states parties can ensure that people with disabilities have access to justice:

> *States parties shall ensure effective access to justice for persons with disabilities on an equal basis with others, including through the provision of procedural and age-appropriate accommodations, in order to facilitate their effective role as direct and indirect participants, including as witnesses, in all legal proceedings, including at investigative and other preliminary stages.*

> *In order to help to ensure effective access to justice for persons with disabilities, states parties shall promote appropriate training for those working in the field of administration of justice, including police and prison staff.*

Kanter (2015) describes Article 13 of the UNCRPD as affirming access to justice for people with disabilities. The UNCRPD, therefore, provides three very useful elements against which equal access to justice can be measured: reasonable accommodation, participation and the training of relevant stakeholders. These three essential elements offer guidance in assessing a judicial system's responsiveness towards the needs of people with disabilities and their families (Carter, 2015).

Clark (2012) asserts that Article 13 of the UNCRPD recognises that both legs of legislation and practice are necessary to attain the inclusion necessary for victims of crime who may have some form of disability. He also argues that such an approach would include policies and procedures as well as sound training programmes to make sure that the purpose and outcome of the training were translated in practice.

When combining all these elements of the UNCRC and supported by the UNCRPD and other policies and legislation, a proper framework is established in order to inform states parties on how to respond to the rights of children with autism to access justice. Responses from states parties, such as legislation and other measures, can be tested against this framework by establishing whether there is compliance with. For instance, the best interest of the child principle, whether children with autism can freely express their views, whether anti-discrimination laws are in place, or whether the justice system allows age-appropriate accommodations for children with autism and training for court officials.

The above emphasised the need for existing rights to be respected in relation to individuals with autism. It places obligations on the states parties to respect, promote and fulfil these rights so as to protect vulnerable individuals. It also supports the social model of disability in promoting the view that the barriers created by society hamper the full participation of individuals with autism in society.

Equality in accessing services, enjoyment of rights and the fulfilment of full potential is stressed by the UNCRPD. This makes the UNCRPD the most comprehensive human rights treaty addressing the rights of all persons with disabilities (Carter, 2015). South Africa is compelled to abide by the principles included in the UNCRC and the UNCRPD in protecting the rights of children and individuals with disabilities. These prominent instruments ensure that where states parties are unresponsive to protect the rights contained in the UNCRPD, persons with autism might have the recourse on an international platform, should they have exhausted all available domestic remedies.

The above is significant for the realisation of all the other rights enshrined in the Constitution discussed in the following sections of this chapter.

12.2.2 Economic and social rights

Section 27 of the Constitution deals with health care, food, water and social security:

- Everyone has the right to have access to health care services, including reproductive health care; sufficient food and water; and social security, including, if they are unable to support themselves and their dependants, appropriate social assistance.

- The state must take reasonable legislative and other measures, within its resources, to achieve the progressive realisation of each of these rights.
- No one may be refused emergency medical treatment.

Children with disabilities are more exposed to risks than their peers (Carter, 2015). It has also been well documented that caring for a child with autism (child with a disability) may be challenging and may lead to hardships not only for the child, but for the family as well children with autism necessitate exceptional levels of care at increased related costs. Often families who care for a child with autism move towards poverty as a result of the financial challenges faced through caring for their child (Clasquin-Johnson et al., 2018).

In the case, Government of RSA and others v Grootboom and others supra, the Court had to consider whether citizens could force the state to act positively to meet their social and economic (or second generation) rights. In question was section 26 of the Constitution which gave everyone the right of access to adequate housing, and section 28(1)(c) which afforded children the right to shelter. Irene Grootboom, who brought the case, was one of 390 adults and 510 children living in appalling circumstances in Wallacedene informal settlement. The High Court had found that the children and, through them, their parents were entitled to shelter under section 28(1)(c) of the Constitution.

The Constitutional Court in a unanimous decision by the honourable Justice Yacoob, noted that the Constitution obliged the state to act positively to help people. The Court further stressed that the rights in the Bill of Rights were inter-related.

In another Constitutional Court judgement, the honourable Justice remarked that the needs of children were the most urgent and the state was obliged to ensure that children were accorded the protection contemplated by section 28 of the Constitution.

This is the powerful impact that the Constitution and the UNCRC (as discussed above) can have when aggrieved individuals approach the courts to ensure that their constitutional rights are upheld.

The United Nations has in the Universal Declaration of Human Rights proclaimed that children are entitled to special care and assistance. The need to extend particular care to the child has been stated in the Geneva Declaration on the Rights of the Child, in the United Nations Declaration on the Rights of the Child, in the Convention on the Rights of the Child and in the African Charter on the Rights and Welfare of the Child. This is recognised in the Universal Declaration of Human Rights and in the statutes and relevant instruments of specialised agencies and international organisations concerned with the welfare of children.

It is necessary to effect changes to existing laws relating to children in order to afford them the necessary protection and assistance. This will ensure that they can fully assume their responsibilities within the community as well as that the child, for the full and harmonious development of his or her personality, should grow up in a family environment and in an atmosphere of happiness, love and understanding. It can be implied from the case Government of the RSA v Grootboom and the case of Minister of Health and Others v Treatment Action Campaign and others, once the care that is provided to children by their parents is lacking, the state incurs a responsibility. The state needs to be "child and disability sensitive" relating to its duties.

This would directly have an impact on children and families with autism, who are often affected by poverty. Parents and families must be given the tools to realise their responsibilities towards children and the state must further provide the legal and administrative infrastructure to ensure that children are afforded the protection contemplated by section 28 (Sloth-Nielsen, 2001). Section 28(2) of the Constitution has been described as "an expansive guarantee" that a child's best interests will be paramount in every matter concerning that child (refer to Sonserup v Tondelli and Another 2001 (1) SA 1171 (CC) at par 29) and has been declared a stand-alone and enforceable right on its own, refer to Minister of Welfare and Population Development v Fitzpatrick and Others 2000 (3) SA 422 (CC) at par 17.

In order for the state to fulfil its constitutional obligations towards children with disabilities (children with autism) in terms of sections 7 and 28 the state must also become disability-sensitive with the purpose of fully considering the rights of this vulnerable group and accordingly determine what may constitute as being in their best interest (Carter, 2015). Access to legal representation plays a central role in realising a right, with reference to children specifically, section 28(1)(h) which stipulates that a legal practitioner must be assigned to a child in civil proceedings affecting the child, by the state at its expense (Zaal, 1997; Sloth-Nielsen, 2008; Du Toit in Boezaart (ed),2009).

The legal representation as stated in section 28(1)(h) may only be required if "substantial injustice would otherwise result". In Du Toit and Another v Minister of Welfare and Population Development and Others 2003 (2) SA 198 (CC) the court indicated that it was important in matters affecting children, that their interests were fully aired before the court, so as to prevent substantial injustice to them (See Also Sloth-Nielsen, 2002).

In Legal Aid Board and Another v R 2009 (2) SA 262 (D), the court held that the Legal Aid Board had the power to render legal assistance to a child, at the state's expense in terms of section 28(1)(h) that failure to do so would result in substantial injustice.

Carnelly (2010) asserts that the appointee should therefore not merely be a practicing attorney or advocate, but he or she should possess additional skills, including the ability to communicate efficiently with the child and to build rapport and a relationship of trust with the child. This requirement is even more important with regard to a child client with autism. As a child with autism may inherently need differential approaches in order to be able to communicate or share their views, the legal representative who is appointed in this regard must have additional skills to allow for effective communication and building rapport (Carter, 2015; see also Chapters 1, Framing Autism and 2, Early Identification in this volume).

Moyo (2015) also points out that the right to legal representation in section 28(1)(h) is not only available to children capable of forming and conveying views. Children facing substantial injustice regardless whether they have the ability to express their own views may be afforded legal representation.

Education, health care, adequate food, housing, water and social security should be enjoyed by all citizens. A family with a child or a person with autism is faced with a higher risk of being poor owing to the vicious cycle of poverty that causes disability and in turn disability causes poverty as discussed above. Children with disabilities (autism) have specific and general rights under the Bill of Rights. They may not be discriminated against on the basis of their disability, they must be protected from maltreatment, abuse and neglect, and they must have access to the courts.

The UNCRC in Article 6 obliges states parties to recognise that each child has the inherent right to life. It places an obligation on states parties to ensure the survival and development of the child to the maximum extent possible. The obligation to recognise the child's inherent right to life includes the duty to address all the needs which safeguard the enjoyment of this right to life (Bartholet, 2010). Article 6 embraces all rights and includes the child's physical, mental, spiritual, moral, psychological and social development. This must also be interpreted in the broadest sense of the word (Carter, 2015).

In the General Comment published by the CORC in 2005 it is stated:

> Ensuring survival and physical health are priorities, but states parties are reminded that Article 6 encompasses all aspects of development, and that a young child's health and psychosocial well-being are in many respects interdependent. Both may be put at risk by adverse living conditions, neglect, insensitive or abusive treatment and restricted opportunities for realising human potential.

It is clear from the CORC's comment that the right to life and survival places an obligation on states parties to pay attention to their policies, programmes, and services affecting children, that those who directly and indirectly violate the right to life, survival and development should be punished. Article 23(3) of the UNCRC recognises the special needs of children with disabilities and provides that assistance be extended in accordance with Article 23(2) free of charge, whenever possible.

Combrinck (in Sloth-Nielsen, 2008) argues that this recognition comes with yet more conditions. Children must be eligible for assistance, an application must be made for assistance, the assistance must be appropriate for the child's condition and to the circumstances of the caregivers or parents. The relevant assistance must be designed to ensure that children with disabilities have access to and receive education, training, health care services, rehabilitation services, preparation for employment and other opportunities.

The author argues that the above does not differentiate between the parents' ability to afford these special services for their children, it states that states parties are obliged to recognise the special needs of children with disabilities which would include children with autism, and that assistance should be afforded free of charge. In respect of South Africa specifically, the CORC has explicitly expressed its apprehension regarding inadequate services and programmes available to children with disabilities in terms of Article 23 of the UNCRC. The CORC further urged South Africa to work towards the inclusion of children with disabilities in society (See Concluding Observations of the Committee on the Rights of the Child: South Africa 23/02/2000).

The Social Assistance Act (2004) provides for social grants to different categories of people, children with autism (when they reach the age of 16) and caregivers of children with autism who qualify can claim these grants. Social grants are in place to improve standards of living and redistribute wealth to create a more equitable society.

Sections 24 to 29 of the Constitution recognise the socio-economic rights of citizens including the right to social security. The government is obligated to progressively realise these rights, meaning that the state must take reasonable legislative and other measures within its available resources to achieve the progressive realisation of these rights. The DSD's proposed National Child Care and Protection Policy dated 19 December 2017 (National Development Strategy 2030) needs discussion here, it is stated that:

> The National Care and Protection policy is a statement of the Government of Republic of South Africa's (GRSA) commitment to pursue a rights-based developmental approach to child care and protection that ensures that all children are guaranteed their rights, not only to survive and be protected from violence, abuse, neglect and exploitation and from unnecessary separation from their families, but also to develop to their full potential; and that advances the country's national development goals as spelt out in the National Development Plan (NDP).
> South Africa is a signatory of the UNCRC and ACRWC. In furtherance of its international obligations, South Africa's Constitution recognises and protects the rights of all children necessary to survive and be protected from violence, abuse, neglect and exploitation, as well as to develop to their full potential. Moreover, the government recognises that achieving sustainable development of the country depends on the realisation of the constitutional rights of children, especially the most vulnerable and marginalised so as to equalise their opportunities to develop to their full potential.
> South Africa's National Development Plan 2030: Our future – make it work (NDP), which is aligned to the global Sustainable Development Agenda, aims to eliminate poverty and reduce inequality by 2030. The foundational strategy of the NDP is to achieve and sustain social and economic development through the development of the country's human capital, from the bottom up, starting with children. It places the development of all children to their full potential, particularly the most vulnerable and socially excluded, at the centre of achieving the lasting elimination of poverty and inequality. The NDP recognises that building human capital is fundamentally dependent on the provision of a universal, rights-based social protection floor for all. Critically, it recognises that it depends on ensuring social inclusion through universal access to services that unlock and optimise the potential of all, starting in the earliest years with children and giving priority to the most vulnerable and marginalised. The NDP identifies several services as critical to equalising and optimising the development of all children, especially the most vulnerable. These include ECE services, education, basic services and adequate nutrition, as well as safe and inclusive communities and families."

The above draft policy document proposes that "the realisation of the country's legal and developmental responsibilities depends on the adoption of a national child care and protection system that ensure nation-wide commitment to, and operationalisation of the developmental approach. The success of this in turn depends on a shared understanding of political commitment to the adoption of measures to realise the overarching purpose of a developmental child care and protection system". It is stated further that there is a disconnect between the country's childcare and protection commitments and the outcomes for children. The reason for this is said to be the limitations of the childcare and protection system, the lack of clarity and understanding of what a developmental approach is, what is required in terms of priorities, programmes and services, who the role players are and what responsibilities they have.

To achieve the legal and developmental care and protection responsibilities of South Africa to support children, the country needs clear and compelling guidance on the developmental approach. Developmental child care and protection is defined as "to ensure the child such protection and care as is necessary for his or her well-being, taking into account the rights and duties of his or her parents ... and to this end, shall take appropriate legislative and administrative measures". The government is duty-bound to ensure this by its international and regional duties.

It further states that the starting point of the developmental model is that all parents and families have the capacity and desire to provide the care their children need to develop to their full potential. However, to do so effectively, they all need access to a number of public services and support that only government is in a position to, and is duty-bound to provide. These include, for example, health care, clean water, sanitation facilities, electricity, play facilities, early education facilities and schools. In addition to the universal support all parents require, the developmental approach recognises that there are vulnerable families and households whose social, economic and related circumstances undermine or limit their capacity to meet their duty of care and protection, and may present a risk to the development of their children. They are entitled to, and must receive support through public programmes to build their resilience to maintain the care, development and protection of their children and prevent the occurrence of abuse, neglect or exploitation.

By implementing this policy the government is duty-bound to establish a system to secure the rights of all children to develop to their full potential. Furthermore, government is duty-bound and committed to establishing a positive, rights-based and inclusive child care and protection policy and system that, inter alia:

- identifies and ensures children receive the comprehensive suite of support and services they need to develop to their full potential;
- identifies and supports parents and families as the primary care and protection duty bearers; and
- defines, regulates and supports role players and their respective roles and responsibilities, including parents, guardians, family, community members, the media, businesses, NGOs and government.

The duty to establish a comprehensive child-centred and family-focused developmental child care and protection policy and system is derived from the following international, regional and national human rights treaties and instruments:

United Nations Convention on the Rights of the Child (CRC)

- African Charter on the Rights and Welfare of the Child (ACRWC), Article 1, Article 3, Article 4, Article 11, Article 13, Article 14, Article 16, Article 18, Article 19, Article 20 and Article 31 is applicable.
- African Charter on Human and Peoples Rights, similar to the Constitution of South Africa is applicable as it was signed and ratified by the government of South Africa.
- Protocol to the African Charter on Human and Peoples' Rights on the Rights of Persons with Disabilities in Africa (ACHPR), this treaty was adopted on 30 January 2018. This is a binding legal document protecting the human rights of persons with disabilities, but will only become effective once is has been formally ratified. This disability rights protocol complements the UN Convention on the Rights of Person with Disabilities (UNCRPD). This protocol highlights and takes into account the lived realities of persons with disabilities in Africa. Both the UNCRPD in Article 24 and the African Disabilities Rights Protocol in Article 16 call for a transformative

approach at domestic level in the provisioning of education for persons with disabilities.

- International Labour Organization (ILO) Convention on the Elimination of the Worst Forms of Child Labour.
- International Convention on Cyber Crime.
- Convention on the Protection of Children and Cooperation in Respect of Inter-Country Adoption.
- Hague Convention on Civil Aspects of International Abduction.
- UN Guidelines for the Alternative Care of Children.
- Optional Protocol to the Convention on the Rights of the Child on the sale of children, child prostitution and child pornography.
- Declaration on Social and Legal Principles relating to the Protection and welfare of Children, with special reference to Foster Placement and Adoption nationally and internationally.
- The Constitution of the Republic of South Africa.

Using the *National Development Plan 2030: Our future – make it work* criteria, a developmental state must be built upon a developmental child care and protection policy and services that address the root causes of poverty and inequality, starting with the youngest children, through:

- The provision of a universal social floor of services required to ensure the optimal development of the capabilities of all children;
- Additional targeted measures to overcome the poverty traps that keep vulnerable children and their families, socially, economically and politically excluded;
- Recognition and accountability by all responsible role players for fulfilment of their collective duty of care and protection by; and
- Evidence-based and responsive child care and protection policies, programmes, budgets and services that are developed, delivered and monitored through inclusive and participatory political and governance processes which involve children and their families, including the most vulnerable and marginalised.

From the above policy, it is clear that the government recognises its urgent obligations to children and families with disabilities. It still needs to be effected, but parents, educators, members of the community and the society as a whole must also advocate change. This brings me to the following section, a discussion of some of the policies, legislation and international agreements applicable to enforce the rights of families with autism.

12.3 Autism and legislation in South Africa

International agreements such as the UNCRC and UNCRPD only become law in South Africa when they are enacted into domestic national legislation. This implies that international treaties in South Africa are not self-executing. For instance, section 231 of the Constitution and Glenister v President of the Republic of South Africa par 96 court elaborates on the role of binding and non-binding international law. It is necessary to look at how South Africa has domesticated the obligations included in these agreements, particularly how South Africa has implemented its obligation in respect of the UNCRC and the UNCRPD.

In the sections above, I discussed some of the rights enshrined in South African Constitution and a host of domestic legislation. In particular, I have elaborated on the right to equality, the right to dignity, the right to education and the right to life and survival, as well as the right to access to justice. In the sections that follow, I examine

- The South African Schools Act (1996);
- The NEPA (1996);
- The Education White Paper 6 (2001);
- The Children's Act (2005);
- The Criminal Procedure Act (1977);
- The Mental Health Care Act (2002);
- The BCEA (1997);
- The Promotion of Equality and the Prevention of Unfair Discrimination Act (2000); and
- The Employment Equity Act (1998.

Although not exhaustive, I discuss how these acts as illustrative examples of their applicability, objectives and aims have been designed to support the rights of children with disabilities and their parents or caregivers.

13.3.1 The South African Schools Act (1996), The NEPA (1996) and The Education White Paper 6 (2001)

In 2001, the government gave itself 20 years to realise the right to Inclusive Education across the country. By 2020, 19 years later and in the reports by Human Rights Watch (2016), and Inclusive Education South Africa (2017) indicate that the government have still not achieved this.

As discussed in the above sections of this chapter (see the discussion about constitutional rights, also see later discussions about the UNCRC, UNCRPD and the Children's Act), this would amount to discrimination by the role players responsible to implement the White Paper 6 (2001), constitutional instruments and international instruments into South African legislation and policies. The White Paper 6 (DOE, 2001) recognises that all children and youth can learn and outlines key steps to ensure educational opportunities for students who have experienced learning and development barriers, or who have dropped out of learning because of the inability of the education and training system to accommodate their learning needs. In the White Paper 6 (DoE, 2001) Inclusive Education is defined as

- acknowledging that all children and youth can learn, and that all children and youth need support;

- respecting and accepting that all learners are different in some way and have different learning needs which are equally valued and an ordinary part of our human experience;
- enabling education structures, systems and learning methodologies to meet the needs of all learners;
- acknowledging and respecting differences in learners, whether due to age, gender, ethnicity, language, class, disability or HIV status;
- maximising the participation of all learners in the culture and the curricula or educational institutions, and uncovering and minimising barriers to learning;
- empowering learners by developing their individual strengths and enabling them to participate critically in the process of learning; and
- acknowledging that learning also occurs in the home and community, and within formal and informal modes or structures.

The right to education is simultaneously the most important right of children with disabilities and the right most frequently denied (Kilkelly, 2002). It is an unqualified and composite right demanding priority (Van Bueren, 1995). Boezart (2012) in "A constitutional perspective on the rights of children with disabilities in an educational context" quote Ex Parte Gauteng Provincial Legislature: In re Dispute Concerning the Constitutionality of Certain Provisions of the Gauteng School Education Bill of 1995, 1996 (3) SA 165 (CC) at para 9, "This constitutional right creates a positive right that basic education must be provided for every person, and not merely a negative right, that such a person should not be obstructed in pursuing his or her basic education".

In the NDP (See discussion in this chapter about the Children's Act), the following is said under the heading of legal imperatives (*of the government*):

> South Africa has ratified a number of international and regional child rights instruments which obligate the adoption of a child care and protection system that promotes the development of children to their full potential through the fulfilment of their full suite of indivisible rights. South Africa has fulfilled its duty through its constitutional recognition and protection of the full suite of children's rights necessary for them develop to their full potential. The ratified instruments and the Constitution recognise the right of all children to develop to their full potential, and the associated duty to adopt measures that ensure children's survival, protection from abuse, neglect and exploitation, their access to parental and family care, protection within the child-justice system, protection from discrimination, to access their socio-economic rights of education, play, recreation, health care, and basic services, as well as to their civil and political rights to an identity, to be heard and to participate in all decisions that affect them.

When the right of children with disabilities are at stake, legislation, international instruments and policies need to be examined. Legislation and International Instruments realising the right to Inclusive Education: The South African Schools Act (SASA) 1996, stipulates that all public schools should admit all learners and should attend to their educational needs without any unfair discrimination. SASA advises that there should be a shift away from the past where children with disabilities were excluded and that the focus must move to acknowledging that there are learners who have barriers to learning but that they have the right to education which suits their needs.

All public schools must admit students and serve their educational requirements without unfairly discriminating in any way. All nine provinces must also ensure that there are enough schools so that every child who lives in his or her province can attend school. The government must take all reasonable measures to ensure that the physical facilities are accessible. The school and education officials must take into account the rights and wishes of learners with special education needs and the rights and wishes of the parents of such learners. SASA also mandates that people with disabilities and experts on special education needs of learners be represented in governing bodies of ordinary schools. Section 5 of the SASA makes provision for all schools to be full-service schools as envisioned by the White Paper 6. Section 12 of the SASA outlines how this should happen by stating that the Member of the Executive Council must, where reasonable practicable, provide education for learners with special education needs at ordinary public schools by providing relevant educational support services for such learners and taking all reasonable measures in ensuring that physical facilities at public schools are accessible to persons with disabilities.

Section 29(1)(a) of the Constitution of South Africa (1996) ("the Constitution of SA") stipulates that everyone has the right to education, including adult education. The policy of "building and Inclusive Education and training system" is embedded in the agenda of EFA, the UNCRC, the UNCRPD and the Millennium Development Goals (MDGs) (Department of Education [DoE], 2001; Assembly, 1993; Assembly, 1989). The right to education is immediately realisable and justiciable (Governing Body of Juma Musjid Primary School v Essay 2011 (7) BCLR 651 (CC) at para 37)

Section 29 needs to be discussed in this context:

> (1) Everyone has the right (a) to a basic education, including adult basic education; and
> (b) to further education, which the state, through reasonable measures, must make progressively available and accessible.
> (2) Everyone has the right to receive education in the official language or languages of their choice in public educational institutions where that education is reasonably practicable. In order to ensure the effective access to, and implementation of, this right, the state must consider all reasonable educational alternatives, including single medium institutions, taking into account (a) equity; (b) practicability; and (c) the need to redress the results of past racially discriminatory laws and practices.
> (3) Everyone has the right to establish and maintain, at their own expense, independent educational institutions that (a) do not discriminate on the basis of race; (b) are registered with the state; and (c) maintain standards that are not inferior to standards at comparable public educational institutions.
> (4) Subsection (3) does not preclude state subsidies for independent educational institutions.

Section 29(1) obliges the government to provide basic education to everyone. This is an unqualified and absolute right. This requires the government to implement measure and make budgetary allocations to give effect to the right as a matter of priority. This subsection should be read with SASA section 12 (supra) which provides that education for learners with special needs should, where reasonably practicable, be provided at ordinary public schools (See Admission Policy for Ordinary Schools published in GN 2432 GG 19377 1888-10-19; Section 3(4)(i) of the National Educational Policy Act 27 of 1996).

In terms of section 29(3), individuals or organisations may establish independent educational institutions. Organisations providing services, such as education to children with autism are a common occurrence (See Western Cape Forum for Intellectual Disability v Government of the Republic of South Africa 2011 (5) SA 87 (WCC)). Section 29(4) stipulates that the state may provide subsidies in these instances (See sections 45 and 48 of the Schools Act; The Amended National Norms and Standards for School Funding GN 869 GG 29179 2006-08-31; Boezart, 2012).

The right to dignity, equality, economic and social rights also apply to the principles of inclusion and non-discrimination. These rights are also relevant to children with disabilities (autism) as discussed previously in this chapter. Furthermore, in line with section 238 of the Constitution of SA which requires the compliance with obligations “diligently and without delay”, the government must urgently fulfil its promise to develop regulations to strengthen provisioning and enforcement of the Constitution and policies.

The NEPA (1996) regulates the drafting, monitoring and evaluation of education policies. Section 4(d) requires the DoE to adopt a policy to ensure that no person is denied the opportunity to receive an education to the maximum of his or her ability as a result of disability. Article 2 of the UNCRC introduces an explicit obligations on governments to assure the realisation of all rights to every child without discrimination, including on grounds of disability. Article 23 of the UNCRC further stipulates that the states parties are obliged to ensure that children with disabilities are able to access education in a manner that promotes their social inclusion. The Committee on the Rights of the Child, in a General Comment on children with disabilities stressed that Inclusive Education must be the goal of educating children with disabilities.

The Committee on the Rights of the Child has identified four rights which must also be understood as general principles to be applied in the realisation of all other rights – non-discrimination, the best interest of the child (see discussion about the Constitution and the Children’s Act in this chapter), the optimum development of the child and the right of the child to be heard and taken seriously in accordance with age and maturity.

The UNCRPD contains detailed provisions on the rights to education, stressing more explicitly than in the UNCRC, the obligation of governments to ensure an “inclusive system of education at all levels”. It also includes a range of obligations to remove the barriers that serve to impede the realisation of rights for children with disabilities, and to ensure more effective protection and a stronger voice for children with disabilities to claim their rights.

South Africa has not yet adopted legislation to enact the provision of the UNCRPD. Boezart (2012) argues that the UNCRPD clarifies the obligations and legal duties of the state to respect and ensure the equal enjoyment of all human rights by all persons with disabilities. Many of the following general principles governing the operation of the UNCRPD have a direct bearing on education:

- Article 3(h) – respect for the evolving capacities of the child with disabilities;
- Article 3(h) and Article 24(1)(b) – the right of the child with disabilities to preserve his or her identity;

- Article 4, 7(1) and 24(1)(a) – full enjoyment of all human rights and freedoms of children with disabilities on an equal basis with other children;
- Article 3, 19, 24(1)© and 30 – full and effective participation and inclusion; and
- Article 3 and 9 – accessibility.

Article 24 of the UNCRPD deals with the right to education in detail. States parties are obliged to ensure an Inclusive Education system at all levels without discrimination and on the basis of equal opportunity. Furthermore, states parties are obliged to ensure that children are not excluded from free and compulsory primary education on the basis of disability (Akinbola, 2010) and to have access to an inclusive quality and free primary and secondary education on an equal basis with others. The UNCRPD obliges states parties to ensure that reasonable accommodation of the individual's requirements must be provided for (see also discussion in this chapter about the meaning of reasonable accommodation). Children with disabilities must receive the support required, within the general education system, to facilitate their effective education. States Parties have to provide effective individualised support measures that maximise academic and social development, consistent with the goal of full inclusion. Section 24(3) examines full and equal participation, setting out measures to be taken by states parties in this regard. For example, this includes the training of professionals and staff who work at all levels of education.

The Children's Act that will be discussed later in this chapter further supports the rights of children and oblige role players to ensure that the rights of children are realised, that in all matters concerning children, the best interest of the child must be prioritised and also comment on measures to realise children's rights. The Constitution dictates that a child's best interest are of paramount importance in every matter affecting that child (See the discussion in this chapter, Children's Act and Laerskool Middelburg v Departementshoof, Mupumalanga 2003 (4) SA 160 (T) para 177 -178, where this principle in education context is discussed). The Children's Act applied to the rights of children with autism provides the primary legal framework for the realisation of the right to social services, parental care, family care and protection from abuse and neglect. Chapter 6 of the Children's Act deals with early childhood development.

- Early childhood development, for the purposes of this Act means the process of emotional, cognitive, sensory, spiritual, moral, physical, social and communication development of children from birth to school-going age.
- Early childhood development services means services (a) intended to promote early childhood development; and (b) provided by a person, other than a child's parent or caregiver, on a regular basis to children up to school-going age.
- An early childhood development programme means a programme structured within an early childhood development service to provide learning and support appropriate to the child's developmental age and stage.

The Act further sets out the strategy expected to implement the programmes and policies with regard to early childhood development. The Minister must consult the Minister of Education, Finance, Health, Provincial and Local Government and Transport. They must include in the departmental strategy a comprehensive national strategy aimed at securing a properly resourced, co-ordinated and managed early childhood development system while given due regard to the principle of best interest of the child and due consideration to the early childhood development of children with disabilities and chronic illnesses. Funds from the money appropriated by the relevant provincial legislature must be used to develop these ECD programmes. The funding of ECD programmes must be prioritised: (a) in communities where families lack the means of providing proper shelter, food and other basic necessities of life to their children; and (b) to make ECD programmes available to children with disabilities.

The prescribed national norms and standards must relate to the following:

- The provision of appropriate developmental opportunities;
- programmes aimed at helping children to realise their full potential;
- caring for children in a constructive manner and providing support and security;
- ensuring development of positive social behaviour;
- respect for and nurturing of the culture, spirit, dignity, individuality, language and development of each child; and
- meeting the emotional, cognitive, sensory, spiritual, moral, physical, social and communication development needs of children (See as discussed in this chapter in the section dealing with the Children's Act, The Constitution).

The Act further stipulates that ECD must be appropriate to the needs of the children to whom the programme is provided, including children with a disability, chronic illness and other special needs.

In the introduction of the National Early Learning and Development Standards for Children Birth to Four Years (NELDS, 2009) it is stated that ECD is defined as "a comprehensive approach to policies and programmes for children from birth to nine years with active participation of practitioners, their parents and other caregivers" (White Paper 5, 2001).

From the above it is clear that it is the intention of the government to protect the rights of children by providing environments and resources for the development of a child's full potential in all aspects of growth and development: cognitive, emotional, social, physical and moral. The South African government has called for an integrated and inter-sectoral strategy in order to manage the care and education for children from birth to four years old.

The White Paper 5 on Early Childhood Education and Social Development (2001), the White Paper 1 on Education and Training (1995) and the Interim Policy for ECD (1996) emphasise the need for different departments to work together on programmes for children from birth to four years old.

This Children's Act read together with other legislation and policies can be used to realise the rights of children with autism, the right to life, the right to standard of living and to benefit from social security, protection from abuse and the right to education which includes ECD and the right to healthcare (Integrated National Strategy on Support Services to Children with Disabilities, 2009).

In 1948, the United Nations (UN) issued the *Universal Declaration of Human Rights (Universal Declaration)* (Assembly 1948). *The Universal Declaration* (1948) states that everyone has the right to education and that education shall be free in the elementary and fundamental phases. *The Universal Declaration* (1948) goes on further to specify that the focus should be on developing the human personality and strengthening respect for human rights and fundamental freedoms.

Has South Africa realised the right to Inclusive Education for children with autism?

In South Africa, Human Rights, Inclusivity and Social Justice are in the foreground in the Revised National Curriculum Statements (RNCS) as priority areas that should be infused across all learning areas (Values and Human Rights in the Curriculum, Department of Education [DoE]).

It is clear from the above that legislation, read together with the Constitution that supports and promotes the rights of all children (inclusive of all children with disabilities) with regard to education and ECD and the international instruments and domestic policies, oblige the government to realise these rights without delay. The government can be held accountable for not providing children with autism with their inherent rights to ECD and education (which would also mean Inclusive Education).

In 2015, the DBE admitted it faces very significant challenges in implementing an Inclusive Education system, particularly ensuring provincial governments comply with the Education White Paper 6. In its progress report, released in May 2015, the DBE advised the government to take "urgent and radical steps" to ensure it is able to reach some of the policy's milestones by 2019.

The Alternative Report to the UN Committee on the Rights of Persons with Disabilities in response to South Africa's Baseline Country Report of March 2013 on the UN Convention on the Rights of Persons with Disabilities, with particular reference to the provisions of Article 24 was published January 2017 by the Inclusive Education South Africa and R2E CWD Alliance. It stipulates that

> In its five-year strategic plan 2015/16-2019/20, the Department of Basic Education (DBE) again made the commitment to prioritise the realisation of Outcome 1, Goal 26 of the National Development Plan (NDP) to strengthen Inclusive Education but has yet again failed to translate this into meaningful action plans, targets or budgetary allocations.

Despite section 12 of the SASA, provincial officials and school principals have not made sufficient provision for the placement and support of learners with disabilities. Parents' experiences are that neither parents' wishes nor the best interest of the child are considered (Inclusive Education South Africa, 2017). Inclusive Education South Africa (2017) recommends that the government must as a priority strengthen sections 5(5) and 5(6) of SASA and obligate Heads of Departments, school principals and governing bodies to ensure admissions policies and practices that guarantee the right of admission of learners with disabilities.

It is further recommended by Inclusive Education South Africa (2017) that the government must fulfil its commitment to urgently review Education White Paper 6 and enact legislation on the right to Inclusive Education before the expiry of the Education White Paper 6 in 2021. This would be consistent with South African constitutional law and the rights of children with disabilities in the Bill of Rights.

In the Report of the International Commission on Education for the 21st century (1996) on page 11, the following is stated as follows:

> Education is not simply a mechanism whereby individuals acquire a limited range of basic skills. Rather, it is a crucial factor in social and personal development, an indispensable asset in (humankind's) attempt to attain the ideals of peace, freedom and justice ... one of the principal means available to foster a deeper and more harmonious form of human development and thereby to reduce poverty, exclusion, ignorance, oppression and war (Report of the International Commission on Education for the 21st Century, Delors, 1996, p11 taken from Values and Human Rights in the Curriculum, Department of Education [DoE]).

The DBE is responsible for delivering Inclusive Education in schools. Other departments also play a key role in implementing this policy as seen in the chart below. This was adapted from a figure in the publication "South Africa's Failure to Guarantee an Inclusive Education for Children with Disabilities / Human Rights Watch" (2015) and clearly indicates what each department (role player) in government are responsible for.

Table 13.1: South Africa's Failure to Guarantee an Inclusive Education for Children with Disabilities, 2015. Adapted from Human Rights Watch.

SHARED RESPONSIBILITIES FOR LEARNERS WITH DISABILITIES	
0-5 years	Department of Social Development • Early Childhood Care Centres • Care Dependency Grant for those who qualify
	Department of Health • Medical Services • Assessment of Disabilities • Referrals to specialized Services • Assistive Devices
	Department of Transport • Adequate and accessible learner transportation
6-18 years	Department of Public Works • Delivery of accessible school infrastructure
	Department of Basic Education (DBE) • Placements in mainstream, full-service and special schools • Pedagogical assessments • Services by district based Inclusive Education support teams • Transportation subsidies
	Department of Social Development • Institutions, including hostels • Care Dependency Grant for those who qualify

SHARED RESPONSIBILITIES FOR LEARNERS WITH DISABILITIES	
18+ years	Department of Higher Education and Training • Inclusive universities • Technical and Vocational Education and Training (TVET)
	Department of Social Development • Protective workshops, skills centres, institutions, hostels • Disability greant
	Department of Basic Education (DBE) • Adult Basic Education and Training programmes

In "South Africa's Failure to Guarantee an Inclusive Education for Children with Disabilities" (Human Rights Watch, August 18, 2015), it was found that the progress on paper for children with disabilities has not translated into equal opportunities or protection on the ground. HRW questions whether government has prioritised children with disabilities' access to a quality Inclusive Education as it committed to do in the Education White Paper 6 (2001).

The key findings of this report were as follows:

- Discrimination accessing education: children with disabilities continue to face discrimination when accessing all types of public schools. Schools decide whether they are willing or able to accommodate students with particular disabilities or needs. In many cases, children with intellectual disabilities, multiple disabilities and autism are particularly disadvantaged.
- Discrimination owing to a lack of reasonable accommodation in school: many students in mainstream schools face discriminatory physical and attitudinal barriers they need to overcome in order to receive an education. Many students in special schools for children with sensory disabilities do not have access to the same subjects as children in mainstream schools, jeopardising their access to a full curriculum.
- Discriminatory fees and expenses: children with disabilities who attend special schools pay school fees that children without disabilities do not, and many who attend mainstream schools are asked to pay for their own class assistants as a condition of staying in mainstream classes. In addition, parents often pay burdensome transport and boarding costs if special schools are far from families and communities.
- Violence, abuse and neglect in schools: students exposed to violence and abuse in many of South Africa's schools, but children with disabilities are more vulnerable to such unlawful and abusive practices.
- Lack of quality education: children with disabilities in many public schools receive low quality education in poor learning environments. They continue to be significantly affected by a lack of teacher training and awareness about Inclusive Education methodologies and the diversity of disabilities, a dearth of understanding and practical training about children's needs according to their disabilities and an absence of incentives for teachers to instruct children with disabilities.

- Lack of preparation for life after basic education: the consequences of a lack of inclusive quality learning are particularly visible when adolescents and young adults with disabilities leave school. Many stay at home after finishing compulsory education and many lack basic life skills.

Segregation and lack of inclusion are visible at all levels of South Africa's education system and reflect fundamental breaches of the UNCRDP, the UNCRC, the Children's Act and the Constitution. Barriers to Inclusive Education begin in the very early stages of children's lives because these children are classified according to their disabilities (Human Rights Watch, 2016).

Often parents with children with autism are faced with uncertainty and have to navigate a complex system without adequate information about their children's special needs, abilities or the best type of education for them. In many cases NGOs (NGO's) fill these gaps in the delivery of public services for children who have been left out of the education system. But most of the NGOs services for children with autism is very expensive and comes with huge financial expenses that not all parents are able to pay (Clasquin-Johnson & Clasquin-Johnson, 2018).

Several organisations have been fighting for the rights and justice of individuals with ASD, like R2ECWD (a National Campaign), Equal Education Law Centre and Inclusive Education South Africa. They have many organisations that are members, among these organisations are autism organisations. The key function of these organisations is the promotion of an education system, that have full participation and inclusion for children with disabilities and that maximises their personal development and enables their ongoing participation and inclusion in society.

The key messages of the campaign are:

- All South African children, including children with disabilities, have the right to basic education under national and international law;
- Education policy in South Africa provides for the increased capacity of ordinary public schools to include children with disabilities, but this has not been effectively implemented;
- There are many kinds of barriers to learning and forms of disability; no single solution is appropriate for all children;
- Children with disabilities who are out of school are being denied their right to basic education;
- Education and support staff need access to appropriate training and resources and to foster and inclusive attitude to meet the learning needs of children with disabilities;
- ECD services are not adequately equipped to support the early identification and intervention needs of children with disabilities;
- Inclusive education can and does work if policy is implemented properly;
- The cost of providing quality, Inclusive Education is small compared with the costs of not doing so (RSECWD Campaign, www.saaled.org.za/R2ECWD).

Traditionally, the education system in South Africa provided special education to learners with disabilities. As the political, social, educational and economic needs of the society changed, it became obvious that the traditional ideas of schools and classrooms were becoming outdated (Du Plessis, 2013). Inclusive Education movements as mentioned above, challenge exclusion and practices in education. It is evident from the reports mentioned above and discussions in the latter part of this chapter that human rights violations and a guarantee that social justice will prevail in education is part of the struggle in a South African context.

The legislation read together with other legislation and policies can be used to realise the rights of children with autism, the right to life, the right to standard of living and to benefit from social security, protection from abuse, the right to education which includes ECD and the right to healthcare (Integrated National Strategy on Support Services to Children with Disabilities, 2009).

In the DBE's, Report on the Implementation of Education White Paper 6 on Inclusive Education: Overview for the Period 2013-2015 (2016), the government highlighted the many challenges and overdue actions which are hindering children with disabilities (inclusive of children with autism) from enjoying quality, equitable, Inclusive Education.

In the NDP: Our Future Make it Work 2030 (2012) deals with the strategic plan for education in South Africa in Chapter 9. The following quote about (and only mention of) Inclusive Education was taken from the NDP:

> *Using the NDP's own* stated criteria, a developmental state must be built upon a developmental child care and protection policy and services that address the root causes of poverty and inequality, starting with the youngest children, through:
> The provision of a universal social floor of services required to ensure the optimal development of the capabilities of all children.

The DSD's draft policy "South Africa's Child Care Policy", which is based on the NDP, but elaborates how this department will implement the plan for South Africa, this was already discussed earlier in this chapter (see discussion about Human Rights and the Constitution), "children with disabilities is mentioned 28 times", this policy shows commitment by the government, acknowledgement, but it is yet to be seen if the proposed changes will be realised for children with autism (disabilities).

The DBE, Revised Five-Year Strategic Plan 2015/16-2019/2020 dated March 2016, the following is stated about the NDP and the commitment by the DBE regarding Inclusive Education:

> The NDP has put forward a number of priorities that will drive all development initiatives from both government and the private sector. The plan gives a 2030 horizon, and emphasises what is critical to the development of human capital starting with the ECD sector, which lays the foundation for development in the country. Alignment of all initiatives and strategies by various sectors will thus be critical in each five-year period towards 2030. Listed below are some of the NDP's critical areas of focus for the Education sector.

Area of Focus NDP Mandate

Early Childhood Development (ECD)

- Expanded access to ECD (covered in Outcome 13) and improvement of the quality of Gr R;
- Standardise the guidelines, norms and standards for ECD;
- Universal access to two years of ECD;
- Improve state funding for ECD; and
- Invest in training ECD practitioners.

Inclusive Education

- Ensuring that all children with disabilities have access to quality education; and
- Provide Inclusive Education that enables everyone to participate effectively in a free society.

It is mentioned in the DBE strategic plan that teacher development and competency must be strengthened relating to Inclusive Education, that the number of schools that effectively implement the Inclusive Education policy must be increased and that these schools must have access to centres that offer specialist services.

The strategic plan sets out how the department will respond to different areas, on Inclusive Education the following is stated:

Inclusive Education

- SIAS Policy: Implement an efficient system for early identification and intervention in addressing barriers to learning;
- Curriculum Differentiation: Teachers are to be empowered to teach and assess in a manner that takes into consideration the diversity of learner needs in the classroom;
- SASL CAPS: There is an urgent need to put programmes in place that will improve retention and completion rates of deaf learners;
- Skills and Vocational Programmes: The existing National Curriculum Statement Grades R-12 is academic and therefore limits options for career paths informed by interest and aptitude. During this term, specific programmes will be developed for learners with disabilities to empower them with skills; and
- Home Education Policy: This policy is to be implemented to promote access to EFA children including those who may not thrive in a schooling system.

The Right of Children with Disabilities to Education (UNICEF, 2011) contains the following recommendations for Inclusive Education:

- Political will and good governance to promote accountability, transparency, access to justice and the rule of law;
- Government structures responsible for the education of children with disabilities must bring an end to the segregation of children with disabilities;

- Financing, a commitment by government to the expenditure to achieve a reform and recognition that Inclusive Education is a cost effective approach to achieving EFA;
- Guarantee the right to non-discrimination, domesticate the UNCRPD and ensure accessible and affordable mechanisms for challenging discrimination;
- Partnership and participation, a commitment to partner with families, children, NGOs, Disability Rights Groups and other role players to ensure that they are involved in all stages of the development and implementation of an Inclusive Education system;
- Respect the contribution of families, who are active parties throughout the life cycle of their children's education;
- Capacity building and awareness-raising, the must be an investment at all levels of government to promote the awareness of the rights of children with disabilities (to Inclusive Education) and other constitutional rights;
- Removing the barriers to Inclusive Education, by investing in public spaces that are not safe and inclusive, by removing physical, communication, mobility, sensory barriers to education;
- Working and supporting parents, by providing parent education programmes to help parents support their child's learning barriers;
- ECD and care services, by investing in early assessment and intervention promote the possibility of effective and appropriate support to children with disabilities;
- Ensuring access and availability of Inclusive education, by introducing legislation, policies and establishing the right to Inclusive Education at all levels, within mainstream settings and classes; and
- Creating inclusive learning environments, by ensuring commitment by all the relevant role players.

In a publication by the DBE, "A guide for parents, caregivers and communities based on the Education White Paper 6" (2003) the roles and the responsibilities for parents/caregivers are discussed in section 4. It is stated that the parents can play specific roles to support their child. Parents must know their rights, they can for example serve on the governing body of the school, write to the National Education Department to report cases where the policy is not implemented, parents must act as activists/advocates for their children's rights, they should set up networks for support, parents should support the educators and parents must raise awareness to campaign for Inclusive Education.

Government still needs to go a long way to realise the basic rights of children with autism, collaboration between different government department, awareness campaigns and adequate allocation for funding specifically earmarked for children with disabilities must be made a priority.

12.3.2 The Children's Act (2005), The Criminal Procedure Act (1977), Mental Health Care Act (2002)

The Children's Act, Act No. 38 of 2005 came into full operation on 1 April 2010, and specifically includes the rights of children with disabilities. The objective of this Act is to give effect to children's specific constitutional rights. These rights, to name a few, are the best interest of the child principle, protection of children against discrimination, enabling the survival of the child, child participation and the promotion of the rights of children with disabilities specifically.

The Mental Health Care Act, Act No. 17 of 2002 is essential for the protection of the rights of individuals with mental disabilities, who are considered a vulnerable part of society. The objective of this Act is to address access to services for individuals with mental health illnesses or intellectual disabilities.

The Criminal Procedure Act No. 51 of 1977 governs criminal procedure in the South African legal system. It sets out legal procedure in terms of matters related to the criminal justice system. For the purposes of this chapter, I will focus on regulations related to witness testimonies of children (but specifically children with disabilities). Although I will discuss The Promotion of Equality and the Prevention of Unfair Discrimination Act No. 4 of 2000 in the next section of this chapter, it needs mention in this section too.

Section 9(4) of the Constitution (as discussed earlier) stipulates that national legislation must be enacted to prevent or prohibit unfair discrimination. This Act is the fulfilment of the constitutional obligations of the government and is the key legislative tool to translate the right to equality into rules that are practical and workable (Albertyn, 2001).

Before this Act came into operation, most people did not have any accessible legal remedies against discrimination, except for utilising civil litigation which amounted to a tedious and expensive endeavour. This Act provides accessible remedies in terms of discrimination (Pityana, 2002). This Act is therefore relevant in respect of non-discrimination against children with disabilities (Carter, 2015).

The Children's Act and the Constitution, and the best interest of the child (with autism)

Every child (including a child with autism) has the rights set out in section 28 of the Constitution. The latter states that "every child has the right to a name and nationality from birth, family care or parental care, or to appropriate alternative care when removed from the family environment, basic nutrition, shelter, basic health care services and social services, be protected from maltreatment, neglect, abuse or degradation."

The rights afforded in section 28 of the Constitution, and all the other rights enshrined in the Bill of Rights, such as the right to equality and the right to dignity, discussed above, entail a declaration of realisable and enforceable rights.

A child is defined as a person below the age of 18 years (Section 28(3) of the Constitution). Section 28 imposes a duty on organs of the state to at all times be child sensitive, as stated in the Constitutional Court in S v M 2008 (3) SA 232 (CC), and address matters relating to family care, protection from abuse, as well as the provision of legal assistance in certain instances.

The state must respect, protect, promote and fulfil these rights. Protection of children's rights leads to a corresponding improvement in the lives of other sections of the community because it is neither desirable nor possible to protect children's rights in isolation from their families and communities.

Section 28(1)(b) of the South African Constitution states that every child has the right to family or parental care. The family component is seen as an integral to the child's enjoyment of childhood and care within his/her family must be promoted as far as possible.

One of the main objectives of the Children's Act is the best interest of the child principle, and as mentioned throughout this chapter, should always be of paramount importance in every matter concerning the child. The legislature's use of the words "in every matter" and in "all proceedings" requires an interests-consciousness with regard to children from all role-players, as there may be very few circumstances, decisions and actions which may not affect children in some way or the other (Boezart, 2013; Heaton, 2009).

Section 2 of the Children's Act (2005) states that the objects of this Act are –

> (a) to promote the preservation and strengthening of families; (b) to give effect to the following constitutional rights of children, namely - (i) family care or parental care or appropriate alternative care when removed from the family environment; (ii) social services; (iii) protection from maltreatment, neglect, abuse or degradation; and (iv) that the best interests of a child are of paramount importance in every matter concerning the child; (c) to give effect to the Republic's obligations concerning the well-being of children in terms of international instruments binding on the Republic; (d) to make provision for structures, services and means for promoting and monitoring the sound physical, psychological, intellectual, emotional and social development of children; (e) to strengthen and develop community structures which can assist in providing care and protection for children; (f) to protect children from discrimination, exploitation and any other physical, emotional or moral harm or hazards; (g) to provide care and protection to children who are in need of care and protection; (h) to recognise the special needs that children with disabilities may have; and (i) generally, to promote the protection, development and well-being of children.

The Children's Act does not distinguish between a child with a disability or a child without a disability, but provide a list of factors that is to be considered when determining the best interest of the child in a particular matter, for example, the child's needs, age and maturity, and the relationship between the child and his or her caregiver. The Children's Act in section 7(1)(ii), which states that any disability a child may have must be taken into account in determining the best interest of the said child (Boezart, 2013). Section 9 of the Children's Act further determines that in every matter concerning the care, protection and well-being of a child, the best interest of the child principle is of paramount importance.

As already mentioned in this chapter, a child with autism would fall under the category of "vulnerable" children as defined by the UNCRPD, UNCRC and the government of South Africa in their NDP 2030 and other policies. This would imply that a child with autism (and their family) would receive protection from not only the Constitution, the UNCRPD, the UNCRC but their interests as vulnerable children will be prioritised as set out in the NDP 2030. One of the other key objectives of the Children's Act is to protect all children form discrimination.

Section 6(2) the Children's Act direct that *all proceedings, actions or decisions in a matter concerning a child must* - (a) respect, protect, promote and fulfil the child's rights set out in the Bill of Rights, the best interests of the child standard set out in section 7 and the rights and principles set out in this Act, subject to any lawful limitation; (b) respect the child's inherent dignity; (c) treat the child fairly and equitably; (d) *protect the child from unfair discrimination on any ground, including on the grounds of the health status or disability of the child or a family member of the child;* (e) recognise a child's need for development and to engage in play and other recreational activities appropriate to the child's age; and (f) recognise a child's disability and create an enabling environment to respond to the special needs that the child has. (3) If it is in the best interests of the child, the child's family must be given the opportunity to express their views in any matter concerning the child.

The Children's Act has the effect that all the planning and development of all strategies and programmes for children with disabilities are required to be aligned to the basic principles entrenched in the UNCRC. The Children's Amendment Act No 41 of 2007 and the Promotion of Equality and Prevention of Discrimination Act lead the way in giving effect to the rights of children as contained in the Constitution, mandating various government sectors to fulfil the obligation in meeting these rights.

Discrimination is defined by the Promotion of Equality and Prevention of Discrimination Act (PEPUDA), as any omission, which directly or indirectly:

- Imposes burdens, obligations or disadvantage on; or
- Withholds benefits, opportunities or advantages from any person on one or more of the prohibited grounds.

The prohibited grounds referred to in this definition include discrimination on the basis of age and disability. The prohibited grounds also include discrimination that undermines human dignity.

Section 9 of PEPUDA creates a very clear prohibition against discrimination on the grounds of disability, and expressly articulates that failing to eradicate impediments that unfairly limit or restrict persons with disabilities from enjoying equal opportunities is tantamount to discrimination. This also includes failing to take steps to reasonably accommodate the needs of individuals with disabilities.

The Mental Health Care Act addresses unfair discrimination. Specifically, section 10 of this Act states that a mental health care user may not be unfairly discriminated against on the grounds of his or her mental health status.

It is clear from the above discussion that children with autism may not be discriminated against, that their dignity must always be respected, that their condition may not be the reason for restriction of the enjoyment of equal opportunities and that reasonable steps must be taken to accommodate their needs.

The child's right and the protection to develop his or her personality is also addressed in the Children's Act. This would include the child's right to be heard. This right is also supported by Article 12 of the UNCRC (discussed previously). Sloth-Nielsen in "Seen and Heard?" (2009) states the following: "The solicitation of children's views runs like a golden thread through the Children's Act, thereby rendering the Act a thoroughly modern text."

Throughout the Children's Act, there are several sections providing children with an opportunity to participate in matters affecting them and for their voices to be heard (Carter, 2015). Children with autism are too often silenced or silent owing to some of them being non-verbal (see Chapter 1, Framing Autism, Chapter 2, Diagnosing Autism, Chapter 5, Voices and Views, Chapter 6, Autism in a Rural Context, of this Volume :)

As indicated above, children must be provided the opportunity to have their voices heard. For example, if a child's constitutional rights or personal rights are at risk, the

Legal Aid Act, Act No 22 of 1969, in its Legal Aid Guide, indicates that the Legal Aid SA grants legal aid in civil matters to all children living in South Africa. The South African Constitution provides that legal representation must be granted at state expense in civil proceedings affecting a child if substantial injustice would otherwise result.

The following criteria are mentioned in the Legal Aid Guide:

> The seriousness of the issue for the child, the complexity of the relevant law and procedure, the ability of the child to represent himself or herself effectively without a lawyer; the financial situation of the child or the child's parents …, the child's chances of success in the case; and, whether the child has a substantial disadvantage compared with any other party in the case.

There is no specific mention of disability or children with special needs. When a child applies for legal aid, the means of the child are considered. If parents or guardians assist the child, their means will also be considered.

As discussed earlier in this chapter, autism is the most expensive disability. Parents having children with autism have extreme financial obligations to assist their children. Against this background, it is sensible for Legal Aid SA to, in the very least, consider that a means test in relation to a child with autism must be understood against a capability as well as the livelihood approach.

Children with autism cannot contribute to a household to ensure the survival of the household. Therefore, a means test should always consider the fact that such a child is unable to care for him or herself. Even with an inheritance or grant, the mere nature of the vulnerability of children with autism seeking legal representation should warrant a negation of the current applicable means test (Carter, 2015).

When considering the means test of the parents of the child with autism seeking legal representation, it must be considered that children with autism are not able to care for themselves in the future (Yeo, 2001). In households that are already financially carrying the exorbitant costs of autism, but still present enough means for the Legal Aid SA to hold them accountable for legal representation fees, children with autism from these families may be excluded and ostracised even further (Carter, 2015).

In a household where there are already limited resources, it may be seen as economically careless to give resources to legal representation. This could leave their child worse off, as the necessary funds to afford costly legal representation takes away from other necessary expenses to afford therapies, for example. This also excludes the child and the family to enforce the rights of their child with autism and the result is further discrimination.

Are lawyers "qualified" to represent, question and assist children with autism?

The training of legal representatives, prosecutors, judges, magistrates (lawyers as a collective) and other law enforcement agencies does not include training to specifically manage, represent or work with a child with autism (or any child with a disability). Article 13 of the UNCRPD is therefore neglected as the accommodation and training required are not addressed.

The importance of addressing the rights of children with disabilities specifically in legislation is grounded in the two-tier vulnerability of these children. This means that legislation addressing children in general may not understand that children with disabilities and *specifically children living with autism* may need separate measures to be undertaken to accommodate their inclusion (Carter, 2015).

Section 11 of the Children's Act explicitly addresses the rights of children with disabilities and states that their needs must be taken into account, "in any matter concerning" that child. Reading section 7 with section 11 of the Children's Act would recognise that organs of the state must take into account the child's disability and recognise the child's disability in any matter relating to the child (Carter, 2015).

Section 11(1) of the Children's Act regulates that for the participation of children with disabilities the specific needs of the child must be recognised. Circumstances must be created to provide conditions that guarantee "dignity, promote self-reliance and facilitate active participation in the community."

Section 11(d) addresses the need for the caregivers of children with disabilities to be provided with necessary support services. Organs of the state must in the application of the Children's Act (section 4(2)) take reasonable measures to the maximum extent of their available resources to achieve the realisation of the Children's Act's objectives and aims. The state is further required to take "reasonable legislative and other measures" to achieve the progressive realisation of these rights.

A very important decision for the Western Cape was the case of the Western Cape Forum for Intellectual Disability v Government of the Republic of South Africa and Another 2011 (5) SA 87 (WC). This case will be discussed in more detail later in this chapter. For the sake of the current discussion it is important to note that the court found that the state infringed on the rights of children with *intellectual* (my highlight) disabilities as there was no rational basis for imposing a shortage in funds and budget cuts on these vulnerable children only, and not on their peers without disabilities.

The court further held that the state had marginalised these children and contributed to the stigmatisation of children with disabilities. The court held that the children's right to dignity was violated. This case is very important when shortages of funds (resources) and services are argued in respect of service delivery for children with autism.

As mentioned above, Article 13 of the UNCRPD obliges states parties to address three elements in respect of access to justice for people with disabilities: reasonable accommodation, participation and training of relevant stakeholders. In order for legislation to adhere to this framework, certain facilities must be adapted to accommodate children with disabilities throughout the justice system. Although the child's right to participation has been addressed earlier in this chapter, a variety of other safeguards must be catered for to facilitate access to justice for children with disabilities (Carter, 2015).

What is relevant for this section is the access to services for children with disabilities in matters relating to discrimination. Like the Children's Act, Chapter 4 of PEPUDA creates Equality Courts. Section 16(1)(a) states that every high court is an Equality Court for the area of its jurisdiction. Equality Courts are created as specialised courts, operating within the structure of high courts and magistrates' courts. Every high court in South Africa is automatically an Equality Court whereas magistrates' courts may be designated as Equality Courts (Government Gazette No 25065 reg 9(1)).

Section 20 of PEPUDA stipulates that any person acting in their own interest may institute proceedings under PEPUDA. Section 20(1)(b) goes further and states that a person *(parent or caregiver of a child with autism)* acting on behalf of another person, who cannot act in his or her own name, may also institute proceedings. It is possible for children with autism to be assisted by a range of representatives because certain children with autism may have communication difficulties and will need a trusted caregiver who will be able to understand and assist the child to share his or her views during proceedings.

The process is inexpensive and no legal representatives are needed in these courts. No fees are required to place a case before an Equality Court. In order to institute proceedings in the Equality Court, the complainant approaches the court and informs the clerk that he or she wishes to institute proceedings. It is incumbent upon the clerk to assist the complainant to complete the prescribed form. The clerk opens a file and allocates a case number to the matter. However, the support given to the complainant by the clerk of the court is crucial in rendering the Equality Court accessible to persons with disability.

As illustrated by the monitoring project of the SAHRC in 2012, these courts are underutilised and opportunities to develop jurisprudence relating to matters of equality were not provided. Therefore, there is limited research available on the effect of litigation in Equality Courts (SAHRC, 2015).

The report expressed dismay at the fact that the adequate resources for these courts to function properly, reflects a lack of commitment from the state in the proper functioning of the Equality Courts as a mechanism to protect and provide recourse to the vulnerable members of society such as children with disabilities (Carter, 2015).

In criminal matters where children with disabilities are witnesses, measures are also taken to accommodate them. Sections 153, 158, 161 and 170(A)(1) of the Criminal Procedure Act will be discussed briefly.

Section 153 of the CPA provides for a child to be able to testify in camera. This means the child will testify in a private room behind closed doors. This is to protect the child's privacy. This section, however, do not protect the child from testifying in the presence of the accused.

Section 158 of the CPA determines that evidence can also be given via closed-circuit television (CCTV) or similar equipment. This may be utilised should it be in the interest of justice. It is also there to prevent "harm" to the child.

Section 161 of the CPA allows further participation by children with disabilities by stating that:

- A witness at criminal proceedings shall, except where this Act or any other law expressly provides otherwise, give evidence viva voce.
- In this section the expression "viva voce" shall ….be deemed to include gesture-language and, in the case of a witness under the age of 18 years be deemed to include demonstrations, gestures or any other form of non-verbal expression.

This section of the CPA clearly allows children with limited communication abilities (like children with autism) to give evidence in the manner that they communicate.

Section 170(A)(1) of the CPA provides for the following:

> Whenever criminal proceedings are pending before any court and it appears to such court that it would expose any witness under the biological or mental age of 18 years to undue mental stress or suffering if he or she testifies at such proceedings. The court may, subject to

subsection (4), appoint a competent person as an intermediary in order to enable such witness to give his or her evidence through that intermediary.

This would allow a child to give evidence through a trained person and therefore not be subjected to an accusatorial direct line of questioning or cross examination.

The list of persons who may act as intermediaries were published in the Government Gazette in 1993 (15024 of 30 July 1993 as amended by Government Gazette 17822 of 28 February 1997, and amended by Government Gazette no 22435 of 2 July 2001). The list is not exhaustive but includes registered paediatricians, registered psychiatrists, certain family councillors, qualified childcare workers, registered social workers with the prerequisite experience, psychologists and certain educators. These include family councillors appointed in terms of section 3 of the Mediation in terms of the Divorce Matters Act, Act 24 of 1987, those who are or were registered social workers, or those who have four years' experience as educators, or those who are or were registered as clinical, educational, or counselling psychologists.

This could be problematic as persons who are able to assist a child with autism are not always available and this can prejudice these children in court proceedings and the procedure before the court proceedings commence (interview and statement taking stage). The financial implication of the use of this person with specialised training to assist a child with autism will also need to be addressed, which could further cause prejudice.

Muller (2015) argues that traditional courtroom procedures act against eliciting complete and reliable evidence from children. In a study published by Hill and Hill in 1987 on the effect of a formal courtroom environment on the ability of children to recall facts and occurrences, the children interviewed in the private room recalled facts more accurately and did not experience the questioning as being as traumatic as the children who were interviewed in the courtroom.

As discussed above, the use of CCTV cameras as the default position for children with autism to give testimony will remove them from the intimidating nature of the courtroom, and be in the best interests of the child principle, which remains a paramount consideration in all matters affecting a child (Sect 9 of the Children's Act).

Section 42(8) of the Children's Act addresses the issue that the relevant courtroom in itself must be as suitable as possible, for a child having no other option, than to be heard in this setting.

Sections 14, 42 and 52 of the Children's Act all support Article 13 of the UNCRPD in requiring some sort of age-appropriate and procedural accommodation when it comes to children with disabilities approaching courts. These sections can only be successful if properly committed to and implemented (Carter, 2015).

Fouche and Joubert (2009) claim that children can be trustworthy witnesses and that they can make meaningful comments about their experiences when questioned correctly. Furthermore, Songca (2004) argues that even through children may communicate in a different way from adults, this does not prevent them from providing information accurately in a manner that can be understood. Generally, children should be questioned in a specific manner as they do not have the same abilities as adults to retain memories and information (Dunn, 1995; See also Chapter 1, Framing Autism, Chapter 11, Classroom assessment, Chapter, 6, Autism in a rural context in this volume). Should a child be coerced into a direction by means of an incorrect questioning technique, the child may attempt to fill in the gaps of his memory with incorrect or suggested information (Dunn, 1995).

Walker (1999) illustrates that linguistic complexities may further contribute to the testimonies of children being brought into question. Vocabularly, word order, syntactic methods and ambiguity in language may be difficult for children to grasp, and much more so for children with learning and speech impairments. The mere use of propositions may also have an effect of a dire outcome in a matter should they be incorrectly used by a child (See also Chapter 1, Framing Autism in this volume).

It is therefore extremely important for any person questioning a child to be alert to the importance of language command. In the light of the status of sign language, the nuances of prepositions, synonyms and ambiguity require alertness from the person questioning the child. As much as it may be challenging to determine the true meaning behind the testimony provided by a child as a result of linguistic intricacies, it becomes ever more complex if the language used by the child can only be understood by a limited number of role players (for example sign language interpreter and the immediate family).

This is extremely relevant for children with autism, as indicated in the other chapters in this volume. Autism is defined in the DSM-V (Diagnostic and Statistical Manual of Mental Disorders, Fifth Edition, 2013), as impairment in social communication and restricted repetitive patterns of behaviour. The criteria for ASD include a deficit in social-emotional reciprocity, ranging from abnormal social approach and failure of normal back-and-forth conversations, to reduced sharing of interests, emotions, or affect, to failure to initiate or respond to social interactions. The criteria also include deficits in non-verbal communicative behaviours used for social interaction, ranging from poorly integrated verbal and non-verbal communication, to abnormalities in eye contact and body language or deficits in understanding and use of gestures, to total lack of facial expressions and non-verbal communication, deficits in developing, maintaining and understanding relationships and difficulties adjusting behaviour to suit various social contexts.

The following are also symptoms that are part of the autism spectrum. Stereotyped or repetitive motor movements, use of objects or speech, insistence on sameness, inflexible adherence to routines, or ritualised patterns of verbal or non-verbal behaviour, this can include extreme distress at small changes, difficulties with transitions, rigid thinking patters, greeting rituals, need to take the same route, eat the same food every day. Hyper or hypo reactivity to sensory input or unusual interests in sensory aspects of the environments is common in children with autism and can include adverse response to specific sounds or textures, excessive smelling or touching of objects.

The symptoms above cause significant impairment in social, occupational or other important areas of functioning, children with autism are not intellectually disabled, but intellectual disability and ASD does co-occur.

From the above it can be seen how important it is for professionals who question children with autism, to be trained to understand the complexities of autism, to develop skills to question, to interview and to assist these children to access justice. A denial of that will be a denial of enforcing their constitutional rights and will amount to discrimination and would be automatically considered unconstitutional.

Section 52 of the Children's Act further calls for rules to be made on the appropriate questioning techniques for children with disabilities which cause difficulties in communication. This is an obligatory provision to protect vulnerable children from certain procedures in court. Role players (Department of Justice, NPA and the DSD) are obliged to make rules designed to address these various types of questioning techniques. However, no such rules have been made.

Although crucial in terms of the rights of children with disabilities to have access to justice and participate during court proceedings, there is no prescribed manner in which presiding officers and other judicial stakeholders (for example police and other law enforcement agencies) should undertake the questioning of children with communication difficulties (Carter, 2015).

On the question posed in the beginning of this discussion, are lawyers (as a collective) and law enforcement officials trained to assist, question and accommodate children with autism. It can further be argued that it is also crucial for presiding officers to be trained to assist children with autism in their pursuit to access justice. In training provided by Justice College to presiding officers on the implementation of the Children's Act (DOJ&CS 2013/2014 Annual Report, 2014), there was no reference made to children with disabilities. The only reference made is about the accessibility of a courtroom to persons who are disabled. This goes completely against the obligations on states parties in Article 13 of the UNCRPD and the Children's Act.

In the matter of George v The Minister of Environmental Affairs and Tourism 2005 (6) SA 297 (EqC) par 7, the court indicated that presiding officers who have been specifically equipped to address the adjudication of equality matters must provide staff to equality courts. It can be argued that any court should be staffed by presiding officers who have been specifically trained to address the adjudication of matters where children with autism are the complainants.

Not only must presiding officers be trained in the relevant legislation to hear matters of discrimination, but must also be trained and sensitised with reference to the social context of disability discrimination. Proper training also becomes imperative in relation to all role players for procedural accommodation in respect of access to justice for children with disabilities. Basic elements such as how to refer to the child's disability (appropriate disability language) can assist in providing the child with equal access to justice in a dignified manner (Carter, 2015).

Appendix 4 of the SAHRC Report, "Towards a barrier-free society" (2002) list a guide to terminology that is preferred by the disability rights movement. It is stated that generally ensure that the person comes first, not the disability. Therefore, the phrase people with disabilities is preferable to disabled people, and definitely not "the disabled".

The UNCRPD has yet to be fully domesticated in 2012 the SAHRC (Submissions to the Portfolio Committee, 2012) recommended to Parliament that South Africa needs to review its current legislation and determine whether there is a need to amend legislation or draft new legislation in order to ensure the domestication of the UNCRPD. These recommendations have to date not been brought to fruition (Carter, 2015).

In the NDP: Vision 2030 (NDP, 2017), the obligations on the government of South Africa and all the role players are discussed and strategies are proposed to implement these changes in legislation and to domesticate the UNCRPD, the UNCRC and other international and regional instruments of which South Africa is a party to.

The DSD's draft policy 2017, South Africa's Child Care and Protection Policy also recognises these obligations and have in line with the NDP: Vision 2030 proposed strategies to implement these changes in legislation.

The Department of Justice, in its Strategic Plan for the period 2017-2020 (amended and updated April 2018) declared "Justice for all in South Africa". The NDP: Vision 2030 is recognised, in the introduction there are no specific mention of children with disabilities but it is stated that there is an obligation to "increase access to justice by providing all services to justice service points, reducing legal costs, providing legal assistance to civilians and establishing new courts".

There is also no specific mention of access to justice for children with disabilities, the obligations of the Children's Act, training for judicial staff, the obligations of the department per the UNCRC and the obligations of the department per the UNCRPD.

It is however mentioned that the state is constitutionally obliged to respect, protect, promote and fulfil the constitutional rights as contained in the Bill of Rights. The plan continues to state that it becomes imperative for the department to ensure that every South African knows and understands the Constitution. It is said that efforts have been made by the department in collaboration with civil society organisations to educate people about their rights and responsibilities, but mush remains to be done.

The NPA, in its Strategic Plan 2013-2018, states that the organisation is committed to transforming itself to meet the needs of society by contributing to the effectiveness of the criminal justice system. The objectives for the NPA in the NDP: Vison 2013 is recognised. However, there is no mention in the strategic plan for training of prosecutors, the obligations of the Children's Act, the UNCRC or the UNCRPD obligations towards children with disabilities or the access to justice of this vulnerable group.

It therefore remains to be seen how the NDP: Vision 2030 where the obligations of the state is recognised to domesticate the UNCRC and the UNCRPD will be implemented in legislation, and how the strategic plans of the role players responsible for giving children with autism's access to justice will recognise the obligations and ensure that this vulnerable group be given access to justice.

12.3.3 The BCEA (1997) the Promotion of Equality and the Prevention of Unfair Discrimination Act (2000), Employment Equity Act (1998)

In this section I will deal with the integration of work and parenting. This is a serious concern for many individuals, societies, governments and families (Dancaster et al., 2008). The aim is to evaluate the contribution or legal regulation of this integration. It is easy to see how society and parenting (in the sense of provision of care to children) reciprocally influence each other (Westman, 1999). Society depends on parents who competently rear their children (Westman, 1999).

Society has to support parenthood (Westman, 1999) and more so there is an obligation to support parents rearing children with disabilities as discussed in the sections above. One aspect of this obligation is to recognise that work and parenting are unable to operate in isolation from one another (Dancaster et al., 2010), and that the demands on paid work should successfully be integrated with the demands of parental care. This means government should provide an appropriate legal basis for such integration (Rossouw, 2018).

The author's personal experiences also contributes to her interest in this chapter and specifically this section, as the researcher is a mother of three children of which one is a child diagnosed with autism and one diagnosed with ADHD and have a very demanding career.

What is autism, what makes parenting a child with autism unique?

Contributors to this volume have provided a range of definitions of autism. Clasquin-Johnson and Clasquin-Johnson (2018), in their autoethnographic reflection on the cost of raising a child with autism, note, "We soon discovered that autism is positioned as the most expensive disability for which parents need impossibly deep pockets". Similarly, Matenge's (2013) exploration of the lived experiences of mothers raising children with autism notes that children with disabilities may benefit from having a mother who does not take up employment outside the home. However, this poses serious financial implications for the family, considering the costs involved in managing the effects of the disability and associated costs, such as therapy, doctors' consultations, special dietary requirements, and special education for a child with autism.

The high number of children diagnosed with autism means that there are many families faced with the unique challenges in caring for a child with autism. As mothers traditionally have served as the main caregivers of children and family (Lutz, Patterson & Klein, 2012), it is clear that working mothers experience more challenges in their journey of parenthood in caring for a child with autism.

For example, children with autism are easily distressed owing to sensory hypersensitivities such as touch and sound, and their highly routinised and stereotypical behaviours characteristic of autism further contribute to this distress, whereby a diversion from normal routine can result in meltdowns (Ooi, Ong, Jacob & Khan, 2016).

Owing to the high demands associated with taking care of child with autism, the personal lives of parents are affected in terms of their career, leisure time and health. The child's inability to withstand changes in work routines and lack of support further restricted parents' ability to work (Ooi et al., 2016).

In the economic climate we live today, the reality is that in several households, the mother is the primary caregiver or the person who provides the larger income. This income is a necessity to provide for the extreme expenses of professional help for their child or children (du Toit-Smit, 2018). In this regard, one immediate (and perhaps the most important) challenge to work-care integration arises from unequal gendered behaviour (which may or may not be voluntary). Women have entered the labour market to a much greater extent than men have increased their household work (Lewis, 2006). The primary caregiver being the mother, who not only bears the practical aspects of taking care of the child but also grapples with numerous challenges. These challenges vary from lifestyle change, limited career progression, leisure time, difficulty in terms of communication and available resources (Mthimunye, 2014).

Research suggests that caring for a child with autism can result in pronounced psychological distress for parents, reflected not only in the impact of diagnosis, but as well as in the specific and on-going psychosocial, developmental and behaviour challenges in the process (Matenge, 2014). This often creates a conflict between a mother's personal and professional life. But when your child has autism, those conflicts can be more frequent and ultimately more costly to your career. The mother often considers giving up her career, but reality is that autism requires additional therapeutic support and one income is simply not enough (Clasquin-Johnson, & Clasquin-Johnson, 2018).

The mothers of autistic children must deal with extra doctor's appointments, conflicts at day care and meetings with teachers on Individual Education Plans. Children with autism and other special needs require the parent to attend to several appointments with professionals for specialised treatments. This requires time off during working hours to take their child to these treatments (see also chapter 6, Autism in a Rural Context).

Ekas and Whitman (2010) indicate that greater severity of autism symptoms is directly related to increased maternal stress. Children with autism can have interrupted sleep routines, waking earlier than a child without disabilities, which is likey to contribute to fatigue for mothers (Glazzard & Overall, 2012). This is known as chronic partial sleep deprivation (Meltzer, 2008). Keen and Rodger (2012) acknowledge the needs of children with autism as extensive and demanding, especially on parents as they need a new set of skills and knowledge to deal with their child's impaired communication and social interactions.

How does international legal instruments, domestic policies and domestic legal instruments support the protection of a family raising a child with autism?

The "family unit" exists in all societies and in this sense are global phenomena (Diduck et al., 2007). The family is entitled to special protection under several international and regional legal instruments. Examples are, Article 16 of the Universal Declaration of Human Rights of 1948 (UDHR) and Article 23 of the International Covenant on Economic, Social and Cultural Rights 1966 (ICESCR) stipulate that "[t]he family is the natural and fundamental group unit of society and is entitled to protection by society and the state". The International Covenant on Civil and Political Rights 1966 (ICCPR) states that "[t]he widest possible protection and assistance should be accorded to the family, which is the natural and fundamental group unit of society, particularly for its establishment and while it is responsible for the care and education of dependent children" (Article 10).

The UNCRC 1990 focuses specifically on child care, as discussed in the sections above, Article 5 provides that:

> States parties shall respect the responsibilities, rights and duties of parents or where applicable, the members of the extended family or community as provided for by local custom, legal guardians or other persons legally responsible for the child, to provide, in a manner consistent with the evolving capacities of the child, appropriate direction and guidance in the exercise by the child of the rights recognised in the present Convention.

The protection of the family and the idea of care are also found at regional level in Article 18 of the African Charter on the Rights and Welfare of the Child 1990, in Article 18 of the African Charter on Human and People's Rights 1981 and in Article 8 of the African Youth Charter 2006 (Rossouw, 2018). In South Africa, the express recognition and support of the importance of the family and parenting can be found in the approval of the Green Paper on Families (Promoting Family Life and Strengthening Families in South Africa (2011) and the approval of the Draft White Paper on Families in South Africa (2012).

The Green Paper on Families aims to promote family life and strengthen families in South Africa. It puts forward proposals how families should be supported in order to flourish and function optimally. The Draft White Paper recommends strategies to support the family in its caregiving functions through mechanisms and policies such as paternity and parental leave, the facilitation of a balance between work and family responsibilities and the promotion of "equal parenting care and responsibility between fathers and mothers."

Both the Green and Draft White Papers recognise that the family is under threat and unable to play its critical roles of socialisation, nurturing, care and protection effectively owing to various societal forces (Rossouw, 2018). As discussed in the above sections, Section 28(1)(c) of the Constitution of South Africa acknowledges that parents have responsibilities towards their children and the child's right to "basic nutrition, shelter, basic health care services and social services". In order for parents to meet these basic needs, they must have the financial capability to do so. The average parent will only have the financial means to support their child(ren) if he or she is employed and generates an income (Rossouw, 2018). Apart from these core (material, safety and health) responsibilities, parents raising children with autism have additional responsibilities related to nurturing and caregiving; for example taking their child to specific treatment appointments, neurology appointments, attend school meetings related to their child's individual development plan and to be spontaneously available when their child needs them (these mentioned are not an exhaustive "list"). Parents do their best to secure the best outcomes for their child (Bartlett, 1988).

Autism is framed as a complex, lifelong yet invisible disability (Hoogsteen & Woodgate, 2013; Leblanc, Richardson & Burns, 2009) accompanied by neurological and developmental abnormalities (Lokhandwala et al. 2012; Wang et al. 2012). Consequently, parents are told their children require costly long-term intensive remediation, therapy and biomedical intervention (Dillenburger et al. 2014). In reality, few South African families can afford this because the typical cost of school fees and therapy exceeds the average household income. Achieving a balance between work and parenting is extremely important for both individuals and society because an appropriate balance between work and family life may help to achieve government's objectives, which are to improve outcomes for family members, thereby improving equity and society at large.

Women, must more than men, juggle dual responsibilities in the home and the workplace (Gornick et al., 2003). Cohen and Dancaster (2009) remark that the South African government and employers have been slow to respond to the needs of employees as caregivers and to prioritise the accommodation of employees with family responsibilities. There is no specific provision in the Constitution of South Africa for protecting family life and care giving responsibilities as it relates to the workplace. The rights to equality, dignity, freedom of association, fair labour practices and privacy may be interpreted to afford protection to the institution of family life (and parental care) related to the workplace (Rossouw, 2018). Section 28 of the Constitution reinforces this, with the right of the child to nutrition, shelter, health care services and social services.

Rossouw (2018) argues that even an implied constitutional imperative to protect the family and parenting is important, as it may and should serve as a catalyst for development of legislation for the legal integration of work and parenting.

Legislation aimed at reconciling work and parenting, or which may be used to reconcile work and parenting, comes in two forms: equality legislation and what may be called employment standards legislation (or "specific rights", typically contained in employment standards legislation) (Rossouw, 2018).

What is care, what are the caregiving needs of children with autism?

Before discussing the legislation, policies and international instruments, the importance of caregiving of children needs to be highlighted. The family environment in which children grow up has been considered a key predictor of their future outcomes (Mokomane, 2012).

As discussed in the other sections in this chapter, it again needs to be emphasised, children are vulnerable and therefore need to grow up in a nurturing and secure family that can ensure their survival, development, protection and participation in family and social life. Families give their members a sense of belonging and are responsible for imparting values and life skills (White Paper for Social Welfare, 1997). The role of the family in rearing a child is essential for the healthy development of any society (White Paper for Social Welfare, 1997).

One of the core functions of the family is the childcare and child socialisation function. The family's affective role of nurturing, supporting and safeguarding the children's health is to make sure that the next generation is productive and socially responsible. Good parenting and adequate care during the first few years of childhood also leads to huge economic benefits later on for both individuals and society as a whole (Department of Education, 2011). The foundation is laid for children to be tolerant of views other than their own and become active and responsible citizens in the future (Draft White Paper on Families,supra).

In Jooste v Botha 2000(2) SA 199 (T) at para 201F, honourable Judge Van Dijkhorst remarked that "There are two aspects of a parent-child relationship. The economic aspect of providing for the child's physical needs and the intangible aspect of providing for his or her psychological, emotional and developmental needs. The best interest of the child demands an environment of love, affection and consideration."

In the DSD's draft policy on South Africa's Child care and protection policy dated 19 December 2017 (NDP 2030), care is defined:

'Care' includes a range of services and support that children require to ensure their well-being and development to their full potential, including the provision of:

- a place to live and living conditions conducive to the child's health, well-being and development, and the necessary financial support (within available means);
- protecting the child from maltreatment, abuse, neglect, degradation, discrimination, exploitation and any other physical, emotional or moral harm or hazards;
- respecting, protecting, promoting and securing the fulfilment of, and guarding against any infringement of, the child's rights set out in the Bill of Rights and the principles set out in Chapter 2 of the Constitution;
- guiding, directing and securing the child's education and upbringing, including religious and cultural education and upbringing, in a manner appropriate to the child's age, maturity and stage of development;

- guiding, advising and assisting the child in decisions to be taken by the child in a manner appropriate to the child's age, maturity and stage of development;
- guiding the behaviour of the child in a humane manner;
- maintaining a sound relationship with the child;
- accommodating any disability or special needs that the child may have; and
- generally, ensuring that the best interests of the child is the paramount concern in all matters affecting the child.

The policy also defines the concepts of ECD and vulnerable children:

'ECD' means the process of emotional, cognitive, sensory, spiritual, moral, physical, and social and communication development of children from birth to school-going age.

"Vulnerable children" are those whose development, care and protection are at risk, and/or whose access to child care and protection services is limited because of the presence of one or more physical, mental, psychosocial, social, economic, geographical, or any other risk factor in the child's physiology, family, caregiving environment, community or broader social, economic and cultural context. These may include, but are not limited to:

- Children experiencing developmental difficulties or disabilities;
- Children with conduct or behavioural challenges;
- Children with chronic health conditions; and
- Very young children under the age of five years.

All vulnerable children require some of, or the full continuum of care and protection services defined in this policy. The combination and intensity of services required will depend on the situation of each child which must be assessed, and they must receive an appropriate package of services that responds to the risk factors pertaining to their specific circumstances.

Bridgeman (2007) states that "caring about, taking care of and giving care to a child" include "feeding, clothing, providing a home, nursing through sickness, securing medical treatment, making decisions about the child's upbringing, ensuring the child is educated, providing appropriate moral guidance and discipline, protecting from harm, promoting and mental well-being, and nurturing social and intellectual development."

The moment a diagnosis of autism is received has been described as a turning point in one's life (Ellis, 2014). Wiese (2014) commented in mothers' experience of their child's diagnosis with an ASD, that according to Janzen (2009), the only treatment that helps every child with autism is a structured early intervention and educational programme. This is confirmed by Fombonne (2006) who reiterates the importance of early, intensive intervention programmes. With early intervention, many families see dramatic improvements in their child's expressive and receptive language and social relatedness (Martin 2010).

Sufficient evidence supports the fact that having a child with autism is life changing for parents. Studies have also shown that the challenges and stressors associated with having a child with autism can substantially reduce the effectiveness of early teaching interventions for the child (Osborne, McHugh, Saunders & Reed, 2007). Parental adjustment and functioning are therefore important issues that are associated with parental ability to care for and teach children with autism (Wiese, 2014). Therefore, effective support of parents raising children with autism is highly important (Braiden, Bothwell & Duffy, 2010; Smith, Seltzer, Tager-Flusberg, Greenberg & Carter, 2008).

Mthimunye (2014) states that in order for a child to be supported fully, the child requires a great amount of services such as physiotherapy, speech and occupational therapy. Comprehensive schooling is also of vital importance. The demands of a child with autism outweigh many other disabilities (Halterman et al.,2009; Biedel & Rao, 2009).

Meeting the high care demands of affected children requires much time, effort and patience. Interventions for children with autism require parents' involvement and also aim to increase parents' caregiving skills, self-efficacy, knowledge of autism, and reduce family stress (McConachie and Diggle 2007). Furthermore, improved well-being of parents could positively influence the effect these interventions have on children with autism (Giallo et al.,2013; Osborne et al. 2008).

As indicated earlier, autism is the most expensive disability. This is attributable to the cost of intensive early intervention, that is, the hourly approved medical aid rate of R 440.00 charged for therapy and the need for small classes because of the weighting of 6 given to these learners (one learner with autism equals six neurotypical learners) (Clasquin-Johnson & Clasquin-Johnson, 2018). Intervention is concentrated in childhood, with the cost of care being the highest during adulthood (Cidav et al. 2013).

Diagnosis typically happens at 3-5 years, followed by intensive therapy, which declines during teenage years and then comes a sharp increase in adult residential and medical care (Lin 2014; Shimabutkuro, Gross & Rice 2008). Families are confronted with long-term economic stress, which is a social issue (Chasson, Harris & Neely 2007; Lokhandwala et al., 2012; Wang et al., 2012).

From the above it is clear that parents raising children with autism need to be involved in the interventions, treatments and appointments of their child. To ensure that these interventions are more effective, parents need to be empowered by educating themselves about autism and the interventions and treatments, which in turn make the interventions more effective. It can further be deduced that enabling the parents to be more effective carers for their child with autism, it will reduce parental stress and could also ultimately lead to lesser financial expenses (for the parents and for the child), as the parents can be actively involved in the interventions. The demands (for example, financial, emotional, educational) on a parent raising a child with autism is simply greater than the typical demands of a parent raising a child without disabilities.

This is a social issue affecting families with autism. It affects the constitutional rights of the children and their parents enshrined in the South African Constitution and stated in the UNCRC and UNCRPD of which South Africa is a signatory.

How is the importance of parental care recognised at an international, regional and constitutional level?

International and constitutional law provide guidance and a potentially definite and important foundation for the effective recognition of family and parenting in domestic legislation. International standards have the potential to impact directly on domestic legislation and have often served as the incentive for much of the legislative reform regarding work-care integration in other countries (Dancaster supra). Section 231 of the

Constitution makes international agreements binding on South African law. It is stated in section 233 of the Constitution: "When interpreting any legislation, every court must prefer any reasonable interpretation of legislation that is consistent with international law over any alternative interpretation that is inconsistent with international law."

The discussion below will provide an overview of Human Rights instruments, which reflect the international community's concern with the provision of "protection for families through their guaranteed and decent existence in keeping with humanity's progress". The domestic instruments which recognise and protect the family will also be discussed.

The International Bill of Human Rights states "[T]he family is the natural and fundamental group unit of society and is entitled to protection by society and the state."

The Convention on the Elimination of all Forms of Discrimination against Women is a human rights treaty for women. South Africa ratified this convention in 1995. This obliges the country to take "appropriate measures to encourage the provision of supporting social services to enable parents to combine family and work responsibilities and participate in public life".

The UNCRC has been discussed in much detail in this chapter, and this was also ratified by South Africa in 1995. This instrument changed the way children are viewed and treated. Article 18(3) of this convention requires states parties to take "all appropriate measures to ensure that children of working parents have the right to benefit from childcare services and facilities for which they are eligible". This has been interpreted to mean that:

> States should create employment conditions within business enterprises which assist working parents and caregivers in fulfilling their responsibilities to children in their care such as: the introduction of family-friendly workplace policies, including parental leave; support and facilitate breastfeeding; access to quality childcare services; protection from discrimination; security and safety in the workplace (UN Committee on the Rights of the Child General comment 16, 2013).

The UNCRPD was already discussed in great detail in this chapter, but the following needs mention: the preamble of this convention declares "that the family is the natural and fundamental group unit of society" and is entitled to protection by society and the State (Ubuntu Centre South Africa, 2012).

The United Nations Declaration on Social Progress and Development aims to promote the full employment and conditions of economic and social progress and development. Article 4 of this Declaration focuses on assistance and protection for the family by stipulating that "[t]he family as a basic unit of society and the natural environment for the growth and well-being of all its members, particularly children and youth, should be assisted and protected so that it may fully assume its responsibilities within the community" (Rossouw, 2018)

The Copenhagen Declaration on Social Development, was adopted at the World Summit for Social Development, held in March 1995. It was agreed that "[t]he family is the basic unit of society and it is acknowledged that it plays a key role in social development and as such should be strengthened, with attention to rights, capabilities and responsibilities of its members" (Rossouw, 2018).

The Beijing Platform for Action is an agenda for women's empowerment, with the purpose to promote gender equality and to empower womEn in all spheres of public and private life. South Africa committed itself to this Platform for Action in 1995. This Platform for Action states the following with regard to women as caregivers and the role that they play in the family:

> Women play a critical role in the family. The family is the basic unit of society and as such should be strengthened. It is entitled to receive comprehensive protection and support. In different cultural, political and social systems, various forms of the family exist. The rights, capabilities and responsibilities of family members must be respected. Women make a great contribution to the welfare of the family and to the development of society, which is still not recognised or considered in its full importance. The social significance of maternity, motherhood and the role of parents in the family and in the upbringing of children should be acknowledged. The upbringing of children requires shared responsibility of parents, women and men and society as a whole... Recognition should also be given to the important role often played by women in many countries in caring for other members of their family.

The International Labour Organisation Conversations (ILO), in its "The workers with family responsibilities convention" (1981) deals with the combination of work and care. This convention provides extensive guidance on policies and measures needed to assist employees with family responsibilities and to reduce work-family conflict. However, South Africa has sadly not yet ratified this convention. Rossouw (2018) asserts that there are a number of ILO conventions and recommendations prohibiting discrimination based on family responsibilities and which require members to accommodate workers with family responsibilities.

The Discrimination (Employment and Occupation) Convention was ratified by South Africa in 1997. This convention prohibits discrimination but also provides that member states are required to "declare and pursue a national policy designed to promote, by methods of appropriate to national conditions and practice, equal opportunity and treatment in respect of employment and occupation, with a view to eliminating any discrimination in respect thereof" (Dancaster supra). Dancaster remarks that this would mean that statutory measures for work-care integration are therefore required in furtherance of this convention if there is to be adequate acknowledgement of the importance of parental care and equality of opportunity and treatment of women in the workplace (Dancaster supra).

The South African Constitution does not contain provisions directly protecting family and care. The Constitution affords indirect protection to the family without prescribing any particular format (Ekelaar & Nhlapo, 1996). The rights to equality, dignity, freedom of association, fair labour practices, privacy, freedom of movement and residence, the right to a non-harmful environment, the right to access to information and the right to just administrative action may be relevant, to a greater or lesser extent, in the "family context" (Visser, 1996) and be interpreted to afford protection to the institution of family life and parental care, also in the context of the workplace (Rossouw, 2018).

Section 28 in the South African Constitution concerns with the rights of the child, in the Constitutional Court case Government of the Republic of South Africa v Grootboom supra, noted that sections 28(1)(b) and (c) must be read together. Subsections 28(1)(b) and (c) provide "Every child has the right to family care or parental care, or to appropriate alternative care when removed from the family environment; to basic nutrition, shelter, basic health care services and social services."

These sections ensure that parents and families properly care for their children (Rossouw, 2018).

In the Constitutional Court decision, the President of the Republic of South Africa and Another v Hugo 1997 (6) BCLR 708 (CC), honourable Judge Goldstone in a majority judgement acknowledged that: "[F]or many South African women, the difficulties of being responsible for the social and economic burdens of child rearing, in circumstances where they have few skills and scant financial resources are immense…"

From the above discussion, it can be seen that the South African Constitution does not contain explicit provisions regarding the protection of family and care, judicial decisions interpreting and applying the Constitution have confirmed the importance of family life and parental caregiving as part and parcel of our fundamental rights.

The protection of the family is highlighted at an international and constitutional level. It is evident from this that the protection and recognition of the family includes, the right to be a parent and to care for your child and the right of children to family care or parental care (Rossouw, 2018).

The mere ratification of these instruments are not enough for proper enforcement. Therefore, it is necessary to ensure adequate integration of work and care provisions in domestic legislation. These international standards can at least play an important role in statutory interpretation on matters relating to work-care integration and have an effect on domestic legislation and its application (Dancaster supra).

An important matter to consider, and the only matter I could find, which does not set a legal precedent on the issue of family responsibility discrimination (because the parties reached a settlement and no judgement was delivered) will hopefully contribute to the development of how courts. More importantly, arbitrators view family responsibility and also encourage employers to consider their employees' family responsibilities, especially in respect of primary caregivers of children with autism, when making decisions in the workplace.

(Hugo v eThekwini Municipality, Case D18/11, Labour Court). The facts of the case were as follows. In 2011, Captain Suraya Hugo, a metro policewoman, represented by the Legal Resources Centre, challenged the conduct of her employer, the eThekwini Municipality's Metropolitan Police, in the Labour Court in Durban, for repeated unilateral, unreasonable and unlawful transfers over a period of one year, resulting in prejudice to the well-being of her minor son with autism. Her son could not cope with change and required a reasonable stable routine. Sudden transfers to other offices and unexpected frequent changes in shifts adversely affected the emotional and physical well-being of her child. Despite requests that her family responsibility to her son required reasonable accommodation, the employer failed to reasonably accommodate the special needs of her and her child (Holness, 2012).

Captain Hugo alleged that her employer unfairly discriminated against her in terms of section 6(1) of the Employment Equity Act, on the basis of both her gender and family responsibility. Her employer did not assess and provide reasonable accommodation for her and her child's special needs. An expert psychologist reported that Captain Hugo's child became highly distressed and experienced "meltdowns" that took the form of self-injurious behaviour. It was recommended that it would be in the best interest of the child that Captain Hugo work regular shifts (day shifts) and be closer to the child's special school. This would enable her to provide the necessary care for the child. A settlement was reached shortly after Captain Hugo finished her evidence in court. This settlement was made an order of court and provided that the employer must accommodate the family responsibility of Captain Hugo, that she shall work at a post at a particular station close to her son's school and that her shifts be fixed day shift from Monday to Friday. The employer was ordered to pay the costs of the court proceedings.

The above-mentioned case demonstrates that family responsibility discrimination might be taking place in South Africa, but rarely come before the courts or tribunals (see the discussion in the previous section on access to justice and the Children's Act), to challenge the discriminatory conduct of their employer, the employee would have to go through the effort of *potentially costly litigation.*

As discussed in the previous section dealing with the Children's Act, the UNCRC and the UNCRPD and the child's right to the access of justice, the best interest of the child should be considered in all matters concerning the child. The key principles of the Children's Act indicate that all proceeding, actions or decisions in a matter concerning a child must respect, protect, promote and fulfil the best interest of the child (Section 2(a)(iv) of the Children's Act).

At the outset of the Children's Act, the preamble posits that children should be provided with the necessary protection and assistance for the full and harmonious developments from one phase to another (Carter, 2105). Society has an inescapable responsibility to protect and support the family and parenthood because rearing children is the foundation of society and without the family, there would be no society (Rossouw, 2018).

On the point of costly litigation to realise parental leave (reasonable accommodations) in work-care responsibilities, it can be inferred from the above discussions that the parents as primary caregivers of the child are responsible for the protection, assistance and development of the child with autism (a disability). When parents are denied the reasonable accommodations to care for their child, this would have the implication that a child with autism (being considered as a "vulnerable" child), who requires extra care, is denied these rights. The above discussions in this chapter would support the argument that this would be litigation where the *best interest of the child* would be considered and where the *appointment of legal representation at the cost of the state* should be granted (See the discussion in the previous section on the access to justice and the Children's Act).

What are the specific rights on the integration of work and care in South Africa?

As mentioned at the introduction to this section, legislation aimed at reconciling work and parenting comes in two forms, namely, equality legislation and employment standards legislation.

The Employment Equity Act 55 of 1998 (EEA) was enacted to give effect to section 9 of the Constitution and its function is to regulate equality in employment (Dupper, 2012). As discussed in great detail, women remain the primary caregivers of children. It can be argued that workplace prejudice based on caregiving responsibilities may constitute gender discrimination (Rossouw, 2018). Section 1 of the EEA prohibits discrimination on the basis of family responsibility, "responsibility of employees in relation to their spouse, partner, dependent children or members of their immediate family that need their care or support".

There is a duty on employers to accommodate employees with caregiving responsibilities, as stated in section 5 of the EEA, that states "[e]very employer must take steps to promote equal opportunity in the workplace by eliminating unfair discrimination in any employment policy or practice". This may be interpreted to mean that, because of recognition of family responsibility as a listed ground of discrimination, there is a direct duty on employers to accommodate employees with family responsibilities and that the absence of such accommodation will constitute discrimination (Rossouw, 2018).

Rossouw (2018) further argues that the EEA further advocates that steps (as affirmative action) must be taken to "reasonable accommodate" women through a modification or adjustment to a job or working environment to promote equal opportunity and treatment in the workplace. This seems to imply that the EEA recognises that in order for employees in general, but women in particular, to combine their work and care responsibilities successfully, proactive measures should be taken to afford protection against discrimination and to reduce their conflict inherent to their dual roles.

In the 20 years since the enactment of the EEA, there is no case law (except for the case of Captain Hugo, which was settled) regarding family responsibility discrimination. As discussed earlier in this chapter, parents of children with autism are already faced with exorbitant financial expenses and do not have the resources to institute potentially costly litigation (See also the discussion in the previous section, access to justice and the Children's Act).

The EEA is also silent on the extent of accommodation required and the determination of reasonableness (Cohen & Dancaster, 2010). In the Research Brief on Disability and Equality in South Africa 2013 to 2017 conducted by the SAHRC, reasonable accommodation as defined in the UNCRPD is "necessary and appropriate modification and adjustment not imposing a disproportionate or undue burden, where needed in a particular case...to ensure ...the enjoyment or exercise on an equal basis with others all human rights and fundamental freedoms".

The Labour Court dealt with the issue of accommodation in the context of discrimination on at least three occasions (Garbers & Rossouw, 2015). In Dlamini v Green Four Security 2006 (27) ILJ 2098 (LC), the court accepted that even if an inherent requirement of the job is found to exist, the dismissal might still be discriminatory if "the impact is not ameliorated by a reasonable accommodation or modification of the rule, or an exemption from it" (see para 13 and paras 31 -32).

In Co-operative Workers Association v Petroleum Oil & Gas Co-operative of SA 2007 (28) ILJ 627 (LC) the court noted at par 48, that South African courts apply a substantive approach to equality to redress imbalances and protect vulnerable groups. The court further noted that the international community acknowledged the fact that workers with family responsibilities constituted a vulnerable group and that special measures must apply to these workers to adjust for the hardships of such responsibilities in order to establish equality among the workforce (see paras 36, 50). The court also stated that the responsibility for addressing the special needs of workers with family responsibilities does not only fall on the state but also on employers (para 50).

The Labour Court in Standard Bank of South Africa v CCMA 2008 (4) BLLR 356 (LC) discussed the content of an employer's duty to reasonably accommodate, where needed, an employee or job applicant with a disability. The court held that the "[r]easonable accommodation of the employee and unjustified hardships to the employer operate as countervailing forces to balance the respective rights of the parties. If the employer cannot reasonably accommodate the disabled employee without unjustifiable hardships, the employer may dismiss the employee" (para 371). The employer who has to provide reasonable accommodation must find an accommodation and prove that it is reasonable.

The above-mentioned decisions show that "reasonable accommodation", which is often associated with disability discrimination, is a versatile mechanism that facilitates equality (Garbers & Rossouw, 2015). When applying this to gender, this then means our equality law recognises – and we can expect – that in order for women to combine their work and care responsibilities successfully, proactive measures are necessary to reduce the conflict inherent in their dual roles (Cohen & Dancaster supra). The above will also imply that parents (mothers) with the unique care responsibilities for children with autism would rightly be able to expect from their employers to reasonably accommodate this and provide for measures such as leave arrangements and flexible working arrangements, which would involve a "more permanent change to the working conditions of female employees" (Cohen and Dancaster supra).

Where an employer denies the imperative to accommodate women with family responsibilities, the employers' failure to reasonably accommodate these women, including a refusal of a request for flexible working arrangements, modified work schedules would be seen as discriminatory unless the employer is able to justify its refusal. As discussed earlier, when dealing with parents of children with disabilities, the rights of the employer and the child with autism (disability) should be balanced to determine what is in the best interest of the child (see the previous discussions in this Chapter dealing with the best interest of the child and the Children's Act).

The principal sources of specific employments rights regulating work and care in South Africa are legislation, collective agreements and the contract of employment. The principal statute giving effect to statutory terms and conditions of employment is the BCEA. Some of the conditions of employment may be varied by agreement between the employer and the employee. Other provisions may be varied by collective agreement and some provisions only by way of a collective agreement concluded in a bargaining council.

Section 7 of the BCEA states that "working time must be regulated by every employer with due regard to the family responsibilities of employees". Section 27 provides for paid family responsibility leave. Dancaster and Cohen remark that this provision is "extremely limited in terms of duration and access" (2010). Three days per year (or five days for domestic workers) are not even enough to provide for the limited care (Dancaster & Cohen, 2010). If one compares the range of care provided for by the discussion above and in the section about the Children's Act, specific care duties relating to children with autism and in the other chapters of this volume relating to the specific needs of these children, "the extremely narrow scope of this section, despite the promise of its heading, becomes readily apparent" (Rossouw, 2018).

The circumstances in which family responsibility leave may be used and the persons in respect of whom this leave may be granted are also too narrow (Dancaster & Cohen, 2010). In view of the different dimensions of parental care identified above, section 27 fails to address leave to employees to attend to these unique circumstances that are in the best interest of their child. It also fails to address leave in the case where the employee needs to attend to the care of their child in an unexpected emergency situation or when the au pair/ nanny does not show up for work. Section 1 of the EEA and Section 1 of PEPUDA could be considered as a starting point to define "family responsibility"... the responsibility of employees in relation to their spouse or partner, their dependent children or other members of their immediate family who need their care or support.

Rossouw (2018) argues that the implication of these sections compared to section 27 of the BCEA achieves a broader approach. The definition contains no apparent limitations as to its application to specific care – it uses care of support in the broad sense. It is evident that the current employment standards in legislation in South Africa in order to regulate and promote a more appropriate integration of work and parental care needs to be addressed. The current inadequate and ineffective employment standard legislation means that employees with caregiving responsibilities (and specifically employees with children with autism that requires specific care) have no other choice but to rely on the generosity of their employers to implement work measure accommodating their family responsibilities or to use their own resources to pursue unfair discrimination claims based on family responsibilities (Cohen & Dancaster, 2009). Rossouw (2018) summarises the key findings of her research, for the way forward for South Africa, the finding relevant for parents with care responsibilities of children with autism is mentioned below:

- The protection and recognition of the family, with the responsibility to care for dependent children includes, inter alia, the right to be a parent and to care for your child and the right of children to family care or parental care.
- South African anti-discrimination law is well positioned to make a substantial contribution to the facilitation of the integration of work and care.
- In a South African context, the rights to time off, or leave for family responsibility, as well as flexible working options are limited and deficient.

Rossouw (2018) makes the following recommendations for change:

- Recognition of the central importance of parental caregiving to society;
- Accommodations that parental caregiving takes place within a variety of structures and accommodation of all these structures – that is, the focus should be on the nature of the care, not so much on who gives the care;
- Recognition that parental caregiving is an ongoing concern that extends beyond birth, with its most acute phase being during the first five years of a child's development;
- Recognition that adequate parental care is about a child's full development (in all its dimensions) – it is not only about the physical health of a child;
- Recognition that parental caregiving is, and should be, a shared concern (that in an equality component should be built into regulation); and
- The elimination of monetary penalties associated with caregiving.

Rossouw (2018) submits that the easiest way to achieve all of these – or at least a good starting point – is to provide for sufficient and paid parental leave over at least the first years after childbirth.

In the report for Citrix (May 2015), it is stated in the executive summary that the benefits of a more widespread flexible working culture include the potential to reduce commuting cost for working individuals while increasing individual's time by allowing them to better manage their work-life balance. If provided with the opportunity to work remotely, 93% of knowledge workers would opt to work from home on average around two and half days in a working week. This would amount to commuting cost savings of R39.5 billion on commuting, while simultaneously reducing 320 million hours a year commuting to and from work. The combined cost saving of the decline in time spent commuting and the actual expenditure on the means of commuting sum to R44.1 billion a year. The increased ability to better manage work activities with care responsibilities will increase production and reduce stress related to work-care conflict. The government has a role to play by creating a favourable environment though policy developments.

Knowledge workers are those whose main capital is knowledge and therefore, think for a living; for example, lawyers, doctors, accountants, engineers and academics. The report further states that parents caring for children with disabilities may require flexitime to be able to attend to different appointments. Flexible working enables employees to be productive at any time of the day and achieve greater productivity and job satisfaction.

From the discussion above in this section and in the other sections in this chapter as well as in this volume, the above recommendations for chance would certainly be in the best interest of the child with autism, arrangement of flexible work times to assist with time management to, for example, attend to meetings at school or emergencies, parental leave to ensure that the child is taken to necessary appointments, attend courses and therapies to ensure his or her full development, and other reasonable accommodations specifically related to the child's needs.

The work-life integration of parents is recognised in the NDP: Vision 2030. It is stated that: "This requires that the national care and protection system provide a protective legal framework which applies to everyone in the country, and a package of quality services that promote safe and nurturing public environments, protect all children, and promote parenting knowledge and practices that optimise the development of children to their full potential".

These include:

- Universal protection of parents in the workplace / regulation of the workplace and employment conditions to enable parents to fulfil their shared parental care and development responsibilities;
- Family promotion and preservation programmes, including parent information and education programmes on child development and protection, including positive parenting practices and the dangers of harsh disciplinary practices;
- Provision of a combination of material, parenting and psychosocial support to vulnerable parents, families and children, that includes, parental education programmes, especially for parents of vulnerable children to enable them to understand and respond to the risks to their children's development; and
- An enabling legal and policy framework with enabling policies, laws and programmes, mandating, obligating, regulating, and harmonising the roles and responsibilities of all role players, including government departments across all levels of government and non-government role players to take measure to advance the policy (NDP) vision, goals and objectives.

It is therefore evident that work-life integration and family responsibility of care for families with autism is recognised that the government and all role players have an obligation to reasonably accommodate these parents.

13.4 South African jurisprudence

Many of the jurisprudence discussed below have been mentioned and discussed in the sections of this chapter (some in detail), the jurisprudence below serves to be a further discussion of how it relates to right to Inclusive Education in South Africa, with mention of international jurisprudence that is also applicable. The information was obtained from the Report by the Equal Education Law Centre (EELC) report (accessed at www.eelawcentre.org.za).

13.4.1 Western Cape ruling (2010)

The Western Cape Forum for Intellectual Disability v Government of the Republic of South Africa and Government of the Province of the Western Cape (2011(5)SA87(WCC)[2010])

Disability associations representing children with severe and profound intellectual disabilities brought this case against the government for failing to accommodate these children in public schools. Cleaver concluded that the government was infringing the rights of the affected children by failure to provide them with a basic education and by not admitting the children concerned to special or other schools. Cleaver declared that the Western Cape's DBE had failed to take reasonable measures to make provision for the educational needs of severely and profoundly intellectually disabled children therefore breaching their constitutional rights to basic education, protection from neglect or degradation, equality and human dignity.

The court *aquo* directed the government to ensure that every child with severe or profound intellectual disabilities in the Western Cape has affordable access to a basic education of an adequate quality. Not all children with autism have intellectual disabilities as autism is a spectrum disorder and each child is affected differently. There are children with higher than the norm intellectual abilities on the spectrum too. This ruling is important not only for children with severe and profound intellectual disabilities but for all children with autism. The schools must accommodate and ensure that every child has affordable access to a quality basic education.

In June 2005 the national Department of Education published the following three sets of guidelines for the implementation of White Paper 6:

- The Conceptual and Operational Guidelines for the Implementation of Inclusive Education: Full Service Schools. These guidelines explain the main principles upon which full service schools are founded, describe their characteristics and outline the institutional development process of such schools.
- The Conceptual and Operational Guidelines for the Implementation of Inclusive Education: Full Service Schools as Resource Centres. These guidelines provide a conceptual framework for an inclusive system of education. They provide inter alia that disability should not be seen in medical terms, but also in terms of the rights

of the person with disability and contain operation procedures for a paradigm shift from special education to Inclusive Education.

- The Conceptual and Operational Guidelines for the Implementation of Inclusive Education: District Support Teams. These guidelines sketch the roll of support providers employed by the national DoE to assist education institutions such as schools and early childhood centres to identify and address barriers to learning and to promote effective teaching and learning.

In 2005, the national DoE developed the SIAS Strategy. This is directed at determining the nature and level of support required by learners with special education needs and also outlines the procedures to ensure that all learners with Level 4 and 5 needs (learners who require moderate and high levels) of support such as learners with disabilities receive social security grants are admitted to schools and receive the necessary support.

In 2007, the national DoE published guidelines to ensure that all special schools become fully functional and contain the preparatory steps for the development of special schools as special schools resource centres.

The UNCRC in article 28 confirms the right to education. Article 29(1)(a) states that "the education of the child shall be directed to ...[t]he development of the child's personality, talents and mental and physical abilities to their fullest potential".

The African Charter on the Rights and Welfare of the Child provides in Article 11(1) and 2(a) that "[e]very child shall have the right to an education and [t]he education of the child shall be directed to ... the promotion and development of the child's personality, talents and mental and physical abilities to their fullest potential..."

Article 15 of the Revised European Social Charter provides for the rights of persons with disabilities to independence, social integration and participation in the life of the community, and recognises the importance of education for those purposes. *(see Autism of Europe v France (Complaint No 13/2002.).*

The UNCRPD and its optional protocol which were ratified by South Africa on 30 November 2007. The preamble of the Convention provides:

> *(m) Recognising the valued existing and potential contributions made by persons with disabilities to the overall well-being and diversity of their communities, and that the promotion of the full enjoyment by persons with disabilities of their human rights and fundamental freedoms and of full participation by persons with disabilities will result in their enhanced sense of belonging and in significant advances in the human, social and economic development of society and the eradication of poverty ... (r) Recognising that children with disabilities should have full enjoyment of all human rights and fundamental freedoms on an equal basis with other children, and recalling obligations to that end undertaken by states parties to the Convention on the Rights of the Child ...*

Article 24 of the Convention provides

> *"1 States parties recognise the right of persons with disabilities to education. With a view to realising this right without discrimination and on the basis of equal opportunity, states parties shall ensure an Inclusive Education system at all levels and lifelong learning directed to:*

(a) *The full development of human potential and sense of dignity and self-worth and the strengthening of respect for human rights, fundamental freedoms and human diversity;*

(b) *The development by persons with disabilities of their personality, talents and creativity, as well as their mental and physical abilities, to their fullest potential;*

(c) *Enabling persons with disabilities to participate effectively in a free society.*

2 *In realising this right, states parties shall ensure that:*

(a) *Persons with disabilities are not excluded from the general education system on the basis of disability, and that children with disabilities are not excluded from free and compulsory primary education, or from secondary education, on the basis of disability;*

(b) *Persons with disabilities can access an inclusive, quality and free primary education and secondary education on an equal basis with others in the communities in which they live;*

(c) *Reasonable accommodation of the individual's requirements is provided;*

(d) *Persons with disabilities receive the support required, within the general education system to facilitate their effective education;*

(e) *Effective individualised support measures are provided in environments that maximise academic and social development, consistent with the goal of full inclusion.*

3 *States parties shall enable persons with disabilities to learn life and social development skills to facilitate their full and equal participation in education and as members of the community. To this end, states parties shall take appropriate measures ...*

4 *In order to help ensure the realisation of this right, state parties shall take appropriate measures to employ teachers, including teachers with disabilities, who are qualified in sign language and/or Braille, and to train professionals and staff to work at all levels of education. Such training shall incorporate disability awareness and the use of appropriate augmentative and alternative modes, means and formats of communication, educational techniques and materials to support persons with disabilities."*

Section 36(1) of the Constitution sets out the requirements for a justified limitation to rights in the Bill of Rights.

"(1) *The rights in the Bill of Rights may be limited only in terms of law of general application to the extent that the limitation is reasonable and justifiable in an open and democratic society based on human dignity, equality and freedom, taking into account all relevant factors, including –*

(a) *The nature of the right;*

(b) *The importance of the purpose of the limitation;*

(c) *The nature and extent of the limitation;*

(d) *The relation between the limitation and its purposes; and*

(e) *Less restrictive means to achieve the purpose."*

When evaluating if a child with autism's right to education could be limited as set out Sect 36 in the Constitution, I refer to SASA 84 of 1996, NEPA 27 of 1996 and Mental Health Care Act 17 of 2002.

It is clear that none of these acts contain any provision which authorises an infringement of the rights of affected children. Budgetary constraints faced by the DoE do not justify the limitation of the rights of the affected children. The concept of reasonableness as explained by the Constitutional Court in Grootboom (2001(1)SA46(CC) Government of the Republic of South Africa and Others v Grootboom and Others was must be observed.

Jacoob held as follows:

> "[43] ... *A programme* that excludes a significant segment of society cannot be said to be reasonable...
>
> [44 Reasonableness must also be understood in the context of the Bill of Rights as a whole ... *The right of access to adequate housing is entrenched because we value human beings and want to ensure that they are afforded their basic human needs. A society must seek to ensure that the basic necessities of life are provided to all if it is to be a society based on human dignity, freedom and equality. To be reasonable, measures cannot leave out of account the degree and extent of the denial of the right they endeavour to realise. Those whose needs are the most urgent and whose ability to enjoy all rights therefore is most in peril, must not be ignored by the measures aimed at achieving realisation of the right. It may not be sufficient to meet the test of reasonableness to show that the measures are capable of achieving a statistical advance in the realisation or the right. Furthermore, the Constitution requires that everyone must be treated with care and concern. If the measures, though statistically successful, fail to respond to the needs of those most desperate, they may not pass the test.*"

Basic education is compulsory in South Africa. All children should be in school by the age of compulsory education mandated as five to six years for grade R or pre-school, and 7 to 15 years for basic education. In 1996, SASA directed the minister of Education to publish a government gazette with the compulsory age requirements for learners with special education needs. As of January 2017, this document had not been published. Children with autism are most often misplaced or excluded from schools owing to a misunderstanding regarding their needs and behaviours.

13.4.2 Constitutional Court ruling

In *the Governing Body of the Juma Musjid Primary School v Essay (2100(8) BCLR 761 (CC))*, the Court interpreted the constitutional rights to an education as a standard of educational adequacy that is measured by achieving specified learning outcomes. More specifically, the Court found that basic education must "promote and develop a child's personality, talents and mental and physical abilities to his or her fullest potential". In defining basic education, the Court also endorsed the definition proposed in UNCRC.

13.4.3 Labour Court ruling

In January 2011, Captain Hugo, a metro policewoman, represented by the Legal Resource Centre, challenged the actions of her employer, the eThekweni Municipality's Metropolitan Police, in the Labour Court in Durban, for repeated unilateral, unreasonable and unlawful transfers over a period of one year, resulting in prejudice to the well-being of her minor son.

Captain Hugo is a single mother of a five-year-old child with autism. Her son cannot cope with change and requires a reasonable stable routine. Sudden transfers to other offices, and unexpected and frequent changes in shifts, adversely affected the emotional and physical well-being of her child. Despite her requests that her family responsibility to her son required reasonable accommodation, the transfers continues without further consultation with her and failed reasonably to accommodate the special needs of her and her child.

Captain Hugo alleged that her employer unfairly discriminated against her in terms of section 6(1) of the Employment Equity Act (1998), on the basis of both her gender and family responsibility. Family responsibility is defined as "responsibilities of employees in relation to their spouse or partner, their dependent children, or other members of their family who need their care or support." Reasonable accommodation is defined as "any reasonable modification or adjustment to a job or to the working environment that will enable a member of a designated group to have access to, or participate or advance in, employment."

After the testimony of Captain Hugo and the report of an expert psychologist of the child's special needs and the impact the changed circumstances had on him, the employer settled the matter and the settlement was made an order of court. It provided that, in order to reasonably accommodate the family responsibility of Captain Hugo, the employer shall transfer her to a post as a particular station, for a fixed day shift from 7 am to 16h00, Mondays to Fridays, as this station was close to the child's school. The employer was also ordered to pay the costs of the court proceedings.

13.5 International and foreign law

South African courts are required to consider international law in interpreting the Bill of Rights and may consider foreign law. Therefore, the definitions adopted by these legal bodies further reinforces and interpretation that an Inclusive Education is included within the meaning of Section 29(1)(a) of the Constitution.

13.5.1 International law

Section 39(1)(b) of the Constitution compels courts to consider international law when interpreting the Bill of Rights. Section 233 also requires the Court to prefer any reasonable interpretation that is consistent with international law over any alternative interpretation that is inconsistent with international law. Therefore, an interpretation of the right to basic education that is consistent with international law will likely take precedence over other interpretations. Relevant international law makes clear that the right to basic education entitles every person to an education that not only meets their basic learning needs but also enables them to develop certain non-academic traits.

The UNCRC ratified by South Africa in 1995, affirms a child's right to education and states in Article 23(1) and

> (3), "State Parties recognise that a mentally or physically disabled child should enjoy a full and decent life, in conditions which ensure dignity, promote self-reliance and facilitate the child's active participation in the community," and state assistance "shall be designed to ensure that the disabled child has effective access to and receives education, training, health care services, rehabilitation services, preparation for employment and recreation opportunities in a manner conducive to the child's achieving the fullest possible social integration and individual development, including his or her cultural and spiritual development."

The UNCRC which was ratified by South Africa in 1995 and entered into force in 1990, adopts a definition of the right and emphasises the purpose of education as a mechanism to empower children. More specifically, "the education to which every child has a right is one designed to provide the child with life skills, to strengthen the child's capacity to enjoy the full range of human rights and to promote a culture which is infused by appropriate human rights values."

The World Declaration for All (1990) states that "every person—child, youth and adult—shall be able to benefit from educational opportunities designed to meet their basic learning needs." The focus of this education must "be on actual learning acquisition and outcome, rather than exclusively upon enrolment, continued participation in organised programmes and completion of certification requirements."

The Committee on Economic, Social and Cultural Rights (1966) makes clear in its General Comments that basic education must be designed to attain "the full development of the human personality and the sense of its dignity, and … [to] strengthen the respect for human rights and fundamental freedoms".

In international law, like the South African Constitution, a child's right to an education is not subject to progressive realisation but rather is immediately recognisable.

In Comment No. 13 of the Committee on Economic, Social and Cultural Rights (1966), the Committee found that basic education is a minimum core obligation for all states and must be implemented immediately.

Accordingly, "the duties in respect of the right to primary education include granting it priority in resource allocation and implementation, taking immediate measures towards the realisation thereof, and providing the service free of charge."

The UNCRPD ratified by South Africa in 2007, also explicitly recognises the right of persons with disabilities to education, and in recognising and realising this right, state parties must ensure that "[p]ersons with disabilities are not excluded from the general education system on the basis of disability" and "can access an inclusive, quality and free primary education and secondary education on an equal basis with others in the communities in which they live."

As referred to earlier in this chapter, the Protocol to the African Charter on Human and Peoples' Rights on the Rights of Persons with Disabilities in Africa (ACHPR) was adopted on 30 January 2018. This binding legal document protects the human rights of persons with disabilities, but will only become effective once it has been formally ratified. This disability rights protocol complements the UNCRPD. This protocol highlights and considers the lived realities of persons with disabilities in Africa.

Both the UNCRPD in Article 24 and the African Disabilities Rights Protocol in Article 16 call for a transformative approach at domestic level in the provisioning of education for persons with disabilities. Once the government of South Africa ratifies this treaty, it will be another effective tool that parents and families living with autism could use to advocate and enforce their rights.

13.5.2 Foreign law – United States

As mentioned earlier, section 39(1) permits South African courts to "consider foreign law" when interpreting the Bill of Rights. Similar to most international bodies, the United States has adopted an interpretation of the right to an education that incorporates an Inclusive Education into its scope.

In *Rose v Council for Better Education*, the Kentucky Supreme Court elaborated on the "right to an efficient school system" to include seven substantive principles that extended far beyond educational outcomes. Majority of states have similarly expanded on their states' right to education. As a result, a consensus has emerged in United States courts that an education "in essence, means a basic quality education that provides students with the essential skills they need to function productively in contemporary society."

United States case law generally holds that additional measures must be implemented to ensure that students with learning disadvantages benefit equally from government education programmes. In the United States, courts have found that a student's barriers to learning must be taken into account and accommodated in order to ensure that they receive the same benefit from the public school system as their peers. This is because students must "equally enjoy the state constitutional protection for the right to schooling." As a result, education "goes well beyond providing accommodative measures for students with disabilities" and "could/should extend to school transportation, school feeding programs and supportive counseling."

13.5.3 Foreign law – Canada

Canadian jurisprudence dictates that special measures must be taken to ensure that the equality provisions contained in Canada's Charter of Rights and Freedoms are correctly implemented. In Canada, where the Charter does not bind private institutions, courts have still found that any entity that implements government policies or programmes has a responsibility to act positively in order to accommodate disadvantaged groups.

Canadian courts have dictated that the purpose of the Charter's equality provision "is not only to prevent discrimination by the attribution of stereotypical characteristics to individuals, but also to ameliorate the position of groups within Canadian society who have suffered disadvantage by exclusion from mainstream society as has been the case with disabled persons."

In this respect, the courts have recognised that exclusion violates human rights and require positive action to remedy these violations. Courts have also recognised the exclusion of persons with disability as a broad, systemic issue in which "exclusion from the mainstream of society results from the construction of a society based solely on "mainstream" attributes to which disabled persons will never be able to gain access."

13.5.4 Foreign law – Europe

The European Court of Human Rights has recognised the damaging effects of education that seeks to divide learners based on ability rather than practicing integration and accommodation. In Horvath v Hungary, the court recognised the intersections between exclusionary education practices and systemic societal divisions. This case dealt with Roma children who were being sent to 'special' schools for mild learning disabilities, and who received a poor education that "compromised their subsequent personal development" and prevented their "integrat[ion] into the ordinary schools… that would facilitate life among the majority population."

The Court in this case recognised that the undesirable effects of sending children to special schools, which prevented them access to opportunities afforded to students in mainstream schools, was in itself a violation of the right to an adequate education and indirectly resulted in a violation of equality rights. They emphasise that, in general, "treatment as a single class of those with intellectual or mental disabilities is a questionable classification, and the curtailment of their rights must be subject to strict scrutiny." The violation of these rights in Horvath represents an instance where a lack of inclusive learning creates a system that is discriminatory on the basis of culture as well as ability.

13.6 Conclusion

Taking all of the above into consideration, we need to reflect on how we as society could reduce stereotypes, advocate for human rights, social justice and inclusivity for individuals with autism.

Consideration for the rights each human being have, social justice and acceptance is a way of life. It starts with parents and all adults being role models, to inform and educate children of values and non-prejudicial attitudes. To not only verbalise this but to act in a way that speaks of a responsible citizen, who are

- informed about the world in which they live;
- able to act with awareness of social, economic and political issues; and
- sufficiently committed to the values of equality, justice and human dignity to be contributors to democracy, human rights, acceptance and inclusivity in their own communities and nations, as well as the global family. (Values and Human Rights in the Curriculum, DoE)

The responsibility to raise children with autism is those of the parents. All parents and families need support to maximise their parenting knowledge, capacities and abilities and all children and their families have the right to safe and nurturing environments in which all children grow, play, learn and develop. This places a duty of care and protection, not just on parents, but on the state to make a suite of parenting support programmes and services, universally available to all parents and to ensure safe and nurturing environments. For example, all parents and children, regardless of their circumstances, require an education system that provides quality teaching and learning that complies with governing legal standards. Similarly, all children and parents depend on the government to provide safety and security in schools and communities, as well as laws of general application that prohibit all forms of harmful conduct against children.

In short, it requires the development of an effective child care and protection system that provides a minimum social floor that is made up of a package of "cash plus care" – a combination of material, parental and psycho-social support and services to support the development of all children, and build the resilience of vulnerable children, their families and caregivers, throughout the child's life, starting at conception – as well as services and support that protect them against harm where the safety net fails (DSD, Child Care Policy,

2017). Government is obliged to domesticate the UNCRPD and the UNCRC in legislation to effectively show its obligation to ensure persons with disabilities (and families living with autism, children with autism) the enjoyment or exercise on an equal basis with others of all human rights and fundamental freedoms. Failure to do this amounts to unfair discrimination on the ground of disability.

In closing a quote by the Former Chief Justice Langa where he explained the concept of "access to participate" in the case MEC for Education: Kwazulu-Natal and Others v Pillay 2008 (1) SA 474 (CC) at para 73,

> At its core is the notion that sometimes the community, whether it is the state, an employer, a school, must take positive measure and possibly incur additional hardship or expense in order to allow all people to participate and enjoy all their rights equally. It ensures that we do not relegate people to the margins of society because they do not or cannot conform to certain social norms.

References

ACPF (2011). *Children with disabilities in South Africa: The hidden reality*. Addis Ababa: The African Child Policy Forum.

African Charter on Human Rights (1986), http://www.humanrights.se/wp-content/uploads/2012/01/African-Charter-on-Human-and-Peoples-Rights.pdf

Akinbola, B. R. (2010). The Right to Inclusive Education in Nigeria: Meeting the Needs and Challenges of Children with Disabilities [article]. *African Human Rights Law Journal*, 10, (2) (2020): 457-477.

Albertyn, R. M, Kapp, C.A, & Groenewald, C.J. (2001).Patterns of empowerment in individuals through the course of a life-skills programme in South Africa [Article]. *Studies in the Education of Adults*, 180-200.

American Psychiatric Association (2013). *Autism Spectrum Disorder Fact Sheet*, APA DSM5. American Psychiatric Publishing. http://tinyurl.com/k77bwpq.

Autism South Africa (ASA), 2012 Shine a light on Autism – World Awareness Day 2 April, http://aut2know.co.za/wp/wp-content/uploads/Issue19-2012.pdf [accessed on 10 August 2018]

Bartlett, C.A. (1988). Organizing for Worldwide Effectiveness: The Transnational Solution. [Article] *California Management Review*, 31 (1): 54-74.

Bateman, A. (2013). Responding to children's answers: questions embedded in the social context of early childhood education, *Early Years*, 33: (3): 275-288, https://doi.org/10.1080/09575146.2013.800844

Benson, P.R, Daley, D, Karlof, K.L. & Robison, D., (2011). Assessing expressed emotion in mothers of children with autism: The autism-specific five minute speech sample, *Autism* 15(1): 65-82.

Biedel, D. C. & Rao, P. A. (2009). The impact of children with high functioning autism on parental stress, sibling adjustment, and family functioning. *Behaviour Modification*, 33(4): 437-451.

Boezart, C.J. (2012). A constitutional perspective on the rights of children with disabilities in an educational context. https://repository.up.ac.za/bitstream/handle/2263/20908/Boezaart_Constitutional(2012).pdf

Boezart, C.J. (2013). Die Rol van die Kurator ad litem en Kinders se Reg op Toegang to die Howe. *De Jure*, 46 (3): 707.

Braiden, H.J., Bothwell, J. & Duffy, J. (2010). Parents' Experience of the Diagnostic Process for Autistic Spectrum Disorder. *Child Care in Practice*, 16 (4): 377-389, http://doi.org/10.1080/13575279.2010.498415.

Bridgeman, J. (2007). Accountability, support or relationship? Conceptions of parental responsibility: legal constructions of unpaid caregiving. *Northern Ireland Legal Quarterly*, 58 (3): 307-24.

Byford, S, Cary, M, Barrett, B, Aldred, C.R, Charman, T, Howlin, P. et al., (2016). Cost-effectiveness analysis of a communication-focused therapy for pre-school children with autism: Results from a randomised controlled trial. *BMC Psychiatry* 15, 316.

Carnelly, M. (2010). The right to legal representation at state expense for children in care and contact disputes-a discussion of the South African legal position with lessons from Australia. *Obiter*, 31(3): 638-661.

Carter, E. I. (2015). Access to Justice for Children with disabilities: The South African Context. Thesis. University of Pretoria in the Faculty of Law.

Chasson, G.S., Harris, G. E. & Neely, W. J. (2007). Cost Comparison of Early Intensive Behavioural Intervention and Special Education for Children with Autism. *J Child Fam Stud* 16:401-413. http://doi.org/s10826-006-9094-1.

Cidav, Z, Steven C. M, and Mandell, David S. (2012) Implications of Childhood Autism for Parental Employment and Earnings. *Paediatrics* 129(4): 617-623. http://doi.org/10.1542/peds 2011-2700.

Cidav, Z., Lawer, L., Marcus, S.C. & Mandell, D.S. (2013). Age-related variation in health service use and associated expenditures among children with autism. *Journal of Autism and Developmental Disorders* 43(4): 924–931 https://doi.org/10.1007/s 10803-012-1637-2.

Clark, M. (2012). The human rights of the disabled to access justice: An imperative for policing. *Police Journal* 225.

Clasquin-Johnson, M.G. & Clasquin-Johnson, M., (2018). How deep are your pockets?" Autoethnographic reflections on the cost of raising a child with autism. *African Journal of Disability* 7(0): a356. https://doi.org/10.4 102/ajod v7i0.356

Cockrell, A. (ed) (2013). *Private law and the Bill of Rights: A threshold issue of horizontality in the Bill of Rights compendium*. Durban: Butterworths.

Cohen , T. & Dancaster, L. (2010). Flexible Working Arrangement for Employees with Family Responsibilities – The Failings of the Employment Equity Act. In O Dupper & Garbers (Eds.). *Equality in the Workplace Reflections from South Africa and Beyond*. (pp.207-226). Cape Town: Juta & Co Ltd.

Combrinck, H. (2008). The hidden ones: Children with disabilities in Africa and the right to education. In Sloth-Nielsen, J. (Ed.). *Children's rights in Africa: A legal perspective*. Burlington: Ashgate Publishing.

Council of Europe, Convention on Cybercrime, 23 November 2001, http://www.refworld.org/docid/47fdfb202.html

Council of Europe, European Social Charter (Revised), 3 May 1996, ETS 163, http://www.refworld.org/docid/3ae6b3678.html

Currie, I. & De Waal, J. (Eds.). (2013). *Bill of Rights handbook*. Cape Town: Juta.

Dancaster, L. & Baird, M. (2008). Workers with Care Responsibilities: Is Work-family Integration Adequately Addressed in South African Labour Law. *Industrial Law Journal* 29.

De Laney A, et al. (Eds). (2016). *South African Child Gauge 2016*. Cape Town: Children's Institute, University of Cape Town.

Department of Basic Education, Values and Human Rights in the Curriculum, A Guide http://www.uct.ac.za/sites/default/files/image_tool/images/250/Pdf/Values%20and%20Human%20Rights%20in%20the%20Curriculum.pdf

Department of Basic Education (2014). *Policy on Screening, Identification, Assessment and Support*. Pretoria: Government Printer. https://www.education.gov.za/LinkClick.aspx?fileticket=2bB7EaySbcw%3D&tabid=617&portalid=0&mid=2371

Department of Basic Education. (2009). *National Early Learning and Development Standards for Children Birth to Four Years (NELDS, 2009).* Pretoria: Government Printer. https://www.unicef.org/southafrica/resources_16275.html

Department of Education (2002). *Revised National Curriculum Statement Grades R – 9*, https://www.education.gov.za/LinkClick.aspx?fileticket=JU1Y7NGqqmk%3D&tabid=390&portalid=0&mid=1125&forcedownload=true

Department of Education (2003). *A guide for parents, caregivers and communities based on the Education White Paper 6.* Pretoria: Government Printer.

Department of Education (2001). *White Paper 5*. Pretoria: Government Printer.

Department of Education. (2001). *Education White Paper 6: Special Needs Education: Building an inclusive education and training system*. Pretoria: Government Printer.

Department of Education (1995). *The White Paper 1 on Education and Training*. Pretoria: Government Printer. https://www.education.gov.za/Resources/Legislation/WhitePapers.aspx

Department of Labour (2018). *Strategic Plan for the period 2017-2020 (amended and updated April 2018)*. Pretoria: Government Printer. http://www.labour.gov.za/DOL/documents/annual-reports/department-of-labour-strategic-plan/2015-2020/strategic-plan-for-the-department-of-labour-2014-2020

Department of Social Development, (1997). *White Paper for Social Welfare,* Pretoria: Government Printer.

Department of Social Development (2009). Integrated National Strategy on Support Services to Children with Disabilities. *The Right to Belong and Participate*. http://www.hsrc.ac.za/en/research-data/ktree-doc/1672

Department of Social Development. (2016). *Comprehensive Report on the Review of the White Paper for Social Welfare, 1997*. Pretoria: Government Printer.

Department of Social Development. (2017). *Child Protection Review: Consolidated Report Department of Social Development*. Pretoria: Government Printer. https://pmg.org.za/committee-meeting/25468.

Department of Social Development's *Draft policy on South Africa's Child care and protection policy dated 19 December 2017 (National Development Plan 2030)*. Pretoria: Government Printer. https://www.sacssp.co.za/NDSD_CCPP_19_DECEMBER.docx [accessed 31/07/2018].

Devenish, G.E. (Ed.) (1999). *A commentary on the South African Bill of Rights*. Durban: Butterworths.

Diduck , A. & Raday, F. (2007). Introduction: Family – an international affair. *International Journal of Law in Context* 8.

Dillenburger, K., Jordan, J-A., Mc Kerr, L. & Keenan, M. (2014). The Millennium child with autism: Early childhood trajectories for health, education and economic wellbeing, *Developmental Neurorehabilitation*, 18(1): 37-46. https://doi.org/10.3109/17518423.2014.964378.

Disabled People's International (1981). https://www.disabledpeoplesinternational.org.

DSM V *Diagnostic and Statistical Manual of Mental Disorders*, (5th ed.) 2013. American Psychiatric Publishing.

Du Plessis, P. (2013). Wetgewing en Beleid: Vooruitgang na die Reg tot Inklusiewe Onderwys. *De Jure*. 46 (1): 76.

Du Toit, C. (2009). Legal Representation of Children. In Boezaart T (Ed.). *Child Law in South Africa*. Juta: Cape Town.

Dupper, O. & Garbers, C. (2012). The prohibition of unfair discrimination and the pursuit of affirmative action in the South African workplace. *Acta Juridica* 224.

Dyches, T. T., Wilder, L.K., Sudweeks, R.R., Obiakor, F.E. & Algozzine, B. (2004). Multicultural Issues in Autism. *Journal of Autism and Developmental Disorders*, 34(2): 211-222.

Ekas, N., & Whitman, T.L. (2010). Autism symptom topography and maternal socioemotional functioning. *Journal Information*, 115, 234-249.

Ekelaar, J. & Nhlapo T, (1998). *The Changing Family: International Perspectives on the Family and Family Forms & Family Law*. Oxford: Hart Publishing.

European Disability Forum (2015). Alternative Report to the UN Committee on the Rights of Persons with Disabilities. https://repository.up.ac.za/bitstream/handle/2263/20908/Boezaart_Constitutional(2012).pdf [accessed on 4 August 2018].

Fombonne, E. (2006) Autism and newborn encephalopathy. *Developmental Medicine & Child Neurology*, 48(2): 84.

Fouche, A. & Joubert, J. (2009). Facilitating disclosure of child sexual abuse victims in the middle of childhood: A seven-phase forensic interview protocol. *Acta Criminologica* 43.

Garbers, C. & Rossouw, E. (2015). Women in the Workplace: On unfair discrimination, affirmative action, reasonable accommodation and special measures. *ISLSSL Labour Law World Congress* 15-18 September 2015, Cape Town, https://islssl.org/wp-content/uploads/2015/10/South Africa-ChristophGarbers2.pdf.

Giallo , R., D'Esposito, F., Cooklin, A., Mensah, F., Lucas, N., Wade, C, & Nicholson, J.M. (2013). Psychosocial risk factors associated with fathers' mental health in the postnatal period: Results from a population-based study. *Soc. Psychiatry Psychiatr Epidemiol.* 48(4) 563-73 https://doi.org/10.1007/s00127-012-0568-8.

Glazzard, J. & Overall, K. (2012). Living with autistic spectrum disorder: parental experiences of raising a child with autistic spectrum disorder (ASD). *Support of Learning,* 27: (1). https://doi.org/10.1111/j.1467-9604.2011.01505.x.

Gornick , J. & Meyer, M. (Eds.) (2003). *Welfare Regimes in Relation to Paid Work and Care*. New York: Russel Sage Foundation.

Green Paper on Families: Promoting Family Life and Strengthening Families in South Africa. (Gazette No. 34 692 – Notice 756) http://www.polity.org.za/article/green-paper-on-families-promoting-family-life-and-strengthening-families-in-south-africa-gazette-no-34692-notice-756-2011-10-03

Hague Conference on Private International Law, Hague Convention on the Civil Aspects of International Child Abduction, 25 October 1980, Hague XXVIII. http://www.refworld.org/docid/3ae6b3951c.html

Halterman, J. S., & Magyar, C. I. , & Montes, G. (2009). Access to and satisfaction with school and community health services for US children with ASD. *Official Journal of the American Academy of Pediatrics*, 124(4): 407-413.

Heaton, J. (2009). An individualised, contextualised and child-centred determination of the child's best interests, and the implications of such an approach in the South African context. *Journal for Juridical Science* 34: 1-18.

Hoffman, E. (2012). Raising a child with Autism: Exploring family support structures. Cape Town: University of Stellenbosch. (Thesis-M).

Holnes, W. & Rule, S. (2014) Barriers to advocacy and litigation in the equality courts for person with disabilities. *Potchefstroom Electronic Law Journal*, 1935.

Hoogsteen, L. & Woodgate, R.L., (2013). Centering autism within the family: A qualitative approach to autism and the family. *Journal of Pediatric Nursing* 28: 135-40. http://www.refworld.org/docid/3ae6b3a10.html

Human Rights Watch (2015). South Africa's Failure to Guarantee an Inclusive Education for Children with Disabilities (August 18, 2015)

International Labour Organisation Conversations, The workers with family responsibilities convention, Convention concerning Equal Opportunities and Equal Treatment for Men and Women Workers: Workers with Family Responsibilities (11 Aug 1983) Adoption: Geneva, 67th ILC session (23 June 1981) https://ecampus.itcilo.org/pluginfile.php/25272/mod_page/content/40/C156_R165.pdf

International Labour Organization (ILO), Worst Forms of Child Labour Convention, C182, 17 June 1999, C182, http://www.refworld.org/docid/3ddb6e0c4.html

Janzen, J.E. (2009). *Autism handbook for parents. Facts and strategies for parenting success*. Waco: Pufrock Press Inc.

Jian-Jun, O., Li-Juan, S., Guang-Lei, X, Chen C., Ren-Rong, W., Xue-Rong, L., Yeng-Ye, Z. & Jing-Ping, Z. (2015). Employment and financial burden of families with preschool children diagnosed with autism spectrum disorders in urban China: results from a descriptive study. *BMC Psychiatry* 15(3) doi: 10.1186/s12888-015-0382-4.

Kanter, A.S. (2015). *The development of disability rights under international law: From charity to human rights*. New York: Routledge.

Kilkelly (2002). Disability and children: The Convention on the Rights of the Child (CRC). In Quinn and Degener (Eds.). *Human Rights and Disability* (2002): 123.

Leblanc, L., Richardson, W. & Burns, K.A., (2009). Autism spectrum disorder and the inclusive classroom: Effective training to enhance knowledge of ASD and evidence-based practices. *Teacher Education and Special Education* 32(2): 166-179.

Lewis, J. (2006). Employment and Care: The Policy Problem, Gender Equality and the Issue of Choice. *Journal of Comparative Policy Analysis* 103.

Lin, J. (2014). Medical care burden of children with autism spectrum disorder. *Journal of Autism and Developmental Disorders* 1, 242-247. https://doi.org/10.10.1007/s40489-014-0023-8.

Lokhandwala, T, Khanna, R. & West-Strum, D. (2012). Hospitalization burden among individuals with autism. *Journal of Autism and Developmental Disorders* 42, 95-104 https://doi.org/10.1007/s10803-011-1217-x.

Lutz, H.R., Patterson, B.J., & Klein, J. (2012). Coping with autism: A journey toward adaptation. *Journal of Pediatric Nursing*, 27: 206-213.

Martin, A. (2010). *The everyday advocate: standing up for your child with autism or other special needs.* London: New American Library.

Matenge, B. (2013). *An Exploration of the Lived Experiences of Mothers Raising Children with Autism*. Psychology Department. University of Cape Town.

Matshedisho, K.R. (2007). Access to higher education for disabled students in South Africa: a contradictory conjuncture of benevolence, rights and the social model of disability. *Disability & Society*, 22(7): 685-699. https://doi.org/10.1080/09687590701659535.

McConachie, H., & Diggle, T. (2007). Parent implemented early intervention for young children with autism spectrum disorder: A systematic review. *Journal of Evaluation in Clinical Practice*, 13(1): 120-129 http://onlinelibrary.wilwy.com/doi/10.111/j.1365-2753.2006.00674.z/full.

Meltzer, L. J. (2008). Brief Report: Sleep in Parents of Children with Autism Spectrum Disorder. *Journal of Pediatric Psychology* 33, (4): 1 May 2008, 380-386, https://doi.org/10.1093/jpepsy/jsn005.

Ministry of Justice and Constitutional Development. *Government Gazette (1993) (15024 of 30 July 1993 as amended by Government Gazette 17822*. Pretoria: Government Printers.

Ministry of Justice and Constitutional Development. *Government Gazette No 25065 of 1998.* Pretoria: Government Printers.

Mthimunye, B.S. (2014). The knowledge and experiences of single mothers raising an autistic child. University of Western Cape. Department of Psychology (thesis) http://hdl.handle.net/11394/4182.

Muller, K. (2001) An inquisitorial approach to the evidence of children. http://www.cirsa.org.za/downloads/ia.pdf.

National Planning Commission, Department of the President (2011). *National Development Plan: Our Future Make it Work 2030.* http://www.npconline.co.za/medialib/downloads/home/NPC%National%Development%Plan%20ion%202030%20-lo-res.pdf.

National Prosecuting Authority, 2013. Strategic Plan 2013-2018. http://pmg-assets.s3-website-eu-west-1.amazonaws.com/130423stratplan_0.pdf

Norma Tarrow, Human Rights Education: Alternative Conceptions, p22 taken from Values and Human Rights in the Curriculum, Department of Education.

Nussabaum, B. & Wiechel, K. (2010). The spirit of Ubuntu. http://www.peacexpeace.org/2010/07/the-spirit-of-Ubuntu.

Nussbaum, M. (2009). The Capabilities of people with cognitive disabilities. *Metaphilosphy* 40, 3-4, https:// doi.org/j.1467-9973.2009.01606.x.

Office of the Deputy President (1997). *Integrated National Disability Strategy White Paper*. Pretoria: Government Printer

Ooi, K.L. Ong, Y.S., Jacob, S.A. & Khan, T.M.(2016). A Meta-synthesis on parenting a child with autism, *Neuropsychiatric Disease and Treatment*, 12: 745-762. https://doi.org/10.2147/NDT.S100634.

Organization of African Unity (OAU), African Charter on Human and People's Rights ("Banjul Charter"). 27 June 1981, CAB/LEG/67/3 rev.5, 21 I.L.M. 58 (1982). http://www.refword.org/docid/3ae6b3630.html [accessed 6 August 2018].

Organization of African Unity (OAU), African Charter on the Rights and Welfare of the Child (ACRWC), 11 July 1990, CAB/LEG/24.9/49 (1990). http://www.refworld.org/docid/3ae6b38c18.html [accessed 6 August 2018]

Organization of African Unity (OAU), African Charter on the Rights and Welfare of the Child, 11 July 1990, CAB/LEG/24.9/49 (1990), http://www.refworld.org/docid/3ae6b38c18.html

Osborne, L. A. & Reed, P. (2008). Parents' perceptions of communication with professionals during the diagnosis of autism. *Autism*, 12, 309-324.

Osborne, L.A., McHugh L., Saunders, J. & Reed, P. (2008). *J Autism Dev Discord*, Jul; 38(6): 1902-103. Epub 2007 Nov 20, https://doi.org/10.1007/s10803-007-0497-7.

Pepperell, T.A., Paynter, J. & Gilmore, J., (2016). Social support and coping strategies of parents raising a child with autism spectrum disorder. *Early Child Development and Care* 186, 1-13. https://doi.org/10.1080/03004430.2016.1261338

Pityana, N.B. (2002). The Promotion of Equality and Prevention of Unfair Discrimination Act 4 of 2000. http://uir.unisa.ac.za/bitstream/handle/10500/407/codi_v44_a1.pdf.

Poverty data is sourced from Stats SA's 2015 General Household Survey data as analysed by the Children's Institute and published in the 2017 Child Gauge (Jamieson L, Berry L, Lake L (Eds), *South African Child Gauge 2017*. Cape Town: Children's Institute, UCT.

Protocol to the African Charter on Human and Peoples' Rights on the Rights of Persons with Disabilities in Africa (2018) adopted 0n 29 January 2018 but not yet ratified, https://au.int/sites/default/files/treaties/36440-treaty-protocol_to_the_achpr_on_the_rights_of_persons_with_disabilities_in_africa_e.pdf

Report by the Equal Education Law Centre (EELC) report on The Right to Inclusive Education, https://eelawcentre.org.za/wp-content/uploads/2016/08/Inclusive-Education-Final.pdf

Report of the International Commission on Education for the 21st Century, Delors, 1996, p11 taken from Values and Human Rights in the Curriculum, Department of Education [DoE]

Republic of South Africa. (1977). *The Criminal Procedure Act, Act No. 51 of 1977*. Pretoria: Government Printer.

Republic of South Africa. (1997). *The Basic Conditions of Employments Act, Act No 75 of 1997*. Pretoria: Government Printer.

Republic of South Africa. (1996). *Constitution of South Africa, Act No. 108 of 1996*. Cape Town: Government Printer.

Republic of South Africa (1996). *National Education Policy Act, No. 27 of 1996*. Pretoria: Government Printer.

Republic of South Africa. (1998). *Employment Equity Act, Act No. 55 of 1998 (EEA)*. Pretoria: Government Printer.

Republic of South Africa. (1969). *Legal Aid Act, Act No 22 of 1969*. Pretoria: Government Printer.

Republic of South Africa. (2002). *The Mental Health Care Act, Act No. 17 of 2002*. Pretoria: Government Printer.

Republic of South Africa (2000).*The promotion of Equality and Prevention of Unfair Discrimination Act, Act No. 4 of 2000.* Pretoria: Government Printer.

Republic of South Africa. (1996). *The South African Schools Act (SASA), Act No. 84 of 1996*. Pretoria: Government Printer.

Republic of South Africa. (2001). *Ministry of Justice and Constitutional Development. Government Gazette no 22435 of 2 July 2001, Categories or classes of persons that can be appointed as intermediaries*. Pretoria: Government Printer.

Republic of South Africa. (2002). *Mental Health Care Act, Act No 17 of 2002*. Pretoria: Government Printer.

Republic of South Africa. (2004). *The Social Assistance Act, Act No. 13 of 2004*. Pretoria: Government Printer.

Republic of South Africa. (2005). *The Children's Act, Act No 38 of 2005*. Pretoria: Government Printer.

Republic of South Africa. (2007). *The Children's Amendment Act, Act No 41 of 2007*. Pretoria: Government Printer.

Republic of South Africa. (2011). *Green Paper on Families (Promoting Family Life and Strengthening Families in South Africa) (2011). Government Notice 756 in Government Gazette 34692 or 19-10-1011*. Printer: Government Printer.

Republic of South Africa. (2015). *White Paper on the Rights of Persons with Disabilities*. Pretoria: Government Printer. https://www.ru.ac.za/media/rhodesuniversity/content/equityinstitutionalculture/documents/White%20Paper%20on%20the%20Rights%20of%20Persons%20with%20Disabilities.pdf

Richter, L; Biersieker, L; Burns, J; Desmond, C; Feza, N; Harrison, D; Martin, P; Sabojee, H; Stemming, W. (2012). Diagnostic Review of Early Childhood Development. *Report for Department of Performance Monitoring and Evaluation (DPME) in the Presidency.*

Rossouw, E. (2018). The Integration of work and parenting: A comparative legal analysis, University of Stellenbosch, Department of Law (thesis).

Shimabutkuro, T.T., Grosse, S.D. & Rice, C. (2008). Medical expenditures for children with an autism spectrum disorder in a privately insured population. *Journal of Autism and Developmental Disorder*, 38, 546-552 https://doi.org/10.1007/s10803-007-0424-y.

Sloth-Nielsen, J. (2009). "Seen and Heard?" New frontiers in child participation in family law proceeding in South Africa. *Juris*, 23(2): 1-9, http://hdl.handle.net/10566/1256

Sloth-Nielsen, J. (2001). The Child's Right to Social Service, The Right to Social Security, and Primary Prevention of Child Abuse: Some Conclusions in the Aftermath of Grootboom. *South African Journal on Human Rights*, 17:2, 210-231, https://doi.org/10.1080/02587203.2001.11827623

Smith, L.E, Seltzer, M.M, Tager-Flusberg, H, Greenberg, J.S, & Carter, A. S. (2008). A Comparative Analysis of Well-Being and Coping among Mothers of Toddlers and Mothers of Adolescents with ASD. *Journal of Autism Developmental Disorders*, 38: 876-889. http://dx.doi.org/10.1007/s10803-007-0461-6

South African Human Rights Commission (2002). Towards a barrier-free society. South African Human Rights. https://www.sahrc.org.za/home/21/files/Reports/towards_barrier_free_society.pdf2002.pdf

SAHRC and UNICEF. (2014). Poverty traps and social exclusion among children in South Africa, https://www.sahrc.org.za/home/21/files/Poverty%20Traps%20Report.pdf

South African Human Rights Commission (2013). Research Brief on Disability and Equality in South Africa 2013- 2017. https://www.sahrc.org.za/home/21/files/RESEARCH%20BRIEF%20ON%20DISABILITY%20AND%20EQUALITY%20IN%20SOUTH%20AFRICA%202013%20to%202017.pdf

Statistics South Africa (2011). Census (2011) STATS SA, Report-03-01-59.

Suid Afrikaanse Onderwys Unie.(2006). The Amended National Norms and Standards for School Funding GN 869 GG 29179 2006-08-31, http://www.saou.co.za/wp-content/uploads/2016/05/40818-SASA-84-1996-amended-national-norms-and-standards-for-school-funding.pdf

The African Decade for People with Disabilities (http://www.achpr.org/network/ngo/435/)

The International Bill of Rights, comprising the Universal Declaration of Human Rights (1948).

The International Covenant of Economic, Social and Cultural Rights (1966)

The International Covenant on Civil and Political Rights (1966)

The Labour Court in Standard Bank of South Africa v CCMA 2008 (4) BLLR 356 (LC)

The United Nations Standard Rules on the Equalisation of Opportunities for People with Disabilities (1993)

The Vienna Convention on the Law of Treaties https://www.refworld.org/docid/3ae6b3a10.html

The World Declaration on Education for All World Conference on Education For All: Meeting Basic Learning Needs. (1990). *World declaration on education for all and framework for action to meet basic learning needs adopted by the World Conference on Education for All: Meeting Basic Learning Needs*, Jomtien, Thailand, 5-9 March 1990. New York, N.Y., Inter-Agency Commission (UNDP, UNESCO, UNICEF, World Bank) for the World Conference on Education for All.

UN Committee on the Rights of the Child (CRC). UN Committee on the Rights of the Child: Concluding Observations: Norway, 28 June 2000, CRC/C/15/Add.126, http://www.refworld.org/docid/3ae6afc410.html

UN Committee on the Rights of the Child (CRC) (2010). Optional Protocol on the Sale of Children, Child Prostitution and Child Pornography: List of issues to be taken up in connection with the consideration of the initial report of Belgium (CRC/C/OPSC/BEL/1), 8 March 2010, CRC/C/OPSC/BEL/Q/1, http://www.refworld.org/docid/50b3565e2.html

UN Convention on the Rights of the Child (1989)

UN General Assembly, Implementation of the World Programme of Action concerning Disabled Persons and the United Nations Decade of Disabled Persons : resolution / adopted by the General Assembly, 14 December 1990, A/RES/45/91, http://www.refworld.org/docid/3b00f1f67f.html

UN Committee on Economic, Social and Cultural Rights (CESCR) , General Comment No. 13: The Right to Education (Art 13 of the Covenant), 8 December 1999, E/C. 12/1999/10, http://www.refworld.org/docid/4538838c22.html

UN Committee on Economic, Social and Cultural Rights (CESCR), General Comment No. 9: The domestic application of the Covenant, 3 December 1998, E/C.12/1998/24, http://www.refworld.org/docid/47a7079d6.html

UN Committee on the Rights of the Child (CRC), General comment No. 6 (2005): Treatment of Unaccompanied and Separated Children Outside their Country of Origin, 1 September 2005, CRC/GC/2005/6, http://www.refworld.org/docid/42dd174b4.html

UN Committee on the Rights of the Child (CRC), General comment No. 16 (2013) on State obligations regarding the impact of the business sector on children's rights, 17 April 2013, CRC/C/GC/16, http://www.refworld.org/docid/51ef9cd24.html

UN Convention on the Elimination of all Forms of Discrimination against woman is a human rights treaty for women (1979)

UN Convention on the Protection of Children and Cooperation in Respect of Inter-Country Adoption

UN General Assembly, Convention on the Rights of the Child, 20 November 1989, United Nations, Treaty Series, vol. 1577, p. 3, http://www.refworld.org/docid/3ae6b38f0.html

UN General Assembly, Declaration of the Rights of the Child, 20 November 1959, A/RES/1386(XIV), http://www.refworld.org/docid/3ae6b38e3.html

UN General Assembly, Guidelines for the Alternative Care of Children: resolution / adopted by the General Assembly, 24 February 2010, A/RES/64/142, http://www.refworld.org/docid/4c3acd162.html

UN General Assembly, Convention on the Rights of the Child, 20 November 1989, United Nations, Treaty Series, vol. 1577, p. 3, http://www.refworld.org/docid/3ae6b38f0.html

Van Bueren, G. (1995). Opening Pandora's Box: Protecting Children against Torture or Cruel, Inhuman and Degrading Treatment or Punishment. https://doi.org/10.1111/j.1467-9930.1995.tb00156.x

Van der Walt, G. (2010) The United Nations Convention on the Rights of the Child – has the bridge been crossed between theory and practice: Mauritius and South Africa? *Obiter* 715.

Van Rooyen, M. (2016). The father's experience: A South African perspective on caring for a child with autism spectrum disorder. University of Stellenbosch, Department of Psychology (thesis).

Visser, P. (1996). Die moontlike uitdruklikke erkenning en beskerming van fundamentele regte ten -aansien van die huwelik en die gesin (familie) in die finale Grondwet van Suid- Afrika. *De Jure*, 351 354.

Walker, A.G. (1999). *Children in the courts: When language gets in the way*. Association of Trial Lawyers of America 2.

Wang J., Zhou X., Xia W., Sun C., Wu L., Wang J. & Tomoda A., (2012). Parent-reported health care expenditures associated with autism spectrum disorders in Heilongjiang Province, China. *BMC Health Services Research* 12, 1–7 http://www.biomedcentral.com/1472-6963/12/7 Westman, J. (1999). Children's Rights, Parents' Prerogatives and Society's Obligations. *Child Psychiatry and Human Development* 29:315.

Wiese, M. (2014). Mothers' experiences of their child's diagnosis with an autism spectrum disorder. North West University. (thesis-M).

Woolman, S. (2006). Between Norms and Facts: The Constitutional Courts Commitment to Pluralism in South Africa's Radically Heterogeneous Public Schools. *PER*, 2015 18 (6), https://dx.doi.org/10.4314/pelj.v18i6.02

Yeo, R. (2001). *Chronic poverty and disability*. Chronic Poverty Research Centre 9.

Zaal, F.N. (1997). When should children be legally represented in care proceedings? An application of Section 28(1)(h) of the 1996 Constitution, *South African Law Journal*, 334.

Cases

Autism of Europe v France (Complaint No 13/2002).

Centre for Child Law and others v Minister of Home Affairs 2005 (6) SA (T) 2005 (6) SA

Christian Education South Africa v Minister of Education (CCT4/00) [2000] ZACC 11; 2000 (4) SA 757; 2000 (10) BCLR 1051.

Co-operative Workers Association v Petroleum Oil & Gas Co-operative of SA 2007 (28) ILJ 627 (LC) the court noted at par 48

Dlamini v Green Four Security 2006 (27) ILJ 2098 (LC)

DPP, Kwazulu-Natal v P 2006 (1) SACR 243 SCA

Fitzpatrick and Others 2000 (3) SA 422 (CC) at par 17.

George v The Minister of Environmental Affairs and Tourism 2005 (6) SA 297 (EqC) par 7

Glenister v President of the Republic of South Africa 2011 (3) SA 347 (CC).

Governing Body of Juma Musjid Primary School v Essay 2011 (7) BCLR 651 (CC) at para 37

http://www.nacoss.co.za/documents/website-White-Paper.pdf

Government of RSA and others v Grootboom and others 2001 (1) SA 46; 2000 (11) BCLR 1169.

Grootboom v Oostenberg Municipality and Others 2000 (3) BCLR 277 (C)

Hugo v eThekwini Municipality, Case D18/11, Labour Court

Jooste v Botha 2000 JOL 5943 (T) 2000 (2) BCLR 187 (T)

Jooste v Botha 2000(2) SA 199 (T) at para 201F

Kirsch v Bhe and others v Magistrate, Khayelitsha and others 2005 (1) SA 580 (CC)

Laerskool Middelburg v Departementshoof, Mupumalanga 2003 (4) SA 160 (T) para 177 -178.

Legal Aid Board and Another v R 2009 (2) SA 262 (D)

M v S (Centre for Child Law as Amicus Curiae) 2008 (5) BCLR 475 (CC)

Mazibuko v City of Johannesburg 2010 (4) SA 1 (CC)

MEC for Education: Kwazulu-Natal and Others v Pillay 2008 (1) SA 474 (CC) at para 73

Mediation in terms of the Divorce Matters Act, Act 24 of 1987.

Minister of Health and Others v Treatment Action Campaign and others 2002 (10) BCLR 1033 (CC).

President of the Republic of South Africa and Another v Hugo 1997 (6) BCLR 708 (CC)

S v M 2008 (3) SA 232 (CC)

S v Makwanyane 1995 (3) SA 391 (CC)

S v Makwanyane 1995 (6) BCLR 665 (CC) at par 328

Sonserup v Tondelli and Another 2001 (1) SA 1171 (CC) at par 29, and has been declared a stand-alone and enforceable right on its own, refer to Minister of Welfare and Population Development v South African Human Rights Commission Report, "Towards a barrier-free society" (2002)

Western Cape Forum for Intellectual Disability v Government of the Republic of South Africa 2011 (5) SA 87 (WCC).

A PRELIMINARY CONCLUSION: TRENDS IN ASD RESEARCH IN SOUTH(ERN) AFRICA

Michel Clasquin-Johnson

In the title of this book we promised to provide African perspectives on autism. The time has come to ask if we succeeded. Formally, we can say that we have. All but one of the chapters in this book were written by authors currently living and researching in Africa, and our two Australian colleagues have long-standing links with our continent. But if we delve in a little deeper and ask if there is anything in this volume that is distinctly African, that could not have been written anywhere else, then we must come up with a more nuanced answer. Three issues immediately spring to mind.

First, every author in this volume (and I must include myself in this) uncritically accepts the DSM-V and its predecessors. In this era of decolonial and post-colonial discourse, how can we Africans allow the American Psychiatric Association to be the final arbiter of our (dis)ability? Is it not time for us to delve into the question of what it means to have a disability in African society? France does not use the DSM, but has developed its own classification system known as the CFTMEA (Classification Française des Troubles Mentaux de L'Enfant et de L'Adolescent). Should Africa not do the same?

That does not mean that we need to discard all the excellent work done by Euro-American researchers, clinicians and educators. But far more thought needs to go into fundamental issues. If we can work out our own understanding of disability, we will be able to evaluate the work done elsewhere in the right context.

Second, our contributions are geographically constrained. Africa is the second largest continent. It has a dazzling variety of cultures and traditions. But our book concentrates on the southern tip of Africa. Perhaps it was presumptuous of us to claim the continent in our title. Here we can only promise to look further afield in future volumes.

Third, some of us have appealed to the concept of Ubuntu. It is an attractive concept, but like all attractive concepts it runs the risk of being absolutised. To what extent is Ubuntu an objective description of an existing pan-African ethos? Could it be more usefully viewed as a condition devoutly to be wished for and worked towards? Is Ubuntu a timeless African ontology or is it an active teleological direction? Our book once again shows the need for a more critical approach to fundamental issues.

Against such shortcomings, we can only plead that this book was always intended to be a first step in the African study of autism. When we started, there was no book produced in South Africa, or Africa as far as we could discover, that focused on the educational aspects of autism. There is one now, and we have optimistically named it Volume One. We trust there will come a day when a different set of editors will bring out Volume Ten, or 20. We hope that they will be able to look back at this humble starting point and feel proud in how far they have come since our day.

APPENDIX: AUTISM-RELATED ORGANISATIONS IN SOUTH AFRICA

Action in Autism
http://www.actioninautism.org.za

Alpha School for Autism
https://www.westerncape.gov.za/facility/alpha-school

Amazing K, Randburg
http://www.amazingk.co.za

Association for Autism
http://www.afa.org.za

Autism and Behavioural Learning Environment (ABLE) Centre, Richards Bay
http://www.ablecentre.org

Autism Eastern Cape
http://www.autismec.co.za

Autism South Africa
http://www.aut2know.co.za

Autism Western Cape
http://www.autismwesterncape.org.za

Boland School for Autism
http://www.bolandautism.org.za/autism

Capulum College, Hilton KZN
http://www.capulumcollege.co.za

Cape Autism Charity Trust
http://www.cact.co.za/what_is_autism.html

Care Centre for Autism, Research and Education
http://www.thecarecentre.co.za

Casa Do Sol School
https://www.casadosolschool.com

Centre for Play and Learning
https://www.centre4playandlearning.co.za

Chere Botha
http://www.cherebotha.co.za

Cornerstone Learning Centre
http://www.cslc.co.za

Craiglands Remedial School Randburg
http://www.craiglandsremedialschool.co.za

ES le Grange School
http://www.espotch.co.za

Faery Glen Therapy Centre
http://www.faeryglen.co.za

Footprints School
http://www.footprintschool.co.za

Free State Association for ASDs
http://www.autismfs.org.za

Johannesburg Hospital School
http://www.johannesburghospitalschool.co.za

Khuluma Education
http://www.khulumaeducation.co.za

Kidstart Early Intervention Centre
http://www.kidstartcentre.com

Little Leaps School for Autism http://www.littleleaps.co.za

L.U.C.C.A Support and Care Centre for Children with a Difference
http://www.luccaspecialkids.co.za

Mind Stretch
http://www.mindstretch.co.za

On the Spectrum
http://www.onspectrum.co.za

Randburg Autism Clinic Centre
http://www.randburgclinicschool.co.za/autism-centre

SNAP Special Needs Adapted Programme
http://www.snap.org.za

Special Kids http://www.specialkids.co.za

The Baby Therapy Centre
http://www.babytherapy.org.za

The Claremont Practice
http://www.claremontpractice.co.za

The Dream Tree School
http://www.thedreamtreeschool.co.za

The Ernie Els Centre for Autism
http://www.ernieelscentre4autism.co.za

The Key School
http://www.thekeyschool.org

The Star Academy
http://www.thestaracademy.co.za

The Talk Shop
http://www.thetalkshop.co.za

Triad Schools, KZN
http://www.triadschools.co.za

Unica School for Autism
http://www.unicaschool.co.za (Accessed 23 May 2016)

Van Kervel Special School, George
http://www.vankervel.wcape.school.za

Vera School for Autism
http://www.vera.co.za

INDEX

For Product Safety Concerns and Information please contact our EU representative GPSR@taylorandfrancis.com Taylor & Francis Verlag GmbH, Kaufingerstraße 24, 80331 München, Germany